Mirrors & Scrims

BOOKS BY MARCIA B. SIEGEL

Howling Near Heaven: Twyla Tharp and the Reinvention of Modern Dance

The Tail of the Dragon: New Dance 1976–1982

Days on Earth: The Dance of Doris Humphrey

The Shapes of Change: Images of American Dance

Watching the Dance Go By

At the Vanishing Point: A Critic Looks at Dance

MIRRORS & SCRIMS

The Life and Afterlife of Ballet

Marcia B. Siegel

WESLEYAN UNIVERSITY PRESS *Middletown, Connecticut*

Published by
Wesleyan University Press,
Middletown, CT 06459
www.wesleyan.edu/wespress
Printed in U.S.A.
5 4 3 2 1

Library of Congress
Cataloging-in-Publication Data
Siegel, Marcia B.
Mirrors and scrims : the life and afterlife of ballet /
Marcia B. Siegel.
    p. cm.
Includes bibliographical references and index.
ISBN 978-0-8195-6875-5 (cloth : alk. paper)
ISBN 978-0-8195-6926-4 (pbk. : alk. paper)
1. Ballet—History. 2. Ballet dancers—History.
3. Ballet companies—History. I. Title.
GV1787.6.S54 2010
792.809—dc22   2009036031

Title page photograph: *Les Biches* (Nijinska).
© Jack Vartoogian/FrontRowPhotos.

Wesleyan University Press is a member
of the Green Press Initiative. The paper
used in this book meets their minimum
requirement for recycled paper.

Contents

Illustrations

Preface

Over the years covered by this collection, I contributed on a regular basis to several publications and wrote occasionally for others. The tone of the writing changes slightly according to the type of publication. In some articles, my extra-performance research is thoroughly documented; other publications discourage footnoting. But as a consistent practice, I try, at least informally, to identify the source of quoted material.

In 1996 I moved from New York City to Massachusetts and began writing regularly for the *Boston Phoenix*. Rather than append a dateline to every entry in this volume, I'm trusting the reader will understand that the performances reviewed for the *Phoenix* were Boston-based and those prior to 1996 took place in New York, except when I traveled to other locations noted in the respective pieces.

I'm indebted to the publicists who made it possible for me to attend performances and supplied additional information, pictures, and recordings when requested.

I'm very grateful for the generous cooperation of the photographers whose fine work illustrates this book.

All writers tremble for the fate of their work once it leaves their computers. I've been fortunate to have understanding editors who not only made space for dance coverage but respected my writing by handling it lightly. In particular I want to thank Bruce Manuel, my editor for five years when I covered New York dance for the *Christian Science Monitor*; Jeffrey Gantz, arts editor at the *Phoenix*, who's kept the paper a principal site for dance coverage in Boston; and Paula Deitz and the late Fred Morgan, whose unflagging enthusiasm has brought my essays into the *Hudson Review* for nearly four decades.

I would also like to thank Suzanna Tamminen, editor-in-chief of Wesleyan University Press, for inviting me to propose this collection and sending it on its way into print.

As always, I thank the dancers, for making dance live.

—Marcia B. Siegel

Introduction

This is a book about history—about the many possible histories that get written on a single subject. It is a document of change, marking a future still being written, not a past that is safely settled. It is about choreographic work, and about those who write the history of that work: the researchers and retrievers, the adapters and promoters, the performers and document-ers, the critics and scholars. And it is about how the idea of dance evolves in the mind of one spectator over a relatively small slice of time.

The literature of dance relies heavily on personal reflection and anec-dote, but serious consideration of dance works requires the application of a critical/descriptive eye, over repeated viewings. Longtime critics return to the great works over the years, understanding that they are looking at objects in evolution. The works can emerge from this writing process as composites. The critic tries to discern and hang on to some essence that informs every performance of the work. We who are not the dancers, who can't know the work in our bones, are negotiating between memory, expec-tation, empirical observation, and subjective response when we report to our readers. They in turn, reading many accounts of many different perfor-mances, may arrive at their own notion of what a given work is.

To focus this collection of my reviews and essays from the past two and a half decades and give it a shape, I have centered the narrative around the historical paradox: We confer great power on the past, even though the past has no fixed meaning. I've chosen pieces that grapple with the floating iden-tity of ballet, and of particular ballets, and with the expanding environment of spectacle in which ballet competes for an audience. I've selected and organized the entries around themes of authenticity and change, rather than notions of chronological progression.

The era of the Diaghilev Ballets Russes is celebrated in our time as a watershed in ballet history, yet the legendary status of the Ballets Russes rests heavily on the personalities of its famous artists and patrons. The innovative ballets themselves are retrievable today as interpretations of the originals, each production asking to be taken as validation of that ballet's reputation. But since we have no eyewitness experience to judge this, we're compelled to look at revivals as self-contained events, detached from the legend. Whether we think the revival is faithful or not, the legend stands intact.

The nineteenth-century Russian classics, even more remote from our experience and more subject to the inroads of time, offer a clearer and more readily understood style to the modern audience. These works undergo constant change—from redesigned costumes, rearranged sequences, and rechoreographed numbers, to shifting interpretations of characters and plots, to the routine addition of new material from year to year. The audience has no trouble recognizing these revised editions as *Swan Lake* or *The Nutcracker*.

The closest thing in recent memory to a distinct style of ballet was the New York City Ballet repertory under George Balanchine. When Balanchine died in 1983, the company entered a period of transition. The Balanchine ballets occupied a less prominent role in New York, but they appeared more frequently in the repertory of other companies. During the same period, the idea of high art itself was in debate. Contemporary ballets, adopting a free-form assortment of dance models, popular culture references, gender and ethnic reforms, have proliferated. In this climate of anti-elitism, even Balanchine has cycled into legend, along with stars like Suzanne Farrell, Edward Villella, and Mikhail Baryshnikov, whose dancing a diminishing number of balletgoers have seen on stage.

Despite their heavy investment in the past, ballet companies are always concerned with new work, as a repertory refresher and a link to the present. Even at its most formal and abstract, ballet tries to reflect the experience of its audience or propose uplifting models. Today ballet is only one element of a performance spectrum that spans circuses and sports, TV dance competitions, animation movies, and fashion shows. All of this new entertainment has reflected onto theatrical dance, just as the glamour, physical expertise, and artistry of dance have influenced the nondance media. Politics, from gender and ethnic struggles to the agonized questions of environment, war, and class dissonance, has found its way into new choreography. With the documentation and ready accessibility of dance repertory on film, video, and the Internet, ballets can be deconstructed, translated to another medium, memorialized, appropriated, or refashioned. Classical icons even become the inspiration for new works and new forms.

As a practice and an art form, dance exalts its landmarks and precedents, while it simultaneously, deliberately, overturns these same defining concepts. The writer of dance criticism is poised between realities. How does the appearance of a historical work alter against the backdrop of our current theater life? Is there something fundamental about a work that withstands rethinking, updating, and even cultural obsolescence? Is a historic work—or any work—to be considered only in the context erected by its producers? Does a work exist when it finally escapes its own mythology?

Dance clings to the idea of authenticity although no one knows what authenticity in a dance performance really is or where its boundaries lie. Big ballet companies today invest heavily in classic works, but this dependency requires that the works be continually refreshed and reconstituted. When one year's *Swan Lake* may be different from its predecessors in small details or large concepts, which is the real *Swan Lake*? Contemporary works—in effect all dances created since 1900—have an even less consistent presence on ballet stages. They are less well known, their "authenticity" is recognized by fewer people, and their audience is ill-prepared for unfamiliar sensibilities.

Given the straitened circumstances of all the arts, especially the expensive theater arts, the unending drive for patrons has intensified during the 1990s and early 2000s. What we read in the papers about dance is more and more the creation of marketing specialists, while the role of critic-responders is shrinking both in the public sphere and within the dance field. But critics leave a record at least as authentic as the testimonials originated by dancers and their spokespersons. Critics document what they have observed on the stage in day-to-day practice. They retrospectively interpret what has occurred over the long run. And they can yield insight into the often clashing claims of art, politics, and popular culture.

Dancers love to assert that what they do can't be talked about, and this is the irresistible challenge all dance critics address. For us, the talking-about-it in writing is the real conclusion to a performance, the place where a loop finally closes between one audience member and the choreographer's idea, as imagined and taught to the dancers and given by them to the audience. Criticism is an act of reciprocity. It may not match up exactly with the original intent, but art allows for—demands—many responses. I suppose the deepest response to a dance would be another dance, but words can make a dance resonate in other ways. I'm principally interested in conveying a sense of what the dance looked like and how it worked, as well as the context in which the dance takes place—its choreographic, artistic, and political influences. I see myself as both a demystifyer and a validator, sometimes an interpreter, but not a judge.

A review can be both an immediate perception and a historical record. My working circumstances have afforded few opportunities to undertake scholarly studies. Some essays of substantial length and depth are included in this collection, but they were all originally intended for general readers. They are all grounded in the empirical experience of the dance at hand, even when I've used other types of research to contextualize and deepen my ideas. As a writing process this is less deliberate, less goal oriented, than setting out to research an arcane subject or taking a new look at previous scholarship. Regular reviewing has its limitations and advantages. It is a discipline, as rigorous as scholarly writing, but different. Perhaps dance is the art form that needs criticism the most; since it cannot be viewed or heard or read except in the singular moment of performance. After that moment it becomes a translation. Critics take their role as witness very seriously.

Many people think of dance as a cultural process that evolves of its own momentum within the social and political parameters of its time. Increasingly in recent years, I've come to think of dance creation and performance as a more calculated product, a sort of tourist attraction, controlled and conceptualized from within, to suit the immediate dynamics of competition and survival. I think to the general public, dance is a foreign destination, exotic, dreamy and inaccessible, surrounded by myth, populated by idealized characters who engage in secret rituals. The dance field reinforces this projection of its own remoteness. It's these shifting, highly mediated representations of dance that I want to consider in this book.

Underlying the concerns of dance producers and creators, as well as those who observe and comment on dance, is the question of what art itself is in the twenty-first century. Art's value as understood for many centuries has been shaken by the countercultural revolution of the 1960s. But even if we know the dances of the distant and recent past only as representations, we can't allow them to disappear without losing a part of what has made us civilized. We must be able to access them—to imagine how they appeared to their first viewers and account for how they've been entrusted to us. This book tries to see into these representations, while acknowledging that it is, itself, a representation.

Mirrors & Scrims

1 Legends

THE ROSE AND THE SCIMITAR

Boston Phoenix, 21 November 2003

The first great choreographer of the twentieth century, Michel Fokine, set out to reform Russian ballet. The classical edifice built by Petipa, Ivanov, and the Maryinsky school in St. Petersburg was suffering from decadence and overfamiliarity, Fokine thought, and it needed to be scraped down to the essentials of training and dramaturgy. Away with virtuosity for its own sake, egomaniacal performances, characters who had nothing to do with the story, overblown productions, generic movement, and mechanical mime conventions. In order to fully realize his choreographic innovations, Fokine had to flee the reactionary management at the Maryinsky. For the best four years of his career he worked as house choreographer for Serge Diaghilev, who imported Russian ballet to Europe with sensational success.

Fokine's ballets were revolutionary. So revolutionary, in fact, that his prescription for a one-act story ballet or poetic evocation, with movement specifically arranged to suit its period, locale, and theme, defined ballet choreography for decades. Calling *Schéhérazade* "classical" in the same breath with *Sleeping Beauty* and *La Bayadère*, as did the rhetoric for the Kirov Ballet's performances in Boston, simplifies what is actually a much richer history, and misinforms the very audience that could appreciate balletic diversity. The Kirov's all-Fokine performances at the Wang Theater reflected this muddled and opportunistic thinking.

Of the three ballets and two bonuses shown opening night, only *The Dying Swan* was choreographed before Fokine left Russia in 1909, as a solo piece for Anna Pavlova. *Chopiniana*, which we know as *Les Sylphides*, did originate at the Maryinsky, as a series of period sketches, but it assumed its marvelous abstract form during Diaghilev's first Ballets Russes season in Paris. *Chopiniana* looks back, not to *Swan Lake*, but to an earlier era, to *Giselle* and *La Sylphide*, and it distills Romanticism down to perfume: three ethereal ballerinas and their noble escort (Daria Sukhorukova, Daria Pavlenko, Irina Zhelonkina, and Danila Koruntsev), with a corps of attendants in long white tutus.

Dance historian Lynn Garafola pointed out to me that *Chopiniana* (as revived in 1931 by Agrippina Vaganova) has remained in the Kirov's repertory pretty steadily, and this may explain the lucid account of it we saw. Aside from a few modern ultrahigh arabesques, the dancers preserved the otherworldly lightness we see in lithographs of Taglioni. I thought the corps was especially effective, wafting with a single impulse to the musical phrase.

Fokine's ballets seem to feature the ensemble much more than any standout solo dancers. I'm aware, of course, that he created for great stars —Pavlova, Nijinsky, Karsavina, Adolph Bolm, Ida Rubinstein—but they all had the ability to transform themselves, subordinate themselves to a choreographic idea. Few dancers today have the magnetism, or the mutability, of these legendary figures. But overinterpreting can throw Fokine's stylistic unity out of whack. On opening night, Uliana Lopatkina made the *Dying Swan* into melodrama, as she caught her breath, flapped her arms frantically, clutched the air with a crooked wing.

Fokine paid more than one tribute to the romantic period. *Le Spectre de la Rose* (1910), for Nijinsky and Karsavina, was a vignette, but a tender one, like rose petals pressed in a diary. A girl comes home after a ball and falls into a reverie—she dreams not of this ball or that suitor, but of an androgynous spirit, the idea of dancing itself. Irina Golub was delightful as the dreamy girl but Igor Kolb seemed to be twining and snaking into the Spectre's delicate shapes instead of floating through them.

It must be a challenge for contemporary dancers to embody these characters so unlike ourselves. *Le Spectre* is intimate, fragile. Nijinsky's mighty leap at the end became legend, but the ballet says something more. For this performance the Kirov omitted Léon Bakst's charming set, of a Victorian sitting room. So Golub reclined uneasily in a chair draped with blue cloth, and the Spectre had to entice her across an empty stage.

When one of the components is missing, you see how thoroughly worked out Fokine's theories of taste and style were, and how perfectly Diaghilev put together his teams of collaborators for each ballet. Rimsky-Korsakov's Russo-Orientalist *Schéhérazade* and Stravinsky's Russian-modernist *Firebird* became staples in the musical repertory, and the Kirov orchestra, under Mikhail Agrest, played with a gorgeous, truly symphonic sensitivity.

But the sense of shock these two ballets ignited in 1910 is hard to imagine today. Both of them were considered savage, sensual, and absolutely transporting in their foreignness. *Schéhérazade*, one of the tales from the *Arabian Nights*, tells of passion, jealousy, and intrigue. The Shah sets a trap for his favorite concubine, Zobeide, and when he catches her and the whole harem engaged in an orgy with the slaves, he orders his soldiers to slaughter them all.

Diana Vishneva as Zobeide and Farukh Ruzimatov as the Golden Slave writhed and twisted tensely, eyed each other obliquely. They and everyone else in the cast seethed with desire every moment. Léon Bakst's original production, with its hangings in saturated greens, orange, and turquoise, looked a bit diffuse on the enormous Wang stage, and the costumes have been scaled down to suit some Las Vegas fantasy. The more Vishneva and Ruzimatov whirled ecstatically, the more I focused on their skin.

Firebird is Fokine and Stravinsky's pageant of Old Russia, with all the elements of the classic fairy-tale ballets compressed into less than an hour. It has folk dances, cavorting monsters, a momentarily thwarted romance, a magic feather, a broken spell, and a stately wedding procession to seal the future of the kingdom. What a reassuring sight this must have been in 1910 Paris, for an audience of aesthetes and expats fleeing as the Bolsheviks dismantled their world.

All the forces make their appearance in orderly succession and dance in formal patterns. The only "classical" dancing in the whole ballet is the pas de deux of the Tsarevich Ivan (Andrey Yakovlev) and the Firebird (Tatiana Amosova). She's on pointe—but only because she's a bird and has to express her freedom by leaping joyously. When Ivan catches her, she flutters and quivers to get loose. The duet looks at first like something a swan and a prince might do, except the danced relationship is one of conflict, not courtship.

One reason Fokine's work is so hard to revive today is its duality. Like George Balanchine a generation later, he wanted to clean up and preserve the classical tradition, but to do it he had to turn it inside out. Even in his own time he was both a radical and a traditionalist. Diaghilev quickly turned to more experimental dance makers.

The Kirov as an institution has come through two wars, a revolution, and the failure of the revolution. It has experienced affluence and poverty, the repression of the Stalinist years, and the freefall of the postcollectivist era. It's a bastion of conservative ballet culture; creative talents have grown restless there and found more receptive sponsorship abroad. Now, with its subsidies slashed, the company must make its mark more forcefully in the world outside Russia. It seems to be groping for a contemporary approach, and at the same time trying to construct a new relationship to its past—both the artistic past and the political.

Christian Science Monitor, 12 November 1987

At this point in history it's hard to tell which is the more astounding achievement, Vaslav Nijinsky's choreography of *Le Sacre du Printemps* or Millicent Hodson's re-creation of his ballet after seventy-five years of oblivion. The mythic status of *Le Sacre*, or *The Rite of Spring*, took root at the scandalous premiere in Diaghilev's 1913 Paris season and was sustained as Igor Stravinsky's still-scathing score made its way into the orchestral repertory. Beginning just seven years after the Nijinsky ballet's advent and quick demise, other choreographers started grappling with the ferocious, dissonant music, and with the original theme of ritual sacrifice— a maiden dances herself to death to ensure completion of the seasonal cycle. And each new *Sacre* stirred memories of the first—which, of course, fewer and fewer people had ever seen.

The Joffrey Ballet now has resurrected this totem of twentieth-century art, seemingly out of thin air. No films or notations of the complete ballet existed. Reconstructor Hodson pieced together the choreography from a hundred big and little clues over almost a decade, working independently with small nonprofessional groups of dancers. Hodson had to excavate four main levels of information—the movements of the forty-six individual dancers, the patterns of small groups, the way the groups were dispersed in the stage, and the way all of it went together with the music. This growing catalog of information existed for all that time only in Millicent Hodson's mind. Not until she began rehearsing with the Joffrey dancers last summer did she see the whole ballet take shape.

This process represents the highest order of scholarship, and something more. Hodson must have tuned in on Nijinsky's vision, understood how he was building the ballet, and absorbed his creative logic, so that she could supply what was missing from her massive but inevitably incomplete documentation. The finished ballet betrays no awkward lapses of style or choreographic floundering. It may be Hodson's work in spots, but by now Hodson essentially *is* Nijinsky.

On opening night at New York City Center the entire dance press, dance luminaries, and a wall-to-wall audience expected a revelation. Well, there were no fistfights or catcalls. The ovation at the end was appreciative, but many turned their backs on the bows and made for the exits. Merce Cunningham, who was in the audience, would probably consider that small dissent a sign of success. Even today, *Sacre* could annoy those it didn't impress.

Le Sacre du Printemps (Nijinsky/Hodson). Joffrey Ballet. Photo © Herbert Migdoll.

For me, the event was overwhelming. The ballet in the flesh exceeds every sensational claim in its dossier. It is tremendous—emotionally powerful, structurally ingenious, and beautiful besides. From the first glimpse of the gorgeous scenic design and costumes, devotedly researched after Nicholas Roerich by art historian Kenneth Archer, the stage is like some great cosmic machine—a cyclotron, a giant radar dish—that sucks in and radiates out the forces of the universe. Nothing in the ballet is naturalistic. All is controlled—preordained. The community must repeat the ritual, step for inexorable step—explosive, dispassionate, unifying, and cruel.

In the opening scenes, small groups gather in conspiratorial circle games. A three-hundred-year-old woman teaches young men to jump over sticks in order to predict their future. Trios of women, joined by others, pitch over from the waist and touch the ground. Lines of people tread the ground and leap like animals. A line of bearded Elders makes its way through the dancers and one ancient stands in the center as everyone bursts into violent stamping fits.

After an entr'acte, we see thirteen maidens, shuffling sideways in a circle, facing out. Their circle widens, contracts; they run, compulsively shifting their places in line. One stumbles briefly. They pause as if uncertain they've seen her, and she quickly scrambles up. They begin again, and again she falls. This time, they're sure. She's the Chosen. Immediately she's standing curled up, almost broken, in the center, and they begin prostrating themselves to her, falling inward, then outward like sunbursts.

On a sudden signal, they cluster to the side, leaving her isolated, ready to begin her final ordeal.

In this Danse Sacrale, the Chosen Maiden becomes the Bride of the Sun. Far from regretfulness or anger or even mundane fear, she longs for her fate, conjures up her own collapse by jumping more and more fiercely into the earth, striving higher and higher toward the sky, and is raised, lifeless, on the triumphant last note by bearskin-clad shamans.

The Joffrey dancers gave this momentous production a fierceness and dedication that's rare on today's ballet stages, led by a transfigured Beatriz Rodriguez as the Chosen Maiden. And I've said nothing about the magnificent music, which at last seems to have found its rightful home.

AFTERNOON OF A LEGEND

Dance Now, Summer 2002

The Joffrey Ballet of Chicago's all-Nijinsky program constituted a historical anomaly, one of those curious gestures that dance routinely flings across the time-space continuum to get a grip on its past. Nijinsky's first three choreographies, *L'Après-midi d'un Faune* (1912), *Jeux* (1913), and *Le Sacre du Printemps* (1913), were created close together, but they were never performed on the same program by their originating company, the Diaghilev Ballets Russes. In fact, they'd probably never been seen on a single evening until the Joffrey staged them in the fall of 2001, on a program titled, probably without irony, "The Nijinsky Mystique."

Vaslav Nijinsky is an unknowable, infinitely manipulable presence in the dance universe. His dancing and choreography come to us through fevered eyewitness accounts and a few photographs, most of them posed. The legend building and the controversy started before he left the stage. According to historian Cyril W. Beaumont: "the evidence of contemporaries is diametrically opposed."[1] For eight decades after Nijinsky's mental breakdown and premature departure from public life, pundits and insiders have contributed new documents, theories, and choreographic information, each discovery provoking reconsideration of the previous signs. Robert Joffrey launched a new round of the debate some fifteen years ago, when he gave Millicent Hodson the resources to complete her exhaustive research on *Le Sacre du Printemps* and bring it to the stage.

Revivals of lost ballets were far from unique at the Joffrey Ballet. Robert Joffrey, who died in 1988, was perhaps the greatest connoisseur and conservator classical ballet has seen in our lifetime. Before the *Sacre* project, he had added works by Kurt Jooss, Frederick Ashton, Léonide Massine, and Michel Fokine to the repertory, along with other nineteenth- and twentieth-century dances and a large complement of newly created pieces. Most of those revivals, but not all, bore some direct connection to original sources: they'd been in fairly active repertory somewhere, or their régisseurs had danced in them or were heirs to the creators or teachers of the applicable styles. Labanotator Ann Hutchinson Guest, with dance historian Ivor Guest, had reconstructed the Romantic era Pas de Six from *La Vivandière*, and several American works of the recent past had been rescued from obscurity.

The elements of any revival tend to be quite shadowy. Even with the finest recall and the most complete documentation, one has to assume some on-the-spot improvising by the directors, to fill in irretrievably lost passages or adapt to the dancers available. At the other extreme, a ballet might be extensively reworked if it looks outdated. Balanchine frequently adopted this practice for his old ballets; he didn't have much use for archival preservation. The Joffrey revival of Massine's 1920 *Pulcinella* couldn't have been much closer to its original than Hodson's *Sacre*, considering that Massine had choreographed it half a century earlier and several other prominent choreographers had set the music in the interim, including Balanchine and Robbins only two years before. The 1974 Joffrey production may even have been a remake by Massine,[2] but it isn't labeled that way in the Joffrey annals.

Even works in continuous repertory sustain slippage no one intends, and a project as massive as the *Sacre* might not have survived into a second season with the best of Ballets Russes care. But the ballet was so complex, so hotly received, and so tinged with the personal circumstances of its creators, that no one at the time could see it clearly enough to preserve it. Hodson and Archer reconstituted their *Sacre* from thousands of pieces of information, and they've been extremely candid about their sources.[3] Some of us find their archeological journeys both fascinating and convincing, but others have branded this kind of research illegitimate.[4] Ballet folk have an irrational faith in the word-of-mouth network, even when its operations can't be tracked. In the United States it's common to see old ballets carried over for years in repertory without a hint of who does the current staging. According to the program for "The Nijinsky Mystique," which premiered in Chicago in October and was repeated at Washington's Kennedy Center in February, the Joffrey *Faune* was "reconstructed by Elizabeth Schooling and William Chappell." You need to do your own research to find out that the team did its work in 1979, for a production headed by guest star Rudolf Nureyev. The ballet has been maintained ever since by a succession of anonymous in-house ballet masters, currently Adam Sklute and Cameron Basden. This *Faune* is imprinted with Nureyev's interpretation, which has been filmed, unlike any performance of Nijinsky. We really don't know how they might have differed.

Schooling/Chappell/Nureyev's *Faune* seems to be accepted as the "real" version. There have been other editions in other ballet companies, and in 1989, the Juilliard School produced a version of the ballet put together from Nijinsky's own notations, translated into Labanotation by Ann Hutchinson Guest and Claudia Jeschke.[5] Except for a few steps, the two versions have the same choreographic outlines, but there are differences in tone, musicality, phrasing. Guest and Jeschke's version is a bit softer, rounder, perhaps more amenable to modern-day psychology. The Joffrey's, danced by Davis Robertson in Washington, is hard edged, almost harsh, and strange. It seems at odds with Debussy's dreamy music, which is one of the objections voiced by its original viewers, and this alone might suggest it's right. But which interpretation did Nijinsky intend? Would he have sanctioned both possibilities? Or was he simply creating a role for himself on a largely instinctive level and ignoring the questions that would become so urgent for his posterity?

Faune was performed pretty consistently through the years, *Jeux* lasted a season, and *Le Sacre* vanished after about eight performances. The future provenance of *Sacre* began to blur immediately. For one thing, Stravinsky pared down the orchestration of his score right away so that it could be performed in concert. The press and public reactions to the ballet were so extreme that its reputation as a scandal soon overshadowed it, and contemporary assessments are colored by the passion of the moment. Stravinsky probably provoked the furor as much as Nijinsky, by breaking with the lush, coloristic effects of his previous ballets, *Firebird* and *Petrouchka*. He gave conflicting opinions of the choreography, although in his 1935 autobiography he delivered the retrospective condemnation that became embedded in the legend.[6] After the end of World War I, when Nijinsky and all his works were gone from the repertory, Diaghilev assigned Léonide Massine to choreograph a new *Sacre* in 1920. The Massine version had some relation to its predecessor from the evidence of photographs, but it too has been lost, unless you believe there were traces of it in Martha Graham's *Rite of Spring* (1984). Graham danced the Chosen Maiden for Massine in 1930.

The *Sacre* was such a monumental choreographic and musical event that it left many traces behind, fueling Hodson's eight-year odyssey to recover it. By the time it got to the Joffrey stage in 1987, the ballet world was almost as excited as the 1913 fans. This time the work had a more lasting success, notwithstanding those who refused to credit it with any authenticity. Leading the opposition was the *New Yorker*'s Arlene Croce, who offered a dizzying argument the crux of which was that there was no way Hodson could have done a credible job. Sidelining Hodson without actually evaluating what Hodson had accomplished, Croce hung her dismissal on "the difference between a scholarly endeavor and a theatrical one."[7] Had a real choreographer like Balanchine undertaken such a project, "we would have had a ballet," she declared, but the Joffrey only delivered "some fragments of curatorship tentatively affixed to the stage." What's in question here is both the comprehensiveness of Hodson's research and her ability as a director, and these are matters of opinion.

Other critics embraced the production, refusing to allow the problems of authentication to interfere with their own pleasure at the result. Alan Kriegsman of the *Washington Post* went to Los Angeles for the premiere; he called it a monumental achievement.[8] The *Los Angeles Times*'s chief music and dance critic, Martin Bernheimer, thought the reconstructors had "pieced together a revelation in the form of a choreographic puzzle."[9] After performances in Vienna, the *International Herald Tribune* arts writer David Stevens proclaimed it "convincing as a scholarly endeavor and tangible, sometimes exciting and moving, as a theatrical experience and as a historical example of collaborative creativity."[10]

Jeux was small in size, duration, and intention to begin with, a wisp of memory, sparked by Debussy's impressionistic score. It puzzled the audience more than anything else, and didn't make enough of a scandal to become a landmark. So when Hodson and her partner, art historian Kenneth Archer, approached the reconstruction, first staged by the Teatro Filarmonico in Verona in 1996, they had less to go on. Around this time they began identifying their work as "after Nijinsky" rather than by him, acknowledging their own contributions to the record. The restoration of *Jeux* was even more severely judged than the *Sacre*. I think the argument that Hodson's reconstructions are somehow a betrayal is a specious one. No one today really knows how far off they might be from the originals, and the doubters offer little information on where they go wrong. Until someone else undertakes to bring them back with as much rigor and intensity as Hodson has applied, we can't make a comparison.

Is there anything we can be certain about regarding Nijinsky as a choreographer? All three of the Joffrey's "Mystique" works were canonized by Lincoln Kirstein among the seventeen greatest works of the twentieth century up to 1970, when Kirstein compiled his eccentric but influential *Movement and Metaphor*.[11] Did Nijinsky anticipate modern choreography by establishing "an entire field theory that ensuing decades have not begun to exhaust," as Kirstein asserted?[12] Or open the door to neoclassicism as part of what historian Lynn Garafola calls Diaghilev's "larger aesthetic project . . . a dialectic of rupture and return in relation to the classical past"?[13] Can we use these revivals to validate these portentous judgments?

⌇ On the Joffrey program in Washington, only *Jeux* was new to me. I'd seen the *Faune* many times, and visited Hodson's *Sacre* as often as I could during its first Joffrey seasons. I'd read about *Jeux* but had no preconceptions as to what it would look like. *Jeux* has acquired a reputation as the first ballet in modern dress. Nijinsky's "Bloomsbury" ballet, it whispers of intrasexual liaisons among the literati, whom Nijinsky and designer Léon Bakst had observed during a visit to Lady Ottoline Morrell in 1912.[14] Nijinsky's ménage à trois for two women and himself may have been a euphemistic reference to Diaghilev and two male lovers, but the inference of lesbianism or even a three-way heterosexual dalliance was titillating enough. Like *Faune* and *Sacre*, *Jeux* was soon re-visualized by other dancers and choreographers, losing its mystery and charm in the process. Time and liberalized sexual mores have finished off whatever shock it might have delivered.

Nearly formless, *Jeux* is a series of events bracketed and given a narrative pretext by the wayward tennis balls that bounce across the space at the beginning and the end. The three players arrive one by one, encounter each other two by two, and finally become an ensemble. After the second bouncing ball, they flee separately. Like Debussy's score, which was written for the ballet, the action passes quickly from one mood to another without apparent reason, and the whole thing has an air of inconsequentiality.

Jeux is modern, not because of the clothes or the trendy games and sex but for the way the movement is devised and sequenced. The dancers' actions are drawn from a wide range of sources—classical ballet, social dance, sport and gymnastics, pedestrian gesture, and perhaps the Russian primitivist iconography Nijinsky was using at the same time for *Le Sacre du Printemps*. The dancers look quite bizarre yet they perform without emphasis, as if it were completely natural to lean toward each other, stiff as boards, their fingers curled, their faces blank, their heads canted over toward their shoulders. Later on, I remembered them as strange—and strangely touching.

Their momentum is often stopped, then continues in a different direction or timbre. All three of the Joffrey reconstructions have this stop-and-go quality. In fact, what distinguishes the Guest/Jeschke *Faune* from the Joffrey version is how much more sequential and therefore humanized the flow of movement is. It could well be that the difference between these two concepts has less to do with Nijinsky than with the reconstructors' sense of how to get from pose to pose. Whether the reconstructor is working from a notation system or a series of pictorial images, the transition between body positions is always difficult to re-create. Nijinsky himself relied on static images—the Russian icons and modern art by primitivists like Gauguin—for some of his inspiration. It was very common at the time, and still is, for dancers to animate paintings, sculptures, and ancient friezes in their efforts to evade the familiar, the traditional. Once the lost poses are found—these days usually from photographs—and put in the right sequence on the music, the reconstructor has to apply an intuitive understanding of how the poses might have been connected. The Joffrey *Faune* uses jerky transitions, the Guest/Jeschke is more legato. The ritual dances in Hodson's *Sacre* don't really continue from one pose into another but drive ahead through repetition; the cumulative force of a phrase seems to hurl the dancer into the next. In *Jeux*, I think the stopped poses suit the ballet's light and changeable atmosphere.

Like the music, *Jeux* proceeds in a series of short episodes. The dancers' fifteen-minute escapade is packed with events, none of them particularly memorable. There's nothing "organic" about the sequencing. In the *Faune*, which is so antinaturalistic with its isolated body parts, awkward two-dimensionality, and mechanical-looking progressions, the movement nevertheless follows obvious motivational patterns: the Faune idly plays his flute, eats grapes; the nymphs appear; he notices them. But in *Jeux*, the players change from one kind of action to another almost arbitrarily. Once in a while they mime swinging a tennis racket, but these moves are as abstract as their sudden jumps with flexed arms and feet. They're playing a game, but the game isn't tennis.

Jeux is like some carefully encoded social transaction—a Baroque minuet or a chess game. Nothing can be what it really looks like; everything stands for more than it seems. The two women are dressed identically, even to their brunette hairdos. They wear pointe shoes but almost never rise from half-toe. When the dancers tilt their heads askew, it's as if they're covertly checking out the status of each other's affections. Cyril Beaumont noted how little acting the original dancers did. Normally so expressive, their features were "expressionless and set," suggesting masks, he thought.[15] Photographs of Nijinsky, Tamara Karsavina, and Ludmilla Schollar confirm

L'Après-midi d'un Faune (Nijinsky). Lubov Tchernicheva and Vaslav Nijinsky, Diaghilev's Ballets Russes. Photo by Baron Adolphe de Meyer. Jerome Robbins Dance Division, The New York Public Library for the Performing Arts, Astor, Lenox and Tilden Foundations.

Beaumont's impression of impassivity. The Joffrey Ballet program offers a sketchy synopsis attributed to Nijinsky, and the cast I saw, Deborah Dawn, Maia Wilkins and Willy Shives, acted it out quite literally, almost as if they were doing an Antony Tudor ballet of much later vintage.

The man seems to prefer one woman at first, and the other sulks, but later he draws her into his encircling arm. When the two women dance together, they move spoon fashion, bodies up against each other, or they mirror each other face to face. The eventual threesome is formed either as a unison lineup or with the man and one woman spooned together so that she faces and mirrors the other woman, with the man sandwiched between them. After a three-way, symmetrical kiss, the music subsides and they lie down, the two women with their heads on the man's chest.

One thing that has always troubled me about Nijinsky's reputation as a choreographer is his inexperience, combined with his withdrawn and naïve personality. Novice choreographers have certainly made spectacular breakthroughs—think of Martha Graham's early work, or Merce Cunningham's. The great careers prove out what might have started as a flash of intuition. The *Faune* and *Jeux* are miniatures, understandably modest in ambition and essentially soloistic in design. The tremendous size of the *Sacre* must have been dictated by Stravinsky's music, and the Dalcroze-trained Marie Rambert undoubtedly helped Nijinsky through the rhythmic challenges of that score. For all these works the choreographer required inordinate rehearsal time, and the dancers had difficulty both attaining the shapes he wanted and remembering the sequencing.

Nijinsky's career ended after only one more ballet production, *Tyl Eulenspiegel*, and the claims that have been made for him seem disproportionate. What if the oddness was not creative genius but a vision insufficiently realized? What if the consistency and foresight attributed to him were actually implanted by the more rational or conventional minds who later took up his thinking? In 1912 Diaghilev needed a major choreographer and was determined to make one out of Nijinsky. He certainly attracted attention, but could he have become a Fokine?

On the basis of these first three ballets, it seems to me now that Nijinsky had an undeniable gift for group choreography. Except for his own role of the Faune, he suppressed his extraordinary ability to create character. The simple but imaginative group patterns in Guest and Jeschke's *Faune* indicate that he may have rethought the chorus of nymphs when he notated the ballet in 1915, but even in the Schooling/Chappell version this ensemble of seven women is beautifully designed. Bronislava Nijinska, the choreographer's sister, noted in her invaluable memoirs that Nijinsky was trying to avoid conventional partnering, even when he danced in classical roles,[16] and the suggestive groupings of *Jeux* are not only unconventional but allusive in a new way. Seeing the *Sacre* again, I was overwhelmed again at the ritualized counterpoint and the wonderfully crafted surges of group violence and ecstasy.

Nijinska, on whom Vaslav worked out key movement ideas for all three of these ballets, declared *Jeux* "the forerunner of Neoclassical Ballet."[17] Nijinska spent several years in Soviet Russia and returned to Europe in 1921, long after Nijinsky's descent into silence. She too was a master choreographer; *Les Biches*, *Les Noces*, and *Le Train Bleu* are the natural successors to his works, but as historian Robert Greskovic points out about *Les Noces*, "What Nijinsky had turned into a modern dance–like antiballet mode of movement [in *Le Sacre*], Nijinska made into austere but undeniable ballet dancing."[18] Nijinska's neoclassical work survived in the Royal Ballet, and her influence spread to Ashton and Balanchine.

But there's another sense in which Nijinsky's modernism veered off from the mellowing evolution of neoclassicism. Diaghilev was justly celebrated for novelty and experimentation, but the Ballets Russes catered to an elitist, conservative audience. Diaghilev's failures—*Jeux* and *Sacre* among them—were the most subversive of his adventures. The first three Nijinsky ballets slashed into the repertory with rakish bodies, aberrant behavior, intractably nonvirtuosic movement. Perhaps, as Millicent Hodson thinks, Nijinsky had a clairvoyant vision of catastrophe. In 1913, all Europe was spoiling for a conflagration, and Nijinsky wouldn't have been the only artist to anticipate the coming war. Hodson also speaks of the constricted poses and groups, the withheld virtuosity and sudden bursts of action, as a way of resisting the easy excesses of ballet and building up tension in the dancer and the audience.[19]

At the same time that Diaghilev was seeking novelty, pushing aside the reformist story ballets of Fokine, and beginning to enlist postimpressionist painters and folkloric musical modernists, Dada and futurism were shouting their defiance of all traditional artmaking. In 1917 Diaghilev tapped Satie and Picasso, for *Parade* (revived, incidentally, during the great Joffrey reconstruction period by its choreographer, Massine). It was the Cubo-futurist line of modernism that led, through Marcel Duchamp, to John Cage and Merce Cunningham, and then to the postmodern dancers. This line of modernism resisted aesthetics and storytelling, the easy satisfactions of form, the sympathetic blandishments of personality. What *Jeux* suggests to me most of all is a dance called *Nocturnes*, choreographed in

1956 by Merce Cunningham, a dance of events and atmosphere, loosely tied to a non-narrative score by Erik Satie.

None of Nijinsky's ballets can be called "abstract." They all follow a scenario. But they feel contemporary in a way that no Diaghilev ballet composed before them does, and few that came after. Looking at them, we see many of the ideas that were taken up decades later by Cunningham and the post-Cunningham avant-garde. I'm especially thinking of the movement drawn from sources outside of ballet; the resisting of personality through a neutral demeanor; the sense of overload and eventfulness, produced by small, unrelated phrases without organic transitions; the absence of a developing phraseology or structure; the collagelike method of organization and its leveling effect, where no one action or dancer is stressed over another. In a 1986 paper titled "Composition by Field," Millicent Hodson built a fascinating account of experimental ideas spanning art, literature, and dance in the 1950s.[20] How much of this research entered her thinking about *Sacre* and *Jeux* is uncertain. One of the issues spiraling around the vortex that is Vaslav Nijinsky involves the unanswered question of how much Hodson has contributed to his choreographic reputation from her own intuitive understanding and choreographic gifts.

Historical repertory has been in decline in America for many years, but perhaps the Joffrey can spark a renewed respect for the treasures of the past. The Nijinsky works, regardless of their controversial provenance or contested authenticity, are worth doing for the sake of the dancers as well as the audience. They're so resistant to contemporary expressivity and ego glorification, they look wrong. For that reason alone, they could be right.

NIJINSKY'S CRIME AGAINST GRACE

DCA News, Autumn 1997

The first Joffrey Ballet performance of *Le Sacre du Printemps* in 1987 wasn't the shocker that detonated when Stravinsky and Nijinsky released the demons of modernism onto the ballet world of 1913. But it was a revelation just the same, confirming the ballet's reputation as a masterpiece. Besides the sheer pleasure of the choreographic design, and the sensual delight of color, sound, and movement, the reconstruction, directed by Millicent Hodson, was a deeply satisfying scholarly achievement.

For Hodson, a gifted researcher, historian, and teaching personality, the professional risk was enormous. Had she brought the project to fruition under a less respected dance archivist than Robert Joffrey, it might have had more detractors. Worse, it might have gone unheralded, as did her revival of Balanchine's *La Chatte* for Les Grands Ballets Canadiens a few years later. But Hodson's *Sacre* was a huge critical success. Joffrey kept it in repertory long enough to be shown internationally. The ballet embarked on a more visible career than its original life span, and Hodson was launched, with collaborator/designer/scholar Kenneth Archer, as a rescuer of what was thought to be the unrecoverable past.

Nijinsky's Crime against Grace is one of the end products of Hodson and Archer's *Sacre* project.[21] The ballet itself left the Joffrey repertory after Robert Joffrey died, but there are more lasting traces of the undertaking: films, interviews, articles, and hundreds of lively drawings in which Hodson first constructed the body attitudes, gestures, and dynamism she intended to elicit from dancers. Many of these form the heart of this book.

Nijinsky's Crime is called a "reconstruction score," but it's no arcane manuscript written in code for the eyes of professional reconstructors. Instead, it's a kind of graphic overview. Maybe somewhere Hodson has notated every inch of this extremely complex ballet, but what she does here is to picture the body movements and groupings, matched with excerpts from Stravinsky's two-piano reduction and brief identifying verbal clues. So you can read through it and see how the choreography evolves through the dance.

One of Hodson's aims in doing the book was to validate her main choreographic sources. Stravinsky himself and Marie Rambert, who assisted Nijinsky in sorting out the music, both left scores with verbal indications to the movement. The artist Valentine Gross-Hugo made sketchbooks, flipping pages rapidly during some of the original eight performances. Hodson also includes some of the few photographs that were taken, nearly all of them posed backstage, a verbal comment or two, and samples of the work of contemporary painters like Kasimir Malevich and Marcel Duchamp.

As a historian, Hodson knows, and, even better, can connect to the cultural iconography that surrounds the ballets she is studying. She sees Nijinsky as a representative of modern art. She shows how the choreography splinters the body to present multiple views of the same movement, in a physical parallel to the work of cubist and futurist painters.

As she exposes the contrapuntal craft of the big group scenes, I begin to understand more clearly how the original audience could have become infuriated. Nijinsky's canonic breakup of the phrase, his compressed rhythms, pounding repetitions, and dissonant shapes—all reflecting the music and incrementally increasing the music's assault—looked like chaos but were actually fanatical patterns. Maybe *Le Sacre*'s creators did unlock the secrets of the ancestors; maybe they were all borderline psychotics.

The book provides grounds for reopening this and other discussions, and it sent me back to the music with a new astonishment. It also evoked Hodson's terrific presence, her contagious excitement on the trail of choreographic treasures and their environments. Since *Le Sacre*, Hodson and Archer have painstakingly reconstructed at least half a dozen ballets from the Diaghilev and early Balanchine periods, and a whole program from the Ballets Suédois is scheduled for Stockholm next June. But ballets come and go on the stage. Provoking theoretical discussions about them, as Hodson's critical insight does, is another way of prolonging their life.

Nijinsky's Crime against Grace could have been two books. Hodson's journey to bring the most famous lost work in the history of twentieth-century ballet back to life was unprecedented. For eight years she not only tracked down and collated all the extant sources of *Le Sacre du Printemps*, but then turned that mass of evidence into living choreography. In her introduction, she gives a tantalizing glimpse of that story, but the step-by-step transformation of Stravinsky's monumental score into the precise movements of forty-six dancers is no academic exercise. I'm not demeaning the reconstruction's authenticity when I say Hodson had to be a gifted choreographer to do it.

NIJINSKY IN TRANSLATION

Hudson Review, Autumn 1999

Shortly after publication of the new version of Nijinsky's diaries,[22] Christopher Lydon invited Joan Acocella, the volume's editor, to appear on his National Public Radio talk show "The Connection." Here's how Lydon introduced the session:

In 1909 the Russian-born dancer Vaslav Nijinsky was nineteen years old when he made his explosive debut in Paris with the Ballets Russes. From the start his performances were so highly sexualized and avant-garde they guaranteed him a place in dance history. The erotic choreography of Nijinsky's *Rite of Spring* to the Stravinsky score triggered a riot in the aisles of Champs-Elysées theater. Nijinsky was known for one other thing in his life—his infamous diary, written at the furious pace of a man losing his mind. He put his creative madness to paper over the course of six weeks. The diary was published after his death as a symbol of the brilliant but suffering artist, though his wife had primed, rearranged and rewritten the diary to hide his obsessions and his bisexual past. Now sixty years later the whole story is being told.[23]

Lydon's clichéd rendition consigns the "new" Nijinsky to the crowded category of history's brilliant but suffering not to mention crazy artists. Though it supposedly improves on the sanitized and/or infamous previous publication, the recovered diary comes off in Lydon's eyes as the colorful but obsessive ravings of a misfit—nothing new in the literature of our times. Lydon also embellishes that other stanza of the Nijinsky legend, his eroticism. As if there were no scandals except sex scandals, he figures *The Rite of Spring* must have had salacious choreography, and he seems to have missed the important Nijinsky roles that didn't exploit his sexuality, in *Les Sylphides, Petrouchka, Carnaval,* and *Giselle,* for instance.

Flaming snapshots are not new to the iconography of dance. In fact, they often attain the status of dance history. It's in the nature of dance that its practitioners—choreographers and dancers—have to rely on others to document what they do. Relatively few people sit in the theater and observe dancers with their own eyes. Audience members alone take away some authentic experience, and even they can have capricious memories. What the rest of us think dance is, or was, depends on critics, interviewers, photographers, filmmakers, notators, publicists, and the images constructed offstage by the dancers themselves. It's no surprise when only the slickest common denominator comes to the surface.

The Diary of Vaslav Nijinsky, edited by Romola Nijinsky, was first published in 1936, when its author had been disabled by mental illness for almost two decades—he was to live in this occluded state until 1950. His motivation for starting the diary, written in 1919 when he and his family were ensconced in St. Moritz at the end of World War I, seems to have been confessional. Converted to a saintly Tolstoyanism, and tortured by a guilty desire to atone for what he saw as his bad behavior in the past, he wanted the world to understand and forgive him. For five years, his personal misfortunes had been compounded by the upheavals of war; his erratic behavior was getting worse and couldn't be concealed. In St. Moritz he was undergoing interviews with a doctor and he suspected his wife intended to have him hospitalized. He realized his mind was coming apart, and he was trying to understand. Verbalizing his confusion may have been the only alternative to dancing it out, which was no longer possible.

For years after Nijinsky was institutionalized and the writing ceased, Romola Nijinsky envisioned the diary as a future bestseller, a solution to their financial needs. It would rectify the real and imaginary injustices done to her famous husband and reinforce his tragic legend. She succeeded in publishing her expurgated version only after strenuous networking among the elite patrons of ballet, including Lincoln Kirstein, and after her own biography of Vaslav appeared, in 1934.

By now the accumulated literature of the Diaghilev era gives us some perspective on the celebrated impresario, his dancers, and the ballets that brought a classical art into the twentieth century. At least three serious biographies of Nijinsky have been published besides Romola's account, which ran to two volumes. There have been memoirs and tributes, and then the innumerable books on the art and times of Diaghilev. Joan Acocella's 1984 doctoral dissertation covered the early years of the Ballets Russes, the years of Nijinsky's eminence.[24]

The full translation does indeed restore material censored by Romola Nijinsky. It runs to nearly three hundred pages, a third longer than Romola's slim volume, and is organized differently, according to what seems to be the writer's original sequence. Acocella has restored passages that would have embarrassed Romola or exposed Nijinsky's priapic interests. She's also reinstated a whole section of letters and chants set in poetic form, as well as many pages of stream-of-consciousness wanderings that make poetic if not logical sense.

> I want to sleep, but my wife does not feel. She thinks in her sleep. I am not thinking, and therefore I will not go to sleep. I do not sleep because of the powders. They can give me any medicine they like, but I will not sleep. If they give me subcutaneous morphine injections, I will not sleep. I know my own habits. I like morphine, but I do not like death. Death is morphine. I am not morphine. My wife has taken a powder containing morphine and is therefore in a daze. She is not asleep.[25]

Millennial readers are drawn to this kind of writing: apocalyptic, hallucinatory, preoccupied with the body's appetites and pathologies. We are incurably voyeuristic about the bathroom and bedroom habits of stars. And any mix of sensuality and mysticism is doubly provocative. Still, Nijinsky's prose, now fully revealed, is hard going. Reading it is like watching an autistic child rocking back and forth, back and forth, absorbed in the patterns of a speeding universe but unable to waylay them long enough to process into purposeful action. It's a terrible sight. We want to stop him, comfort him. But we know he's doomed.

Peter Ostwald, a professor of psychiatry, thoroughly explored the workings of Nijinsky's mind, through the diary and through extensive studies of the diagnoses and treatments to which the dancer was subjected.[26] His book is probably the definitive explanation of Nijinsky's psychosis. Ostwald also considered some of the ways in which Nijinsky's life as a dancer might have aggravated his clinical symptoms. As a performer, Nijinsky was used to role-playing, and his diary has powerful histrionic overtones. His life in the ballet required incessant practice and repetition of the same moves in order to perfect them, a process not unlike his verbal tics.

> I want to tell you that I love you you
> I want to tell you that I love you you
> I want to tell you that I love I love I love
> I want to tell you that I love I love I love
> I love but you do not. You do not love that which He
> I love that He that He. You are death you are death.[27]

Nijinsky seems to have been cursed with bad genes—madness ran in his family—and science had not yet found ways to moderate the effects of schizophrenia and manic depression. His mind at the time of writing the diary must also have been burdened by a terrible dependency. Jobless and copeless, with a wife and child to support, the twenty-nine-year-old Nijinsky had never even had to take care of himself. He entered the Maryinsky theater school as a child. Lower-class parents prayed that their children would have the talent to be accepted in such schools; not only would they be educated and provided for, they would be assured of decent employment afterward. The precocious Nijinsky was taken into the Imperial Ballet while still a student; a couple of years later Diaghilev whisked him off to Paris.

Though he must have earned enormous fees from his dancing, he probably turned them over to his boss and lover, Diaghilev. Romola was still litigating to recover them years after Nijinsky was dismissed for marrying her. Diaghilev encouraged him to choreograph, and never has a neophyte been so amply surrounded by high-powered collaborators and resources. Ousted from the Ballet Russes, he tried to take control of his artistic life. With no experience in business affairs and a distinctly unaggressive personality, he bungled badly. Others tried to help him start a school or a company, including his gifted sister Bronislava, but the war made such schemes impossible. Bronislava returned to revolutionary Russia; Vaslav and Romola were caught in Budapest as prisoners of war in the household of his overbearing mother-in-law.

Diaghilev, in possibly the most misguided act of his career besides the firing of Nijinsky, extricated the dancer from this predicament only to set him a more severe sentence. Otto Kahn of the Metropolitan Opera, principal backer of the 1916–1917 Ballets Russes North American tour, had demanded Nijinsky's stellar presence as artistic director, dancer, and choreographer. Nijinsky couldn't cope with any of it, and the tour was a failure although it remains in the mythology as one of only two opportunities Americans had to see the fabulous Ballets Russes. Even then, the company was making myths. Kirstein tells how, when he was an impressionable nine-year-old, his mother wouldn't let him see the company in Boston; ironically, he learned later that the performance he missed turned out to be one of those occasions when Alexander Gavrilov substituted for Nijinsky, unannounced.[28]

The Nijinskys returned to their temporary exile in St. Moritz. If, as Joan Acocella theorizes, Vaslav wanted above all to preserve his relationship with his wife, he must have realized that she was his sole lifeline at that point. In the diary, Nijinsky talks very little about dance, almost never about his fabulous early success or his later catastrophes. He's obsessed with sex, money, and the people around him—his wife, daughter Kyra, the servants, the doctor—and with his own identity in relation to the dominant figures in his life, Diaghilev and God. His fellow dancers remember him as inarticulate even before his decline. The ballerina Tamara Karsavina's reflection is typical: "Nijinsky had no gift of precise thought, still less that of expressing his ideas in adequate words."[29] Yet, once he embarked on the diary, he became fascinated with his own words and the effect they would have on others. After some irreverences about the Church and the Pope, he says:

> I speak crudely on purpose, so as to be better understood, but not in order to offend people. . . . Tolstoy was ashamed of being a writer, because he thought he was just a man. Man is a writer. A writer is a journalist. I like journalists who like people. Journalists who write nonsense are money. Money is journalists. I am a journal without money. I like journals. A journal is life. I am a journal in life. Man, journal, life, writer, tolstoy, dostoevsky.[30]

His endless reconfigurings of these identity markers seem to be his attempt to hold on to a persona that was slipping. They remind me of the black outlines with which van Gogh nailed down the shapes in his late paintings.

I'm not as convinced as Joan Acocella that Nijinsky might have been "trying to create a work of literature."[31] In fact, Acocella makes many claims in her introduction that tend to imprint the Nijinsky mythology more deeply, and even extend it. She tries to counter the common perception of Nijin-sky's naiveté: "genius of dance, helpless in all else." He was well read and even sophisticated, Acocella says, and "knew something about painting."[32] But when he refers to Russian authors, mainly Tolstoy and Dostoyevsky, they're no more substantial than the frequent walk-on appearances of politicians who'd been in the war news. Nijinsky's familiarity with such figures is extremely selective. He's read their books in school, or learned of them in the newspapers or from hanging around Diaghilev's literary circle, but he derives only symbolic meanings from their lives. To make a case for Nijinsky as a product of the "intellectual trends of the day"[33] is like calling Joan of Arc a theologian.

The one thing Acocella does not address in her revaluation of Nijinsky is his choreography. She's resigned to the fact that choreography disappears only a little less instantaneously than dancing. "Of these works [*L'Après-midi d'un Faune, Jeux*, and *Le Sacre du Printemps*]," she says, "only one, *The Afternoon of a Faun*, survives today, but it is enough to show that Nijinsky ushered ballet into modernism."[34] Rather than probe for some idea about great choreography that outweighs scandals, accolades, and posthumous canonizations, she insists on Nijinsky's genius while asserting that "never was so much artistic fame based on so little evidence."[35]

Nijinsky's "father of modernism" label may have been initiated by Kir-stein. As early as 1935 he ventured that as a choreographer Nijinsky "either demonstrated or implied theories as profound as have ever been articu-lated about the classic theatrical dance."[36] By 1970 seventeen works by nine choreographers occupied Kirstein's pantheon of twentieth-century greats,[37] and three of the four Nijinsky ballets made it onto that select list. These three, *Faune, Jeux,* and *Sacre*, were all originals, way outside any of the Ballets Russes self-made modernist formulas, before or after Nijinsky. But fate didn't allow him to follow up these ballets; they might have started a revolution or they might have been meteoric accidents. Nijinsky had no direct successors other than his soul mate sister Bronislava, nor can his influence on other individuals, styles, or schools be clearly identified. Bal-anchine, Tudor, Ashton, and Robbins were all much more instrumental in creating modern ballet.

Once Nijinsky was expelled from the Ballets Russes, his ballets were too. They were oddities in their own time, and one can only imagine what kind of a repertory he'd have had to collect around them if he'd been capable of assembling another company—the nine-minute *Faune*, archaic in style, provocative in theme; the sexually ambiguous *Jeux*; the gigantic and incon-ceivable *Sacre*; and the strange, pantomimic and possibly unfinished *Tyl*

Eulenspiegel. Nijinsky planned other ballets that never came to fruition, and during his more lucid periods in Switzerland he devised a notation system and recorded at least one of his finished works, *Faune*.

Acocella is willing to leave all of this in the mythological realm, along with Nijinsky's dancing, which seems never to have been filmed. And in a footnote, she adds the opinion that "there have been attempted reconstructions . . . but the choreographic evidence is so meager that these productions must be considered constructions rather than reconstructions."[38] Acocella, who became the dance critic of the *New Yorker* in 1998, has adopted her predecessor Arlene Croce's regrettable habit of not naming those whose work she considers substandard. Acocella's dismissive remark about the extant or revived Nijinsky oeuvre clarifies nothing, not even the nature of the supposedly credible *Faune* on which she plants his choreographic reputation.

Faune is the only ballet in Nijinsky's notation that has been found. The notators Ann Hutchinson Guest and Claudia Jeschke deciphered his system and translated it into the more commonly used Labanotation, and the dance has been taught and filmed from this score.[39] Comparing this production with the more widely known word-of-mouth stagings of the *Faune* (evidently after Rudolf Nureyev's performances) in the recent repertories of the Joffrey and the Paris Opera Ballets, you can see quite obvious differences. We don't even know which is Acocella's definitive and defining version.

And to claim that only "meager evidence" prompted Millicent Hodson's eight-year reinstatement of *Le Sacre du Printemps* is an insult to one of the most scrupulous and dedicated scholars in the field of dance history. Hodson's *Sacre* reveals her own directorial and creative talent. Her *Sacre* was a tremendous success when the Joffrey premiered it in 1987, and it has since been taken into the repertory of several ballet companies around the world. Hodson and Archer went on to retrieve many other iconic twentieth-century ballets, including *Jeux* and *Tyl*, and to create new works from styles long thought to have disappeared. Since Acocella ignores it, we don't know why she thinks Hodson's *Sacre* is inauthentic, nor, for that matter, why the original *Sacre* or anything else validates Nijinsky's choreographic greatness.

Unless some miraculous discovery is made—a film taken during a performance by some phantom photographer at the back of the theater—we can only know Nijinsky's choreography and his dancing by secondhand means. I think dance history from the point when the artist ceases to function has to be debatable. People will find documents, they'll search their memories, they'll try to match up visual relics with verbal accounts, and they'll disagree about what that all means. Acocella offers nothing but a *Faune* reconstruction with an unidentified provenance to prove Nijinsky's crucial position as the founder of modernism. So we're left with this deeply disturbed diary as his artistic testament. As a vehicle of mystification, it encourages those who'd like to think of Nijinsky as just another glam boy with a problem.

WHEN BALLET LEAPED INTO TODAY

Christian Science Monitor, 5 January 1990

Sixty years after its termination the Ballets Russes de Serge Diaghilev holds a mythic allure for audiences and scholars that seems to increase over the years. This fall some new productions and a new book gave us another opportunity to think about the Russian impresario who, with his artistic collaborators, carried ballet into the modern age in two extraordinary decades.

No one can deny the glamour of Diaghilev's fast-evolving circle—Nijinsky, Fokine, Karsavina, Stravinsky, Picasso, Massine, Balanchine were among them—or the impact most of them made on dance in their subsequent careers. The Diaghilev ballets that survive don't look anything like the dance of today, and the public basically doesn't care much about history. Yet Diaghilev is something of an industry in the ballet world. Books keep coming out, long-dormant ballets keep being resurrected. Each arrival evokes curiosity, controversy, and sometimes revelation.

Diaghilev's Ballets Russes by Lynn Garafola examines the company's popularity in its own time from three perspectives: art, enterprise, and audience. This is not a study of choreography or a gossip's field day—both approaches which have been amply applied to the Ballets Russes by others. Instead, Garafola sees the company's power as stemming from political, artistic, economic, and social forces that came into play in varying combinations during the company's existence. The ballets almost recede into the background as she fits the Ballets Russes into the culture of modernity that was emerging, mainly in Paris and London, before and after World War I.

The usual ballet history, self-preoccupied and inbred, makes ballet seem a kind of religious practice, available only to initiates, who gather in overheated studios to enact arcane rituals and then collectively, intuitively arrive at elusive metaphors of Truth and Beauty. The mundane world, when it intrudes on their incantations at all, disturbs them very little.

Lynn Garafola doesn't see it that way. For her, ballet is a product of the times, bearing the indelible marks of world events. The early years of Diaghilev's dynasty were provoked by social conscience and republicanism—the ideals of the Russian revolution—and by the modernist breakthroughs of the revolutionary Russian stage. Almost from the first Paris season in 1909, Garafola thinks, Diaghilev responded to both the siren song of modernism and the detaining clutches of conservatism. At different times one or the other could rescue his company from chronic insolvency. He aligned himself with futurism, fashion, vernacular dancing, the music hall, retrospective classicism, new waves, old waves, whichever hand seemed likely to pay off at the critical moment.

In the process, he not only brought into being a repertory of persistent novelty and frequent genius, he changed the way Europe thought about ballet and ballet dancing. Garafola sees Diaghilev as propelling ballet from the rarefied status of high culture to a popular and accepted theatrical form. As one of the first independent ballet companies, not attached to a state institution, the Ballets Russes had to create a name and a style for itself in order to survive, and sometimes it was forced to fit itself into opera seasons, or even provide half-hour acts on a variety bill. Ingeniously, Garafola looks at the circles of artists, literati, and social climbers that adopted the Ballets Russes, the tastemakers who presented it, and the influence its supporters exerted on the repertory.

Garafola focuses on three choreographers as successively shaping the Ballets Russes character: Michel Fokine, the first, democratizing force; Vaslav Nijinsky, a modernist who definitively gave ballet a Western sensibility; and his sister Bronislava Nijinska, whose ballets criticized modern society and its sexual mores. After 1924, Garafola thinks, straitened economics led Diaghilev to a more eclectic mix of styles as he courted a popular public. The company's modernism was transformed in the last five years "from a radical statement into a socially palatable style."

As she details the social and artistic surges in which the Ballets Russes were swept along, Garafola doesn't attempt to single out any one significant breakthrough or culminating style. This is a refreshingly evenhanded view of history, designating neither the exoticism of Fokine nor the neoclassicism of Balanchine as Diaghilev's principal legacy. Considering the turbulent artistic currents of the period, the many areas of private and public life that were drawn to the Ballets Russes and that had some part in shaping its course, Garafola demonstrates that there's no one way to write history, and that even after this fascinating book, the history of the Ballets Russes can still be worked on.

⌒ This, I think, is the premise with which we can also view each new reconstruction of a Ballets Russes work. Since authenticity is so much in debate in the ephemeral realm of dance, even revivals coming from the same hand can look different, and no audience can say for sure which version is closest to the original ballet. The Joffrey Ballet's new production of Bronislava Nijinska's *Les Noces* (1923) was staged by the choreographer's daughter Irina and Howard Sayette, the same team responsible for the Dance Theater of Harlem (DTH) version. Yet the ballet looks quite different on each company. While DTH had a strong sense of ensemble when they performed *Les Noces* last spring, I thought they overacted and romanticized the parts of the bridal couple and their parents. The Joffrey cast I saw, headed by Julie Janus and Daniel Baudendistel, treated the characters more impersonally, more like icons, and created the strange, modernistic sculptural designs with a solemn and beautiful formality.

An even more drastic account of what's come to be the accepted version of a classic is the "new" *Après-Midi d'un Faune* (1912), shown recently in New York by the Juilliard Dance Theater. Most Americans know *Faune* from the version taught to Rudolf Nureyev and the Joffrey by Elizabeth Schooling in 1979. This ballet, much inscribed with Nureyev's personal mannerisms and ideas, has remained in the Joffrey repertory, looking more and more peculiar as the years go by. Now Ann Hutchinson Guest and Claudia Jeschke have discovered and read the notations Vaslav Nijinsky himself made for his ballet. Their account of the *Faune* is softer in line and less extreme in every way.

Instead of simply using Debussy's familiar score as background, the Faun's naive approaches and the nymphs' fearful retreats flow out of the musical line. Instead of all the movement being grounded and quirkily angular, some of the transitions are smoother and the traveling steps vary in texture, even including little jumps and springy runs, so that we get a sense of both languorousness and urgency in this encounter between virginal innocence and seductive primitivism. Lynn Garafola discusses *Faune* as an erotic conquest that inadvertently illustrates Nijinsky's own attitude toward sex. Later she quotes E. M. Forster as seeing the Faun as "a humorous and alarming animal." With these discrepant versions of the ballet, the audience now has its own choice of interpretations.

The interest in reconstruction has even given us startling new ways to look at Diaghilev ballet. This fall the Joffrey was able to offer *Faune* and *Noces* on a program with Millicent Hodson's reconstruction of Nijinsky's *Le Sacre du Printemps*. This could never have happened in historical time, since *Sacre* was withdrawn during its initial season in 1913 and rechoreographed in 1920 by Léonide Massine. So, unlike Diaghilev's contemporaries, we could see together the Nijinsky-Nijinska works that have often been compared.

For me, *Les Noces*, in spite of its rigor and abstractness, is an altogether more accessible ballet. The "plot" is familiar and is told in a graphic, even cinematic form. Stravinsky's music is more melodic, more ongoing, the themes longer, the rhythms more sustained than in his barbaric *Sacre*. Choreographically this is represented in large, clear group movements, a minimum of complex counterpoint, and an easy-to-read offsetting of principal characters against the corps.

In *Sacre* the rhythms are foreshortened, the melodies fragmentary, the harmonies crudely dissonant. Similarly, the choreography is almost confused; you can't follow it or assemble it into neat counterpoint. The motifs are very curtailed, almost cursory, but each one is an outcry. The sparse individual characters and choreographic markers are not set apart, but rise to the surface for a moment like bubbles bursting. You may miss them entirely, or only become aware of them after a delay.

Le Sacre is ritual at its most raw and primitive stage. *Les Noces* shows a community that is already more socialized, submitting itself to a more prescribed, confining religious order. What they have in common is a non-balletic, nonvirtuosic, severe, and sculptural movement style and a tight massing of groups that Garafola attributes to constructivism.

DANCE THEATRE OF HARLEM'S NIJINSKA

Christian Science Monitor, 28 July 1989

Bronislava Nijinska's choreographic reputation is based on two splendid works, made within a year of each other for Diaghilev's Ballets Russes. Because *Les Noces* (1923) and *Les Biches* (1924) are virtually the only ballets of hers that survive, critics and historians continue to wonder whether they were the fortuitously preserved vestiges of a closetful of treasures, or if they're just the trinkets from an otherwise dowdy wardrobe.

Dance Theatre of Harlem, celebrating its twentieth-anniversary season at City Center, presented both ballets, plus another Nijinska work, the ballet spoof *Rondo Capriccioso* (1952), which has never been seen in this country. The choreographer's daughter, Irina Nijinska, staged all three works for DTH, assisted by Howard Sayette for *Les Noces* and Rosella Hightower for *Rondo*.

Set to music of Camille Saint-Saens, *Rondo Capriccioso* is basically a pas de deux in an all-purpose exotic style, for a Bird of Paradise and a Prince, Stephanie Dabney and Ronald Perry, framed by Two Hunters, Dean Anderson and Marck Waymmann. The Prince, dressed in shocking pink, stalks the ballerina, who wears a lavender bodice and a tutu and bathing cap made of white feathers. She leaps slowly away from him while checking to see he's not too far behind. Eventually he catches her, of course, and arranges her in a variety of lifts, the hardest of which are delegated to the Hunters. The higher she's hoisted, the more surprised she looks and the faster she flutters her hands. When the Hunters aren't otherwise occupied, they ripple a long orange cloth to float over and behind the couple's most decorative effects, and in one deft maneuver they drape it over the ballerina's extended leg in the final lift, just as the Prince throws her completely upside down over his shoulder.

From the initial moments of the piece, when the Prince spies on the Bird of Paradise by sticking his head out between the two Hunters as if they were bushes, *Rondo* is a collection of clichés and decadent devices cribbed from the late-nineteenth-, early twentieth-century showpieces that filled up the idle moments in every ballet company's repertory for all the years of Nijinska's career. The audience at DTH's first performance, however, didn't emit a giggle, even though Dabney intermittently signaled that it was supposed to. Maybe this was because Dabney and Perry play the same roles straight in *Firebird*, elsewhere in the repertory, but that should have made the double entendre funnier.

Dance humor is an intriguing subject. With Bronislava Nijinska it's even more elusive than usual, because she had a subtle wit, often characterized as "feminine" in the male-dominated world of Diaghilev, and because she could count on her sophisticated audience to recognize her sly allusions with very little prompting from the dancers. *Les Biches* (Poulenc) is the most mysterious ballet I've ever seen—a strange cocktail party where the women outnumber the men five to one, where the three male guests are brawny types dressed as if they've come straight from the gym, and where the guests play boisterous games with a large, moveable sofa.

There are some halfhearted flirtations, and some more serious, offbeat ones. Two girls in gray (Kellye Gordon and Erika Lambe) do a close-harmony duet that culminates in a surprised kiss. One of the athletes (Eddie J. Shellman) is attracted to an androgynous creature (Virginia Johnson) in

Les Biches (Nijinska). Virginia Johnson and Eddie J. Shellman, Dance Theater of Harlem. Photograph © 1983 Jack Vartoogian/FrontRowPhotos.

a blue velvet tunic and white gloves. The Hostess, draped in pearls, commandeers both of the other two men.

One of the most remarkable things about *Les Biches* is that it's all dancing, no miming or trademark gestures to build characters or plot. The DTH corps looked wonderfully vain and sensuous promenading on their pointes, shoulders swaying with their arms straight down and hands angling out at the hips. Francesca Harper was terrific in the Hostess's allegro variation; for some reason she doesn't make an appearance till late in the party, and her bubbling solo gives the whole ballet a second wind. Virginia Johnson was opaque, remote, as the Girl in Blue, bouréeing sideways and shielding her face with one flat hand. But Shellman and his cohorts, Marck Waymmann and Robert Garland, continually muffed the multiple air turns that are supposed to make the athletes so irresistible.

Les Noces is a masterpiece of massed designs and rhythms, a theatricalized version of a Russian peasant wedding. What Stravinsky and Nijinska celebrate is a ritual of continuance and community that supercedes individual, romantic choice. The company looked a bit unsure of the music's fiendish meters at first but then locked into its massive, implacable logic.

WEDDINGS

Boston Phoenix, 12 May 2006

Classical ballet is full of third-act weddings. With the bad guys disposed of, plot complications untangled, and everyone matched to the proper partners, they don their best tutus and tiaras for a grand party that spells happily ever after. Bronislava Nijinska's first choreography for the celebrated Diaghilev Ballets Russes, in 1921, was a revival of the nineteenth century's most majestic tale of love and royal succession, *Sleeping Beauty.* Her second big work for Diaghilev, *Les Noces,* in 1923, overturned the whole kaboodle and in the process launched the Ballets Russes into its last years as the leading producer of ballet modernism.

Boston Ballet staged this groundbreaking work of strangeness and emotional truth for a stingy six performances last week, hardly enough to let either the dancers or the audience savor its tremendous challenges and rewards. *Les Noces* pictures a wedding in an indeterminate past of the Russian countryside. The nuptials in *Raymonda Act III,* which opened the same program, take place in a royal court of medieval Hungary. The audience raved about the nineteenth century's *Raymonda* and cheered its head off for a package of Imperial and Soviet Russian trifles that are usually reserved for encores and festive galas. It greeted Nijinska's masterpiece with dutiful appreciation.

Les Noces strips away the finery and the flattery of ballet's wedding conventions and gets to deeper realities. Nijinska staged the nuptials as a turning point for a whole community, not just the bride and groom. She had spent nearly a decade in Russia before joining Diaghilev in France, learning her choreographic craft among the constructivist experiments of the early Soviet period, collaborating with the avant-garde artist Alexandra Exter, and absorbing new ideas in theater and cinema. *Les Noces* is both a collectivist work and a classical one.

Depersonalized, monolithic, and severe, like Byzantine religious icons, the dance is all massed movement and tightly packed group poses. The bride (Karine Seneca) stands still for the entire first section as her friends surround her and eventually drape her with long ropes symbolizing her hair, which must be cut short at the end of her maidenhood. The Groom (Roman Rykine) solemnly takes leave of his friends, his parents. He stands in the center of the men's chorus as they circle him with downward-swooping leaps.

The scene changes, and we see the wedding couple and their parents, seated in a room above the ensemble, who celebrate with raucous but organized dances. The bride and groom meet for the first time, embrace deliberately, bid good-bye to their parents, and are led into the bridal chamber. There's no emoting or expression except for these few deliberate gestures of embracing, blessing, farewell, but in the very stillness of the characters amid turbulent activity, you imagine their thoughts. Things we all feel at weddings but aren't supposed to admit: loss, apprehension, even panic.

Driving all the action is Igor Stravinsky's harsh and monumental score for singers (the New World Chorale and soloists Margaret O'Keefe, Gale Fuller, Ray Bauwens, and Aaron Engebreth), four pianos, and percussion. Solo exclamations break into a throbbing regular pulse, and a triumphant bell tolls above the final tableau.

The dance doesn't imitate the music's folk suggestions the way czardas steps and arm movements are woven into the classical *Raymonda*. Instead, the corps of thirty surge back and forth in repetitive patterns, the men striding and plunging, the women with pistonlike bourrée steps to the side. Nijinska undermined the pretty line of the women's turnout and decorative arms with dark pointe shoes and white legs stabbing straight into the floor. Both men and women jump endlessly on both feet.

You can't say *Les Noces* is violent, but there's discord, even menace, beneath its tightly controlled surface. The company achieved a thrilling sense of power, showing us ballet's rarely invoked capacity to wound and heal and fortify.

BECAUSE I MUST

Dance Ink, Spring 1994

Every age gets the ballet fantasy it needs. In the 1930s, when big-production Russian ballet was romping across the land via the expatriate companies that succeeded Diaghilev, ballet was the object of satire. Both George Balanchine and Fred Astaire spoofed its pretensions, in "On Your Toes" and "Shall We Dance." That was the era of acute American self-consciousness about "culture," especially the kind that emanated from Europe. Movies were full of bumbling professors, plain-faced good girls who gave piano lessons, and dotty impresarios. When star danseur Astaire is discovered tap-dancing in his dressing room, company director Edward Everett Horton is scandalized. "Fun? The great Petrov doesn't dance *for fun*. I forbid that. That's not Art!"

By the 1980s ballet had become a household word, so Herbert Ross and company portrayed it like the tear-drenched corporate battlegrounds on TV's "Dallas" and "Dynasty." Its fictions were laid, à clef, in the upper ranks of American Ballet Theater, whose personnel comprised most of the cast. In "The Turning Point," dancing isn't much more than another poker chip in the deadly game of ambition that all the characters are playing. It represents not only sexual desire but youth and power. The movie even tries to counter ballet's effeminate image by making the star, Mikhail Baryshnikov, a lady-killer. As one ballet boy says to another at a party: "You know what this fantastic little Russian is gonna do, don't you? He's gonna make it respectable for American boys to be dancers."

In 1993, with traditional and contemporary ballet companies gripped in desperate combat for survival, we got *The Red Shoes*, a sanitized, even rosy version of the 1948 movie, a Broadway musical as upbeat as . . . well, a Broadway musical. It enjoyed an overpublicized half year of production, a month of previews, and a three-day run after its official opening. I suppose we shouldn't have expected otherwise. The show's old-pro composer and director, Jule Styne and Stanley Donen, practically defined the postwar Broadway and movie musical between them. Writer Marsha Norman (book and lyrics) followed their sunny lead, when she wasn't simply quoting the prototype. Choreographer Lar Lubovitch, no jaded pessimist himself, came closest to lifting the show off its mundane Marley, but the book and the music engulfed him too often in romantic platitudes.

Lubovitch knows ballet life—early in his career he danced for the American impresario who most closely approximated Diaghilev, Rebekah Harkness—and he tucked some smart allusions to ballet history into his dance numbers. For instance, when the company celebrates the birthday of their ballet master, Grisha Lubov, they dance the Charleston and other popular dances of the time (1921). Grisha first leads them and they follow from force of classroom habit. Then they do their own variations, which Grisha copies intently, including a pseudo-Spanish number. This I took to be a reference to Grisha's real-life prototype (and creator in the movie) Léonide Massine, who soaked up every broadening influence Diaghilev threw in his path. Massine solidified his name as a character dancer–choreographer in *Le Tricorne* (1919), with a *farruca* lifted from a virtuoso dancer they picked up in the streets of Seville.

But the producers of this Red Shoes cared little about historical fidelity, either to Diaghilev or to the fevered imaginary zeitgeist surrounding Boris Lermontov on the screen. The show opens with *Swan Lake,* which tells us right away that this company is conservative, not cutting-edge. A little bit later Lubovitch sets a fast montage of repertory to make a cinematic bridge and show the company on tour. But the ballets excerpted here are the four most popular potboilers in anyone's repertory, *Swan Lake, Coppélia, Sleeping Beauty,* and *Les Sylphides.* Anyone's, that is, except the Ballets Russes alias the Ballet Lermontov.

Neither one of these celebrated ensembles made its name doing the classics, even though many of Diaghilev's innovations quickly graduated to that status, including *Les Sylphides* (1909). Novelty was their game. Around 1921 Diaghilev was cashing in on the characters and modernisms of Massine. *Parade, Good Humored Ladies, Boutique Fantasque* represented a relatively conservative period for Diaghilev—*Les Noces, Les Biches,* and Balanchine were just around the corner. In the late '40s British and French ballet were embarked on some daring adventures in surrealism, which is the idiom that attracts the Ballet Lermontov audience. The first bit of dancing we see in the Red Shoes movie, the new ballet those excited student fans mob the theater to see, is a modernist essay that might be a bit from choreographer Robert Helpmann's famous *Adam Zero.* This existential allegory also had big troops of people on the floor, masses of hands holding up the principals in fervid but distorted poses.

The cast of *The Red Shoes*—the students, the impresario and his entourage, the jittery dancers backstage, and Victoria Page, the young ballerina on the brink of fame—comprised everything I knew or believed about ballet in 1948. They, and their world, didn't resemble anything I'd encountered up to that time. They were oblivious to everything in the world except the special universe within it that they were creating. Their tedious hours of practice were as transfiguring as their moments on the stage. They played and loved as desperately as they died. They said devastating things to each other like, "She is impossible!" and "I can't *bear* amateurs" and "You shall dance. The world will follow." As soon as the LP was issued, I bought the score. I wanted to go to Paris and Monte Carlo.

It never occurred to me to try dancing.

But I pictured what it would be like to live in that world—and thought I would never get near it in a million years. I was a quite ordinary girl from the suburbs who wanted to be a writer, and I saw my future work as grubby and practical. I certainly didn't presume I was touched with any magic wit or talent.

It's precisely the sense of otherness, of the artist as exceptional, that makes *The Red Shoes* memorable. It isn't for a realistic portrayal of ballet that we cherish this film, but for the way it raises the ballet enterprise to the level of metaphor. The producers of the Broadway version misunderstood this when they tried to humanize the characters, make them more sympathetic. *The Red Shoes* takes Hans Christian Andersen's fairy tale for its text. A girl falls in love with a pair of red shoes; in the movie they stand for dancing. When she gets them, she can't take them off. She can't lead a normal life. In fact, society shuns her, she's even rejected by her lover and her church. Finally she dies of exhaustion.

It seems to me the only way we could accept modern characters reenacting this story is if all of them were obsessives. The movie is driven by three remarkable personalities. Lermontov, the company director, as played by Anton Walbrook, is no mere autocrat. He is a snob, a manipulator, and an emotional cripple. ("He has no heart, that man," says the first ballerina he dismisses because she dares to get married.) Call it repressed homosexuality, call it the sublimation of all sex into art, this man's feelings are definitely distorted. No one actually likes him. His all-male collaborators on the business end of the company are his professional intimates, but he doesn't seem to have friends. The dancers respect him out of loyalty and the traditions of a hierarchical art form. He is, of course, lonely, another weakness that must be covered up. No one who's seen the movie can ever forget Walbrook's cold, sneering smiles, his eyes narrowed and penetrating, like knives, his lips drawn back from his teeth as if he'd bitten off something horrid but he's too polite to spit it out.

I knew something was wrong with Steve Barton's Lermontov immediately. From the moment he swept into the middle of the *Swan Lake* rehearsal, grandly ignoring the company's elaborate révérence, he was conceited, a poseur. Yet Barton—or Donen—couldn't resist making him susceptible. This was a tyrant with an unfortunate antisocial side, but definitely no misogynist. As soon as Victoria Page comes into his life, she makes him miserable because, you see, he really loves her. The show gets even worse when he admits this to himself, in the second act. But even before that, he gives her fatherly advice, tries to inspire her when she's discouraged. "You can live in a world that few others do," he sings to her. Sings!

Roger Rees, the original Lermontov, left the show in previews, supposedly because he couldn't sing. I'd bet Rees had a more stringent concept of the character, but I doubt if anyone could have made a unified persona out of a neurotic misanthrope who harbors song within his breast. *The Red Shoes* musical's Lermontov was a latter-day Scrooge, ripe for reform and lovability.

The other characters in the show were similarly limp around the edges. George De La Peña's ballet master, the one consistently satisfying performance for me, was sweeter and more exposed than the irascible, exacting Massine/Lubov in the movie.

Margaret Illmann, the young Australian who was picked from an audition of thousands to play Victoria Page, veered wildly in her acting from vacuous bunhead to breathless parvenue. She reacted to everything with random, inappropriate grins. Her Vicki wanted to be a star all right, but perhaps dancing was just the thing she happened to be good at.

Now Moira Shearer's Vicki is another character, perhaps the first and only movie ballerina with both brains and self-possession. When Lermontov meets her for the first time in the movie, they are immediate and well-matched adversaries. He's been lured to the party by her wealthy aunt, a possible patroness of the ballet, and he quickly stifles a plan to subject him to a captive audition of Vicki's dancing. She realizes immediately that the ploy was a mistake and admits it to him. This intrigues him and he fires the famous question "Why do you want to dance?" She shoots back, "Why do you want to live?" He's thrown off guard, and after hesitating, answers, "I suppose I must." "That's my answer too," she replies calmly.

Shearer's Vicki is a sophisticate. Rich, extremely privileged, she's traveled, knows how to talk to people, knows her own needs, and has the certainty of one who has looked at alternatives. Her belief that she's one of the elect, an artist, comes not by accident, but by the careful cultivation of a gift. Illmann's Vicki is immature, easily swayed, polished on the surface but empty beneath. Her answer to Lermontov is almost offhand, like the chic repartee she uses at parties. She might have been modeled after Leslie Browne's neophyte in *The Turning Point*, who responds to her father's similar question about her ambitions: "I know what I want for now . . . just to dance." For a seventeen-year-old, this is an easy choice, almost a banality.

The Red Shoes is about impossible choices, and fate. Vicki's lover, composer Julian Craster, played in the movie by Marius Goring, is equally immersed in his own creative passion. I'll always dislike him, almost as much as Lermontov, for making the either-or demand on Vicki that drives her to suicide. But you can see how such a character would be ruthless. As played in the show by Hugh Panaro, Julian is callow, a really nerdy guy who probably never changes his socks, and who belts out rhapsodic tenor melodies and looks as if he meant to be writing fight songs for the cheerleading squad and stumbled into the theater instead.

I always have moments in the movie when I'm repelled by these characters. When filmmakers Michael Powell and Emeric Pressberger close in on the beautiful Shearer, in full makeup for *Swan Lake,* with grotesque eyes and a furious look of effort on her face, I see not a vision but a nightmare, a witch. Goring at times is almost sloppily sensual, and of course Walbrook is an unrelenting villain. You could call them travesties, but I think that's the point.

The Red Shoes is a metamovie. That is, it's simultaneously a story and a commentary on the story, a fable. When the film appeared, England was recovering from the war's devastation, and, like the opulent Sadlers Wells production of *The Sleeping Beauty* around the same time, it was a powerful symbol of renewal. A nation that could mount ballets and films on such a magnificent scale, that could find time and tranquility for art, was truly on the road back to civilization.

Helpmann's Red Shoes ballet may not have revolutionized the choreographic art but as a cinematic achievement it's still stunning. Surreal images that could be conjured up only on film, propelled by Brian Easedale's expressive score, seemed to place the ballet in the hectic mind of Vicki. It's *she* who dreamt of dancing forever, who whirls through theatrical carnivals and ballrooms, who glimpses dancing's morbid side and flees in imagination as a flower, a cloud. It's Vicki who realizes she can never be like other people and can only die in peace if the shoes have been taken off her feet by her former lover.

Lubovitch tried to match this on the stage, creating spectacular effects— a corps of red-shod wilis rising out of the ground, a burning cross, and the dancer's desperate leap off the church roof. We could see they were the ravings of the demented ballerina, but Illmann's Vicki was too rational, too shallow, to have imagined them herself. Her real-life reenactment a moment later was pure melodrama, not predestination.

The movie's message is double. While showing us the glamour and intensity of ballet life, it also shows us the danger. The characters are brilliant and destructive, and perilously close to madness. We aren't meant to love them, we aren't meant to sympathize. They make art for us, but only because they're super-real themselves.

If I were going to do *The Red Shoes* today, I'd junk the whole milieu of ballet. I'd have this flamenco dancer from the Bronx who goes to film school at NYU. She's torn between her brilliant lesbian lover and a director with dreams of glory and a big part for her. If anyone in it sang at all they'd sing rap, and there wouldn't be any other dialogue. I'd shoot it in black and white, except for the shoes, which would be crimson spike heels. Or maybe hightops . . .

BALLETOMANIACS

Boston Phoenix, 18 November 2005

When Serge Diaghilev died in 1929, his company, the Ballets Russes, expired with him. Instantaneously, twenty years of glamorous, innovative performances became legend. The dancers dispersed all over Europe and beyond, to plant the idea of "Russian Ballet" across four continents over the next forty years. In America, two main touring companies carried on the exotic tradition that became synonymous with ballet, until the culture boom of the 1960s certified the primacy of our own indigenous ballet companies.

It's hard to imagine the nearly fanatical excitement generated by the itinerant Ballets Russes companies in the 1940s and 1950s, but an extraordinary new film by the San Francisco team of Dayna Goldfine and Dan Geller evokes the charisma and the competition of the era. Seldom has a two-hour documentary inquired so deeply into the heart of dance culture.

Goldfine and Geller interviewed seventeen dancers over a two-year period around the time of the Ballets Russes reunion in New Orleans, June

2000. Some were in their '80s or '90s at the time, some have died since they spoke on camera, but they share their priceless memories, insight, and gossip.

You might think it would be depressing to see these ancient, crumpled ballerinas and arthritic danseurs reminiscing, but actually the film sparkles with their vivacious personalities. We encounter icons: Dame Alicia Markova, the last of the great stars to have danced for Diaghilev; two of the famous "baby ballerinas," Irina Baronova and Tatiana Riabouchinska; and great principal dancers Mia Slavenska, George Zorich, Maria Tallchief.

Gifted with lifelong vitality, these seniors talk about what drew them to the ballet in the first place and you can still feel the attraction. Nathalie Krassovska, in jewels and décolletage, rehearses a scene from *Giselle* with Zorich, who wears a T-shirt over his still-muscular torso. Riabouchinska finishes teaching a class and trundles away in a dented red convertible. Frederic Franklin, now ninety-one, performs and coaches revivals to this day. It's he who provides the anchoring voice in the film with his informative and funny commentary.

All the speakers contribute to a collective history that isn't easy to sort out. The two big Russe companies, that of Colonel Wassily de Basil (1932–1952) and that of Sergei Denham (1938–1962), overlapped to some extent in time and repertory, and dancers went back and forth, periodically forming short-lived spin-off groups of their own. The film's narrative, with brilliantly layered talk, music, and visual images, keeps a clear bead on these surging and waning fortunes.

It's a story of success, hardship, intrigue, and finally, of history moving on. With the rise of American Ballet Theater and the Balanchine ascendancy, ballet aesthetics began to change. We lost our taste for eccentricity and ego. The older generation of Russe dancers settled into more permanent teaching and choreographing opportunities in New York and elsewhere. Some found new careers in Hollywood.

If one person could represent what made the Ballets Russes fabulous and then obsolete, that person would be Léonide Massine. A novice choreographer and fabled character dancer for Diaghilev, Massine went on to recreate Diaghilev favorites and made his own repertory of bubbling post-Diaghilev party ballets like *Gaîté Parisienne* and *Le Beau Danube*. Beginning in the 1930s he created a string of allegorical, abstract "symphonic ballets" that astounded audiences and perhaps stimulated the modernist tendencies of his rival George Balanchine.

The film gives us glimpses of Massine's forgotten works, together with generous footage of the other repertory, the dazzling personalities and daring designs. The only critic in the film is Chicago's Ann Barzel, who preserved countless bygone performances from the wings and the balconies, wielding a silent, stop-and-go camera. As the Russes phenomenon was winding down, television entered the culture, and pretty soon we had high-tech video to preserve the performances of our time. But the era of Russes had already ended. This film is a poignant but heady memoir.

ROBERT JOFFREY, 1930–1988

Christian Science Monitor, 1 April 1988

For most of his life Robert Joffrey was obsessed with one project: to have his own ballet company. The single-minded tenacity with which he pursued that goal, and the nearly selfless way he realized it as a showcase for the notable achievements of ballet history, gained him not only the company he had always desired but the wholehearted respect of the ballet world.

Born in December 1930 in Seattle, Joffrey studied ballet through his teens with Mary Ann Wells. He came to New York in 1948, where he not only studied ballet but took modern dance classes with Martha Graham alumnae Gertrude Shurr and May O'Donnell. Almost immediately he began teaching too, establishing a distinguished parallel career in which he became head of his own school, the American Ballet Center (now known as the Robert Joffrey Ballet School), and a much sought-after guest in the United States and abroad.

The Robert Joffrey Ballet began in 1952 on a shoestring. With no outside financial backing, Joffrey and five other dancers performed in out-of-the-way auditoriums, toured the country in a station wagon, and danced in operas. Joffrey supplied some of the choreography. What is probably his best-known work, *Pas des Déesses*, based on the famous divertissements for competing nineteenth-century ballerinas, dates from 1954. But choreography was never his main preoccupation, and his partner, Gerald Arpino, served as chief choreographer during the entire history of the Joffrey company.

The Joffrey Ballet made its transition into the big time during the 1960s, when it was first adopted, then abandoned, by dance benefactress Rebekah Harkness. The Harkness patronage enabled the company to expand its repertory and personnel and to make two important international tours. By the time Mrs. Harkness decided to create a new company bearing her own name, Joffrey had gained enough credibility in the dance world to regroup his forces. Within two years he mustered start-up foundation support; gave prestigious performances at the White House, Jacob's Pillow, and the Delacorte Theater in Central Park; and accepted an invitation to install the new company in residence at the New York City Center, where it made its debut in March 1966.

With regular spring and fall seasons scheduled there, the company thrived during the next two decades, filling in the calendar with tours; regular seasons in Houston, Washington, Los Angeles, and other cities; and summer teaching residencies. Robert Joffrey dominated the company as director, teacher, and coach, but choreographed infrequently. His real love was repertory, and the remarkable living archive of ballets that he gathered was as impressive an achievement as the survival of the company itself.

The Joffrey Ballet style and programming always contained a mixture of elements. Especially in its early years it was known as a youthful company, and the explosive, topical choreographies of Gerald Arpino helped to establish the whole speeded-up, athletic, and glamorous genre known as modern ballet. Joffrey invited interesting fusion choreographers such as Jiri Kylian, William Forsythe, and Laura Dean to supply contemporary works. He got the elusive Jerome Robbins to revive two of his jazz ballets from the 1950s, *Moves* and *N.Y. Export: Opus Jazz*. He also began an association with modern dancer Twyla Tharp, commissioning her first venture into the classical arena, the extravagantly successful *Deuce Coupe*, in 1973, and three subsequent ballets. He himself made the first big mixed-media ballet, *Astarte*, a sensuous, psychedelic piece for film and dancers, in 1967.

Complementing Robert Joffrey's instinct for the modern was an unerring taste in classics. Having set his sights on a particular work or choreographer he wanted to appropriate, he would pursue his quarry, sometimes for years, until a production could be mounted. His most recent and triumphant accomplishment was the recovery last fall of the 1913 Vaslav Nijinsky/Igor Stravinsky/Nicholas Roerich production of *Le Sacre du Printemps*. Joffrey had become interested in this lost landmark in the mid 1950s, joining the company of aesthetes and fanatics who were convinced of this ballet's crucial significance to dance modernism.

He was equally adventurous in capturing the first New York State Council on the Arts grant for a major reconstruction, to bring back Kurt Jooss's famous antiwar ballet *The Green Table*, in 1967. The time was right for this strong and heartfelt statement, and audiences responded to it as if it had been made as a Vietnam war protest instead of a bitter 1932 comment on diplomatic impotence. *The Green Table* was followed by all three remaining recoverable Kurt Jooss works, and when Joffrey had accumulated them, he gave an all-Jooss evening to celebrate the choreographer's seventy-fifth birthday.

The Joffrey repertory also became an anthology of ballets from the Diaghilev Ballets Russes with faithfully restored productions of *Petrouchka* (Michel Fokine); *Le Tricorne*, *Pulcinella* and *Parade* (Léonide Massine); and Nijinsky's *L'Après-Midi d'un Faune* as well as *Le Sacre*. He formed a long-term alliance with the great British choreographer Frederick Ashton that brought such marvels as *Les Patineurs, Monotones, The Dream*, and *A Wedding Bouquet* to American audiences. His affection for the Romantic period resulted in a reconstruction of the Pas de Six from Arthur Saint-Léon's *La Vivandière* and Ashton's version of the pastoral story-ballet, *La Fille Mal Gardée*. Joffrey's last acquisition was the popular Russian classic *The Nutcracker*, set by Arpino and Richard Englund, director of the Joffrey II company

Although he was a superb teacher and a beloved director, Robert Joffrey is not noted for the individual dancers he produced. Unlike a Balanchine or an Ashton, who inspired and shaped dancers to embody their creative visions, Joffrey didn't project his personality or his genius through choreography. In a field almost totally constructed around individual egos, Robert Joffrey didn't force himself into the public eye. His company developed as a flexible, versatile ensemble that undertook the protection of history as seriously as it saluted the rapidly evolving present. In that, he was, and his company is, both exemplary and unique in American ballet culture.

THE HUM OF THE TURBINE,
THE ROAR OF THE CROWD
Dance Now, Summer 2005

The Steel Step, Princeton University's translated title for the newly recreated Diaghilev-era icon *Le Pas d'Acier*, just doesn't scan. *Ballet of Steel* would come closer, but there really isn't a decent way to convey it in English. One of the things this flat-footed verbal rendering brings into focus is the mixed provenance of the ballet. Diaghilev's French gloss may have sweetened his stated intention to honor the social and artistic advances of the Russian Revolution—*en français*, even the plight of the workers could be chic. But the ballet's title is only one symptom of its problematic identity.

Le Pas d'Acier / *The Steel Step*, presented for three performances at Princeton's Roger S. Berlind Theater (April 7–9), was a massive undertaking, funded out of nine pockets at the university as well as the Arts and Humanities Research Board of the United Kingdom. It was realized through a collaboration between Princeton's Department of Music, the Department of Theater and Dance, and the technical resources of McCarter Theater. The three main architects of the production were dance historian Lesley-Anne Sayers, based at the University of Roehampton London; musicologist Simon Morrison of the Princeton music department; and the choreography-staging team of Millicent Hodson and Kenneth Archer.

I've seen just about all of Hodson's archival productions that were performed in North America, starting in 1987 with Nijinsky's notorious 1913 *Sacre du Printemps* and including *Jeux* (Nijinsky, 1913), *Cotillon* (Balanchine, 1932), *La Chatte* (Balanchine, 1927), and three pieces from the Ballets Suédois (1920–1923). I find Hodson's projects tremendously stimulating, but *Le Pas d'Acier* has been the hardest to pin down. The Princeton production added new and unfathomable depths to the arguments about authenticity and ownership that surround a dance property few living persons have seen or performed. Who is qualified to attempt such retrievals, where do they come from, and should they be staged at all? What the Princeton team undertook was a double impossibility—to complete a concept which existed only on paper and in the process correct a production that departed from this never-performed scheme. Were we watching a revival, a deconstruction, or a premiere?

In 1925 Serge Diaghilev was declining in health and finding it harder to keep his Ballets Russes afloat. Alexander Tairov's experimental Kamerny theater had visited Paris in 1923, refueling the impresario's fervent Russian nationalism and his continuing curiosity about the latest trends in modern art. Not incidentally, the mysteries of collectivism presented an enticing prospect for scandal. He commissioned designer Georgii Yakulov and composer Serge Prokofiev, who did the scenario together. When the ballet reached the stage two years later the choreographer was Léonide Massine.

Most of the 1925–1927 collaborators were expatriates, although Prokofiev was having second thoughts about his self-imposed exile. It was Yakulov who knew Revolutionary Russia firsthand. Based in Moscow, he was deeply involved with theater artists during the remarkable post-1918 period that saw the development of constructivism, machine art, and agit-prop; the visionary work of photo-collagist Rodchenko, utopian designer Tatlin, theater director Foregger, visual artists Popova, Vesnin, Exter, Malevich, Lissitsky; as well as the monumental figures Meyerhold and Eisenstein. Yakulov designed a set that was both sculptural object and working parts, a railroad station that converted into a factory. The flimsy story line was only a pretext for a demonstration of collectivist empowerment.

Once the ballet was written, Diaghilev wanted to bring a theater director, Tairov himself or Meyerhold, to stage it, and the experimental choreographer Goliezovsky to do the movement. None of them accepted his invitation—probably fearing they wouldn't be allowed to return to the Soviet Union, where the avant-garde was already being stifled and the grim cloak of Stalinist social realism was about to descend. In Massine's hands, what started out as a hymn to the Revolution became an entertainment to some viewers, a betrayal to others; either a dramatic modernist experiment or a trendy addition to the Ballets Russes repertory. The 1927 production wasn't filmed or otherwise decently documented, but Sayers's 1999 research concluded that it misrepresented the intent of its initial collaborators.

The ideal choreographer for Yakulov and Prokofiev's project might have been Bronislava Nijinska, who had returned to Russia in 1915 after her brother's disastrous breakup with Diaghilev. She began her choreographic career and worked productively there until 1921. Nijinska made her best ballets (*Les Noces, Les Biches,* and *Le Train Bleu*) on a second go-round with Diaghilev, but left him again as the ascendancy of Balanchine became clear. Nijinska was probably the most adventurous modernist of the Ballets Russes's second decade. During her Soviet years, in her teaching, producing, and her developing theories of movement, she embraced constructivism, explored the relationship of bodies and machines, revitalized classical technique, and worked to bring the image of the ordinary worker into the ballet stage.

Le Pas d'Acier would surely have suited Nijinska's admiration of technological advances like the automobile and the airplane. In her notes on movement she spoke of "the dynamic rhythm of these machines, their breath—speed, deceleration, and the unexpected, nervous breaking." She would have understood Yakulov and Prokofiev's scenario as a parable of how the oppressed masses rally under the Bolshevik banner and through their coordinated efforts bring about industrial productivity.

The adaptable Massine reoriented the ballet's aesthetics and threw the politics and symbolism into ambiguity. He countered the depersonalized effect of the first act by alluding to a series of old Russian folktales, establishing a rural tone instead of following Prokofiev's indication for a more urban and contemporary marketplace crowded with Vendors, Cigarette Sellers, Thieves, and Hungry Citizens. Instead of a generic Sailor Hero and Working Girl as protagonists, Massine created contrasting pas de deux for two sets of company stars, himself and Alexandra Danilova in act 1 and Lubov Tchernicheva and Serge Lifar in act 2. Viewers spoke of his first act as a divertissement, hampered by the complicated sets. According to critics, the second act came closer to the authors' intent, and impressed the Paris and London audiences. The whole scene came alive with robotic energy as wheels spun and pistons heaved up and down, lights flashed, and the dancers shuttled back and forth in a surge of well-calibrated precision movement.

The 1920s in Russia and Europe abounded in machine dances—symbolic experiments where dancers imitated mechanical processes, constructed geometric patterns, and massed together in groupings to signify electric power or the dynamism of an idea. The first principles of Meyerhold's biomechanics exercises for actors asserted a dual affinity: the body is a machine and the actor is a machine operator. So constructivist stage action could be both a highly energized form of movement and a symbolic activity. Even Balanchine inserted human pyramids and pistonlike propulsions into *La Chatte* and *Prodigal Son* to express solidarity, skill, and power. Given their metaphoric aspects, there were always questions whether the machine dances and films glorified the machine age or condemned it. Diaghilev's audience of displaced aristocrats and culture snobs would have despised the communist experiment, and *Le Pas d'Acier* was sometimes taken as satire.

At Princeton, a fifty-four-piece student orchestra played the score and the re-creators returned to Yakulov and Prokofiev's cast of character-types. Workers and Commissars replaced Massine's Crocodiles, Devils, and Mice. The action at the train station was a turmoil of petty crime and scrabbling hardship. One Sailor emerged, and after a duet with a Worker Girl, he shed bits of his uniform, signifying his disenchantment with the regime and his dedication to new ways. The scene changed from street to factory, and the whole cast was eventually recruited to work as one throbbing, plunging, leaping ensemble, everyone with a job to do that contributed to a symphonic visual climax.

Without trying to assess its faithfulness to the unproduced production, my reaction to the single performance I attended remains shadowed by history. That seems appropriate. I don't see the necessity for every ballet to "read" according to the dance trends of 2005. I don't rule out an old dance because it looks "dated." In fact, a historical artifact would fail if it didn't make us think about history.

When I look at Hodson's staging, I see echoes of the busy, counterpointed clusters of ritual participants in Hodson/Nijinsky's *Sacre du Prin-*

temps, and the ensembles in other people's revivals of Fokine's *Petrouchka* and *Firebird*. We don't know exactly how these scenes played out choreographically, but all three of those classics belonged to the early Ballets Russes period, when story, character, locale, and dance style were compressed for the first time into one-act ballets. Small groups danced in choral sequences, to maintain a visual coherence within a stage space that might otherwise have been chaotic.

In Hodson's *Pas d'Acier*, and maybe Massine's as well, character and incident dominated the first act. Looking at it was a lot like being in an actual crowd, your attention shifting from one thing to another, without time to discover if they're related. I remember someone pulling a lamp or a vase out of a suitcase to sell, people climbing ladders and swinging on gymnastic rings, a card game going on underneath one platform. I remember a man I took to be a teacher haranguing a small group that gathered around him. Sailors entered but I don't remember what they did. Individuals emerged but I didn't know who they were. Not until the second act did the commotion resolve into a more organized design and rhythm, as people in tandem wielded big mallets or yanked levers, ganged up to form a chugging motor, turned cartwheels.

Morrison and Sayers's scenario tells of a management crisis at the factory, a shutdown, and a restoration of production when the politicized workers take over. All this escaped me. I don't know if I'd have tracked it on additional viewings, or if the staging itself lacked clarity. The cast of twenty-four student dancers worked feverishly to activate the busy movement patterns at the supercharged energy levels that were essential to the constructivist style. What did come across was the vitality of all the components—the kinetic scenery, the illustrative music, and the unruly populace that transformed itself into a working unit.

And something else: the makeshift feeling of it all. You see this in the surviving artwork and posters of the early Soviet period too. The colors are faded, the materials are rotted and torn. Artists were simply too poor to buy proper paints and canvas; they built sets out of raw wood and found objects. Their graphics and stage designs looked like wreckage from a doomed civilization they wouldn't miss. They wore jumpsuits and gym outfits on the stage and dreamed of Martian goddesses.

2 Movable Classics

FARM FROLIC

Boston Phoenix, 17 March 2006

La Fille Mal Gardée (1789) leads off Cyril Beaumont's indispensable thousand-page reference to the first 150 years of European ballet. Like many classic works that followed it, *La Fille* survived till Beaumont's time by way of successive reworkings, each preserving elements of previous productions and inserting new ideas. Beaumont's 1938 libretto sounds quite authentic, although no one by that time could have known exactly what the original Jean Dauberval ballet looked like. In fact, the *Fille* we recognize now as the real thing is quite modern. Frederick Ashton choreographed it in 1960 for the Royal Ballet, and one of its greatest interpreters, Alexander Grant, supervised the staging that returned to Boston Ballet last week after a three-year absence.

Boston Ballet doesn't maintain a repertory of standards except for *The Nutcracker*, but *La Fille Mal Gardée* deserves to be performed more consistently here. Despite Ashton's Anglicized rendering of the French subject, the ballet retains its flavor as an early work. It predates the Imperial period *Swan Lake* and *Sleeping Beauty*, and the Romantic era *Giselle* and *La Sylphide*. It's a story of simple folk and simpletons, who've never seen a king or a princess, never imagined fairy godmothers or menacing trolls. They understand three things: work, money, and love.

This poses a very different performing situation, at least for an American ballet company in the twenty-first century. Today's dancers know how to wear splendid costumes and behave nobly, with superb technique exemplifying social order. Ashton asks something else of them: they have to create a community that enjoys itself. The main characters scheme to protect their families and their property, but neither magic nor monarchy controls the outcome.

A prosperous widow wants to make an advantageous match for her daughter. despite the fact that Alain, the prospective groom, is missing more than a few marbles. Lise stages a whole repertory of tricks to evade her mother's beady eye and rendezvous with her boyfriend, Colas. In the end, it's the mother who unwittingly defeats the unsuitable betrothal by being overprotective. Lise and Colas get her blessing at last.

The corps of farmer friends form the usual lines and background framing for the principal dancers, but also they produce important group designs and circle-dance romps. They dance for each other and with each other, not solely for the audience. Ashton's ingenious choreography requires real cooperation. The men dance around in a ring, bonking sticks together in precise rhythm. The women construct pinwheels, geometrics, and a pony cart with pink satin ribbons. They all celebrate around a maypole, weaving a mesh at the top of the pole with the ribbons they hold. Four women back up the Widow Simone's clog dance with a collective call-and-response pattern. By the time they all rollick away singing at the end, you're convinced they must have been having as much fun as you have for the past two hours.

The other part of what makes *Fille* a challenge is the character work, and here I thought things were less believable. Most of the principals in the two casts I saw seemed to be working with studied eccentricity but little through-relationship to the plot. As Lise, Lorna Feijóo fired off a battery of expressions as formidable as her dancing, but she overpowered Nelson Madrigal, her Colas, in both categories. Misa Kuranaga mustered one charming smile after another but never appeared to be in love with Reyneris Reyes.

Christopher Budzynski played the drag role of the Widow Simone more modestly than Viktor Plotnikov, but neither one of them seemed to have decided whether they were playing a mean social climber or a softy. And both Joel Prouty and Jared Redick, as Alain the nitwit suitor, danced with fabulous spirit and extreme mugging. It's possible to play all these characters for their flaws and faux pas, but what makes *La Fille Mal Gardée* endearing is how sympathetic they can be too.

〰 BOLSHOI WRAP-UP

Christian Science Monitor, 29 July 1987

The Imperial Russian ballet lives. Despite the Soviets' efforts to purge all the arts of their monarchist connotations, ballet's pivotal teaching institutions in Leningrad (the Kirov) and Moscow (the Bolshoi) survived the revolution. Through them, classical virtuosity was preserved against efforts to democratize the theater. Acrobatics, cabaret, vaudeville, agitprop, and signature gestures of the Common Man all make their contribution to Yuri Grigorovich's reformist choreography, but these modernisms remain subordinate to the ongoing idiom, which is classical ballet.

Giselle. Nina Ananiashvili and Andrei Uvarov, Bolshoi Ballet. Photo by Costas.

Somewhere during the four performances of the Bolshoi Ballet I attended at the Metropolitan Opera House, I realized that not only does the company excel in pyrotechnic dancing, it's laden with the creaky devices and affectations that prompted Americans to develop truly modern alternatives.

The Bolshoi is a big company—the thirty principal dancers and eighty-seven corps de ballet members touring the United States this summer represent only one unit of the larger aggregation—and that circumstance underscores ballet's inherent class differences. The chorus members are doomed to anonymity, while the stars indulge in subtle privileges, like wearing their own jewelry even though impersonating slaves. In *Giselle Act II*, while the ghostly Giselle was dancing to save the remorseful Albrecht from being slaughtered by the wilis, both Albrecht and Myrtha, queen of the wilis, wandered offstage as if looking for something more interesting to do. Extravagant bows followed every solo or duet of consequence, breaking the stride of the scene and encouraging the audience to applaud even more ostentatiously. This cuckoo-clock bowing could backfire as a dancer rushed on for the second or third time only to freeze in a ghastly grin because the mini-ovation had run out.

The productions were attractive, even in scaled-down touring versions, but chief designer Simon Virsaladze has an irritating preference for splitting the body vertically and making each half of the costume a different color. This jester effect appeared in every ballet I saw. Lighting at the Met was primitive—schematic flat blue for fantasy scenes, amber for broad daylight, follow-spots for the stars.

More disturbing than the hack scores (Khachaturian, Drigo) and lapses in visual taste were Grigorovich's choreographic mannerisms. Certain tried-and-true effects are dragged into view whenever possible. Some character in nearly every Grigorovich ballet owns a large piece of fabric to match his or her costume and is sure to find a moment to run with it flung across the chest or to turn while swirling it decoratively around the body.

Since Grigorovich's choreography is nonstop dancing, acting takes a secondary place in his ballets. Character is established as perfunctorily as plot, by means of symbolic gestures or stances. Crassus, the villainous Roman general in *Spartacus*, stands with his hip out and one hand propped on it. Whenever he comes to a halt, and sometimes when he's dancing, he assumes this imperious yet effete pose. A whole chorus of Roman ladies in the same ballet mince around with downcast eyes and one arm caressing the opposite shoulder. The point—that they're snooty but decadent matrons—is made by repeating the same step and pose combination till the idea is established.

Having seen several of Grigorovich's poster-style modern ballets, I awaited the classics more hopefully. But the *Giselle* looked lifeless, as if, deprived of hyperbole and athletics, the dancers felt they were going through meaningless motions. The complete *Raymonda*, a ballet we know better from George Balanchine's several splendid condensed versions, hasn't often been done successfully in the West. The Bolshoi program notes suggest that while Marius Petipa's original ballet (1898) was something of a masterpiece, Grigorovich has improved on it throughout. So much for authenticity.

Evidently thinking to clarify and strengthen the plot, Grigorovich has added more stereotyped poses and attitudes, more pedestrian sequences of steps. The entire second act is a divertissement of supposed exotica by the the entourage of the visiting Saracen knight Abderakhman. Each one is a ludicrous pastiche, neither ethnically credible nor choreographically effective. The Saracen, a typical Grigorovich Bad Guy, crouches and leers obsequiously, jumps with one foot dragging as if he hasn't quite disengaged himself from his horse, and assaults the virtuous Raymonda rather than seducing her. Since the point of the story is that despite his sensuous appeal she repels him and remains faithful to her crusader fiancé, this interpretation of the Saracen's character doesn't clarify anything.

Raymonda's third act, the conventional wedding celebration of the noble lovers, looked choreographically truer to Petipa than the rest of the ballet, but by that time even the Glazunov music couldn't relieve Grigorovich's rhythmic and spatial banality. I longed for the sparkle of Balanchine.

CABRIOLES AT DAWN

Boston Phoenix, 22 February 2002

Sectors of the ballet world think the nineteenth century is due for an overhaul. Okay, some historic ballets might improve if the princess turned up in combat boots and the supernaturals arrived from Mars in a dream sequence induced by bad cocaine. *Giselle* is not one of these. Since it has fairly credible characters and a wonderful score by Adolphe Adam that powers a dancing throughline, it deserves to be revisited for itself alone. So it's good news that Boston Ballet's production, directed by Maina Gielgud, resists the urge to update.

This is about as traditional a *Giselle* as you're likely to see anywhere. Gielgud even restores some of the assets that have gotten excised from the ballet in the interest of modernizing. The tasteful sets and costumes by Peter Farmer, borrowed from the Australian Ballet where Gielgud first did this revival, suggest the rustic village and neighboring forest. A front curtain depicts a dreamy landscape framed by Greek pillars with a gauze curtain draped around the edges, thus establishing the whole ballet as a kind of theatrical genre painting.

There's no way to recover the authentic original *Giselle*, or even to identify the specific contributions of the formative choreographers, Jean Coralli, Jules Perrot, and Marius Petipa. Like all historic ballets, *Giselle* is a mutable object, shaped by what worked and who danced it, what was forgotten and how new things were pasted in, and a thousand other accidents over time. But there's a greater degree of consensus about *Giselle* than there is for other classics; the steps and the music seem as if they could fit together in no other way.

My one reservation about the Boston Ballet production is that it has "romance" but no sex. It's unfortunate that the contemporary idea of romanticism is so sugary and innocent. The Romantic movement seized the imagination because it included what was forbidden as well as what was morally approved. In *Giselle*, death, sex, and the unknown determine the main characters' lives as much as their station in life and their virtue.

Giselle is indeed deceived by a nobleman pretending to be a peasant, and as a spirit she saves him from being punished by her fellow wilis. But that's not all there is to the story. I don't even think the program note's flowery introduction, "*Giselle* is a story of unrequited love," is accurate. The slumming Count Albrecht may (and may not) have deceived Giselle about his true identity but he certainly cares for her, and after her death he mourns her sincerely. And even if we believe that Giselle and all the wilis are virgins, we shouldn't assume they've never experienced desire. There's more to this than broken hearts.

Though the story is set, and the steps carefully stitched onto the score, a lot remains for the dancers' individual interpretation. In fact, each of the three casts gave me different answers to some of *Giselle*'s mysteries. Adriana Suárez and Yury Yanowsky hinted most successfully at the erotic potential—that is, the danger—in the meeting of two social unequals. Suárez may be just a village girl but she's a sensualist. She enjoys being courted by this stranger with the good manners. Yanowsky's Albrecht seems the more innocent of the two. He may even imagine giving up his life at court to stay with Giselle. He makes his fatal mistake by reflexively acknowledging his fiancée, Princess Bathilde, when she unexpectedly appears. Not only does he lose Giselle; when her ghost saves him from the wilis, he'll have to return to his old life.

It's easy to believe a girl as impetuous as Suárez could actually die of shock, and her forgiveness in the second act carries a lingering tragic fervor. Yanowsky danced almost casually in the village, released from the ritual demands of his courtly life. When the wilis put him through his trial in the forest, he seemed to get tighter, straighter. Maybe more noble. Maybe his experience reforms him.

Larissa Ponomarenko and Gaël Lambiotte made an unlikely pair, both frozen in carefully etched impersonations. Her Giselle seemed passive, acquiescent to her fate. Her smile never changed until she had that weak spell while dancing; then she seemed to age twenty years. Lambiotte's Albrecht was so conceited, so engrossed in his line and the height of his leg extensions, that he seemed to take it for granted that his beauty alone would win her. In the second act, he seemed to expect her to come to his rescue, and I thought, he may be sad she's dead but it isn't going to ruin his life.

Pollyana Ribeiro seemed relentlessly and unconvincingly ingenue. In other roles she doesn't always go for the equation that a small woman has to be coy and helpless. Simon Ball, ardent and delighted in his conquest of this charming, trusting girl, has the confidence granted only to the upper classes. He has no idea of the disaster he's about to precipitate. His conversion in the second act seems drastic, his sorrow won't be easily repaired.

Giselle is tempted not just by Albrecht's physical attractiveness but by his upper-class status. Her would-be boyfriend, the gamekeeper Hilarion, is a constant reminder of the life she's meant to have. Paul Thrussell made him a clumpy woodsman, maybe not terribly bright but crafty and capable of dogged devotion. Viktor Plotnikov looked more refined but possibly ruthless. Hilarion precipitates the tragedy out of simple jealousy, but also he's offended by Albrecht's violation of class distinctions.

You can't really take account of *Giselle* without a healthy respect for the supernatural. This production includes the crucial mime scene where Giselle's mother foretells her death—it's often reduced to a memo, when directors assume the audience will be bored with it. But Laura Young made my skin crawl as she described the evil spirits ready to claim her daughter. Giselle won't rest in her grave, but will rise and dance with the wilis in their eternal, demonic mission of revenge. In her vision the wilis threaten the whole village. What's in jeopardy is not just the lives of young girls, but the comfortable order in which everyone lives.

Giselle, premiered in Paris in 1841, has a libretto by the poet and proto-balletomane Théophile Gautier. As translated by the English critic Cyril Beaumont, the "book" represents a ballet fully committed to the Romantic period's fascination with the erotic. The wilis are jilted girls with an unfulfilled passion for dancing. They hate all men, and they avenge their own betrayals by first seducing their victims, then dancing them to death.

Gautier's wilis were quite individual, even international, in their costumes and their dancing, but this is undetectable in the choreography now. In Gielgud's and most other contemporary productions, the wilis have become anonymous shades, the perfect corps de ballet, whose technical accomplishment and total togetherness are their attraction. These wilis don't seem seductive or evil. It's not even clear that their encounter with Hilarion ends in his death. After making him jump till he's exhausted, they sort of push him out of their space and he runs away into the forest. Myrtha, the queen of the wilis, can stir them to fury with her big leaps and implacable hauteur, but I thought all three women in this role looked stiff rather than commanding.

Probably the main reason ballet companies want to perform *Giselle* is that it puts them to the test. Its choreography is rigorous and recognizable; the principal dancers have to meet both technical and dramatic challenges. The music helps them, and conductor Jonathan McPhee gave them a spirited first act, with skipping, running rhythms and celebratory ensemble numbers. He slowed down the tempo for the second act, sometimes stretching out the phrase to make the dancers use their last ounce of breath.

The thematic musicality of Adam's score has often been noted. He reminds us of Giselle's lost happiness when its tune recurs in the mad scene. The musical motif that underlined their courtship is inverted as Albrecht lifts her ghost. Their duet is drawn-out on the strings when she emerges from the grave, then becomes jumpy and urgently orchestrated when time is running out. Giselle is playing for time; if she can delay and keep Albrecht dancing till dawn, the wilis' power will be broken. The wilis glide across the space in arabesque, echoing her feverish, hopping circle when she first emerges from the grave. Later, as Albrecht makes his last exertions, he carries Giselle across the floor in the same arabesque and her foot merely touches the ground. The same music is playing, but faster, with a lift in it.

In a way, the whole second act is an inversion of the first. The lively, productive village community is brought to a halt by a process of unsuspecting transgressions. Giselle goes from health in the real world to madness and death. Then, in a cold blue light, the unearthly community of the wilis spins out its mission—and they're foiled by something even they can't control.

WHY WE NEED THE CLASSICS

Boston Phoenix, 22 November 2002

Whenever a ballet company programs one of the half-dozen classics in the repertory, a chorus of blasé groans arises from the dance community. I admit I was underwhelmed when FleetBoston Celebrity Series and the Wang Center informed us the entire week of performances by American Ballet Theater would consist of a single story ballet, *Le Corsaire*. The prospect improved significantly when logistical problems necessitated a switch to *Giselle*, but the threat of encroaching Disneyfication remains. Do local dancegoers always have to be coaxed to buy their tickets with promises of the most palatable, tried-and-true, escapist dance fare?

Ballet can't survive on its past alone, but good recensions of the classics are something we need to have around, as touchstones, models, and a source of purest dance pleasure. *Giselle* is perhaps the most admirable of these historic survivors. It can hold psychological, theatrical, and choreographic challenges for contemporary interpreters with its finely wrought score by Adolphe Adam and a plot no less plausible than a James Bond movie.

ABT's lost world of peasants and nobles who make fatal mistakes and are punished by supernatural forces achieved a tricky balance: it looked authentic but not generic or dated. Authentic is a loaded word, since *Giselle*—like every other nineteenth-century ballet and many more recent ones—is a pastiche of things handed down and newly reproduced, things remembered and gaps repaired, adaptations to modern theater practice and dancers and audiences. None of us was there in 1841 to verify what the original *Giselle* looked like, and no documentation would have been foolproof enough to ensure that every step, every gesture, every floor pattern would stay the same for a 150 years. A modern *Giselle* is always a supposition, a best guess.

ABT's version incorporates choreography by half a dozen ballet masters besides its successive "original" creator-adaptors, Jean Coralli, Jules Perrot, and Marius Petipa, but its current staging is credited to artistic director Kevin McKenzie. The décor (by Gianni Quaranta) and costumes (Anna Anni) are holdovers from the 1985 movie *Dancers*, and the score has been orchestrated by John Lanchbery. All these hands have artfully retrofitted the ballet for modern eyes and ears. What I liked so much about it was its clarity and its attention to the many interwoven themes in the story.

Giselle takes place in two contrasting but mutually accommodating spheres, the real and the supernatural. The country winemakers live an orderly, predictable life under their royal patrons, while at night, spirits inhabit the forest, with their own social codes and magic. The inclusion of peasants, princes, and wilis obviously makes for a spectrum of dance opportunities, but in narrative terms, I've never been so aware of three distinct social strata as in this production.

The villagers wear pale green and gray against an autumnal landscape. When the Prince of Courland's hunting party stops by for a rest at the inn of Giselle's mother, the peasants gather excitedly to watch the royal visit. As the entourage sweeps in, with its wolfhounds and spear-carriers and courtiers dressed in silk and velvet in shades of maroon and black, the pastoral space suddenly becomes more vivid, perhaps even harsh. Later, in the haunted forest, a luminous sky can be seen beyond the trees, but the woods are really dark except when something flashes by in the distance, lightning perhaps, or a passing wili. These things happen much the same way in all versions of *Giselle*, but Jennifer Tipton's masterful lighting transforms the scene and intensifies all the effects.

The story of the ballet is based on class differences anyway, but Tipton and the other creators of this production have emphasized the social context in which a fate like Giselle's could happen. Seduced by a nobleman, she risks her whole future by giving herself to him. Her mother knows the secret of the wilis, that jilted girls will die and return to take revenge on their deceivers. It's a certainty that Albrecht will betray Giselle, and her mother foresees the consequences, although she issues a more practical warning: Giselle has a weak heart and overexertion is dangerous. But Giselle invites her girlfriends to dance with her, foreshadowing the feminine community of the wilis she's doomed to join. They crown her Queen of the Harvest, but she'll trade this earthly existence under the royal patrons for a restless afterlife ruled by a spirit queen, Myrtha.

The whole ballet is filled with echoes and portents. Giselle teaches Albrecht a little country dance. After discovering he's engaged to the princess Bathilde, she stumbles through the same steps as if trying to cling to her reason. Feverish from shock and too much dancing, she dies. In act 2 a deeply repentant Albrecht visits her grave in the forest, and she sets out to save him from being danced to death by the wilis. When she first appears to him, they recall their first companionable, side-by-side courting with a parallel dance, only now they face in different directions on crisscrossing paths; they can't inhabit the same world any more. Another example, the wilis and Myrtha cross their arms over their breasts in the mime gesture for death. When Albrecht tries to capture the ghost of Giselle, his empty embrace closes into the same corpselike pose.

Despite the melodrama and spectacle—or maybe precipitated by it—the heart of *Giselle* is its dancing. Unlike the later high classics (*Swan Lake, Sleeping Beauty*), in which dance is a separate action that interrupts the story, the Romantic ballets weave dancing into the story, through style, steps, and staging. The peasants in *Giselle* act 1 do folklike dances. Special friends and Giselle's village suitor Hilarion can behave with more classical refinements, and when Giselle asks two friends to dance for the nobility, the Peasant Pas de Deux expands into a more virtuosic entertainment. Opening night, this was performed by Herman Cornejo, who jumps without any seeming effort at all, and Xiomara Reyes, who stressed the frilly soubrette qualities of the role.

Albrecht and Giselle get most of the bravura dancing—in the first act it sprouts directly out of their courtship, and in the second it's an extended adagio that begins in sorrow and broadens into urgent lifts and leaps as the couple tries to thwart Myrtha and the wilis. The unison dancing of the wilis has become a test of classical fidelity for a corps de ballet. They don't just pose and shift their lineups in obedience to Myrtha's commands. They surge forward like arrows in pursuit of Hilarion and Albrecht. They travel in hopping arabesque, as creatures eternally bound to both the earth and the air.

The first of ABT's four casts offered authoritative dancing and thoughtful characterizations by all the principals. Paloma Herrera's Giselle, a beaming, happy girl at first, began the famous "mad scene" with an interesting denial. When the jealous Hilarion exposes Albrecht as a nobleman in disguise, Herrera closes her eyes. She's not refusing to believe this deception; she's probably known it all along and accepts it if Albrecht loves her. What really unhinges her is the subsequent discovery that he has a noble fiancée already. She descends into hysteria and runs frantically back and forth among the assembled villagers. A moment of recognition in her mother's arms, and then she rushes toward some invisible command and dies as Albrecht tries to catch her.

Herrera's Albrecht, Marcelo Gomes, was big and beautiful. He focused on her totally, instead of trying to get her to look at him. You could almost believe that he was going to keep his promises. Ethan Stiefel the next night clearly was infatuated by Xiomara Reyes, but his admiration was tempered by a playboy's self-assurance, a knowledge that he'd leave as soon as he tired of her.

Karin Ellis-Wentz as Giselle's mother opening night was thin and wary, almost puritanical. The next night Susan Jones in the role was ample and warm. Both of them performed the prophetic mime scene in a spacious way, showing everyone the place beyond the village where the mysterious spirits lurked, the untimely death that lay in store if Giselle weren't careful, and the way she'd rise from the grave as a wili to fly through the trees.

Two characters who usually get portrayed in stereotyped ways gained vital new identities. Princess Bathilde, the fiancée of Albrecht, is usually a haughty woman who's probably picked him as a suitably aristocratic marriage partner. It was odd to see Monique Meunier, who joined ABT last year after some promising years in New York City Ballet, playing a mime role, but she did it wonderfully. She was not only grand but a snob, and the rest of the aristocrats followed suit, treating the peasants like servants and discreetly holding their costumes clear of the dust.

The Myrtha on opening night, Gillian Murphy, can only be called sublime. Murphy is tall and red-haired, pale and implacable. She materialized with a series of pas de bourrée—tiny, rapid sidesteps across the stage, so light and smooth she might really be a shadow. She circled regally in arabesque, invoking whatever evil magic wilis use to possess a space, and then, with the most chilling gestures, commanded her subjects to rise from the ground for their nightly ritual. You knew Giselle was up against a terrific power, and when she defeated Myrtha by keeping Albrecht alive until dawn, you realized a remarkable act of love had taken place.

 SHAZAM!
Village Voice, 12 March 1985

Creating a ballet is never as easy as rubbing a magic lamp, but Ballet West's restoration of the 1855 August Bournonville spectacle *Abdallah* qualifies as a miracle. Due to ballet politics, the public's fickle taste, and just plain chance, *Abdallah* survived only a couple of seasons at the Royal Theater in Copenhagen and one in Vienna before it was consigned to the great ballet repertory in the sky, and only a similar convergence of improbabilities has brought the work credibly to life in 1985 Salt Lake City.

Ballet West director Bruce Marks and principal teacher Toni Lander came across the original scenario, and—ten years later—a musical score partially annotated by the choreographer. On the basis of this and other documentary information, they decided to mount the ballet, filling in the gaps out of their firsthand knowledge of the Bournonville tradition. *Abdallah* comes as close to being an authentic replica of a big Bournonville piece as anything in the repertory of its native company, the Royal Danish Ballet, where lapses, modernization, and inevitable adjustments to contemporary bodies and temperament have altered even the most scrupulously and continuously preserved of these nineteenth-century treasures.

Ballet West's fine rescue job realizes for us another rare example from the fantasy stages of the Romantic era—an escapist dream where the audience is transported from the snowbound rectitude of northern Europe to a lavish and uninhibited landscape, in this case the never-never Muslim city of Basra. In return for a good deed, the shoemaker Abdallah is given a magic candelabra, which turns his cottage into a palace. He succumbs easily to drink and the head harem girl. But in true Bournonville fashion, before he can be totally seduced by sybaritic pleasures, he makes one wish too many and is recalled to his senses as the idyll goes up in smoke. Luckily the girl back home forgives him, and the sheik adopts him and makes him rich anyhow.

The plot hasn't much dramatic grit, or much logic either, but for Bour-

Swan Lake. Black Swan pas de deux. Cynthia Gregory and Bruce Marks, American Ballet Theater. Photo by Costas.

nonville it served to demonstrate the evils of greed and sensuality, while showing the audience a generous sample of them at the same time. In Ballet West's production, designed by Jens-Jacob Worsaae, the pleasure dome that rises out of the fleshpots is a miasma of filigreed casements and gauzy hangings looking out on a painted oasis. Turbanned squads of slaves and girls in bare midriff tutus are the main dancing population, but the ballet also provides character roles, comedy, and a plaza full of peasants and children in the first act.

Superseding the entertainment and the scenic beauty, Bournonville's ballets offer us dancing, lots of it, which gives them an advantage over the stagy but often static Russian classics. It may look a bit tame to eyes accustomed to the alternating flash and tableau of *Swan Lake*, because it isn't aggressive. Instead it flows and sparkles along on wonderfully effervescent waves of rhythm. You respond to the quality of it as much as to the height of the vaulting jumps or the faster-than-the-eye batterie. Bournonville choreography plays on contrast: the difference between smooth progressions and spiky ones, little finicky steps and lordly space-covering ones. The dancers splurge into the air on the downbeat or delay a step just long enough to prevent synchronization with the infectious, untroubled music.

The Ballet West dancers proved surprisingly adept in this subtle style under Toni Lander's devoted tutelage. They have a natural reticence and a generally clean line that allows you to see the movement's detail. I felt most of the principals in the two casts I saw were less engaging as actors than they might have been, but Miguel Garcia, the Abdallah on opening night, had somehow acquired an authentic Bournonville nobility, charm, and technical aplomb en route to Utah via Toronto and Rego Park.

DANES AT THE MET

Christian Science Monitor, 30 June 1988

The New York audience has always had a special place in its heart for the Royal Danish Ballet, and this year's one-week engagement at the Metropolitan Opera House hardly got rolling before it was over. The spring ballet events here have stirred up hot debates over taste, style, and classical integrity, with the New York City Ballet's controversial American Music Festival, American Ballet Theater, the Danes, the Paris Opera Ballet, and William Forsythe's Frankfurt Ballet all claiming our attention in one dense six-week period. As we ricochet between Balanchinian neoclassicism, Imperial Russian classics, postmodernist formalism, and virtuosic neuroticism, it's a shock to enter the sweet Old World of the Danes.

In both full-length August Bournonville ballets that formed the repertory this spring, *Napoli* (1842) and *Abdallah* (1855), the curtain goes up on a bustling marketplace in a harbor town. Only the Danes today can produce a scene like this with such clarity and verisimilitude. Vendors and shoppers bargain over their wares. Children skitter about excitedly, get into mischief, are given perfunctory spankings by their parents. There'll be a stone drinking fountain with real water, a boat that pulls up beside the quay. Boys and girls will flirt, and the heroine's overprotective mother will try to break up what she considers a poor match by dragging off the girl, who will dig in her heels and shake her fists and eventually find a way to elude parental custody. And then the characters will go off on theatrically marvelous adventures from which they emerge unscathed, saved by their religious faith, to marry their true hearts and live happily ever after.

So what's so appealing about this in the midst of our high-fashion, high-octane ballet culture? I don't think it's pure escapism, though the Danes are still doing brilliantly what most other stage institutions have abandoned to the meta-realistic capabilities of the movies. When Abdallah lights a magic candlestick, his bare, dusty lodgings are transformed into a palace, with a burst of flames and smoke that not only masks the changing of scenery but startles and maybe frightens the audience a tiny bit. We feel we've gone through some danger, and when the tableau of harem girls is revealed behind a gauzy curtain, it seems like a beautiful reward. This, of course, is one of the timeless messages of all fairy tales.

So is innocence and courage in action, which for Bournonville means dancing—refined, bouyant dancing, infectious rhythm, speed, precision, and detail. You get to know the Danish dancers quickly, and you pick your favorites. I admit I missed some of mine this time. The company is still in transition after three years under the artistic direction of Frank Andersen, and there are many new faces. Some, like Nikolaj Hübbe, who I saw in the lead of *Napoli*, look more suited to the company's modern repertory. Hübbe is a fine dancer but his attack and his acting style seem more forthright and abrupt than the smoother, modest Bournonville heroes exemplified in our time by Peter Martins and Ib Andersen, both now ensconced at the New York City Ballet.

Alexander Kølpin, the lead I saw in *Abdallah*, is both a classically clean and stylistically satisfying Bournonville dancer. Kølpin's little tailor who earns a fortune by doing a good deed is engagingly awestruck by the riches and power that materialize when he lights those magic candles. At the same time he pretends this sort of thing happens to him every day, so his newly acquired slaves won't think he's just a nouveau prince.

Heidi Ryom was the leading lady both evenings I attended, and filled that role at most of the seven performances. In *Abdallah* she had some of the charm I remember from former years, but she's become somehow harder and broader in her acting. In fact, Ryom and Hübbe chewed the scenery too often for my taste. There are enough comic characters in Bournonville so that you don't mind if the principals are soft-spoken. Kirsten Simone played the anxious mother in *Napoli* as solicitous and loving, while in *Abdallah* she was a shrewish fortune hunter. When Kølpin and his magic candlestick made her go up in smoke, the audience almost cheered.

200 YEARS OF GENIALITY

Hudson Review, Autumn 2005

August Bournonville served as ballet master at Denmark's Royal Theater for the better part of fifty years. The dozens of ballets, operas, divertissements, and pièces d'occasion he made over that time have dwindled to a handful, but, scooped from the bottomless well of dance history, that constitutes a significant legacy. At the beginning of June the Danes celebrated the choreographer's two-hundredth birthday by staging just about all the surviving works in one tremendous ten-day bash, an extraordinary opportunity for dancers, audience, and over one-hundred journalists and scholars to savor this miracle of preservation.[1] The third Bournonville festival surpassed its predecessors in 1979 and 1992, with a panorama of dancing surrounded by exhibitions, publications, open classes, talks, tours, and conviviality. Bournonville ballet, as a style, an archive, and a way of experiencing dance, seems way out of the orbit of the twenty-first century, but over the days of the festival, a kind of euphoria took over the whole community that had assembled. The festival accumulated force like a gospel service or a great political rally, generating not only heat but belief.

So little is known of ballet's Romantic period that Bournonville emerges as a singular presence in the modern repertory. Scholars have researched the French and Italian counterparts of Bournonville ballet, and paintings, music, and literature convey the greater cultural ethos of the early nineteenth century. But Copenhagen is the only place where you can see a living dance tradition that stretches back to its roots in the period. The festivals in Copenhagen have showcased Bournonville's repertory and effectively established the choreographer not just as a generic label but as a creative citizen of his time.

This is no small achievement. The 2005 festival had been the focus of artistic director Frank Andersen and the entire Royal Danish Ballet organization for three years. I can't imagine an American ballet company with the foresight and the courage to bring off something like it. Andersen first of all was determined to revitalize the Bournonville technique, which had lapsed during the 1990s, and to bring the ballets gradually back into the repertory. The technique was structured into a set of daily classes by one of Bournonville's successors at the Royal Theater, Hans Beck, and subsequently worked on by various teachers. Over the past two summers the classes were filmed by a team headed by Anne Marie Vessel Schlüter, an exemplary Bournonville ingenue in the 1970s and now an instructor and ballet master in the company. A two-disc DVD and two books documenting the steps and the accompanying music were issued during the festival. Andersen feels the survival of the technique is ensured now.

The festival itself plunged us into full-scale saturation. Several exhibitions were prepared, with accompanying catalogues and lectures. Vessel Schlüter presented daily lecture-demonstrations of the Bournonville curriculum with company dancers, children, and guest speakers. Dinna Bjorn, one of the principal regisseurs for the Bournonville repertory and now the artistic director of the Finnish National Ballet, hosted a fascinating session on the relationship between ballet mime and the theatrical pantomime tradition, opening up a seldom-noted link between ballet and popular culture. Festival-goers could visit Bournonville's country house down the street from the royal palace at Fredensborg. We toured the restored eighteenth-century Court Theater, the new multimillion-kroner Opera House at Holmen, and the Old Stage in Kongens Nytorv where the ballets were performed. We attended shows in the Tivoli Pantomime Theater, looked at old and new costumes up close, observed company class, and strolled through the same streets Bournonville knew in the old city center.

Seen all at once, Bournonville's ballets reveal a sensibility nourished by contradictions. Denmark, perched off the edge of Europe, countered its geographic isolation with a seafaring tradition that established connections around the world, and brought the world home. Bournonville was a deeply religious and home-loving person, but also a dedicated traveler, a ballet anthropologist who collected folkloric customs to use on the stage. His ballets are models of good taste and good behavior, but most of them pit virtue against temptations of the flesh, or Christian faith against alien magic and danger. This paradox of oppositions ultimately produced a balanced stage universe. The moral imperative may be challenged but the benevolent instincts usually prevail, and the audience gets to savor plenty of forbidden exotica along the way.

The existing Bournonville repertory ranges from full-scale story ballets to divertissements and small showpieces. What seems to distinguish them thematically from the classical ballets of the later nineteenth century is that they don't want to impress us with the power of hierarchy. They're class conscious, but few kings and queens make an appearance. They're populated by gentry, religious, working people, strangers, supernaturals, and an occasional chieftain; and at some point, everyone dances. The ballets distinguish clearly between students and masters, officers and swabbies, elder statesmen and servants, rich folks, weirdos, renegades, and bums. But the interesting thing is how easily these cadres come together on a social basis and how often individuals cross the porous borderlines from one class to another. The ballets are full of disguises, crossdressing, and transformations. Characters become suddenly wealthy or fall into disgrace; they marry different people than they expected to, they get rescued from calamity. They pursue extravagant adventures only to discover that happiness lies at their doorstep, and then they celebrate with raucous parties, not pompous processions.

A *Folk Tale* (1854) exemplifies the Bournonville temperament, perhaps even better than the more familiar *La Sylphide* (1836) or *Napoli* (1842). The choreographer thought it his most perfect and finest work. Three communities live side by side. The home world is populated by villagers of Christian faith and aristocrats. The residents of the nearby troll-hill in a sense mirror the everyday folk. They work, dance, and make mischief, and they capture souls. Like the Sylphide and the undersea monarch Golfo in *Napoli*, trolls have magic powers and they offer temptations—erotic dancing and erotic love, material indulgence and the satisfaction of a natural world under their control.

The story has been set in motion when two troll brothers, in flashback, stole a little girl from her cradle and put a troll infant in her place. Both young women are experiencing adolescent discontents at the beginning of the ballet. Junker Ove, a young aristocrat, is engaged to the troll changeling Birthe, who taunts him by flirting with the worldly Sir Mogens. Put off by her mercurial behavior and despite warnings of danger, Ove wanders off to the troll-hill. He encounters the beautiful Hilda, who tries to seduce him, in a nice way of course—though raised by trolls, she's inherently decent.

He's about to follow her into the troll-hill but something scares him off at the last minute. A chorus of menacing elf-maidens encircles him and puts him under a spell.

In the second act, Hilda sees the cradle switch in a dream, along with two special objects, a crucifix and a goblet she had offered to Junker Ove. She realizes that she has to escape her adoptive family. During a party to celebrate her engagement to Diderik, the nasty troll brother, she sneaks away, assisted by Viderik, the brother with lovable human instincts. Once above ground, they find themselves among the villagers. Hilda cures Ove of his madness with holy water from the spring of Saint John, and makes her way to the manor house. There, her old nurse recognizes the goblet, which the trolls had stolen when they abducted her long ago. Hilda is welcomed home. Viderik and Diderik's mother Muri confers a dowry on her lost daughter Birthe, who elopes with the rakish Sir Mogens. The trolls take off for new territory and Hilda and Ove's wedding is celebrated with a classical divertissement and a waltz.

A Folk Tale is a web of dualities: the good-bad troll brothers, the kindly nurse Catrine and the imperious troll mother Muri, the noble but dissipated Sir Mogens and the simple Junker Ove, and of course the conflicted changeling girls, Birthe and Hilda. Even the trolls' party looks like a soiree in the big house gone berserk, with rollicking explosive music that imitates a Viennese polka. Birthe realizes her true nature in front of a mirror, with a dance alternating between willful bad temper and carefully tutored gentility. I think it's the pervasive presence of these dualities that makes a Bournonville ballet so much more interesting, and even modern, than classics like *Swan Lake* or *Sleeping Beauty*. In those Imperial works, the main characters may have flaws but they understand their roles in life. Only the supernaturals, Rothbart the sorcerer, Carabosse the evil fairy, and the magicians Drosselmeyer and Dr. Coppelius, have any mystery about them. In Bournonville, the "evil" characters aren't thoroughly bad, and the "good" ones are susceptible to their own worst instincts. The magic is absorbed or conquered by the Church, good deeds are rewarded. Even Madge the Witch, who punishes James for treating her badly by tricking him into poisoning the Sylphide, acts as matchmaker for James's rejected bride Effy and the kindly Gurn.

The psychological dimension is even more evident in Bournonville's domestic ballets. Neither the religious nor the supernatural world has much of an influence in *Far from Denmark*, *Konservatoriet* (renamed, for some reason, *Le Conservatoire*), or *The King's Volunteers on Amager*, although disguises and sentimental tokens are used as plot devices. Alchemy and magical objects control events in *Kermesse in Bruges* and *Abdallah*, but the ballets feature comedy and spectacle, and the magic spells ultimately serve to teach the protagonists the lessons of humility and moderation.

Love is constantly being tested in Bournonville's ballets. Husbands and fiancés pursue attractive dalliances—fatal in the case of James and the Sylphide, trifling for the military men on duty in *Far from Denmark* and *The King's Volunteers*—and repent their indiscretion before the curtain falls. Contemporary critics debate the motivations of these characters, and dancers interpret them differently. Is James now the protagonist in *La Sylphide*? When he sees the Sylph and, infatuated, runs into the forest to catch her, is he mad, or dreaming? Scholar Knud Arne Jürgensen suggested he's a proto-existentialist. In Thomas Lund's performance, I saw a modern man teetering on the edge of marriage, fantasizing that he can still back out, and gorgeous Gudrun Bojesen as his imaginary soul mate. And should the Sylphide have a touch of evil about her, or is she a total innocent? In another performance, Caroline Cavallo seemed to taunt Mads Blangstrup; he went unhinged almost the moment he saw her.

The role of Madge has become celebrated as a challenge to all kinds of dancers—old and young, male and female, Bournonville-trained or not. In Copenhagen, where principal dancers go on from romantic leads to dramatic roles, the frisson of the aging ingenue adds depth to the demonic aspects of Madge's character. Last spring I'd seen New York City Ballet's Merrill Ashley do Madge in a sort of method-acting style, a ravaged beauty half in love with James and gloating over his defeat. That production was staged for Boston Ballet by former RDB principal Sorella Englund, who gave a devastating performance as Madge, triumphant but with a shiver of compassion as she stood over James's fallen body. In Copenhagen Jette Buchwald was relentless and powerful, Lis Jeppesen, a charming Sylph in former years, was skinny and defiant.

Bournonville ought to be having a popular renaissance today, given the audience's addiction to story ballets and the opportunities they offer for character interpretation. But his ballets don't import very well. They're "old-fashioned" in a particular, homey way, like the genre paintings of the period. Even the dancing is domesticated; you don't scream over it, you savor it. Bournonville dancing is defined by a sense of momentum, lightness, and protean detail. Not many dancers can manage this, even very good ones, unless they really live in the Bournonville realm. As shown in

Anne Marie Vessel Schlüter's Bournonville class sessions, the step vocabulary is as demanding as any classical style, but it gets deployed almost decoratively.

Working from a centered body and a soft, secure plié, the dancer spins out long chains of steps that are like enthralling little stories in themselves: phrases with interesting descriptive modifiers and dependent clauses, parentheses, and concluding exclamations that lead straight into new thoughts. Little beats and expansive jumps don't simply repeat for cumulative effect; each return of the step can take a different form or direction from the one before, or issue from a differently modeled body. A dancer makes a series of jumps without pausing to adjust his balance, springing off from the foot that just landed and shifting into a new direction or a carving new path with the working leg. You get a terrifically airy feeling from these big leg gestures, sailing out in all directions, swooping in toward the body and out again before they finally close into a precise fifth or fourth position. The dancer can insert small beats or connecting steps between jumps or turns. She can come down out of a relevé while she's still turning, for a quiet deceleration, or descend into plié to start a new jump or traverse. Bournonville enchaînements don't finish with a self-satisfied, applause-inducing sense of consolidation. Without pausing and re-preparing, the dancers just seem to be carried forward into the music, with the irrepressible, gotta-dance quality you find in folk dance.

Epaulement, the carriage of the head and shoulders, is very important in Bournonville, apart from the specific mime gestures and expressions which tell the story. The dancer's whole upper body is active all the time, referring to the steps, extending their scope in space, creating a diagonal line of tension through the body. Interviewed on the DVD, Thomas Lund says he thinks of the legs as carrying the rhythm of the phrase and the arms as carrying the tune. The music features the same kind of continuum as the step sequences; dotted rhythms, dancelike figures, long phrases, and few stops for breath. The many balleticized folk dance interludes blend into the stories, and folk rhythms spill over into classical variations. Dancers speak of the joy of dancing, which comes through even when the choreography is difficult.

We see these refinements and technical wonders in the best Bournonville dancers. But the company also does a contemporary repertory, and acknowledges some conflict between the two. For the very reasons Bournonville ballet is special, it robs dancers of the chance to do their hottest moves and earn today's most vociferous praise. In a men's company class one day we saw them hurling themselves into multiple pirouettes and air-turns without troubling about how they finished. Another day we saw women stretching into eye-high extensions and arabesques that would have improperly exposed their upper legs under a tutu. Some of the women aren't good turners; they tend to skitter off their center of gravity. Modern ballet technique doesn't require the niceties of placement and reticence; Bournonville ballet doesn't sanction force and flash. There are those who think the two styles are technically incompatible, but Vessel Schlüter insists Bournonville training prepares a dancer to do anything.

When you watch the ballets, you're not so aware of these thin spots in the technique. Nor do we necessarily notice changes in staging—how could we, when the international audience only sees a ballet once in a decade? Dinna Bjorn demonstrated mime sequences that had been deleted from Nikolaj Hübbe's new production of *La Sylphide*. Mime is considered a needless accessory in classical ballet today, but Bjorn's example showed how the characters and their relationships could be deepened by explanatory mime passages.

Much of the informal conversation during the festival carried the sense of experiencing a milestone. Were the Danes moving into a new Bournonville era or did the festival mark the end of one? Only two of the ballets will be done next season, and it's uncertain how many of the rest will ever be restored to the repertory. Facing even a temporary loss, you start to long for recordings to keep them in mind until the next round. So far almost none are commercially available. Seeing the whole lot at once is impressive but superficial. You can be convinced that what you're looking at is authentic. But is it? No one disputes that the ballets and the style are changing all the time. The Danish teachers and scholars are as scrupulous about explaining the lineage of the ballets as they are about placing them in context. We accept these productions as the real thing, even though they comprise tiny updatings, scenic modernizings, and "as ifs." For the dancers' sake and the audiences', this continual refurbishing is necessary to stave off boredom and obsolescence. But how much modern sensibility or shrewd historicizing can you apply to the aesthetic before it turns into a theme park?

Bruce Marks, Toni Lander, and Flemming Ryberg's *Abdallah*, recovered in 1985 for Ballet West and taken into the RDB repertory a year later, holds a slightly ambiguous place in the Bournonville canon. It arrived as a finished piece in 1855 in Vienna, where Bournonville was fulfilling what turned out to be a less than satisfying sabbatical. He seems to have inserted an inordinate amount of showy dancing to please the cosmopolitan Viennese audience. *Abdallah* disappeared when he returned to

Copenhagen, and the reconstruction may be somewhat stigmatized because of its semi-American provenance. I've seen it in Salt Lake City, New York, and Boston, but set among all its fellows in Copenhagen, it looked like a transitional work, or a premonition about ballet's future.

Abdallah starts out with a typical village scene; instead of Denmark or Italy, we're in Basra, in what's now Iraq. There's a shoemaker hero, his girlfriend and her social-climbing mother, a good deed prayerfully undertaken, and a reward in the form of a magic candelabra. The hero wishes for the obvious things; he gets a palace, heaping platters of food, magnificent clothes, and a harem of beautiful girls. He blows the whole thing, of course, with one wish too many, but everything works out all right in the end. Still, *Abdallah* doesn't follow the usual trajectory.

In most Bournonville fantasies, the characters live to regret their adventures into the supernatural. They wake up, as Bournonville did after his ambitious escapade in Vienna, with a strengthened appreciation for home and home folks. This happens in *Napoli*, *Far From Denmark*, *Kermesse in Bruges*, and even *La Sylphide*. But Abdallah and Irma's union isn't celebrated in the village square. They're inducted instead into the real Sheik's royal court, which looks suspiciously like the illusory one Abdallah wished for in act 2. I started to see ballet history reeling forward, from the homely first act with its chatty neighbors, local characters, and quasi-ethnic dances, to the visions of the second act, complete with a corps de ballet of harem girls, to the opulent finale with its men's and women's formal dances, classical variations, pas de deux, and implied dynastic order. The whole process looked like the evolution from Romantic ballet to Petipa's Imperial Russian style.

The Danes are not an unreasonably nostalgic people. In spite of the key position Bournonville has won in ballet history, the RDB is still a little self-conscious about him. The company prides itself on an eclectic repertory that bounds from Bournonville to *The Nutcracker* to Balanchine, and on to Kylian, Tharp, and contemporary Nordic choreographers. Flemming Flindt, trained in the RDB school, choreographed an early sex-and-violence ballet, based on Ionesco's *The Lesson*, in 1963. Modernism and bad taste have surfaced intermittently in the repertory ever since. Kinky sex even made a walk-on appearance at the 2005 Bournonville Festival.

On Tuesday afternoon we climbed the circular ramp of Copenhagen's Round Tower to see a photo exhibit, "Sylphs & Trolls," curated by art historian Mia Okkels. Surrounding the archival display, a series of large color prints suggested a different, postmodern Bournonville. Photographer Per Morten Abrahamsen had posed the dancers in views and collages that disclosed what he considered the repressed subtexts of the ballets. The pictures had been published by the RDB as a sold-out 2005 calendar called "Absolute Bournonville."

January's picture looks at an open field. Perhaps it's sunrise. Mists rise from the dark grass. Under a colorless sky stained with clouds, ten sylphs dance in a ring. They usher in a scenario without a story, as scenes of wispy innuendo and lurid glamour unfold month by month. In hard-edged artificial light, the dancers enact feverish beach parties, orgies, murders, and seductions. They play at bondage, voyeurism, goofy disguises. They pose balletically in studios, chase each other underwater, admire themselves in store windows. Naked women encircle a man with ropes of fire. One sylph, multiplied six times, inspects a man suspended like a puppet from a tree branch, where another sylphic sister is holding the strings. All the characters seem absolutely banal in their embrace of naughtiness.

Abrahamsen's pictures take the ballets beyond realism to "reality," a state where danger is so patently faked that it no longer holds any mystery, and where sex comes in as many flavors as ice cream. Trendy and amusing as all this may be, Romanticism in the long run is both more ephemeral and more lasting.

KITRI'S CABOODLE

Boston Phoenix, 7 April 2000

Don Quixote the ballet has gone through many changes since its premiere in 1869, from freshening-up to major rehab. This often happens with the old Russian classics, but the Boston Ballet *Don Quixote* has outgrown both its title and its original story line. Cervantes's quixotic seeker after the feminine ideal may have been a dreamer but he was an adventurer too, charging after supposed villains, rescuing maidens in peril, duelling for affairs of honor, and getting mocked for his fanaticism. The Boston Ballet Don and his dopey sidekick Sancho Panza have become fixtures, peripheral to the thwarted romance of the young couple Kitri and Basilio, and to nearly three hours' worth of dancing prompted by a colorful Spanish locale.

Boston Ballet acquired Rudolf Nureyev's version of the ballet in 1982 and has reworked it extensively since then. Artistic director Anna Marie Holmes and ballet mistress Caroline Llorca have understood intuitively that *Don Q* works best as a pretext for classical and character dancing, but they haven't been daring enough to clean out the dramaturgical dross.

Holmes's introductory note in the program tells us to expect "scads of bravura dancing and scores of people on stage at any moment." In this case, less would be more.

The production got off to a rough start last Thursday night, but the second performance displayed the company's dancing to great advantage. Pollyana Ribeiro and Paul Thrussell as Kitri and Basilio, the mischievous couple who are the ballet's real subjects, overcame the adversities of opening night.

Any time a dancer falls onstage, the audience is momentarily traumatized. The dancer usually picks up the pieces and goes on, but Aleksandra Koltun's injury at the end of the second act was serious, a torn Achilles tendon, it turned out, and she couldn't get to her feet. The Don Quixote, Arthur Leeth, chivalrously carried her off and Larissa Ponomarenko, one of the alternate Kitris, finished the ballet in her place. Before that point, there had been opening night glitches and a persistent nervous hyperintensity throughout the cast. Ponomarenko threw herself into the breech but she hadn't rehearsed with Koltun's Basilio, Yury Yanowsky, and there were more scary moments.

The whole production Friday night was calmer and smoother, but it was Ribeiro and Thrussell's performance that really made the difference, giving the work a focus if not a dramatic credibility. Ribeiro has charm without affectation; she seems to enjoy being playful, and Thrussell reacted boyishly, fondly. If she was unpredictable, he loved her more for it. If she taunted and pulled away one minute, he knew she'd be in his arms the next.

Even with Ribeiro and Thrussell's light touch, the ballet is riddled with clichés and extraneous characters. The frequent scenery changes seem to necessitate mime scenes played in front of a black curtain: a procession of townspeople, all—curiously—walking in the same direction; the Don whacking away at some ineffectual ghostly intruders; the foppish wealthy suitor in a reprise of the fussing and preening with which he's been upstaging the rest of the ballet.

Many people are credited with having an artistic hand in this production, and some of the overextended and undermotivated mime seems to originate from Russian traditions carried over into the Soviet period and brought to Boston Ballet by dancers and coaches. Vadim Strukov's Gamache, the vain suitor, was an encyclopedia of pratfalls and powder puffs, way out of scale with Leeth's Don, who seemed to be sleepwalking all the time, and the dithery Sancho Panza (I saw Christopher Budzynski and

Reagan Messer). Piotr Ostaltsov, as Kitri's father Lorenzo, opted for either hand-wringing or fist-shaking as his response to the meandering plot.

Then there are what can only be called "roles"—characters who appear only as a pretext to interpolate more dancing. There were so many I soon lost track, but Simon Ball was impressive as Espada, a matador who dances a lot but has no involvement whatsoever in the story.

What's missing from *Don Quixote* and some of Boston's other block-busters is firm editing: a look at the logic of narrative, the balance of plot and dancing, the way things fit together.

To take just one example, Basilio is supposed to be a comic as well as a virtuoso dancer—Nureyev said that's why he took the role. The romance plot—how to get Kitri's father to agree to the barber Basilio as a son-in-law instead of the rich and totally inappropriate Gamache—is resolved when Basilio fakes a suicide. Boston's Kitri appeals to her father and to the inef-fectual Don: I really *really* love him, let me marry him instead of that space cadet Gamache. They agree. Huh? The Don, as played by Arthur Leeth, hadn't by then made the slightest impact on the townspeople. He clanked in and out; people stared at him, then forgot him. If he was in love with Kitri—who in literature represents the Don's eternal fantasy, Dulcinea—he gave no indication, either before or at that decisive point.

The much more persuasive reason for the resolution, and the funnier one (I remember Mikhail Baryshnikov's version in 1978), is that marrying Kitri is Basilio's dying wish, something no religious person could ignore. Kitri falls in delightedly with his whispered plan. Just let us get married so he can die in peace, and then I'll have Gamache, Kitri wheedles. Of course, Basilio jumps up in perfect health the minute the ceremony is performed.

Dancing redeems some of the Boston production's dramatic perfunc-toriness. It has, indeed, scads of faux-gypsy, faux-Spanish, and generic-peasant dancing. The Russians perfected the idea of adapting nonclassical dance styles so that they could show off classically trained dancers and give variety to these long ballets. New to the Boston production is a men's seguidilla in silence—they accompany themselves with stamping and anti-phonal clapping, as in flamenco performances—and two women's dances, one with big red shawls and one with castanets.

And then there's the "pure" classical second act, where Kitri dons a tutu and dances in some heavenly dreamscape with spirits and nymphs of all ages. And the final pas de deux, often done alone as a showpiece, where Kitri and Basilio celebrate their marriage. To Ludwig Minkus's most rousing music, they have their most demanding solo and partner work.

Opening night, you could count Ponomarenko's thirty-two fouettés, she was so dead-on to the music. I couldn't tell you how many Ribeiro did, but her performance was thrilling, because she inserted a double-turn about every fourth time.

Boston Ballet CEO Jeffrey Babcock assures us in a program note that we can expect more productions like *Don Quixote*. I think this is regressive, not to mention expensive. In the age of nightly dance entertainments on television, of stand-up comedy, and multiple stories told and resolved in fifty-two minutes, ballet has to say something else to us. These extravagant gestures to the past don't do it for me.

KIROV ON TOUR
Christian Science Monitor, 6 June 1986

Excitement over the North American tour of Leningrad's Kirov Ballet is based on the pursuit of an ideal. Like the hero in a nineteenth-century ballet, the dance community believes in a physical perfection, a nobility of soul, that has somehow survived from an earlier, purer time; and the Kirov embodies that ideal. It was the Imperial Russian ballet, of which the Kirov is the direct descendant, that crystallized classical ballet's technique—its movement language—and created its grandest theatrical works. The Kirov and its immediate predecessor, the Maryinsky school, have also produced some of the most extraordinary dancers, teachers, and choreographers of the twentieth century, including Anna Pavlova, Vaslav Nijinsky, and George Balanchine, and the contemporary artists Rudolf Nureyev, Natalia Makarova, and Mikhail Baryshnikov. The Kirov is where you go in the ballet world to look for impeccable training, elegance and expression in dancing, and faithful productions of the classics.

Philadelphia's sprawling, 5,000-seat orchestra shed, the Mann Music Center, was not the best place to savor a full-length Kirov classic, let alone assess the company after its twenty-two-year absence from the United States. In fact, the whole rationale of the tour—seven American and Canadian cities in just a month—belongs to theater of the absurd: last-minute bookings; no appropriate theaters available; no date in New York, the nation's dance capital; pressurized travel and rehearsal schedules; limited repertory. Nevertheless, the performance I saw in Philadelphia did show off the Kirov resources and reveal some of its stylistic priorities.

Swan Lake in the first place is a mixture of elements—magic and majesty, romanticism and spectacle, frivolity and moral instruction. Originally it had two choreographers, Marius Petipa, the Maryinsky ballet master who devised forty years of entertainments for the tsars, and his musical, self-effacing second-in-command, Lev Ivanov. Petipa's first and third acts celebrate the grandeur of the court, with processions, fanfares, toasting, and flourishes. They show off the panoply of Empire that will be the inheritance of Prince Siegfried and the woman he chooses for his bride. Ivanov's lyrical, formal second and fourth acts depict the mystery and allure of the outer world—enchanted swans, craggy moonlit landscapes, and love that transcends earthly power.

Even though *Swan Lake* has been handed down in an unbroken line through the Maryinsky/Kirov ballet masters since its definitive form was reached in 1895, what we see today is only relatively authentic. Contemporary taste, politics, even the size of the stage can affect the look of a ballet, and the current Kirov *Swan Lake,* staged in 1950 by Konstantin Sergeyev, is streamlined in several ways.

Modern ballet everywhere seems to go in for reduced clutter, and this *Swan Lake* has cut miming and dramatic byplay to a minimum. Siegfried's mother doesn't gesture to him that he must choose a wife, and Odette neglects to explain how she came to be under the spell of the evil magician Rothbart. The audience is informed about these things by a synopsis in the program. However superfluous, these mime passages can add depth to the characters and texture to the dancing. But character differentiation is not a major concern for the Kirov either.

The first act no longer mingles courtiers and peasants at the prince's pre-birthday party; everyone attending appears of equally high station. Perhaps even such an innocuous reference to a class system is not suitable for Soviet consumption, but throughout, this production goes for a more homogenous, less complicated cast of characters. The visiting delegations who entertain at the birthday ball with national dances of Spain, Italy, Hungary, and Poland retain very little ethnic distinction. The dances now seem mainly composed of ordinary ballet steps with a few typical gestures —the arms and torso sweeping backward in the Spanish dance, the elbows folded and heels clicking together in the czardas—but no rhythmic emphasis or exotic fire.

On the other hand, more opportunities have been made for use of the standard classical vocabulary. Benno, the prince's friend, long banished entirely from American productions, has been reinstated as a jumping, twirling jester (Vitaly Tsvetkov in the performance I saw), who dances the equivalent of impertinent remarks and distracting bons mots. The villain Rothbart (Elidor Aliev), usually played by a mime with mask and enveloping costume, is also a danced role, which makes him seem more like Siegfried's rival for Odette's affections than a demon who already possesses her.

These changes make for a certain theatrical blandness in the production, which was reinforced by the principals. Evgeny Neff, the Siegfried, made very little effort to project a character, and Lubov Kunakova was a monotonously tragic Odette and a uniformly triumphant Odile in the third act, where, as Rothbart's daughter, she tricks Siegfried into betraying Odette.

All this deemphasizing of the theatrical elements had the effect of focusing attention on the dancing—on the Kirov's superlative corps de ballet and attractive demi-soloists, and on Ivanov's choreography for the "white" acts. Although the success of the Imperial Russian ballet is usually credited to the showman Petipa, Ivanov's reputation is more and more appreciated. The Soviet critic Yuri Slonimsky attributed *Swan Lake*'s vitality to him, and it's his two acts that George Balanchine distilled for the version now done by the New York City Ballet. Some people consider Balanchine's *Swan Lake* eccentric; to others it contains everything expressive about the ballet that anybody needs.

On a hot night in Philadelphia, with cameras clicking nearby, and neighbors humming familiar bits of the music, this dancing expressiveness came through to me and seemed to convey the whole argument for the tradition. It's not just that the Kirov corps is precise, that all the women's legs go up into the exact same angle of arabesque, or that they leave the ground exactly together for a jump. More than that, they seem connected to each other through space—perhaps it's the music that links them, but the link is palpable. They can sense how far they are from each other even when moving backwards or in circles. They flutter—you can feel the agitation in their feet—when the music runs fast. They float when it slows. When Kunakova lifts her arms to simulate the wings of a woman-turned-swan, she makes me see an expanse of sky around her, with clouds and wind whipping past, an effect more real than what's painted on the backdrop.

In the last act, when Siegfried returns to the lake in remorse, eight black swans appear and thread their way through the lines of white swans. They seem to be Rothbart's envoys, symbolizing the presence of evil among the noblest spirits. And that presence overshadows a hokey, happy ending. This is metaphor without acting; perhaps it's the beginning of modern choreography.

Boston Phoenix, 8 April, 2005

Critics look at *Swan Lake* differently from the rest of the audience. The prospect of viewing this long, demanding classical ballet for the tenth or fiftieth time can arouse anything from anticipation to dread, but no critic can approach it without some comparative machinery clicking on. No matter how you try to take the performance on its own terms, you can't completely erase the layers of images previously imprinted on your memory screen.

We're not talking photographic authenticity here. Ballets can't be cloned from one performance to the next, or even preserved more or less intact for one hundred years, as music can. *Swan Lake* has undergone continual cleansing and retrofitting since the canonical 1895 St. Petersburg prototype. Choreographers have tweaked Marius Petipa and Lev Ivanov's creation to suit changing tastes and politics. Not to mention revisionists who've turned it into gender-bending satire (Matthew Bourne), Hollywood kitsch (George Balanchine), and popular parody. All this lurks beneath one's conscious observation, waiting to be triggered by Tchaikovsky's luscious score.

The Russian National Ballet Theater production, opening a two-month American tour at the Cutler Majestic last Friday, revealed something about the ballet's reworked choreographic history but left its iconic attributes submerged. This production's creators, after Petipa and Ivanov, included the Soviet choreographers Alexandr Gorsky and Asaf Messerer, with amendments by the company's artistic director Evgeny Amosov and general manager Vladimir Moiseev. In the Soviet years, the Russians cleared away a lot of *Swan Lake*'s old-fashioned mime and concocted a happy ending. Gorsky sought a more naturalistic acting and pictorial style. Later, the milling peasants and nobles were eliminated from the background of the party scenes as a distraction.

Superficially, this performance made the right motions, but the standard was low, and I looked for explanations. For one thing, the Majestic stage is too small to accommodate a large-scale ballet. At times an ensemble of twenty-four dancers did squeeze on, but whenever they moved out of their positions, the movement looked cramped and cut off. It didn't breathe. The soloists seemed to be calculating how many steps or turns they could make without bumping into the scenery. The corps started out looking disciplined, but by the last act they seemed demoralized.

Act 1 opened with a Jester (Khasan Usmanov) center stage, surrounded by a neatly lined up corps. This character, added and danced by Gorsky in around 1920, launched his bent-legged clowning and high scissors-jumps into the middle of the corps' decorous dances. He held the party scenes together like a jovial ringmaster, but his hyperbravado was out of scale with the rest of the action.

It was hard to tell much about the quality of the Siegfried (Maxim Romanov) and Odette/Odile (Ekaterina Evseeva), or the lesser soloists, because the choreography was simplified and repetitive as well as spatially constricted. Some of the usual tricks were there but few of the subtle step-embellishments. Romanov looked bewildered all the time, a shy person making dutiful princely moves. Evseeva seemed a potentially commanding dancer, both as the unfortunate White Swan and the spiteful alter ego who seduces Siegfried into forgetting his promise.

The Moscow-based ballet company usually performs with taped music, I've learned, but for this tour, they're accompanied by the Sofia Symphony Orchestra led by Sergey Kondrashev. The orchestra had continual difficulties with intonation, entrances, keeping together, blurred passages; I'm told they received badly printed scores.

You can sympathize with dancers when they have to perform in these conditions, but you can't pretend that approximate musicality, insecure line, and wobbly pointe work don't make a difference. The soloists insisted on the Russian affectation of taking at least two bows after every important number, whether or not the audience wanted them. Why would they assume they could whip up our excitement when they'd displayed none in their dancing?

SWANS UNDER GLASS

Boston Phoenix, 17 November 2006

The third act of *Swan Lake* is a ritual, signifying the transfer of royal power. The heir to the throne celebrates his coming of age, representatives of his future colonies pay him tribute, and he's supposed to choose a bride. All this takes place in the presence of his mother the Queen and members of the court. In this quasi-public way the continuation of the monarchy will be assured. Prince Siegfried has already fallen in love with an enchanted Swan, though, so after a round of waltzing with six would-be fiancées, he goes down the line and rejects each one.

The way the Kirov Ballet performs this scene, the princesses are virtually identical partners in a formal dance. Only after they've been passed over do they each react differently—one is disappointed, one huffily turns away. I bring this up because, thinking back over the performance Friday night at the Wang, it seems symptomatic of the ballet's whole style: *Swan Lake* down to the bone, all dancing with only the merest, conventionalized suggestion of acting verismo to create a plot. Everybody in it looks like their peer group, and all of them dance classical steps in strictly formal patterns with small inflections to indicate their station. The courtiers are a dutiful corps de ballet, the Swans hop sorrowfully in arabesque, the Spanish women do deep backbends.

"Revised Choreography and Stage Direction" for the production are credited to Konstantin Sergeyev, and this explains a lot of its even tone. Sergeyev, who died in 1992, rechoreographed the 1895 *Swan Lake* in 1950, at the beginning of his nearly three decades as artistic director of the Kirov. We don't know how many alterations have been made to Sergeyev's reproduction, but it premiered deep in the Soviet period and still bears the respectful but revisionist attitude that brought the classics—scathed—through the revolution.

The production looked choreographically credible to me, but subtly sanitized. When the curtain went up on act 1, the first thing you saw was dancing people wearing all-alike beige, white, and mauve costumes in a generic ballet Russian style, with the women in calf-length, high-waisted filmy dresses. No way to tell if they're villagers or gentry, friends or attendants. They dance neatly, drink toasts, dance some more.

While this is going on, the Prince's tutor (Petr Stasyunas) pulls two girls aside and introduces them to his charge. A bored playboy, Siegfried is polite but nothing more. The tutor shrugs; he's tried this before without success. After this promising piece of character sketching, the production foregoes even the pretext of psychological complexity and falls back on standard types, or no types at all.

Diana Vishneva, the Swan Queen Odette, projected exquisite despair throughout her second-act encounter with the Prince (Igor Kolb), and he looked stunned by her. In the third act he could do nothing but smile in goofy submission to her haughty glamour as the impostor Odile. I'm not saying they didn't dance well. Vishneva unfolded tremendous extensions and beautiful pointe work, Kolb ripped off some lofty jumps. They looked really correct, and their every effect seemed really *really* studied.

Besides the tutor, who disappeared after the first act, dramatic texture was provided by an interpolated Jester (Andrey Ivanov), who spins around a lot and pleases the audience, and the evil Swan abductor Rothbart (Maxim

Chashchegorov), who loses one of his wings and dies after a collision with Siegfried in the fourth act. The evening's grandest moments came from the massed designs of the large ensemble of swans.

Probably if you didn't know *Swan Lake* in more traditional versions, you wouldn't miss the naturalistic detail—the peasants and potentates, the mimed storytelling and conversations, the simulated ethnicity of the third act divertissements. I never thought I would either, but after three hours of this anti-extravaganza, I longed for some hearty huntsmen and tipsy serving girls.

KINGDOM OF THE SWEET

Hudson Review, Summer 1997

Every year the signs of Christmas turn up a little earlier and last a little longer. In my local mini-mall the department store put out the plastic wreaths and trees before they sold all the garden hoses, and citizens were encouraged to leave the lights up on their houses till Presidents Day, to twinkle up the landscape. But you really know it's Christmas when *The Nutcracker* makes its appearance. According to a *"Nutcracker* Alphabet" compiled for the New York City Ballet program book by Maitland Mc-Donagh, there are more than a hundred different versions of the ballet in America. This is a gross underestimate. The first Sunday in December the *Boston Globe* listed approximately 130 performances of 14 different productions, just in the Boston area. This list doesn't discriminate between the professional Boston Ballet version and a whole range of semiprofessional, student, civic, regional, children's, and even puppet renditions of the theme.

The Nutcracker is a ballet spectacle and a moneymaking showcase for struggling dance organizations, but I think it's more than that. It can be reconstituted in seemingly limitless ways to serve different needs and populations. Despite its roots in nineteenth-century Imperial Russia, it's become almost a folk-art form in middle America. I wanted to explore what this phenomenon means, and I felt pretty certain it didn't mean the Balanchine paradigm that dominates the landscape in New York.

If I think of the New York City Ballet version, which will always be *the Nutcracker* to me, I see wonderful stage effects and contrasting moods: a family party full of loving relatives and benign surprises, snowfall in deep night woods, treats that come to life, and a flight in a sleigh with a chivalrous little boy for an escort. And ballerinas, dancing children and toys, the Christmas tree that grows as the dreaming little girl seems to shrink, and the scary/comical battle of the mice. All this, as well as the dance action, changes drastically from one version to another, but no matter how limited the producers' resources or how diverse their goals, *The Nutcracker* gets told in essentially the same terms. Its two-part structure inverts, by magic, from a family party to a utopian fiesta where the parents are nowhere in sight. Maybe one reason little children can sit still for the second act, which has no story and virtually no mimetic action, is that it projects them into the Kingdom of the Sweets, where they can indulge their greedy appetites, their longing to be free of parental control, and their fantasies of regal indolence.

This reversal of circumstances is facilitated by the mysterious Drosselmeyer and the dolls he brings to the Stahlbaum children. Clara, the child/protagonist (for some reason the NYCB Clara is called Marie), either from overstimulation or preadolescent wish-fulfillment, dreams the toys to life. In a nursery tempest, they defend her against a horde of attacking mice, and after she helps their commander, the Nutcracker, defeat the Mouse King, he turns into a handsome prince. He takes her on a magic journey to his home, where it's Christmas all the time and a child can have as much candy as she wants. (The NYCB, perhaps anticipating parental objections, has replaced some of the nutritionally incorrect goodies in the second act decor with fruit.) The characters who entertain them there are reminiscent of the party dolls but no one except the translated Nutcracker normally goes along with Clara into the second act, not even Drosselmeyer.

The party scene introduces the characters, sets up the transformation, and features social dancing ensembles of children, parents, grandparents, and friends, rather than ballet dancing. Some versions omit or downplay this, perhaps to deflect one criticism that has followed *The Nutcracker* since its premiere in 1892, its lack of unity. The rift between narrative and technical display, typical of the nineteenth-century ballets, is at its most serious here. Not merely alternating story and poetry as in the acts of *Swan Lake*, or mime and dancing as in *Coppélia*, *Nutcracker* breaks into two distinct theatrical units. But the phenomenal popularity of the ballet overcomes this flaw, if it is one. One could just as well argue that the contrast between the acts is an asset, and that the galop and Grossvater dance reinforce the party's cordiality. Balanchine certainly emphasized the discrepancy, by withholding all ballet dancing, except for Drosselmeyer's mechanical dolls, until after the mouse battle and the transformation.

The party dances not only fold easily into the social atmosphere in which they occur, they make a place for dancing children. Modern *Nut-*

*cracker*s face a problem: if the first act is about children, are real children to be used in staging it, and if so, what will they be able to do? When the producing organization is backed up with a fine ballet school, as of course was the Imperial Theater in St. Petersburg where *The Nutcracker* originated, the work can provide a training ground for children preparing for a professional career. Balanchine himself played various roles in this and other classics when he was a student at the then Maryinsky. In his own stagings of the nineteenth-century repertory, and sometimes in new choreography like *Mozartiana*, he made as many opportunities for children as possible. I once heard him say he felt this guaranteed at least two people in the audience for every child on the stage, but I doubt that his motives were entirely crass.

He demanded so much more dancing from them than was needed just to show them off. Stagewise children are good at fooling around when the curtain goes up. A bigger test is whether they can actually dance. In Balanchine's *Nutcracker*, children not only act, they do two contradances in the first act, perform as mice and toy soldiers in the battle scene, and appear in the second act divertissements. From the tiny, gliding angels, to the Candy Canes and Polichinelles who have real ballet steps to do, they have to conform to the lines and focus of the group, maintain spatial patterns, preserve musical accuracy, and stay in character in front of an audience.

Unfortunately, many dance teachers follow Balanchine's example without his resources. On public access TV one night last Christmas season, some small automatons wove across a strip of stage in front of the local symphony orchestra, captured in fuzzy focus by a stationary camera. These products of a dancing school in the area labored joylessly through several *Nutcracker* divertissements. Some looked too young to be wearing pointe shoes, and they all looked unprepared to use them. Nervous and wobbly, lacking any notion of turnout, they struggled to stab their legs into the floor and execute the shapes they were assigned. I imagine recitals like this go on everywhere. Of course, a doting audience loves them no matter what.

Boston's enterprising James Reardon, director of the Boston Dance Company, doesn't have a major school to supply a juvenile component, but he's worked out a decent, full-stage *Nutcracker* that cycles several communities into the ballet. Reardon's associate director and ballet master, Clyde Nantais, gathers a youthful supporting cast in each of about five suburban areas around Boston. They rehearse weekly through the fall, then give both public and school showings several times in each locale, with a basic cadre of adult dancers from the company taking care of the technical numbers.

I attended a performance one freezing morning in a barnlike audi-torium at Salem State College, with about two hundred bused-in primary and middle schoolers. The production was condensed and adapted to the situation, but not unrecognizable, and it came with a program book full of advertisements that said things like: "Good Luck!! Akilah & Arantya. We are proud of you. Love, Mom & Dad." The children here were more than charm-ing; they danced with spirit and technical ability, in choreography suited to them but not apologetic.

At one point the taped music went awry and the perky Clara, a thirteen-year-old from one of the participating dance schools, was trapped alone onstage for at least five minutes while miscued bits of music went on and off. This trooper managed to keep the fidgety audience from going out of control. Building with unerring stage instinct on the balletic situation—she was supposed to be watching the divertissements in the Kingdom of the Sweets—she gazed expectantly at the empty stage, then turned with a smile to the audience, including us in what seemed a delightful suspense. I've never seen a professional make a better recovery from a technical gaffe. Backstage, she was surrounded by a flurry of smaller girls pleading for her autograph.

Reardon's *Nutcracker* demonstrates how the ballet can be a true chil-dren's occasion, without condescending either to the children or to the ballet itself. And though the NYCB version is a fully professional ballet, it too is a family show. When I saw it in New York at a matinee, the audience comprised children and adults almost equally.

Besides the advantage of holding back on choreographed classical glam-our, Balanchine's first scene balances home values against escapism. The lure of what Clara sees on her journey can't quite supercede the comforts of her own fireside. Although this version doesn't show us Clara/Marie's re-turn, it implies that her yen for adventure has been satisfied, and she'll be happy to wake up in the loving arms of her mother when the reindeer sleigh reaches its destination. Balanchine's *Nutcracker*, perhaps because it doesn't show the heroine's awakening, leaves us suspended between dreaming and reality. A curiosity that appeared on TV this season assumed a viewer couldn't be expected to read the events as a dream unless it literally showed her waking up safe.

One night, trolling through the channels in mid-November, I snagged the end of an anonymous *Nutcracker* that BRAVO was apparently screening several times. I wouldn't have known what it was except for the music. It had that gelatinous look of early-television ballet: orange crinkly cello-phane sets, fluffy tutus with satin bodices, and dancing hunched into a performance space no bigger than a nightclub. The dancers had the smooth, impassive faces of mannequins, but my first reaction was "Melissa Hayden!" "Edward Villella!" I dismissed this notion; what would these stellar dancers have been doing in a vehicle like this? A few minutes later the show ended and to my amazement the credits listed Hayden, Villella, Patricia McBride, and the German modern dancer and mime Harald Kreutzberg. After a successful home taping and some research, I knew that it had been choreographed for Bavarian TV by the German freelancer Kurt Jacob sometime in the early 1960s.

On full viewing, the Jacob version proved to be the most revisionist of all the *Nutcrackers* I saw this season. Compressed to fit a one-hour format, but determined to supply a postparty plot, it has Drosselmeyer alias Uncle Alex (Kreutzberg, trying, I suppose, to look mysterious but only looking sedated) taking Marie (McBride) and the Nutcracker (Villella) on a sleigh ride to find the young man's lost home. They encounter some of the usual divertissements on the way—rechoreographed without distinction—plus what looks like a complete Bluebird pas de deux from *Sleeping Beauty*, danced by Niels Kehlet of the Royal Danish Ballet and the German ballerina Helga Heinrich. Eventually the travelers come to a palace with golden doors. Inside is the Sugarplum Fairy (Hayden), who turns out to be none other than the Nutcracker's mother. After she "changes him back to what he was before—a prince," according to the voice-over, they dance the Grand Pas de Deux together. The duet fades out on Marie as a child, waking up in bed with the Nutcracker in her arms. "It was all a dream," says the narrator, "and no one would ever know. Except maybe Uncle Alex." Kreutzberg hovers next to the bed, and he and Marie share a wink.

This tintype *Nutcracker* is fun to watch, the way minor silent movies are. It offers first of all the rare pleasure of revisiting dancers in their vanished youth. Despite the cramped choreography, you can still see McBride's luxurious stretch, Villella's eager elegance, and Hayden's strength and poise. The video also shows us how far dance on TV has come in thirty years. Jacob's capsule version of the ballet does somehow hang onto the main elements, cleansed of all subliminal eroticism and danger. There aren't even any mice. As Tchaikovsky's mouse music plays, the trio are sailing along in the sleigh, and the narrator talks about the "strange creatures" they see below them. They encounter storms and a flock of blue birds, done with animation, but nothing scarier than the music intrudes on the screen.

Television at its most conventional is a story medium, trying for the intimacy and realism of the movies. Early TV dance gave up on trying to reproduce the spectacular aspects of ballet and often brought whatever narrative there was to the foreground. Jacob and the German producers center their *Nutcracker* around the protagonists, with reaction shots, close-ups, and lots of nondance activity. As much as possible the camera encloses people in a steady tracking shot and avoids the constantly shifting space-body relationships that occur during dancing. The production is really a divertissement, without shadows or revelations, a passing pleasantry, like *I Dream of Jeannie*.

Balanchine's *Nutcracker* is also stress free and deeply middle class, but also deeply glamorous. When the NYCB finally filmed it in 1993, in an adaptation by Peter Martins, it pulled back slightly into a romanticized subtext. Clara/Marie's dream is touched off by a crush on the nephew, played with embarrassing affectation by the boy actor Macaulay Culkin. All the gender-specific aspects of the party scene, which the NYCB has been trying to downplay in recent years, glare out of the video. Boys always dance with girls and failing that, their mother. As presents, the boys get drums and the girls get dolls. The boys are aggressive, the girls simpery and fearful. In other small ways, including a redundant narration by Kevin Kline, the video seems to be pandering to a conservative audience.

Producers with a more modern turn of mind have probed the relationships between Clara, Drosselmeyer, and the Nutcracker-boy-Prince to uncover troubling but trendy issues of motivation, conflict, and desire. Drosselmeyer and Clara may have some subliminal sexual attraction for each other. Incestual implications can be raised, then safely side-stepped by transferring Clara's affections to the Nutcracker. He is, after all, only a toy, although in the dream the reincarnated Nutcracker is often played by the same child who comes to the party as Drosselmeyer's nephew. Some choreographers have suggested a more-than-familial bond between this boy and his uncle, or a rivalry between them for the nascent affections of Clara. The potential for triangular interplay becomes further complicated when Clara is played by an adult dancer. But I doubt if these racy undercurrents add much appeal for the children in the audience, whose fantasy world encompasses exploding spaceships, dismembered robots, and sportive battering, but not psychological intricacy.

Essentially every *Nutcracker* is an interpretation. Even the Balanchine version, which we consider the most authentic we have today, was retrieved in 1954 from the choreographer's memory of the versions he knew before leaving Russia in 1924, and it has since gone through another four decades of evolution. *Nutcracker* is not like *The Messiah*, which may differ from performance to performance in instrumentation, vocal forces, and expressive style but will almost always consist of the same notes, in the same order. Not even the score of *The Nutcracker* remains intact to the same degree, let alone the staging. Composed to the prescription of the ballet master, Marius Petipa, the score is laid out in a series of scenes that have musical relationships but no overall symphonic structure. Parts of it get moved around or omitted or laced with swatches from other ballets. Nobody thinks a thing about it.

Each new *Nutcracker* is a creative challenge, an attempt to uncover what the ballet might mean in a way that pleases both children and adults. Provided it keeps hold of the basic ingredients, we're prepared to become innocents or sophisticates; we're ready for almost any amount of patchwork, embroidery, or redesign. The Boston Ballet version, reconceived by artistic director Bruce Marks and choreographed by Marks and Daniel Pelzig, seems like one of those nineteenth-century musical exhibition pieces, a rhapsody or a fantasia on the theme of *Nutcracker*. It's not that the ballet is gone, but that so much has been tucked in around it you can hardly recognize it.

As the overture plays, a tableau of assorted Dickensian characters parade across the front of the stage, most of them making no further appearance in the ballet. I suppose this is meant to set a tone for the story. All I could think of was the Balanchine version, where during the entire overture nothing happens. We simply look at a drop painted with a village of snowy rooftops and a heralding angel, and listen to the music. Similarly, at the beginning of the second act, Boston gives us a panorama of angels, smoke, moving scenery, props, landscapes, and characters, while Balanchine, to the same music, offers tiny angels in long white dresses skimming along in clean linear formations.

Rather than hone down to the bedrock, which was always Balanchine's instinct when revisiting the nineteenth century, Marks builds, elaborates, overloads the idea. Wherever possible there are two of something instead of one, people upstaging other people, byplay off in the corners. Drosselmeyer, a batlike apparition in a huge flapping cape, is shadowed, literally, by his nephew, who dresses the same way and imitates his movements. Since the nephew neither turns into the Nutcracker nor reappears after the party scene, the doubling device is simply clutter. Drosselmeyer, on the other hand, is in charge of the action till the end. What were just parlor tricks at the party become supernatural powers. Not only can he transform the room and the toys, he tells Clara what to do in the mouse war, commandeers transportation, and makes the whole second act happen. The divertissements aren't gifts from the Sugarplum Fairy but animated denizens of Drosselmeyer's toy theater.

The Boston *Nutcracker* seems afraid to leave anything alone. The party scene is a tumble of tricks and schticks, a disapproving governess and a tippling maid, a larger-than-lifesize toy bear, a clownish grandmother. Amid the constant activity, the remains of the traditional story are hard to detect, and the audience is encouraged to abandon those simple lines in anticipation of the next coup de théâtre, and the next. The production is highly touted for its expensive sets and effects, and the audience is meant to feel thrilled by them. As if Clara and the Nutcracker couldn't get all the way to the "Palace of the Sweets" in the sleigh, Drosselmeyer transfers them to a decorated balloon, and then soars up after them on his own wire. The mice not only fight with the dolls, they dance in a troll-like ring around the Nutcracker, they are obsessed with food, and they do a rickety version of the clichéd four little swans from *Swan Lake*.

It's nearly impossible to settle down from all this and look at dancing in the second act. After Clara and the Nutcracker are ushered into fake stage boxes, they watch the divertissements emerge from a stage within the stage, against new backdrops representing each country of origin. What I noticed about the choreography—I think the Soviets started this—is how most of the numbers had shaken down to conventional partnered ballet turns. In some, a principal couple was flanked by a complementary ensemble: umbrella-twirling children for the Chinese, fluffy little lambs for the Marzipan. In most, a male partner or a small male cohort steadied and lifted a woman soloist with various site-specific quirks. Since there's also an added pas de deux couple in the Snowflakes scene, the production gives out a major message that partnering is what traditional ballet is about.

Balanchine was hardly one to stint on partner work, but his second act ranges in scale from the slinky solo woman in Coffee (the Arabian dance) to the three Chinese to a female quintet (Marzipan), the hoop-twirling Candy Canes, and finally the big women's group Waltz of the Flowers. He even detaches the dance of the Sugarplum Fairy (the famous celesta music) from the Grand Pas de Deux and relocates it as a solo, presented before Clara and the Nutcracker arrive. This shift gives the Sugarplum greater autonomy. Her dancing skills don't need to be displayed or assisted by any partner. For Balanchine, dancing itself is a variety show, a spectacle with many facets. You could almost read the whole second act as a subtle lesson in the way dancers, and dancing itself, can develop from the simplest childish beginnings to the majestic ensemble of Flowers and the virtuosics of the pas de deux.

Marks and Pelzig's *Nutcracker* is like a big bazaar, with Drosselmeyer as the pitchman for the attractions within. In a way, it's also the central booth in the larger marketplace that's selling the Boston Ballet to the public. *Nutcrackers* everywhere capitalize on the popularity of the Christmas perennial to pull in the biggest audiences; it's no secret that *The Nutcracker* often subsidizes a ballet company's whole operation for the year. In Boston this promotion has reached a level of expertise that rivals the stage performance itself. Beginning with the company's enthusiastic director, Bruce Marks, *The Nutcracker* is first hyped from within. The local media then take up the cry, and the process loops around for weeks, with feature stories, interviews, film clips on TV news, more press releases, special events eliciting more coverage. None of this is paid for, but the city is also plastered with ads and special ticket offers. When the ballet finally began its run of fifty-two performances, local papers frontpaged the reviews. The ballet generates hype; the hype makes the ballet seem more hype-worthy.

Boston Ballet, like its siblings around the country, creates spin-off products and occasions to generate additional revenues: a *Nutcracker* gala ball, a storybook, an audiotape of the music with sound effects. The New York City Ballet features not only a boutique full of toys, games, books, advent calendars, tapes, and videos. You can also have your child's picture taken with a Snowflake—during the intermission, a corps de ballet dancer in costume will pose for a $20 Polaroid photo, and you get her autograph thrown in.

Boston Ballet's hyperbole circus reached its height when the local headlines started calling it "the most popular in the world," evidently upgrading Bruce Marks's ambiguous program note: "*The Nutcracker,* the mainstay of Boston Ballet, is the most attended ballet performance in the world." José Mateo's Ballet Theatre of Boston retaliated by advertising its modest but dreary version as the one you went to for the dancing. In any case, a month after the season ended, Boston Ballet officials admitted that revenues had been lower than anticipated this year.

To stage *The Nutcracker* now, a company either risks a yawn-inducing traditional version, or breaks the bank on new spectacle and effects. One more possibility, no less hazardous than the others, is deconstruction; that is, pulling apart the texts (story, dancing, music) and putting them back together in an entirely different framework. Deconstructions are tricky. Expensive but not necessarily durable, they take tremendous imagination, a real idea. Mark Morris's pop art *The Hard Nut* (1991), set in the sexually liberated 1970s, had a few years of successful touring, but seems to be out of circulation now. This season, *The Harlem Nutcracker* arrived at Brooklyn Academy after a brief national tour. It deserves a longer life.

Choreographer-director Donald Byrd not only transplanted the scenario to a contemporary setting in an African-American family, he reconceived the plot quite drastically. The original *Nutcracker* is a rite of passage. In Clara's dream, she begins the process of growing up, and confronts the sexual demands of adulthood through the possible roles she assigns to the Prince and Drosselmeyer. Donald Byrd sees the whole story through the eyes of a grandmother, and her journey as a look back on her loving relationship with her husband. At the end, she is ready to join him in death. The one mysterious character is Death himself, enticing Clara to let go of her comfortable home and pass gracefully into another existence.

With this as a premise, the elements fall into place. At a Christmas party attended by her large family, Clara withdraws into reverie. Her dead husband appears with a toy nutcracker he gave her long ago, and she dances with him in her dream. Clara's children and neighbors, an assortment of amusing character types, dance and visit the punch bowl; a band of carolers troop in and sing a gospel chorus; the grandchildren dance an exuberant frug–macarena–hip hop number with arm movements borrowed from the traditional toy soldiers.

One of the most ingratiating things about this production is the score, an expansion by arranger/composer David Berger of the 1962 Duke Ellington–Billy Strayhorn *Nutcracker Suite,* which inspired Donald Byrd to revamp the ballet. Berger preserves the well-known Ellington sound, but the Tchaikovsky themes are all inside it and all in the right places. The big-band beat drives the whole performance, and dictates the dance styles.

The production is generous, with wonderful costumes, visions, transformations. Byrd wasn't so successful with the obligatory but often intractable mice—here they're gray lumpy devils, accomplices of Death. What he did do splendidly was Clara and the Nutcracker's arrival at Club Sweets, in a taxi. Dressed in evening clothes, they're ushered to the fabulously lighted doorway by fawning attendants. This was as magical a stage effect as any second-act opener I've seen. The divertissements were done in tab show style—trashy, flashy, and fun. Throughout the ballet, Byrd put the women in high-heel shoes. Perhaps an uptown version of the pointe shoe, the three-inch spike must be at least as demanding to dance in as classical ballet footwear.

The shoes, and the other finery in which the production is dressed, create a kind of glamour we readily recognize. So does the dancing, and the other ways people behave. Although Byrd's choreography lacks the inventive nuance of the Balanchine model, the vernacular chorus lines and raunchy comic turns in the second act make perfect sense in the smart ambience of Clara's flashback to the Harlem Renaissance.

Despite the down-and-dirty club acts and the misbehaving party guests, the underlying tone of this *Nutcracker* is one of warmth and affection. I think that's what the *Nutcracker* stands for, why the ballet survives, but we often can sense it only in token gestures, almost absent-mindedly inserted between virtuosic effects. Byrd's production style is consistently approachable without being mundane. The characters and the dancing are real, but they're not so simple they could be any one of us in the audience. Flamboyant and sexy in ways ballet is too stylized to convey, *The Harlem Nutcracker* is a contemporary romance, like an Astaire and Rogers movie. When Clara and the Nutcracker (Eleanor McCoy and Gus Solomons Jr.) drift into a slow foxtrot in the first act, the attraction between them is palpable. And what a lovely thing it is to see two older dancers, portraying even older characters, dancing with such regard. More often the *Nutcracker* grandparents are stiff and dotty caricatures.

Donald Byrd says he wants his *Nutcracker* to invoke basic ideas of love and respect, to counter the negative picture we often get of African-American family life, and without being preachy he achieves that. In fact, I think his ballet falters only when he counterpoints the darker aspects. Death, perhaps his stand-in for Drosselmeyer, symbolizes Clara's fear of the unknown. In the scariest hallucination, near the end, he makes her look at a tableau of violent happenings, perhaps out of her past. Crime and danger do stalk the Harlem streets, but their actual depiction seems unnecessary. Drosselmeyer/Death and the mice stand for all the terrors from which Clara's strong family network will insulate and protect her.

Long after any viewing of *The Nutcracker,* we retain these images, of celebration, of dreaming, and of successful journeying. How Clara imagines herself in the fairy-tale world, what kind of power Drosselmeyer wields over her, whether she grows up at the end or reverts to childhood—or dies—these fasten themselves in the audience's memory the way movie patterns do. The role models may be deeply conservative or parodistic, or intentionally idealized. The dancing may be classical or exotic or contemporary, highly polished or humbly aspiring. But through its long history of renovation, deconstruction, downsizing and upscaling, its amplifications and simplifications and shifts to new locales, *The Nutcracker* always seems to revolve around an idea of a stable, sustaining home. Our own lives may be different, but we make the annual pilgrimage to reassure ourselves, to satisfy this primal longing, if only in the theater.

EVERYBODY'S TREAT

Boston Phoenix, 5 December 2003

The first Christmas catalogue came in the mail just after Labor Day, and Jennifer Fisher's book, *Nutcracker Nation*, arrived soon after that.[2] Fisher sets out to examine the perennial ballet favorite as a money-making cultural product with significant redeeming value. In spite of its own opportunistic timing, her study might even provide a momentary antidote to the cash-register mentality that infects the holidays.

The Nutcracker, as Fisher demonstrates in this thoughtful survey, is no monolithic artifact. Since its first production, choreographed by Marius Petipa in 1892 for the Maryinsky (now the Kirov), it has become a theme to be riffed upon as much as a masterpiece to be preserved. Fisher thinks when it "immigrated" to this side of the Atlantic in the twentieth century, it began a versatile career as a conduit for psychological, artistic, ethnic, and community aspirations as diverse as North America itself.

For Fisher and devotees of the traditional *Nutcracker*, just the thought of it triggers comforting memories of family holidays, childhood pastimes, scary monsters easily defeated, beautiful ballerina role models, and magical escapes into the world of theater. As long as a production adheres to this "template," Fisher thinks, it can evoke powerful and personal responses.

Fisher points out early in the book that the *Nutcracker* was never a "virtuosic showpiece for its leads." Only half of its two-act scenario is devoted to classical dancing. The first act depicts the world of children: the party, the loving or strange grown-up Others, the dreaming, the irrational fears. The second act divertissement is pure fairy tale, a reward with no ambiguities. It's the interplay of the real and the unreal, reinterpreted in the image of a local audience, that keeps the *Nutcracker* ballet alive.

Clara, the heroine, can be played by a real girl or an adult dancer. The Nutcracker, once liberated from his identity as a fancy kitchen utensil, can be a boy or a man. The relationship between them and the godfather/magician Drosselmeyer can be as simple as a visit from Santa Claus or as complicated as pre-adolescent sexual angst. Both the protagonists and the fairy-tale characters can be choreographed up or down according to the local talent; they can be surrounded by accomplices, extra effects, and comic turns.

Different editions of the ballet can engage in ethnic stereotyping or promote ethnic pride. There's a *Nutcracker* with dancing wheelchairs, and one for endangered plants and animals, and a dance-along for any enthusiast with access to a tutu and tiara. Of course the theme can be modernized, glamorized, and imported into popular media like film, TV, or ice skating.

Fisher gives a fascinating account of two contrasting productions: the massive community effort staged annually by the Loudoun Ballet of Leesburg, Virginia; and the professional version done in Toronto by the National Ballet of Canada. Or versions in the latter case, since the Celia Franca standard was thrown out during the period of Fisher's research (1995–1997) and replaced with James Kudelka's remake when he became director of the company. The backstage operations Fisher traces in Toronto and Leesburg reveal a whole insider culture that probably forms the nucleus of every *Nutcracker* audience.

Disturbing contemporary questions underlie *The Nutcracker*'s spirited history. How far can the ballet stretch in alternative directions without disappearing? And, perhaps more ominous, can a classical ballet compete with the megafinancing and blanket visibility of commercial spectacle? The impending invasion of the Rockettes' Holiday Show at the Wang Theater is neither new nor limited to Boston. As Fisher notes, the "lavish sets and special effects" of Kudelka's *Nutcracker* in Toronto were perceived as a bid to compete with "lavish musicals that were taking away business."

Nutcracker Nation invites us to think about the reasons for this ballet's enduring appeal despite its often perilous prospects. *The Nutcracker* may make money for its sponsoring organizations, but the budgets increase and, in places, the attendance is declining. I wonder who constitutes the "community" of *The Nutcracker* for companies like Boston Ballet. If Boston's production can't make money in the 3,600-seat Wang, can it pull back and still be economically viable? It's no accident, and no disgrace, that both professional and community *Nutcracker*s have tapped into new audiences with small-scale touring and large-scale local participation.

Fisher describes wonderful moments of communitas that sometimes occur when a performance speaks to the experience, the longings, and the collective energy of an audience, moments that make *The Nutcracker* something more than entertainment. Fisher herself acquired ownership through her early ballet classes and a euphoric teenage career as a Snowflake with the Louisville Ballet. Others may make the connection as production volunteers, as performers, or as witness to a single moment of beauty in one performance.

Nutcracker Nation began as a doctoral dissertation at the University of California at Irvine, and it retains a few scars from that process. But the academic conceits are mostly unobtrusive, and Jennifer Fisher, who is a dance critic as well as a teacher, writes in a lively, readable prose.

Christian Science Monitor, 8 June 1989

The Royal Ballet's new production of Marius Petipa's *La Bayadère*, staged by Natalia Makarova, is a big attraction this spring at Covent Garden. For two performances the excitement rose even higher, with the appearance of Altynai Asylmuratova and Sylvie Guillem as the rival ballerinas. Asylmuratova is perhaps the finest young star of the Kirov Ballet in Leningrad, while Guillem has joined the Royal as a principal guest artist from the Paris Opera Ballet. They were partnered by Kirov principal dancer Faroukh Ruzimatov.

Makarova has made a few choreographic additions and changes and some clarifications of action that brought the plot into focus. *Bayadère* is one of the more interesting of the nineteenth-century vehicles for Imperial Russian classicism, with its psychological twists and theatrical variety. Set in a mythical kingdom somewhere in deepest Asia, the plot concerns Nikiya, a temple dancer, ostensibly consecrated to her religious vocation and, by class, only a little higher than a slave.

After spurning the advances of the High Brahman, she reveals her love for the warrior Solor. Although he swears his devotion to Nikiya, in the very next scene Solor agrees to marry the beautiful Gamzatti, daughter of the Rajah. Everybody thus is mad at everybody else, except Solor, who's confused, and by the time the first act is over, Nikiya has been fatally bitten by Gamzatti's gift of a poisonous snake.

So the plot gives plenty of opportunity for dramatic contrasts—between sacred and profane love, between innocence and wealth and power—and for dancing that illustrates all sides. In the famous second act, a repentant Solor escapes in an opium dream to the Kingdom of the Shades. In this divinely ordered realm, he and Nikiya dance an idyllic pas de deux, attended by twenty-four corps de ballet maidens and their leaders, young Royal Ballet soloists Karen Paisey, Darcey Bussell, and Viviana Durante. Upon awakening, however, Solor submits again to the worldly attractions of Gamzatti. As they take their marriage vows, the ghost of Nikiya appears, to preside over the destruction of the temple. For poetic if not dramaturgical reasons, Solor is rewarded and goes off to the Kingdom of the Shades with Nikiya in an apotheosis.

Examining the theatrical logic of these old plots isn't fair, but Asylmuratova brought such unusual depth to the character of Nikiya that I began to see her almost in realistic terms, and to wonder about the other characters too. Her initial dances suggested that eroticism wasn't so far from godli-

La Bayadère. Apotheosis. Irina Dvorovenko and Maxim Beloserkovsky, American Ballet Theater. Photo © Gene Schiavone, courtesy of American Ballet Theater.

ness; perhaps it wasn't only her chaste status that made her turn down the High Brahman. Her sensuous attraction to the handsome, amoral Solor contained a spirituality to which he proved unequal, as played by the passionate, intense Ruzimatov. The High Brahman was the super dancer Anthony Dowell, director of the Royal Ballet. His jealous fury and later his monumental grief at Nikiya's death made this character believable to me for the first time.

Of course, at the heart of *La Bayadère* is the contrast between the two ballerinas, and in style Guillem and Asylmuratova are totally different. Asylmuratova is classically magnificent and dramatically gifted. Guillem is a modernist—not strong in classical technique but endowed with long, flexible limbs. Her acting seems to be all on the inside, with only an attitude of icy grandeur showing, except when she offers one of her split extensions to the audience. Then she looks quite pleased. The audience ecstatically approved Guillem's tricks. Her coming to the Royal has been a coup of sorts, giving a boost to the company, which has been badly in need of some glamour.

Bayadère's designer, Pier Luigi Samaritani, was also responsible for American Ballet Theater's production of the work in 1980, but there's very little resemblance. The Royal's production looks Victorian, with Yolanda Sonnabend's lush, cumbersome costumes and Samaritani's decors dissolving in a brownish, Pre-Raphaelite gloom.

CLASSIC IN RETROGRADE

Boston Phoenix, 19 July 2002

We're into the second century since the great Russian classicist Marius Petipa choreographed *La Bayadère* for the Maryinsky Theater of St. Petersburg (now the Kirov) in 1877. *Bayadère* survived as an evolving stage work, woven from remnants, updates, and successive interpolations, but the ballet as originally done is effectively lost, with only its reputation intact. Last year the Kirov decided to go back to Petipa's final revision, for which considerable documentation exists, and it's this 1900 relic that opened the Lincoln Center Festival and the Kirov's two-week engagement early last week.

La Bayadère was very successful at its premiere, cementing Petipa's reputation as a creator of stage spectacle and dance novelty. It went out of the repertory when the ballerina for whom it was choreographed, Yekaterina Vazem, retired. Petipa brought the work back in 1900, with changes, and the dances in this version were recorded at the time in Stepanov notation by regisseur Nikolai Sergeyev. The score is presently housed in the Harvard Theater Collection; it was one of the major sources consulted when the Kirov undertook a full-length restoration. Despite the extensive research and authentication, with a team headed by Sergei Vikharev, the ballet is still a mix of old and new ideas.

This *Bayadère* occupies an odd position in history. Having the dances in notated form adds to their credibility, but we don't know the relationship of the 1900 choreographic score to the 1877 *Bayadère*. Petipa was eighty-two in 1900. He had been in charge of the Maryinsky for thirty years; his ballets were grand—and formulaic. The era of art modernism was germinating, not to mention the Russian revolution. Michel Fokine, the great reformer and first choreographer of the Diaghilev Ballets Russes, was standing in the wings. It seems reasonable that a twenty-three-year hiatus would have inspired Petipa to fresh thoughts about the revival, even if he couldn't have anticipated the vastly different ballets and ballet dancers that would emerge in the next twenty-three years.

When Natalia Makarova staged a gorgeous, streamlined *Bayadère* for American Ballet Theater in 1980, the first full-length production outside the Soviet Union, it provoked dance history's eternal questions. How much can we expect from a revival of a nineteenth-century ballet? Should it satisfy us in modern terms? Can it satisfy us in its original terms, even if we think we know what those terms were? I longed to see the mime and divertissements that Makarova had omitted. Well, the Kirov's new production supplies these, along with fussy, semi-period costumes, and reams of Ludwig Minkus music that we've mercifully never heard. Now I think Makarova's *Bayadère* made sense. It wasn't an abstraction, like the all-dance ballets of George Balanchine, but it brought a new appreciation for the old genre by acknowledging modern taste.

The plot of *La Bayadère*, set in a fictional ancient India, has love, jealousy, secrets, murder, disloyalty, and despair; exotic dancing girls; the dazzling rituals of two coexisting potentates, one secular and one monastic; a drug-induced vision of heaven and a cataclysmic earthquake. None of the characters is thoroughly good or evil but the spiritual life, symbolized by classical dancing, triumphs over worldliness.

Ballet was one of the few opportunities the public had to see mass effects before the development of movies. Given the limitations of indoor photography in the late-nineteenth century, most of our impressions of the Russian ballet spectacles come from highly exaggerated engravings that were widely published. In the fine-drawn graphic style of these images, the stage looks detailed and expansive. There are immense, vaulted banquet halls, forests and fountains, crowds of curious villagers, battalions of Amazons and hussars, live animals, and innumerable busy servants. On stage these productions may not have been quite so extravagant, but the operatic scale and density was what struck the audience.

Ballet shared the Maryinsky Theater with opera in those days. The performances were long and the audience could wait for the spectacle to unfold. Possibly they came late to miss an act or so. Extensive miming was needed to tell the story and reveal the characters. When Fokine came along he threw out bombast, pared down miming to a few essential gestures, and integrated dancing with story line in smooth-flowing, stylistically coherent one-act formats. *Bayadère* circa 1900 shows why Fokine's reforms were so badly needed.

Although the Kirov production labored on for three and a half hours, it somehow didn't seem grand enough. Processions introduced several scenes, but they looked skimpy and rushed, as if the company hadn't adjusted its timing to the huge stage of the Metropolitan Opera House on opening night. The group dances in diverse styles seemed like diligent exercises, each with an exotic twist or device—a garland dance, a dance for girls with parrots on sticks, a dance for a girl balancing a water jug on her head. As they streamed out one after another, they looked more and more academic to me.

The first two acts have almost no dancing at all, and we plod through long mime passages of "You! Renounce him!" "I won't give him up!" "He's mine!" "But he swore to me." "[two vigorous hand claps] Servant! Take this woman away!" The dancers on opening night whaled into this claptrap, led by Svetlana Zakharova, as Nikiya the temple dancer, a thin, snaky modern ballerina with arms and legs like vines and a torso that seemed pushed forward and sprung backward at the same time. Igor Kolb, her lover, looked a bit bumbly and you could see why he would fall for a glamorous Rajah's daughter at the first opportunity, though he turned out to be a surprisingly good dancer when given the chance. The Gamzatti, Elvira Tarasova, looked a little bit like Barbara Stanwyck, a bad girl who invites your sympathy, if only because she was compelled to wear low-heeled shoes until the fourth and last act, when she also proved to be a fine dancer.

By the time act 3 rolled around, the audience applauded deliriously for the Kingdom of the Shades, whether because they recognized the scene that has come down the most consistently through time as a paradigm of pure classicism, or because they were so happy to get their teeth into some dancing at last. In fact, the Shades worked wonderfully well although the impressive thirty-two-member corps de ballet was only two-thirds the size of the 1900 ensemble. There were moments, with the lines of white tutus floating forward in unison, when you seemed to be flying in a clear space above a cloudscape.

RAYMONDA REDUX

Boston Phoenix, 15 October 2004

Marius Petipa, the great Russian ballet master, had been choreographing for fifty years by the time he created *Raymonda*. Fifty years of stories and spectacles including *The Nutcracker, Swan Lake, Sleeping Beauty, La Bayadère,* and dozens of others that didn't outlive the nineteenth century. It can't have been easy to find new twists on the standard ballet plot: girl and boy fall in love, fate separates them, but they're reunited after two or three acts devoted to entertainments, dueling, treachery, magic, and maybe a thunderstorm. You can see why Petipa settled for the feeble plot that became *Raymonda*.

Last week *Raymonda* kicked off the Bolshoi Ballet's six-week American tour at the Wang Theater. The legendary Moscow company hasn't visited Boston in fifteen years, but we didn't get to see their most modern creation, a scandalous update on *Romeo and Juliet* that goes to Minneapolis, Seattle, and Berkeley.

Raymonda owes its longevity to its wonderful, danceable score by Alexander Glazunov and its generous dance opportunities for the ballerina, her two rival swains, and the ensemble. Yuri Grigorovich's *Raymonda*, choreographed in 1984, is a curiosity that tilts backwards, leaning on both the prerevolutionary Imperial ballet model and the Soviet revisionism of the 1950s and 1960s, a style mainly invented by Grigorovich. With its eviscerated classicism and proletarian virtuosity, it gives us dancing, dancing, dancing, but not much theatrical juice.

By the time Grigorovich got to *Raymonda*, he had already rewritten several other classics and he was making a new repertory about slave uprisings and deservedly punished capitalists—*Spartacus*, *Ivan the Terrible*, *The Stone Flower*, *Golden Age*. The original *Raymonda* actually hints at a class dialectic, but Grigorovich doesn't explore it beyond routine social typecasting. Raymonda, a member of the medieval French nobility, is in love with a Hungarian knight, Jean de Brienne. While he's away at the Crusades, a Saracen general visits the palace and tries to seduce the unwilling Raymonda. De Brienne returns just in time to slay the barbarian and marry the ballerina.

According to ballet convention, racial and national differences can facilitate variety in the dance material. Noblemen dance in the purest classical style; villains, outsiders, slaves, and sensualists have movement that's dramatic, exotic, or pantomimic. The Saracen, as an Oriental, is not only an exotic but an infidel and a potential invader—a triple threat. So how does he get invited to the palace in the first place? Raymonda recognizes him as a bad guy right away because of his overwrought acting and acrobatic jumping.

The foreigner is accompanied by an obsequious retinue of prancing primitives and passionate Spaniards, who get to entertain the gentry and aren't troubled by their lowly rank in the dance hierarchy. For the famous Grand Pas Hongrois in the third act, Jean de Brienne and the King of Hungary bring along packs of mazurka and czardas folk to dance at the

wedding alongside the nobility. But despite these differing dance charac-
teristics, one number begins to look like the others.

All cleaned out and rearranged as a dance show, Grigorovich's *Raymonda* grows monotonous. It's partly the fault of the production, and
partly a company style that seems to value neutrality. The big presentation
scenes that dominate all three acts lack the bustle of realistic onlookers
in the background. The tempos are universally spirited. An ill-conceived
lighting design focuses follow-spots on the leading dancers and consigns
the hardworking corps to a gloomy background. They fade into anonymous filler even when they're making interesting patterns, and the principals aren't much more individual.

The opening night Raymonda, Nadezhda Gracheva, was bold and correct, but expressively inert. At the second performance, the audience responded readily when Maria Allash rushed on with a smiling impetuosity.
She danced well, but she wore the same smile most of the evening, so it lost
its effect. The two knights, Sergey Filin and Alexander Volchkov, were well
behaved, but neither one of them looked smitten.

It's mind-boggling to consider that the other great reformer of the twentieth century, George Balanchine, shared with Yuri Grigorovich the desire
to cleanse ballet of excess but preserve its essential dance values. After
staging a complete *Raymonda* in 1946 (with Alexandra Danilova), Balanchine revisited the Glazunov several times, leaving the plot behind altogether. His *Pas de Dix*, *Raymonda Variations*, and *Cortège Hongrois* are studies in brilliant technique, texture, scale, variety, and dynamics for every
dancer. There's no deeper way to experience ballet tradition than this.

⟢ BEAUTIFICATION

Boston Phoenix, 9 July 1999

More than just another showpiece in the grandest classical style,
The Sleeping Beauty is a symbolic ballet. Its theme—the continuity of benevolent but absolute power despite trials and historical accidents—places it
in close proximity to many of the twentieth century's cultural and political
struggles.

The Sadlers Wells (now the Royal Ballet) staged *Beauty* in 1946 as a
symbol of England's recovery from World War II, as well as British ballet's
entry into the ranks of world culture and its rescue of then-eclipsed Russian art from the neglect of the Soviets. An opulent Oliver Messel version

constituted American Ballet Theater's shot at world-class balletdom in 1976. And the New York City Ballet mounted a complete though semi-updated *Beauty* as a sign of its determination to survive the death of George Balanchine, himself an inheritor and reformer of the Kirov/*Sleeping Beauty* tradition.

Now we have the Kirov (Maryinsky) emerging from recent economic and administrative turmoil to invest enormous resources in a reconstruction of the original 1890 production. With decor and costumes copied from the earliest designs and photographs, and Marius Petipa's choreography reconstituted from Stepanov notation scores housed in the Harvard Theater Collection, the new *Sleeping Beauty* aims to be purer, more authentic, and in every way more the paradigm of Russian classicism than all of its variously modernized descendants.

I got to see one of the four performances the Kirov brought on its tour to New York's Metropolitan Opera House last week, and it raised some provocative questions for me. The nineteenth-century classics are always pastiche productions today, having gone through big and small changes as they traipse from one company to another, adjusting to the capabilities of dancers, the creative urges of resident choreographers, the inevitable shortcuts and economizing, the stylistic tastes of this or that decade. My idea of what Petipa's ballets looked like is probably a composite of selections I've seen that "look right," rather than any fixed template of a choreographic scheme or style.

The Kirov's solo work seemed authentic, but the solos of any big ballet do become quite standardized across the repertory. They get taught personally by one dancer to another. Because they're performed by the stellar personages in any company, we remember them clearly; and we notice more acutely if steps are left out or changed. I've always thought Petipa was great at ensembles as well as sparkling, virtuosic solos, perhaps because of the remarkable inventions of his latter-day disciple Balanchine. But the Kirov's corps de ballet numbers seemed staid and, except for some clever contrapuntal groupings in the Prologue, obsessively locked into lineups facing the audience.

A big dramatic ballet like *Sleeping Beauty* is more than choreography though. The sparer, more concentrated tendencies of the recent past may have pointed away from spectacle, but ballet at the Maryinsky was also a popular entertainment, so it featured acting, extravagant stage effects, acrobatics, and pageantry as well as dancing. Here I thought the Kirov's efforts weren't always an improvement.

Having restored a lot of the mime that's been dropped over the years,

Sleeping Beauty. Apotheosis. Kirov Ballet. Photo by
Valentin Baranovsky, courtesy of *Boston Phoenix*.

they went for an extremely broad, formal but low-key acting style. The
dancers playing the King (Vladimir Ponomarev) and the wicked fairy Carabosse (Igor Petrov) looked as if they were a bit embarrassed to be playing
these rival superpowers, or afraid that if they let loose their characters'
passions, something really terrible would happen.

What I liked a lot about the production was the restoration of courtly
pomp and circumstance. Each of the three acts and the Prologue started
with all-out processions, not just formal arrivals. Russian Imperial ballet, and this ballet in particular, proudly showed off the attributes of the
monarchy. Set roughly in the seventeenth century of Louis XIV, *Sleeping
Beauty* celebrates the era of French culture so admired by the Russian tsars
who presided over the building of St. Petersburg and the great imperial
theaters.

But the court entertainments at Versailles also projected back, back,
to the Renaissance and to antiquity. The six well-wishing fairies at Aurora's christening bring symbolic gifts and are accompanied by exotic attendants, all in the style of the ballets de cour, those masquelike enter-

tainments that linked the aristocratic spectators to the marvels of Greek mythology. The final apotheosis, with backcloths unrolling and tunic-clad cherubs settling into place, revealed a wonderful tableau: Apollo/the Sun King/Tsar Alexander in his (painted) horse-drawn chariot, welcoming the Lilac Fairy, Aurora and Prince Desiré, and all their courtiers and subjects— and the audience—into his realm of light. Modern technology couldn't have done this half so marvelously.

TWO TALES RETOLD

Boston Phoenix, 15 June 2007

The big ballet companies are shackled tighter than ever to the idea of the story ballet. The *Swan Lakes* and *Cinderellas* are a fail-safe audience draw, but the problem is, they seem to need freshening up every so often. It's a paradox: you must preserve the successful formula while getting attention for something new. The rehab job can involve anything from touching up the costumes to tearing the poor old structure down to the bones and building a McBallet. Or, what's considerably harder, you can find another story to tell.

With *The Nightingale and the Rose*, which premiered Friday night at New York City Ballet, Christopher Wheeldon has come up with a rarity, a new fairy-tale ballet. Even rarer, he's made a piece of poetry for the stage. The ballet, based on one of the fairy tales of Oscar Wilde, has a commissioned score by Bright Sheng and a spare visual presentation (costumes by Martin Pakledinaz, animation by James Buckhouse, and lighting by Mark Stanley). In a single act, Wheeldon and his collaborators create a mood and a look— a dream-message about how little we understand the cost of beauty.

The Nightingale and the Rose isn't your usual happily-ever-after fantasy. It does have a hero in love and a wild creature who helps him. But the story turns bitter. The Nightingale promises to bring the student a red rose for the girl he loves. The only red rosebush in the garden is dried up and dormant, but it agrees to produce a flower if the Nightingale will sing all night with her breast pressed against its thorn. As she dies a blood-red rose blooms. The girl proves fickle and rejects the rose gained at such sacrifice. The student shrugs off his bruised ego and walks away, dropping the rose carelessly and stepping over the expiring bird who gave her life for it.

The wonderful thing about Wheeldon's ballet is that he's found a way to get this across without literalness or melodrama. His unsentimental eye sees the harshness of this bargain, and also the beauty. There's a simplicity, a starkness to the ballet that resembles some Asian theater forms. You may not know exactly what's happening at every moment, but you feel the injustice and the inevitability.

The ballet begins in silence and then the sounds of birds filling the dark theater. We find Wendy Whelan center stage, encircled by two large calligraphic brushstrokes projected on a front scrim. She doesn't do a conventional ballet-bird imitation, but moves the way birds actually do, with angular, stopped gestures aimed in all directions, hands fluttering behind her, upper body and head thrust out. All of a sudden she runs across the stage and lofts into the air, courtesy of some black-clad men who catch her and fly her off. They're like the near-invisible stage managers who help Kabuki actors make magic transformations. Just as Whelan leaves the ground, the orchestra plays its first note, and a large moon appears.

Whelan dances then, streaking around the stage with the same sort of jutting shapes, a solitary bird-woman singing to herself. The student (Tyler Angle) pursues the girl (Sara Mearns), who coyly rebuffs him and runs off. Then in a duet he tells the Nightingale of his longing and they seal their bargain with a flower gesture that looks like the lotus mudra in Indian dance, upturned hands pressed together, the fingers opening like petals.

Groups of four women, as white and yellow rosebushes, cluster together like closing blossoms. They're not the flower the Nightingale seeks. When she finds the shriveled red rose, the scrim flies out and a huge blinking eye veils the moon. The red rosebush, at first two men knotted together like a gnarled brown twig, accepts the Nightingale, and as she perches on their writhing shape, patches of red appear on their legs and arms. More and more men add to the growing plant. Eventually there are sixteen in all, with bigger and bigger red patches on their brown unitards.

Whelan languishes against them, not using her arms, as they support her and wrap themselves around her. They create a succession of blossoming shapes. Whelan grows weaker, pushing through the solid bark they're forming around her, until she's absorbed into their midst and a single flower rises where she disappeared.

Bright Sheng's music—he conducted the two performances I saw over the weekend—is atmospheric, lightly Chinese influenced, with strings, brasses, flutes, and a lot of percussion. Like the ballet it's full of gorgeous color and pitiless clarity, fastidiously modern.

⤳ I don't know what American Ballet Theater had in mind with its new production of *Sleeping Beauty*. The brainchild of ABT artistic director Kevin McKenzie, former star ballerina Gelsey Kirkland, and teacher/dramaturge

Michael Chernov, this *Beauty* incarnation leans toward tradition but at points veers sharply off toward some kind of not-quite-contemporary theatricality. One aspect kept interfering with the other, till I lost my sense of the ballet altogether.

First of all, the production is gaudily expensive, a visual hodgepodge that breaks up dance patterns and actions that might otherwise be clear. In the Prologue costume designer Willa Kim pits fairies in spangled gumdrop-colored tutus against an entourage of powdery pastels. The interweaving designs of the Garland Dance look jumbled because the peasants wear goldenrod costumes with turquoise sleeves, and you can't tell which arms belong to which bodies. In act 3, when the courtiers wake up in the eighteenth century, they wear extremely elaborate, sculpted white and gold period costumes that look awkward when they're sat down in. Tony Walton's scenery alternates between dreamy forests and gaudy throne rooms.

More distracting to me were the scenario and character elements injected into the story. Carabosse, as played for half of Saturday evening by Gelsey Kirkland, was a grande dame of the theater, raging and rampaging through Aurora's christening scene. Kirkland's acting, though out of scale, was truly majestic, physically invested every moment, and psychologically motivated. She didn't appear after the intermission due to an injury (Kristi Boone substituted for her), but Carabosse's demented fury, unabated after Aurora's century-long sleep, twisted into an inscrutable plot to ensnare Prince Desire in a giant spider web made out of what looked to me like the evil fairy's entrails.

The collaborators dredged up an extinct *Sleeping Beauty* plot involving a river of tears shed by Aurora's mother—where have I heard that before? *Swan Lake?*—with an ensuing scene for the Prince which interrupted the hunting scene. These new turns of the plot, and even the small ellipses like the omission of all the third-act divertissements except the famous Bluebird pas de deux, kept claiming my attention, thwarting my expectations. Neither the story nor the dances built in any sustained way. Lasting three hours with only one intermission, the ballet seemed to have no real momentum. It just went from well-preserved gem to eccentric appendage and back again all evening.

I was hoping to see Diana Vishneva in the one performance I was able to attend, but she cancelled, necessitating the substitution not only of Paloma Herrera as Aurora, but Angel Corella for Vishneva's partner David Hallberg, who had been substituting for the injured Vladimir Malakhov. And so forth. It was the end of *Sleeping Beauty*'s run in the Metropolitan Opera House season, and for all I know, the bad reviews had demoralized everybody.

Herrera was a perfectly behaved but bland Aurora. She cranked up her considerable technique for some spectacular things in the last act, probably spurred on by Corella, whose dynamism and real charm got the audience excited. Sarah Lane and Carlos Lopez (also substituting for the announced dancers) had warmed the audience up for them in the Bluebird pas de deux. Stella Abrera's Lilac Fairy was a cipher despite her role as presiding benefactress. The production retained much of *Sleeping Beauty*'s fine dancing, but the repetitious group choreography, the lack of individualism in the solo dancers, and the excruciatingly stately behavior of the royals bogged down whatever survived its scenic and narrative excesses.

3 Postlude & Prelude

GEORGE BALANCHINE, 1904–1983

Hudson Review, Autumn 1983

A few years ago, after the premiere of his spooky ballet about Robert Schumann, *Davidsbündlertänze*, George Balanchine said in an interview that for the finale, after the tormented artist-hero (Adam Luders) wandered away into the mists of madness or death, what he had really intended was for a flood to engulf the stage. To me this extraordinary statement revealed a great deal about Balanchine's relation to his own work. Despite his denials of autobiographical intentions, the *Davidsbündlertänze*, like all Balanchine ballets, is intensely personal. Besides, it's riddled with à clef references to the choreographer/composer, his moods and his muses. For Balanchine to say essentially "après moi le déluge" was an astonishing admission and perhaps a bleak prognosis for the future of the New York City Ballet.

George Balanchine's presence was so dominant in NYCB that the dancers, the scenic presentation, and the musical investiture all seem to operate with the same value system, even in ballets not choreographed by Balanchine. The company's look is not like any other: pared down to the essentials, even in its most flowery gestures toward traditional nineteenth-century ballet; opulent in its use of the classical idiom, even when it veers into modernism. Balanchine shared with nearly all contemporary dance artists a severe ambivalence about the past and an indifference to the future. He treasured his own roots in the Russian classical tradition and seemed at times even more devoted to the literature of nineteenth-century music and art. But he had no taste for turning the repertory into a stable of warhorses or for keeping his own past work in some kind of perpetual animation where it could be experienced and savored by the audience. What he cared about was the ballets he was making. I think it must have been this attitude, reinforced and institutionalized by those around him, and not pure ego, that made the New York City Ballet the uniquely contemporary and personal company that it was. As long as Balanchine's genius could supply the repertory with invention, who needed museum pieces? Only this spring Lincoln Kirstein, chief apostle of the Balanchine mystique, was quoted as saying the NYCB's mission was to "annihilate history . . .

to canonize the New." But actually, Balanchine's purpose was neither to create something entirely new nor to perpetuate something entirely traditional. It was simply to make ballets. In the process, his originality permeated everything. The same could be said of most great artists, including Balanchine's musical mentors, Stravinsky, Tchaikovsky, and Mozart.

Still, no great ballet company can survive on the day-to-day production of a single artist. Repertory—the dance equivalent of a library or a museum —serves the present as much as the past. It not only shelters the works of former times, it furnishes the dancers with things to do, helps them learn range and expression, offers the audience a variety of attractions. The New York City Ballet is a true repertory company in spite of the fact that it doesn't do standard ballet classics. Thanks to Lincoln Kirstein's perseverance, Balanchine was provided with the means every choreographer needs, and few Americans are granted, to reach his fullest development. What the NYCB is today—what it has been for the past thirty-five years—is as accurate a record as there will ever be of George Balanchine's art. It is not, however, a static record. It evinces the same reservations about the past that Balanchine himself did, and, being committed neither to totally fixed images nor to totally ephemeral ones, it gives out an aura of precariousness that's not entirely unpleasant.

To provide a working environment for a resident artist, a ballet company manipulates an intricate and unstable mix of conditions. It must keep a big enough repertory of old ballets to attract a big enough audience to sustain enough performances to keep enough dancers on the payroll for enough of the year, so that that process of making new ballets isn't subordinated to improvised allotments of time, space, and bodies. Even when he had to put up with less than optimum resources, Balanchine was able to create. He made some of his masterpieces as a freelance choreographer working with unfamiliar dancers (*Symphony in C*, for the Paris Opera Ballet in 1947), others as classroom exercises for his School of American ballet student recitals (the legendary *Serenade* in 1934), or as once-only items for special ballet evenings at the Metropolitan Opera, where he found a temporary refuge for his dancers in the '30s (the first *Jeu de Cartes* and *Baiser de la Fée* in 1937). Once the City Ballet was established in 1948, he managed to turn the cumbersome machinery of permanence to his own account.

He avoided the worst pitfalls of repertory—the staleness and mechanical delivery that comes with repeating works many times—by keeping at his old works as if they were new. Not only did he rehearse the ballets himself, galvanizing the dancers and inspiring them with his ideas, but he worked at the choreography. Scarcely a season went by that he wouldn't change things a little—adding and subtracting passages, respacing, revising steps. When ballets had been inactive he'd forget them and have to rethink the music. For the audience, which became increasingly familiar with NYCB over the years, surprises were always a prospect. Instead of having to witness the erosion that usually befalls old ballets after a few seasons, we found invention everywhere.

The loss of these small renovations is going to be the first sign of Balanchine's leaving us. His hospitalization for most of the 1982–1983 season meant there were no new ballets, but I always imagined him sending bulletins off to the theater about changes he'd thought up for this or that standard work. Perhaps, I thought, he even asked one or two dancers to come see him and gave them new things. And I realized, the first performance I saw after his death, that the extra attentiveness with which I'd always watched Balanchine ballets would no longer be rewarded. By keeping dancers and audience from growing too sure of the ballets, Balanchine created a climate of immediacy and alertness that was very modern in character. Merce Cunningham had to overthrow all the rules of academic ballet and devise a completely new set of hierarchies to achieve the same thing.

Along with changes in the choreography came changes in the dancing style and the dancers themselves. Films of New York City Ballet dancers in the '50s or even the '60s show us a very different set of bodies, skills, dynamics from the ones we know now. The positive side of ballet's ephemerality is its affirmation of life and change. New York City Ballet, through its school and its performing ranks, simultaneously hands down an old tradition and fosters the learning of new standards. What an Edward Villella could do fifteen years ago, boys in the corps can do today. Students in the school are already learning Merrill Ashley's feats. Never satisfied with what the dancers could do, Balanchine invented ways to make them surpass themselves. There are different versions of Balanchine ballets around, and different ways of dancing them. These are interesting, and we may even be fond of them, but the best way to see Balanchine is the way he's danced at the New York City Ballet.

The size and longevity of the company have also made possible a tremendous individuality. In the journalistic backlash that has followed quickly on the journalistic canonization of Balanchine, we hear a lot of sour comments about the supposed tyranny of his taste in physical types. Some people—who evidently never look at performances—would have us believe that the New York City Ballet dancer is an anorectic, inbred freak with disproportionate measurements and a head full of fluff. No doubt there are dancers like that, but there are far more who are not. Sometimes I look at the NYCB corps and think I've never seen so many stunning women at one time. Even more than the ill-perceived heterogeneity among physical types, what makes the dancers so singular is the individual way they dance. This too is sometimes counted against the company. They are accused of looking rhythmically and spatially imprecise in the mass formations of their rare academic-reproduction ballets. But the dance spectator's standards are totally conditioned by the performances he or she has witnessed. Perhaps we judge any *Swan Lake* ensemble on the basis of productions that have been petrified through over-reverent repetition. For all I know, the original Maryinsky corps was as eccentric as NYCB is now.

When I look at contemporary European or American companies that are supposed to be the most respectably classical—the Basel Ballet, for instance, or the Houston under Ben Stevenson—some essential quality of dancing seems left out. I note the neat formations, the clean line, the good taste, but I'm not excited; I'm not even caught up in the stage event. As soon as I get to the NYCB again, I see what I missed. All NYCB dancers dance like soloists. Not only do they have above average technical ability, they command the space around them. They don't make some mimetic pretense of authority but possess it through their dancing. They don't merely show you a shape, a direction, a step; they energize a gesture all the way out to the fingertips, articulate their movement through the whole of its trajectory. They can phrase the music like vocalists, show you minute inner rhythms, take expressive liberties. You can see faces in the back row of the NYCB corps, not purposely neutral masks. You can see that what the dancers are doing affects them—gives them a high, gives them a pain.

One of the reasons they behave this way is that Balanchine's choreography is an extraordinarily soloistic, intimate form, even when it swells into huge productions like *Union Jack* and *Vienna Waltzes*. His choreographic structures, big or small, symmetrical or free-form, all seem to begin with the irreducible unit of one principal dancer or couple. What happens in the ballet is an extension or a reflection of the principal dancers' actions. In a Balanchine ballet you seldom see the corps in decorous, metronomic ranks filling up the stage with unremarkable motion. Instead you see small groups of three to six dancers working together doing difficult steps, intricate counterpoint, inventive floor patterns. In any other company, corps dancers exist to provide some choreographic cotton batting for the soloists' designs. In NYCB, despite the size of the company (over sixty-five dancers below principal and soloist rank), you learn many of the corps dancers' names because Balanchine demands that you see them.

Even when he employs his corps in hierarchical ways, Balanchine tailors their gestures and rhythms to the style, role, or mood of the solo subject. He seems to have thought of each ballet as an interactive event between the soloists, the ensemble, and the music. No other ballet choreographer can be "read" in such an integrated way. Though they seldom resort to stories or even to the boy-meets-girl-boy-loses-girl-fate-reconciles-them scenarios typical of ballet lore, Balanchine ballets are nevertheless dramatic events of the most gripping kind, because we either don't know what the resolution will be, or we don't know how a foregone conclusion will be arrived at. And the only way we can find out is through the dancing.

The most balletically conventional of his situations is the one where the ensemble acts as a frame to set off the soloists. In its most grandiose and pristine form this is *Symphony in C*. In each of four sections, a central duo is accompanied by two secondary couples and a small group of attendants who echo, amplify, and display their movements. Each section is a small ballet in itself, and the scale is dramatically enlarged in the finale, when all the dancers return and a total ensemble of twenty-eight women backs up the eight auxiliary couples and the four solo couples in a spectacle as forthright as a chorus line. The 1945 *Symphonie Concertante*, originally made for Balanchine's School of American Ballet students and reconstructed for American Ballet Theater this year from a Labanotation score, seems related to *Symphony in C* in its formality, its purely classical architecture, and its academic steps. But its basic unit is a two-woman duo that metamorphoses partway through into a trio, with the entrance of a lone male. The twenty-two-woman corps sets off these two central units by showing us the different floor and step patterns possible in multiples of two and three dancers. The corps almost always works in symmetrically divided blocks of eight, eight, and six dancers. The point seems to be that symmetry, or at least equality, can be maintained whether there are two dancers or three at the core of the pattern.

When he becomes even more inventive, the strict rankings and role-identifications break down; more and more importance is given to the secondary dancers, fewer and fewer of the expectations he sets us up for get fulfilled. Balanchine ballets all have the hidden agendas of the classics; what occurs in them always has reference to classical suppositions—the primacy of the ballerina star, for instance, or the set form of the pas de deux—although the suppositions are often questioned or denied. I think of the tiara-and-tutu ballets in which he invents an extra woman, who has no designs on the man but who refocuses the ballet when the central pair is absent. (In *Tchaikovsky Concerto No. 2*, I see her as a modern descendant of the Lilac Fairy.) Or the two-woman ballets where a man is introduced long after we've forgotten he's missing (*Concerto Barocco*). Or the partner ballets where no one is the exclusive partner of anyone else (*Divertimento No. 15*), or the ones where no one gets a partner until very late in the game (*Who Cares part I, Stravinsky Violin Concerto*). Or the story ballets without a story (*Bugaku, Donizetti Variations, La Sonnambula*). Or the modern ballets where it looks like all bets are off, until you realize you're seeing the whole classical game through a trick lens (*Agon*) or possibly in reverse (*Four Temperaments*). This list goes on and on. Because he stuck to classicism, Balanchine gave his audience and himself a field for exploration.

In *Serenade* he tore himself drastically from the classical anchorage. He had, after all, just abandoned Europe and cast his lot with Kirstein in the great American experiment. *Serenade* preserves almost none of the conventional roles, spacings, proportions. And yet, it never loses its formality or throws away the classical vocabulary. With it Balanchine made a virtue and maybe even a practice of expediency. He had only students at his disposal when he made it, not a professional company, and it's said he devised it out of what his forces could do and who showed up each day to rehearse. Whatever the cause, the ballet's form and its order keep shifting. The ensemble of seventeen women splinters into subgroups of many different sizes—some of them flit amorphously across the stage before you can do more than sense their passage; others gather in staid ranks and didactically perform unpredictable gesture sequences; still others do slightly deranged fragments of nineteenth-century ballets, as if the phrases had been taught to them by someone with a fond but faulty memory. Certain women emerge momentarily into prominence, but only quite late in the ballet is there any extended, properly displayed dancing by principals. What looks at the beginning as if it's going to be a classroom demonstration transforms itself subtly into something like another couple ballet, but before we settle into this mode, it all turns into a tragic allegory of, perhaps, the struggle between youthful beauty and death.

Serenade might be the model Balanchine ballet if we had to make such a choice. It's like an impressionist painting, with its glimpses of mood, tone, period that dissolve into each other before any fixed image can be captured. Balanchine puts glints and streaks of suggestive movement into a floating background, evoking a whole array of illusions that might have remained below the surface. In great measure his success depends on the way he used Tchaikovsky's *Serenade for Strings* as an unstoppable tide on which the action is carried along. The dance neither gathers in little pointed rhythmic clumps, nor lingers for effect, nor forces the momentum into emphatic strokes—things that nineteenth-century ballet assumes you can do to music. And although he didn't often use such sweeping, romantic music, the sense of movement as an urgent, overriding propellant is characteristic of all his ballets.

Though it's easier to notice the crooked wrists or the sometimes aberrational placement or the deliberately exaggerated line of a Balanchine dancer, these are less important aspects of his style than his concept of dance time. Balanchine choreographed what is called in music a "through-line." That is, his notion of dancing was that the movement keeps on going just as the melody does in a score. He didn't choreograph isolated steps, or neat 4/4 mouthfuls, or even strenuous blasts of virtuosic show followed by self-satisfied poses. Important steps like jumps or pirouettes are, in Balanchine, treated like transitional steps; the dancer lands only to take off again without adjusting, centering, or resting in between. This was one of the things Mikhail Baryshnikov had the most trouble with in the year he danced with NYCB; he was used to conventional stop-and-go dancing. In thinking of movement as a progression rather than as a series of exclamations, Balanchine also considered as dancing certain elements of the vocabulary usually thrown away as mere linkages, like the five foot positions or the functional walking step. And in thus bringing movement into a closer analogy with music, he made possible for himself a variety of musical game plans far more sophisticated than anyone else has devised. Dancers are heard to speak a lot of starstruck mystical stuff about why they adored working for Balanchine, but I should think the tremendous possibilities he made for them to exercise their art would have been reason enough.

No one who loves Balanchine wants to think about what will become of the many things he means to us now that he's gone. We can't hope for the miracle of a choreographer to fill his shoes. The company and school, I suppose, will survive as institutions are meant to do, changing season by season to accommodate the lesser leaders who will have to replace him. I have less confidence than some people in the future of the repertory. It will be preserved, of course, and some pains have been taken in recent years to document it in film, videotape, and notation. But probably it will slip in tiny ways—detail will fuzz out, new dancers will try to capture its drive and not know how, vitality will ebb away. Dancers will be afraid to take liberties as they do now, because the people in charge will be more concerned with keeping ballets the same than with giving them room to grow. But they'll still be deeper and more interesting than other ballets. I think we can count on that.

Ballet News, October 1983

I can't remember when I first met Edwin Denby, but by now he is thoroughly embedded in my dance writing—and my life. Whenever I talked to him he gave me something to think about, some new way to look at things. I used to resolve to memorize our conversations and write them down later, but I never did. His talk had an elusive quality that I never could write down. As words it didn't quite make sense. So much of the idea was left unsaid, you had to be mentally following the same track with him. Perhaps that's why he found writing so hard too. He was trying to put down on paper the way his mind worked.

Unlike the expansive, proliferating imagery of other poets, his effects came from condensation, compression, reduction to the most concrete yet the most inexplicable terms. The way he arrived at these mysterious specifics told as much about them as the ultimate nomenclature with which he secured them. In a poem he referred to the telephone's "armorplated speech," and I saw why he called me every few weeks and we talked long and safely there, free of the unnerving, distracting rituals of face-to-face meetings.

Some of his most indelible effects on me he made without being present at all. His reviews of course were masterly, but they didn't quite serve me as models. As a journalist I knew myself and my circumstances to be entirely different. But his article about criticism in the Chujoy/Manchester *Dance Encyclopedia* reassured me that there was indeed some reason for pursuing so quixotic a profession. Rereading the title piece in his second book, *Dancers, Buildings and People in the Streets*, I see the confirmation if not the source of nearly all my ideas about seeing dancing. He knew long before I did that dancing is like living, and that the better we can perceive the ordinary specialness in living, the better we'll see the out-of-the-ordinary specialness of dancing.

He was fond of the literary contradiction. His writing drew sensuality and strength from exploring the dualities in things. It was more than a word game. It was a way of searching out the tension that makes a dance or a person exciting to us, of detailing more finely how a thing works. His criticism reads very simply—yet he often skipped right over the obvious. He could get to the psychological or visceral core of the matter immediately, without waffling or pages of buildup.

People often talk about how clear and precise and descriptive his criticism is. Actually, what little pure description he employed is extremely selective and subjective. It wasn't *what* he saw but *how* he saw that gave his criticism authority. His insights went so deep, so far beyond ego projections or utilitarian accounts, that one was forced to stop and consider them.

He spoke of rhythm as no other dance critic has ever done. ("Markova's rhythm is not only due to her remarkable freedom in attacking her steps a hair's breadth before or after the beat. . . . In musical terms there is a rubato within the phrase, corresponding to the way the balance of the body is first strained, then is restored.") He allowed the full force of personality to assail him and he surrendered to it. (Merce Cunningham and John Cage, after their first concert in 1944, had for him "an effect of extreme elegance in isolation.") He discerned metaphor of the most intense resonance while the rest of us were laboring with logic and historical precedents. ("*Serenade* in its dreamlike speed and poignance uses the ensemble less to corroborate the principals than to weave their fragments of adolescent romance into the unwearied rush of immortal space.") And he could look straight at the ludicrous (the self-conscious primpiness of French dancers in 1953, for instance) while everyone else was pretending not to see.

Reading his collected reviews one is struck on every page with the provocation of incredibly risky ideas. But never with any oppressive partisanship or bitchiness.

To look at Edwin Denby you would think him the mildest and frailest of men—an aristocrat, with his white hair and his Harvard accent, his disinterested way of wearing out-of-style clothes. Yet this creature of rarefied sensibilities was also a lover of cats and the Maine woods, an insomniac prowler of nighttime streets, a destroyer of chronically imperfect manuscripts. Somewhere in him was a burly illiterate, a nameless citizen among the city's masses.

I learned this with amazement from his poems, and from his inspired acting of raunchy comic roles in Rudy Burckhardt's movies, and it made me think we had something more in common than a love of Balanchine and Cunningham. He made me aspire to flight in my writing, even though I'd thought myself earthbound and proletarian. If you were his friend, he gave you the priceless gift of his courteous appreciation. He made you feel that your work was of great importance to him, and he spent a good deal of his meager energies going to his friends' concerts and exhibits, reading their books, and trying to get other people interested.

Yet he felt that too many people were doing too many things for him. He couldn't see well, his feet hurt, his mind and his health were lapsing more often into peril—his recoveries were less and less complete. He could only have foreseen diminished pleasures, diminished control. I think now he must have been saying good-bye to us all spring, having decided to end his life before his dependency on others became unbearable to him. So he made his public appearances, gave interviews. Then in midsummer he quietly slipped away to Maine and took pills.

It would be selfish of us to wish he'd stayed on and given us more. His gift is already so large and so unheeded.

Once in a poem he lamented the loss of one of his many feline familiars:

Cat-heart that knew me gone, I cried
It stopped beating drugged in a cage
Dear, mine will too, and let go rage.

You wouldn't have imagined him an angry man. I remember his quick, brilliant ideas, tumbling out sometimes in confusion or with memory lapse pauses that I could usually fill in, to his relief, allowing him to continue. And I remember his laughter at the world's crazy antics. But there was underneath it a hermit's howling fury. I hope he's quiet now.

BALANCHINE AND BEYOND

Washington Post Book World, 18 July 1982

Dance criticism can be something of a performance itself, Arlene Croce says in her introduction to *Going to the Dance*, and this new collection of Croce's reviews from the *New Yorker* (1977–1981) is a virtuosic example of the critic's craft.[1]

Croce is the star of the intellectual dance elite that finds its inspiration in the New York City Ballet—writers, artists, and devotees who see George Balanchine and his company as the center of the universe. As leading raisonneur for the NYCB aesthetic, Croce has written some of the most careful, detailed, and enlightening analyses of its dancers and choreography ever published. She goes to performances often enough to know the dancers intimately, to steep herself in the repertory. When she writes about them, she seems to have arrived at the Elysian state that every critic longs for but most of us only snatch at, where the dance becomes a retrospective world you can inhabit with your own mind, probe at will, explore, extend, and experience with a pleasure that increases rather than fades with time.

Croce can transmute performances from memory into vital word images: Suzanne Farrell in *Chaconne* making a "sly sforzando attack . . . brightening each step like sunlight behind a cloud." The enduring quality of Patricia McBride's Columbine, "made of ovenproof porcelain." A whirling passage by Merrill Ashley in *Ballo della Regina* that "cuts like flying glass."

Her discussions of historical and musical matters in such classics as *Apollo* and *Don Quixote* testify to a scholar's thoroughness and a leisurely deadline. When she surveys the repertory she sees beyond any individual ballet. Of Balanchine's one-act *Swan Lake* she says: "I am caught up in it as in no other version of the ballet, because, although it isn't *the Swan Lake*, it's the essence of what attracts me in *Swan Lake*." And for audiences who want more than an essence, she recommends his equally plotless *Tschaikovsky Concerto No. 2*: "a secret-cabinet, stifled-melodrama ballet. Somewhere deep inside the ballerina-danseur relationship we sense the dagger, the tea rose, the chain-mail glove; all the fun, in short, that *Swan Lake* should be."

Croce's writing, like the world she describes, may be exemplary but it is not inclusive. Its boundaries can stretch back into history—to Bournonville, Petipa, and Fokine—and encompass the other classical companies as well as the perversities of modern ballet. But for Croce a significant range of other things aren't even on the map, like non-Western dance forms and contemporary experimentation. Taking the dynastic view that all dancing evolves upward toward Balanchinian classicism, she seems uncomfortable where academic standards might not apply.

American dance in the twentieth century has been in large part an effort to find alternatives to the balletic solution. To discuss modern dance choreography using balletic vocabulary, as Croce does repeatedly, or to set it aside as mime, acrobatics, drama, anything but *dance*, is to deny that people from Martha Graham to Laura Dean have been trying to develop movement systems independent of balletic precedent. Croce tells of modern dance's musical correspondences, narrative developments, poetic qualities (Merle Marsicano's "simultaneous delicacy and deliberation"), without giving the reader a visual image of the particular physicality which gave rise to these allusions.

In her introduction, Croce explains that she doesn't find much "postmodern dance" interesting, and doesn't look at it very often. But her occasional forays into this field show a dismaying lack of insight. She's had the grace to include in this collection the controversial piece on the avant-garde that she wrote in the summer of 1980. On that occasion she divided all experimental dancers into the "mercists," an unfortunate term she invented for followers or sympathizers of Merce Cunningham; and the "mysterians," a group related only, as far as I can tell, by their reliance on their own intuition and the pre-verbal, their use of "ritualistic repetition," their adoption of a "contrived primitivism" which Croce seems to dislike or fear inordinately in the theater. Croce's mistaken assumptions and hostility brought forth a sheaf of outraged letters from dancers, and she has added an unrepentant, still uncomprehending postscript to the scandal.

There's a difference between brilliant analysis and categorizing snobbery. A critic's taste is one thing, but Croce often resorts to labeling people as unworthy when she really means she's not in sympathy with their terms. She crops the names of artists she hasn't ever dignified with a full review, insults others under the impression she's complimenting them. Sara Rudner, for instance, she considers a great dancer but not a true choreographer. Rudner takes herself for a choreographer. Why doesn't Croce? Lucinda Childs and Trisha Brown are reducing dance from a theater art to a scientific exercise. Laura Dean's dance is "folk art," for participants, not spectators.

I think a critic has to take even mavericks and crackpots at their word. In not doing so, Arlene Croce places herself above the artists. She implies she knows better than they do what's right for dance. To my mind, that's the one thing a critic isn't allowed.

THE MAGIC OF MR. B.

Washington Post Book World, 23 December 1984

Personal fame was not George Balanchine's trip. Like most really productive dance people, he was preoccupied with drudging, mundane work that takes place indoors at all hours of the day and night, and didn't have any interest in cultivating a personality that glowed in the limelight. As head of the New York City Ballet and the School of American Ballet, and choreographer of a remarkable repertory that has extended the concepts of twentieth-century dance, he was an authentic culture hero. In life he declined that role, but now, less than two years after his death, the rush is on to canonize him. Several new books about his life and work, in addition to the two volumes considered here, have been issued in the past year. None of the current Balanchiniana contains much that will add in a startling way to the existing legend, but I assume that strengthening the legend is its purpose.

Bernard Taper's biography, *Balanchine*, grew from a *New Yorker* profile into a 1963 book, with an updated section added for a 1974 paperback. The new edition has been extended up to the choreographer's death in 1983 and renovated throughout with new material and editorial second thoughts.[2] Photographs seem scattered even more generously throughout the book than in the earlier editions, and Taper has unearthed rare material and made some intelligent juxtapositions—a two-page spread of four successive *Apollos*, for instance. My favorite picture, from the '20s, shows a dapper Balanchine with cigar and cane, regarding the camera enigmatically, shadowed by the real owner of the cigar and cane, Serge Diaghilev, a blurred but smiling figure in the background, bundled in overcoat and scarf against the Monte Carlo sunshine.

Taper's book is still the most readable and reliable introduction to the sphinxlike Russian who inspired his own brand of balletomania from the Diaghilev era to the present day. Taper draws on personal interviews with Balanchine and his associates beginning in 1958 (unfortunately, none of his sources are thoroughly documented) and on information he gained watching classes, rehearsals, and performances. His view of Balanchine, concentrated and anecdotal, shows the human side of a career that was celebrated as much for its unpredictability as for its persistence. Taper notes the milestones: the flight of an ambitious twenty-year-old and four other renegade dancers from the traditionalist confines of jittery post-Revolutionary Russia; his triumphs and reverses after being brought to America by Lincoln Kirstein in 1933; the increasingly assured position of the New York City Ballet. Taper reports on great moments like the prodigal's return to Russia in 1962 as head of a world-class ballet company and adds some colorful detail to the long, sympathetic collaboration with Igor Stravinsky.

Taper's view, though privileged, is limited. Part reporter, part chronicler, he doesn't analyze or question why things happened the way they did. We learn nothing about how Balanchine, a foreigner and a visionary in a passionately partisan field, managed to build the empire he did. It's inconceivable, for instance, that control of the dance component of Lincoln Center or acquisition of a multimillion-dollar grant from the Ford Foundation in the '60s could have been won on artistic merit alone, but that's how it's told by Taper. Balanchine's relation to the dancers, to the press, to his students, to the producing organization that he headed—none of this is probed by Taper, who only sees and hears and reports what's offered to him by his principals.

Lincoln Kirstein's role is pivotal, but Taper doesn't indicate anything beyond the official and public dimensions of their partnership. How the team worked is one of the aspects of the Balanchine dynasty that's still to be written. Kirstein not only sponsored Balanchine's immigration and gave him a working foothold here, he knocked over impediments of every sort for fifty years; he raised money, enlisted powerful friends, excoriated the competition and the doubters, explained and rationalized an aesthetic Balanchine couldn't be bothered to articulate.

Kirstein's obituary essay for his friend and protégé is the most extravagant I've seen of all his gestures on Balanchine's behalf. First printed in the *New York Review of Books*, it now forms the centerpiece of a memorial volume, *Portrait of Mr. B.*, published by Viking together with the Ballet Society, the umbrella organization Kirstein and Balanchine set up in 1946 to foster their aims.[3] The book's photographs, unlike Taper's selection, are focused on the man as teacher, mover, molder of ballets and of ballet dancers. Except for a few performance shots, they show the master in action—placing, adjusting, prodding, exhorting, showing how—a Dr. Coppélius who with his vitality and faith elicits life from his pliant pupils. The *Portrait* also includes Edwin Denby's famous essay on *Agon*, two brief interviews Balanchine gave to Jonathan Cott, and a refreshingly concrete estimate of the man's personality by his successor as head of the New York City Ballet, Peter Martins.

What Kirstein sets out to do in "A Ballet Master's Belief" is reveal that we've been in the presence of no mere mortal, no mere genius, but a heavenly being. Balanchine was deeply religious himself, and he believed that dancing is a moral pastime. He was also fond of playful metaphors, like comparing dancers to angels, and of semi-mystical references to his artistic preceptors, Kirstein takes all this with deadly faith; he intimates that Balanchine had a personal pipeline to the Infinite, and warns all nonbelievers and dissidents that engaging in other forms of dance is the practice of not just folly but sin.

Building his ponderous case for the moral superiority of Balanchine's art, Kirstein tries to make ballets into icons, their creator into a saint. This is not only extreme but premature. It's Balanchine's ballets that will ensure his immortality, if anything, and though he denied over and over that he was interested in seeing to their continuance after his death, he accepted totally the idea that wonderful composers live on through their music. We must trust his heirs not to seal him off in a shrine of myth making and sentiment, but to keep his ballets around long enough for history to make its judgment. If he *was* blessed, he deserves no less.

Peter Martins's new *A Schubertiade* came at the end of the New York City Ballet's first long season without George Balanchine. It turned out to be a romantic ballroom ballet with lush, intricate partnering that shows off the company's splendid reserves of dancers. Martins hasn't yet struck me as a choreographer with anything pressing of his own to say, and he does nothing new in *A Schubertiade*. Yet the idiom in which he casts a set of well-known options employs a kind of extravagance that Balanchine avoided for all but the most compelling occasions. The choice of theme and style for this ballet has to be significant: what Martins does artistically as Balanchine's successor in these initial years will be read as a statement of how the company intends to carry out its pledge to keep the master's spirit alive. Nothing can be surmised yet, except that they're going for broke.

Couple dancing in the ballet is now a highly conventionalized image and a universally popular one. Beautiful ladies in long swirling skirts are attended by ardent gentlemen, and the music sweeps us up into romantic motion. Everyone remembers the dance floors of adolescence, so this is one of the few situations in classical ballet where the audience can have a real reference to what the dancers are doing. The type was probably fixed in the 1930s and 1940s by Léonide Massine, whose costume ballets *Le Beau Danube*, *Gaîté Parisienne*, *Vienna—1814*, *Symphonie Fantastique*, and others evoked nostalgia for Europe's crumbling social order—the ballet equivalent of Lehar's operettas.

Despite the success of Massine's ballroom ballets and their many imitations, George Balanchine had seized much earlier upon both the dramatic and the virtuosic possibilities of fusing social dance with the classical pas de deux. From descriptions in the encyclopedic listing of Balanchine's choreography issued by Eakins Press (1983), he may have begun these explorations even before he left Russia in 1924, but there is at least a surviving fragment from the 1932 *Cotillon* that shows him already far along on this road. The "Hand[s] of Fate" duet, preserved in the repertory of the Tulsa Ballet by its directors Roman Jasinski and Moscelyne Larkin, who learned it in the Original Ballet Russe in the '40s, is simple and mysterious at the same time. The man and the woman apparently are only dancing a Chabrier waltz. But the tone of oddness, established at the opening when the woman covers her face with both long-gloved hands, is not dispelled by the rhythmic intimacy of their dance. In fact, certain dramatic gestures intrude suddenly—I remember once the man pulling away and shielding his eyes as if he'd seen something awful—without breaking into the flow of the dance. These gestures, unprepared for and unstressed, become part of the dance's step vocabulary, reinforcing the aura of strangeness. They are not "signature" or mime actions, they're not there to create character or embellish an ordinary social dance form. They seem, rather, to grow out of the dance form and belong to it, like a fungus on a tree—organic but disturbing.

Often later on, Balanchine allowed the romantic impulse to exert its power, leading his couples into wonderfully enigmatic situations—forebodings of death and corruption (*La Valse*), visions of Paradise (*Emeralds*), conjurings of lost lovers (*Vienna Waltzes*, last movement)—all without any prior indication of character or plot. But this aspect was not Balanchine's primary interest, however good he was at it, and it was pursued more thoroughly by Antony Tudor, who could erect whole social structures upon a glance over a partner's shoulder or a hand raised in farewell, and by Jerome Robbins, who heightened the gesture to the status of a virtuosic act.

Balanchine led the way too in ever more elaborate reworkings of the pas de deux's introduction/adagio/variations/coda format—transforming the ballroom into a showcase for dazzling partnering displays laced with spectacular lifts, balances, and counterpoint. *Liebeslieder Walzer* (1960) was and is the great exemplar of this genre. With couple dancing now back in vogue, contemporary choreographers like Jiri Kylian and Glen Tetley may dispense with the ballroom trappings, but they too rely on the unstated premise of romantic love. Otherwise the athletic convolutions they've invented would look like wrangling and manipulation.

Peter Martins has taken all this heritage to heart in *A Schubertiade*, even the Massine, and has come up with a ballet that is sumptuous, beautiful, and technically admirable and that somehow makes you wish there were less of everything the longer it lasts. The scene is an 1830-ish drawing room in what I imagine to be a wealthy Viennese suburban house. A pianist (Gordon Boelzner) sits in a charming windowed alcove and supplies continuous Ländler and waltzes by Schubert for the eight dancing couples at a party. Later the set breaks away and turns into a formal garden with the piano installed in a little Grecian pavilion.

Although great pains have been taken with Federico Pallavicini's decor, unquestionably the most beautiful and well conceived I have ever seen at NYCB, the illusionistic detail it embodies is not carried through in the action of the ballet. As though only the right architecture and a few courtly stances were necessary to sustain the period and place, the ballet proceeds as a succession of display pieces—duets and trios mainly, with a few larger ensembles and brief solos. Taken on the level of realism established by the mise en scène, the party should be about dancing, everyone dancing. Instead, everyone seems to have urgent business elsewhere. Or while one couple at a time goes out on the floor, scattered individuals may watch idly from the sidelines. We have no idea how well any of these people know any of the others. We glimpse them only in attitudes of conviviality or passionate floods of dancing.

Bart Cook and Heather Watts have a serious, meditative early duet; they seem darkly involved with each other. Yet they end their dance and go off in opposite directions. Ib Andersen and Joseph Duell strike up a rivalry over several different women. Which one they win seems to matter less than their getting the best of each other. Nichol Hlinka and Jock Soto are young, playful, literally wrapped up in each other. They finish, move to the sidelines, and the current of warmth and animation between them is completely quenched by the time she sits on a chair and he stations himself at her side. Martins seems to be saying there's no bonding between any of these pairs, just momentary attraction. They change partners, ignore the people with whom they apparently came, look devastated by small inattentions, and ignore brush-offs. Stephanie Saland dances the only extended solo in the ballet, a melancholy, almost tragic cry, perhaps the lament of a wallflower. Because somehow she hasn't got a partner. But this is unaccountable because she's clearly the most beautiful woman in the place, and later three men cluster around, begging for just a smile.

After the change in setting, the party metaphor disappears almost entirely. A pit orchestra begins to play the longer, more dramatic *Fantasie in F Minor*. (This jarring switch, from intimate salon music to full stage sound, was remedied at a later performance when Schubert's original four-hand piano version of the piece was restored, with Jerry Zimmerman materializing beside Boelzner in the gazebo.) Dancers return two or three at a time, now in streamlined versions of their party clothes, and dance some more exaggerated dramatic dances without any pretext of showing us who they are and why they're attracted to each other. The extended, melodramatic entrances and exits, the excited bendings and twinings, the inspired lifts and complicated partnerings eventually lead into a completely formal finale with all sixteen dancers paired up. The other principals were Maria Calegari, Kyra Nichols, and Sean Lavery, but I can't remember who ended up with whom.

Twyla Tharp doesn't specialize in dramatic dances at all; her subject is usually style. Yet it's she who's inherited the Balanchinian genius for inferring character out of dance gesture. Unlike Martins and Robbins, she doesn't have to apply character on top, because her dance is so directly whatever it is; human contradictions and failings are built in along with human heat. Tharp's is a dance of events, sequences of swelling and subsiding mastery, approach-impact-dispersal, a tide of thrilling circumstance out of which the human authenticity emerges almost uninvited. Her dances don't have story lines or literal characters, yet she has given me some of the most profoundly joyful and profoundly disturbing moments I've ever experienced in watching dance.

In her recent work Tharp has been developing three quite different strains of choreography: a purely musical exploitation of dancing (*Telemann*, *The Golden Section* from *The Catherine Wheel*), a continuing romp through the popular music of the twentieth century (*Nine Sinatra Songs*), and, I think most important, a dark, often violent probing of the modern situation (*Bad Smells, Fait Accompli*). All these attach to facets of Tharp's own creativity—her classical braininess and musical intuition, her knack for style and the zeitgeist, and her seeming conviction that there's a long-standing enmity between the artist-individual and a predatory social system. Tharp is a loner, both unique as an artist and unapproachable as a dancing persona. Yet she pushes herself toward contact, leans over the brink of togetherness. Sometimes the results are engaging, sometimes they're chaotic and alienated.

Her struggles to socialize herself—that is, to function in a more and more inclusive social universe—are an ongoing subtext in her choreography. The progression was evident this season at Brooklyn Academy. In *Eight Jelly Rolls*, dating from 1971, when she still had an all-female company, tuxedo-clad women assume what are traditionally male roles—jazz musicians and barroom drunks—in the unself-conscious manner of girls' school theatricals. *Sue's Leg* (1975), a quartet incorporating what were then the only two resident males, comes from her fooling-around period; men and women compete playfully, collapse on each other and gently shove each other away, and join in friendly tumbling and showing off. By the late '70s and *Baker's Dozen* (1979), the company was larger and more accomplished technically; the dance is suave and amusing, based on an acute sense of coordination in partnering that can only occur in a finely tuned ensemble. She's built this virtuosic teamwork into the sublime speed and skill of *The Golden Section* (1981), and into the seven sets of ballroom personalities in *Nine Sinatra Songs* (1982), where each couple has its own particular relationship embedded in a different dance-floor style.

Apart from its sheer danciness and wit, *Sinatra*, the most overtly romantic of Tharp's current dances, gets its charm from the fact that each couple is individual. The dance is meant as an exposition of dancing types. It's airtight, distanced. Like many of Tharp's dances, it's grown sharper and less subtle since it was made. I first saw it in the fall of 1982 on the West Coast, and two major changes have tipped the balance of the dance, making it more of a comedy that it was originally. On the Coast, guest artist Gary Chryst substituted for John Malashock in the tango "Strangers in the Night," with Mary Ann Kellogg. The incomparable Chryst was able to commit himself totally to the dance's reckless glides and stops, its extreme swivels and switches of focus, so that however bizarre the pattern was, you could see that it all contributed to his and Kellogg's mutual seduction. Malashock, back in the part created for him, is unable to take it seriously, and turns the eroticism into camp. Then, the naive waltz "I'm Not Afraid," for Richard Colton and Christine Uchida, has been scrapped. Uchida left the company, and now Colton dances a cute but also arch "Somethin' Stupid" with Barbara Hoon. These changes, and some less obvious ones, have made the whole dance coarser and less emotionally wide-ranging.

The audience, of course, is always ready to take Tharp as a great joke, and before *Sinatra* had run five minutes almost every move caused hilarity. Perhaps neither Tharp nor her audience can tolerate serious sentiment for long. When she danced an adaptation of four of the *Sinatra* numbers with Mikhail Baryshnikov on the last night, she seemed uncomfortable, even awkward. She couldn't seem to find a persona for herself as a conventionally feminine type who could wear a smashing Oscar de la Renta gown and high heels, and dance with the most sensational partner in the world.

Yet, in her more androgynous guise—and the more egalitarian roles she's made for the company—she's capable of sexy dancing. And it's the darker pieces in the repertory where Tharp is truly erotic—*Short Stories, Bad Smells*, and the new *Fait Accompli*, and even in the neoexpressionistic cartoon sections of *The Catherine Wheel*. Tharp has discovered how to use real sensuality in partnering, rather than the airy, pictorial semblance of it we usually see on a ballet stage. Natural rhythm and the sense of body weight are essential components of Tharp's movement style, and when she began to explore partnering, she allowed them to come into play.

Several years ago on one of her television tapes Tharp said she hated to be lifted, it made her sick. From then on she seemed determined to overcome this weakness, and her choreography has accumulated an extraordinary number of duet situations and solutions. Whoever is being lifted or swung or supported—this happens to men in Tharp's work as well as women—can permit the full force of his or her weight to fall on the partner for a moment before rebounding or suspending. Often in a lift the woman will intensify her weightiness while changing position in the man's arms, transforming acrobatic strength into embracing or caressing contact. Women launch themselves full out across huge spaces and land securely in the men's arms. The floppy fall that's come to be almost a Tharp trademark can be a pleasurable giving in, a sign of willingness to accept help.

In the middle of her long, astonishing *Fait Accompli*, to David Van Tieghem's electric rock score, Tharp dances with all eight men in the company, creating a whole lexicon of male-female support images of which she is the center. For a large part of this sequence she's carried, manipulated, slung around by groups of the men. They handle her protectively but always leave her casually, on her own two feet. She dances duets with several of them. With Raymond Kurshals she has a sort of disjointed prizefight; they throw punches, lunge for each other, miss, grab, clinch. With Keith Young she's harmonious, balletic, supporting him as often as he supports her. She keeps falling as if in exhaustion out of Tom Rawe's arms, and he pulls her up so they can go on dancing a routine together. Each man leaves her after a while and she's finally alone.

As a whole, *Fait Accompli* might be about this duality of Tharp's—the need for other dancers/people to surround and support her, and the need to fight out her most personal battles for herself. Except for the section just described, the dance is completely formal, with the company working in strictly designed groups, displaying their technical prowess, their athleticism, and their ability to turn themselves into mechanical monsters with equal preciseness. The dance is frequently grotesque, the movement aggressive and fractured. The dancers grimace and gesture without evident cause, always in close coordination but spread slightly apart, as if they had some substance on their skins to repel all aliens venturing near. At other times, it's theatrically beautiful, as the dancers advance from an upstage void beneath banks of harsh sports-stadium downlights, and scatter again into nowhere when their dance is played out. Lighting designer Jennifer Tipton has surpassed herself here, with slanting, cathedral-like beams, fogs, projections. One change was so dramatic Tharp left the stage empty for it, and the audience burst into applause.

After the middle section, Tharp leads the men and the women into another front-facing, formal movement sequence that seems to contain references to some of her other dances. The others leave one by one, and Tharp is alone, shaking, gesturing, stretching with such a severe intensity she seems almost spastic by the time she grinds to a stop in ballet's first position, with a tortured grin on her fact. The she turns and makes her way with a tight strolling step away from the audience toward that now-familiar void—only a row of footlights has come up and she's walking straight for them.

Critics differed about the meaning of this dance, and especially about the final image. I don't see any reason to take it as a sign of Tharp ending a career, as some have. It could as easily have been an affirmation of challenges yet to come. Nothing in the season showed any sign she's slacking off.

PUTTING A LITTLE ORANGE IN THEIR LIFE
Hudson Review, Fall 1987

Four years after the death of its founder and stylistic architect, George Balanchine, the New York City Ballet is beginning to show signs of transition, and Peter Martins's new *Ecstatic Orange* may be a portent of the company's future course. Much as the NYCB's fans would like to see it preserved forever in a state of peak Balanchinian classicism, no one has yet discovered how a ballet company can be arrested and held in one performing mode. Subtle signs of change were everywhere during the NYCB spring season, even in the audience. The group of regulars who used to occupy the left-hand corner of the upper lobby at intermissions has diminished noticeably, and a new kind of patron, not very knowledgeable about ballet or the company, is now in evidence. An orchestra seat on a weeknight now costs thirty-two dollars, putting the ballet in the entertainment class with a Broadway show. One night I heard a woman behind me explaining to her friend: "*Square Dance* is a ballet about square dancing, but it doesn't have a story." (*Square Dance* is a classical ballet.) The same night half the audience left before *Liebeslieder Walzer* and half of the remainder left during that ballet. It may be significant that *Ecstatic Orange* came between those two Balanchine classics.

Marketing is the biggest word in today's dance world, and without a living, breathing genius to market, NYCB faces an image crisis. The Balanchine legacy is extensive and durable and is bound to dominate programming for a long time to come. But NYCB's repertory will gradually shade off until the Balanchine ballets make up a smaller and smaller proportion of it. Everyone agrees that maintaining a repertory or even reviving old works is not enough to motivate a dance enterprise over the long term. Dancers seem to do their best when new works are made on them, and the presence of a few premieres over a season is a virtual prerequisite to the press coverage that stimulates the box office. During the last

Ecstatic Orange (Martins). Heather Watts and Jock Soto, New York City Ballet.
Photo © Steven Caras, courtesy of New York City Ballet Archive and Peter Martins.

two weeks of the nine-week 1987 spring season, only half the scheduled ballets were Balanchine's.

So where are these new works to come from, and what kind of works will they be? At present the non-Balanchine repertory originates almost entirely from the two chief ballet masters, Jerome Robbins and Peter Martins, with Martins the most prolific producer of novelties. Martins has proved a competent classical choreographer—he can put together a coherent, attractive display of the academic vocabulary in a variety of period guises. *Les Gentilhommes*, new this spring, was a classical showpiece for nine young men, set to music of Handel, with simple costuming that suggested the eighteenth century. In addition to filling the never-ending repertory gap, it demonstrated that the company has male talent in the ranks.

But Martins is also trying to make ballets with a more modern look. *Ecstatic Orange*, the latest effort in this vein, illustrates very well how narrow is the borderline between classicism and modernism—or between a classic and an efficient contemporary product. It looks like innumerable other ballets that have come out of the European opera houses in the years of the Dance Boom, and purists immediately dubbed it "Agent Orange." The company certainly has done modern ballets—Balanchine was peerless in that form too, and Robbins dabbles in it from time to time. But the genre of *Ecstatic Orange* is peculiarly inimical to classicism though it exists only because of classical skill. I have difficulty talking about the piece without employing paradoxes.

First, there's Michael Torke's score, which dictates both the form and the style of the ballet. For a large orchestra, the music is itself an attempt to coax mileage out of a theme no longer in fashion. It's a kind of bombastic minimalism, based in repetition, with no real structural development, with flamboyant harmonic and coloristic effects borrowed from nineteenth-century music, and with infectious but not always predictable rhythms. Shallow and of no compelling interest, this music is too blatant to ignore. The ballet is like that too. Martins dresses his nine couples in black Milliskin, with the tights anachronistically cut off at the calf. The women wear ponytails. The vocabulary is classical steps with stretches and twists, skewed positions, rubbery torsos, each series of moves underscored by prominent pauses or surrounded by walking/running passages.

Where Balanchine's modern ballets used an expanded vocabulary to deepen the discursive and structural possibilities of steps, Martins cuts his ties to classicism by abandoning structure. Each of the dance's three sections offers dancing, seemingly uninflected or developed, in different energies and tempi. Though there's a principal couple (Heather Watts and Jock Soto) and two solo couples (Helene Alexopoulos and Mel Tomlinson, Victoria Hall and Peter Frame), they scarcely distinguish themselves from the rest of the dancers, who often pose in mass formations within which small groups sidestep or assume different shapes for a measure or two. The movement thus pans across the ensemble without any member of the ensemble dancing all the way through. In the final section (premiered in January), the music and the movement are so undistinguished that many dancers were still counting to themselves, to find their cues. The middle section, a duet for Watts and Soto, is set to a quasi-Latin rhythm with modernish harmonies that reminded me of the slow rumba in Robbins/Bernstein's *Fancy Free*. The dancers wind around each other and corkscrew outward in the trickiest shapes imaginable. I thought their dance was possibly about sexual avoidance and capitulation, but definitely not about desire.

Desire—or any other emotionality that demands commitment—is not something I've seen in Martins's ballets. Disengagement is what makes his work, so far, less than great. He demands sweat from his dancers but not love. *Ecstatic Orange* exhibits a kind of dispassionate, egalitarian objectivity that many European ballets share today. The dancers display; the audience admires. Nobody gets involved. To see Balanchine-trained dancers doing this style, you realize the uniquely humanizing influence of Balanchine. Classical ballet is an exhibitionistic pursuit, and in the past its fierce impersonality has been tempered by the interpolation of stories, the sensuality of exotic trappings, or the earthiness and swing of assimilated folk dances. Without resorting to any of these devices, Balanchine allowed us to see dancers as both technical exemplars and individual interpreters.

As the Balanchine temperament recedes from the repertory and the training, NYCB as a dancing ensemble is also changing. I find it difficult to distinguish some of the youngest dancers featured so often in Martins's ballets, and the fans' favorite game of picking out promising newcomers in the corps seems less interesting. Among the leading dancers, we see less of great individualists like Patricia McBride and Bart Cook, more of people trained outside the School of American Ballet, like the Kozlovs, Otto Neubert, Robert LaFosse. For some devotees the retirement of Suzanne Farrell irrevocably changed the look of the company. Without her as a supreme model for personal style adapted to Balanchine style, younger dancers opt for either bland proficiency or the exploitation of physical shortcomings: quirkiness as style.

Following a Balanchine tradition of casting opposite types in the twin-ballerina roles of *Concerto Barocco*, the company paired Heather Watts and Judith Fugate, allowing us to see how Fugate's whole body is energized in maintaining a clean line, the rhythm of her step flowing through from the center to the extremities; while Watts compensates for a nearly inert torso by exaggerating every head and shoulder articulation until it becomes almost a distortion of line. In the pas de deux in *Agon*, Watts has to work hard to do the steps, while Mel Tomlinson's effort goes into slurring through them. Together they draw out the transitions between the extraordinary poses, so that they seem to be enjoying his bizarre manipulations of her limbs. Another peculiar pairing was Christopher d'Amboise with Merrill Ashley in *Square Dance*. Ashley, still in fabulous technical shape though a trifle slower, is best matched with a strong, secure partner like Sean Lavery, who was out most of the season with an injury. D'Amboise is thin and wispy. He collapses in the middle and flaps at the extremities, is flexible without being articulate, and looks as if the basic gestures and positions are foreign to his body. He jumps high and the audience finds him charming. In the Melancholic variation of *Four Temperaments*, he seemed to be trying misguidedly for a "real" effect, sinking into his hip and dropping his energy level to neutral in between steps.

Balanchine could achieve expression without resorting to naturalism; the reason we don't think of his ballets as expressive primarily is that his expressive devices were contained in steps and subordinated to the refining process of music. The dancers who are the most expressive within his ballets, like Farrell, can make character and sometimes even story emerge out of their inner sense of the movement. In *Prodigal Son* this spring Darci Kistler did the Siren, a role I've associated in recent years with the steely cold and implacable Karin von Aroldingen. Kistler lured the hapless Prodigal (La Fosse) by being truly sexy and truly feminine. She looked as if the erotic pleasure of seducing him turned her on as much as the triumph of destroying him afterward. Kistler also made a striking debut in *La Sonnambula*, the most otherworldly sleepwalker since Allegra Kent.

Late in the season, one of the most atypical ballets in the repertory offered a surprising demonstration of the resources a truly great institution can bring to bear. As other companies ostentatiously load the nineteenth-century story ballets with more elaborate stage magic and decorative schlag, the NYCB's *Coppélia* comes as a shock. Balanchine revived it, with Alexandra Danilova, in 1974, retaining what they could remember of the 1884 Petipa choreography and inventing the rest. The controversial result looks clean and focused in spite of its discordant Rouben Ter-Arutunian sets and Karinska costumes. Dispensing with most of the traditional, distracting business, peasants, parents, Balanchine and Danilova concentrated on dancing but preserved the story with clearly visible mime scenes.

Shaun O'Brien, their original Dr. Coppélius, now has his role sharpened to the most exquisite details. As the dotty, slightly sinister doll maker, his toy creations are far more real to him than the unsympathetic villagers. In his workshop domain he's mastermind and, O'Brien suggests, ballet master too, as he shadows and directs the movements of his magically animated doll in a paternal pas de deux. The doll, of course, is the mischievous Swanilda. But even when her trick is discovered, Coppélius drags the real doll around with him as if she were his own flesh and blood.

The Swanilda, Patricia McBride, was also the creator of the role in this production, and it was moving to see her again in it. McBride has made minor technical adjustments in the choreography as she's grown older, but they aren't obvious, and Ib Andersen partnered her solicitously, making the trickiest lifts look beautiful. Both of them acted their adolescent roles with the restraint and generosity that only maturity can permit. The performance also delivered fine solos by some of the most interesting second-rank featured dancers, Lauren Hauser, Helene Alexopoulos, and Melinda Roy; and the unbeatable bonus of twenty-four little girls in the Dance of the Hours. The matinee audience cheered at the end, and I suddenly found myself choked up when a young man stepped out of the corps and handed McBride a bouquet.

With Ashley nearing forty and McBride forty-five, the great ballerina in the company now is Kyra Nichols, an extraordinary technician who is capable of surprising me no matter how many times I've seen her. Nichols keeps alive in the upper body without sacrificing the clarity of her leg action. You can see exactly what she's doing, no matter how subtly she phrases things. In *Walpurgisnacht Ballet* she played with sudden legatos and tenutos, speeded up, got increasingly detailed in one variation, without looking either fazed or insistent. I didn't see enough of her, though. In most of the ballets where I would have expected Nichols, Valentina Kozlova appeared. Pretty, accomplished, and almost totally amusical, Kozlova seems to be carrying on the NYCB's tradition of hardworking, attractive, inexpressive principal dancers.

A more endearing tradition is the staging of festive occasions for close supporters and friends. Midseason, the company and school celebrated Lincoln Kirstein's eightieth birthday with an evening of surprises that included a preview of the forthcoming—not yet fully financed—*Sleeping Beauty*. While the NYCB orchestra, onstage for once, played the overture and Prologue music, I mentally cast the ballet—it would star Kistler, of course, with Nichols as the Lilac Fairy, and a little-known youngster in each of the fairy variations. . . . Before I got to the prince and the other characters, Peter Martins came out to introduce a semi-promotional film that showed off David Mitchell's proposed designs. Over a condensed version of the score, Martins told the story of the ballet while cutout figures flashed through model sets. After that, the corps and children of the school performed Balanchine's Garland Dance, choreographed for the 1981 Tschaikovsky Festival, with all ten principal female dancers as benevolent fairies. Other bonbons of the evening included Jerome Robbins's *Circus Polka*, with unannounced guest Mikhail Baryshnikov in the role of the ringmaster, and the little girls spelling out the initials L. K. at the end. And there were speeches—short ones—and a big birthday cake onstage, and music, dancers, flowers, balloons, and a toast by Farrell and ballet mistress Rosemary Dunleavy.

Only the New York City Ballet knows how to put on events like this with aplomb. What's so extraordinary about them is how democratic they are.

I always feel warm and proprietary after one of these bashes, the way I imagine people in much smaller towns feel about their local orchestra or art museum. Lincoln Kirstein, the principal articulator of the company's ethic and aesthetic over the years, likes to picture NYCB as the people's ballet, though his recent statements in print have grown more emphatically exclusionary. Perhaps trying to counter the Balanchine backlash incited by the memoirs of various disaffected dancers, Kirstein jousts with dance history like some literary Don Quixote, skewering the modern dance pioneers for not establishing academies, relegating all contemporary modernism to the status of therapy or jogging, lopping off rival ballet heads, and swiping at the experimentalists who've had the only new ideas about dancing in several decades.

Kirstein's dilemma is a tragic one. He fought this battle for fifty years in order to establish and hold Balanchine's position as the culminating genius in the history of theatrical dancing. Now that Balanchine is no longer alive, the trashing of everyone else has left the Balanchine institution with few access routes to the future. His direct heirs are, so far, academic journeymen without any burning revelations to offer. The company has never seen the virtue of maintaining an archive of ballet classics, so the twentieth-century repertory of Fokine, Nijinsky, Nijinska, Ashton, Tudor, and the Americans has fallen into less likely hands.

At the end of the season, the company delivered another surprise: for next spring, not the *Sleeping Beauty*, but an American Music Festival. Barrels of new works will be done over the three-week event, and the choreographers announced so far include Jean-Pierre Bonnefoux, Laura Dean, Eliot Feld, William Forsythe, Lar Lubovitch, Paul Taylor, Helgi Tomasson, Peter Martins, and the late Joseph Duell. The omissions on this list are as interesting as the inclusions—most of whom never got near the company in Balanchine's lifetime. Missing are young company members who have ventured into choreography recently—Bart Cook, Daniel Duell, Miriam Mahdaviani—or any alumni working elsewhere like Bruce Wells (Boston) and Kent Stowell and Francia Russell (Seattle). Even more glaringly, Twyla Tharp is absent. Besides Merce Cunningham, who may be represented with a revival of *Summerspace*, Tharp is the modernist most seriously and successfully committed to reshaping classicism in contemporary terms. In addition, she collaborated last year with Robbins on *Brahms/Handel*, which invigorated the NYCB dancers as no new work since Balanchine has done. Come to think of it, no contribution of Robbins has been promised either—what an opportunity this would be to recover one of his psychological ballets of the '50s. The American Music Festival is obviously intended to follow in the glorious footsteps of Stravinsky (1972 and 1982), Ravel (1975), and Tschaikovsky (1981), all of whom produced some wonderful ballets. What's needed even more than that is a clear direction, a line of thought that can carry the company into a new era. Dancers and critics will be working hard to seize it, and hoping for the best.

IVES AND ROBBINS

Christian Science Monitor, 24 February 1988

Jerome Robbins is not scheduled to do one of the twenty new ballets on the New York City Ballet's American Music Festival in April and May, but his new *Ives, Songs* makes a perfect curtain-raiser for the revels to come. There are practical reasons why it was wise to have this premiere at the end of the company's winter season instead of in the thick of the festival, not least of which is the dancers' availability for rehearsals. But the piece itself makes a convincing case for early scheduling. Its meditative, sparse theatricality might be hard to appreciate amidst the hectic novelty and thrills of festival time.

Ives, Songs belongs to that special genre called the piano ballet. Accompanied by onstage musicians instead of a pit orchestra, it conveys an intimacy, a personal feeling that's rare in the usual grand setting of classical ballet. Besides the great Balanchine works *Liebeslieder Walzer* and *Davidsbündlertänze*, *Ives, Songs* is preceded in the NYCB repertory by Robbins's *Dances at a Gathering* and several other romantic works.

Ives, Songs is reflective, even somber. A solitary older man (Laurence Matthews and his alter ego, baritone Timothy Nolen) looks back on his life with affection, nostalgia, and a lot of still unanswered questions. The eighteen songs are skillfully arranged (no credit is given for the musical choices) to create an almost narrative sequence, leading from childhood reminiscences to spiritual revelation, to patriotic fervor that turns bitter with the devastation of war, to love, doubt, and finally farewell. Nolen, seated at the edge of the stage with pianist Gordon Boelzner, sings with a clean, simple delivery that makes the words easily understood. This is not only helpful to the ballet, but very pleasant to hear, since Charles Ives used some wonderful texts from the likes of Byron, Keats, and Longfellow, as well as some enigmatic words of his own.

Robbins's vocabulary for the ballet is reserved, deliberately unvirtuosic. Even his sense of eventfulness is curtailed. Though there are thirty-eight dancers in the cast, you never see them all till the end, when they cluster

Ives, Songs (Robbins). Lourdes Lopez and Alexandre Proia, New York City Ballet. Photo by Paul Kolnik, courtesy of New York City Ballet Archive and The Robbins Rights Trust.

together and confront Matthews, then disperse like fading memories. They are grouped to represent different periods or ideas in the man's life. Some are semirealistic in their actions, like the little girls who play twittery games ("The Children's Hour"), ooh and aah on their visit to the opera house ("A Very Pleasant"), and flirt with oafish boys at dancing school ("Waltz").

A more sedate group of older girls and men waft through, mostly with partners, but they don't do anything spectacular. Their main expressivity comes from lifts, which Robbins distributes sparingly to them, and in odd contexts. The two spiritual pieces ("At the River" and "Serenity") seem to consist entirely of walking patterns. The men raise the women in reclining positions and carry them aloft. At the end of the two songs, each man turns his partner upside down and takes her off. The effect, which ought to be clumsy, is brought off with such seriousness and, well, serenity, that as they go, one by one, the audience inhales in wonder.

The most interesting songs, to me, were the really strange ones. In "The Cage" Ives pictures a leopard stalking around its cage, and a boy watching it, wondering, "Is life anything like that?" A very diminutive man and a very tall one tiptoe back and forth, all bent over into S curves. Helene Alexopoulos and Alexander Proia float through "In Summer Fields," and as he lifts her she twists and spirals outward, seeming to escape his hands like dandelion fluff. And in the strangest one of all ("Incantation"), a gaunt, vacant-eyed Stephanie Saland steps on her pointes with arms spread, and Jeppe Mydtskov supports her from behind, until finally they merge into a single searching shape.

The most striking effects in the ballet are cinematic ones, not danced ones. A family clusters around the parents (Florence Fitzgerald and Otto Neubert) in "Tom Sails Away." With the singer, they recall the father's homecoming, the babe in arms. Suddenly Ives moves forward in time, to visualize the baby grown up and going off to war. The family group wheels and re-forms, and a young man in a helmet steps out and moves away from them.

Ives, Songs is Robbins at his most affecting. Its introspective mood, so intently maintained by the dancers, depends on limited action and simple images set in empty space. At first the audience seems to mind its length and its lack of virtuosic dancing, but you somehow end up being drawn into its spell.

The City Ballet set off late-season fireworks with dancers this year, rather than choreography. After double hip-replacement surgery, Suzanne Farrell returned to the stage in *Vienna Waltzes*, looking wonderful, and the audience welcomed her adoringly. Nina Ananiashvili and Andris Liepa, principal dancers of the Bolshoi Ballet in Moscow, made their debut as visiting artists in *Raymonda Variations*. This is one of Balanchine's most endearing showcases for dancers, and I'd seen a miraculous performance starring Kyra Nichols the week before. When Ananiashvili appeared among the delicate, crystalline NYCB corps, she looked as though she'd come from another planet, and so, later, did Liepa. Big, muscular, and soft in their movements, they had the haughty, gracious manners of conventional classical stars, yet they looked curiously uncertain in the intricacies of the choreography. They hadn't, in fact, learned it all, and two of their variations were omitted. But seeing what they had trouble with—the ballerina's re-adjustments of balance, the danseur's substitution of spectacular fouettés for the choreographer's more ordinary but rhythmically daunting steps— gave me new insights into the richness and originality of Balanchine's achievement.

Christian Science Monitor, 20 June 1988

The first time modern dance and classical ballet encountered each other on the New York City Ballet stage, in 1959, Martha Graham made a psychological narrative about Queen Elizabeth and Mary Queen of Scots for her own company with one NYCB dancer, and George Balanchine created the abstract, modernistic *Episodes* for his own company with a solo for a Graham dancer named Paul Taylor. Three decades and a lot of cross-referencing later, the two genres met again during the last week of the NYCB's American Music Festival, and it seemed the battle had been rejoined.

The protagonists were the same Paul Taylor and his own modern dance company, with NYCB soloist Peter Frame, and on the ballet side Merrill Ashley and Adam Luders, in NYCB artistic director Peter Martins's choreography for them and two exemplars of the Taylor style, Kate Johnson and David Parsons. It was by far the most stimulating evening of the festival.

Martins took a conventional, even regressive view of the confrontation. In *Barber Violin Concerto*, to the 1941 score, he seems to see modern dance as "primitive," threatening to the composure and maybe even the morals of ballet dancers. He offers us two paradigms: Ashley and Luders, tall, elegant, and aristocratically aloof; Johnson and Parsons, a complementarity of physical extremes—tiny and light, big and weighty. Right away you could see that Martins was exploiting the kinkier aspects of modern dance, giving Parsons and Johnson what he thinks of as Taylor movement, with emphatic turned-in legs and crooked arms and bent-over bodies.

The two couples state their terms alone, then dance simultaneously but almost unaware of each other. Then they exchange partners. The Ashley-Parsons duet is the princess and the frog all over again. Parsons galumphs along behind Ashley, his arms splayed out as if he needed them to balance an ungainly bulk. (Parsons, by the way, has to work hard to make himself look this clumsy and menacing.) She seems terrified of his embrace and tries to slither out of it, but finally succumbs, and is transformed. I've never seen Ashley so totally confident in a partner, and she seems to abandon herself to his solid support. But she recovers quickly from this indulgence, and my last image is of her trying to straighten his arms and turn him into an unwilling prince.

If modern dance represents physical license to Ashley, to Luders it's a maddening itch. Johnson streaks around him as he sleepwalks across the

Barber Violin Concerto (Martins). Kate Johnson, David Parsons, Adam Luders, Merrill Ashley, New York City Ballet. Photo © Steven Caras, courtesy of New York City Ballet Archive and Peter Martins.

stage, leaping on his back, buzzing near his face with her hands. His struggles to fend her off are hilarious, and you'd think, what with her superhuman speed and his inability to focus on her, that she'd get the better of him. But the ballet ends as he throws her decisively to the floor.

Meeting Martins's defense of ballet territory with an equally polemical challenge, Taylor's *Danbury Mix* insisted on the grotesque, dark proclivities of modern dance. Set to selections from Charles Ives, *Danbury Mix* is almost a pastiche of Taylor themes and phrases. Karla Wolfangle, dressed in a handsome silver jumpsuit by William Ivey Long, is the totemic leader of seventeen dancers dressed in simple black dresses and pants. She strides ahead and they tumble after her, anarchic, clotting together in little groups that threaten to overrun each other and her as well. Momentarily, they shape up ("Circus Band Music") with Peter Frame as their drum major. But pandemonium breaks out again as they all start doing their bits and stunts as fast as they can, falling, sliding, cartwheeling, sometimes slamming into each other.

The music for this last section is Ives's "Three Places in New England," with its overlapping, discordant musical ideas, and as it lurches to a closing consensus with the first two measures of "The Star Spangled Banner," Wolfangle is suddenly left all alone, and a row of black-and-white American flags unfurls on cue behind her as the curtain falls.

I thought it was brave of Taylor, who has made several pretty dances that conveyed themselves easily into ballet repertories, to risk the audience's displeasure by making such an earthbound and chaotic festival piece. I decided he was aiming to show how his personal vocabulary can be cast, unsanitized, in a formalistic mode. It's invigorating to think modern dance can still be distinguished from ballet when it wants to be.

~ CHANGING THE GUARDS

Hudson Review, Winter 1989

The New York City Ballet's American Music Festival was Peter Martins's first independent move since the death of George Balanchine, and it pushed the company out of a five-year holding pattern. In this extended period of mourning, Martins and co–ballet master Jerome Robbins acted as willing caretakers of the Balanchine tradition. They preserved the Balanchine repertory, even reviving some ballets that had been out of circulation, and Martins created ballets in a Balanchinian classical style to complement Robbins's more free-ranging forms. It didn't do any harm, either, to use Balanchine as a feature attraction while paying respect to his memory.

With the company's position stronger than ever, Balanchine's reputation solidified to a degree he never reached in life. Accolades, books, tributes poured out. Disciples and detractors said openly what they hadn't dared to say in his presence. Come-lately critics jumped on the bandwagon. Now they could praise him without risk, since his work—now an oeuvre—was already figured out, defanged, and fully certified as a great thing. The bereft fans clung ever more tightly to his legacy, knowing there wouldn't be any more. And the dancers were philosophically and physically bred to carry on his style. An institution fifty years in the making, a phenomenon in the feckless world of dance, the New York City Ballet would always be a Balanchine company, a Balanchine shrine. Or so we thought.

The safety of the ballet repertory is always in doubt. Ballet changes all the time, a step here, a notch of tempo there, a smoothed-out accent, a shade of emphasis. These never get noticed in the day-to-day performance of repertory, but if they're not corrected, they accumulate until the work is transformed. Ballet needs constant shoring up. It needs the prod of personal imperative, the systematic scrutiny of an eye that knows what to look for and sees what wants changing. More than anything else I think, it's the power of personal vigor and vision that creates style in dance. We the audience aren't sharp enough to see when style slips, only to notice when the cracks have gotten so wide they drastically change the look of a passage or a whole work. Despite the scrupulous efforts of his designated heirs and coaches, Balanchine's ballets have begun to deteriorate. Some people love the relaxed, slurred style and the friendlier delivery of the younger dancers, and they don't miss the lost details. Some people think the whole enterprise is getting flabby.

What NYCB is facing now—and Martins must be praised for recognizing it so publicly with his festival—is an identity crisis the magnitude of which no ballet company in modern times has experienced. Precisely because NYCB is the product of a single, evolving creative persona, its post-Balanchine leadership, no matter how dynamic, must either seek new directions or be content as curators. Unlike other ballet companies which lacked a prolific, propulsive force to shape them, NYCB never had to hustle for choreographic drawing cards; it had the biggest. Not only didn't it have to search for talent, it never had to consider what would attract an audience. As Balanchine recedes into the company of the Old Masters, the New York City Ballet is having to think about what ballet is supposed to be in the 1980s and 1990s. The American Music Festival put this process on display.

At first announcement, the festival seemed to be another sign that things were still status quo. Institutions need periodic events to break the regular seasons, and the NYCB staged festivals with flair under Balanchine. Perhaps 1988's participating choreographers, five imported and thirteen from the NYCB stable, would come up with one or two wonderful works that could justify the vast expenditures of money and effort these occasions always require. But the results were disappointing. For me, there were no premieres that felt truly memorable, many that were inferior or trivial. In fact, the pleasantest parts of the 1988 festival were the Balanchine works interpolated among the new material. And thinking back over the NYCB's record of splashy events that yielded only one or two good ballets, I have to recognize that nearly all the rewards were provided by Balanchine then too.

As the festival progressed, I began to feel I was watching a momentous event, an elaborate and secret rite of passage. The elements of a longer and less perceptible process were revealed in symbolic form—changes were hinted at and sometimes declared in fiery, disappearing letters. Balanchine's direct influence was evident in many works by present and former NYCB dancers, but aspects of the Balanchine style that have been eroding over the past five years were also acknowledged, even built on by new choreographers. Ideas that Balanchine never considered despite his modernity made full, confident appearances. The dancers looked convinced too, not just contented. They seemed to believe they might still be the carriers of innovation, and to welcome being given permission to revert to the state of naturalism and flamboyance adopted by most other contemporary dancers. By the end of the three weeks, I felt some kind of transition had been negotiated, unintended perhaps by those who engendered it, and that the future of the company was now quite undefined.

I think the key aesthetic issue of the festival, and of this whole year in ballet, was just what constitutes contemporary work, and how some dance form might be devised in which classical rigor and integrity don't drain away in eclectic compromises.

Balanchine proved a master at solving this problem. For the first thirty years in America he successfully blended classicism and modernity. After that his contemporary sense may have slipped a bit, but by then he had his audience well in hand. Philosophically, he never uprooted himself from Europe, and his unwavering adherence to the high-art European traditions brought him his initial gloss and prestige. He offered a dance form that was elitist in origin even when it wasn't so elevated in tone, a form the culture climbers were—and still are—more willing to pay for than a humble homegrown product. Throughout his career, his ballets to American music were overtly aimed at popularizing the classical idiom, often through the use of Hollywood images, but his most startling and difficult works were those in which he grafted American rhythms and dynamism onto the music of the European moderns, Stravinsky especially, rather than American scores. Making little attempt to glamorize or humanize the look of the dancers, he disguised the American qualities by merging them totally into classicism.

I suspect Balanchine had an aristocrat's affectionate disdain for American culture—at least, he couldn't take it quite seriously. *Ivesiana* (newly revived for the festival), *Stars and Stripes*, *Slaughter on Tenth Avenue*, *Tarantella*, *Who Cares?* and *Western Symphony* apparently represent all the retrievable ballets Balanchine set to American music, and they're probably the most impressive of what is anyhow a very small assortment. Excepting *Tarantella*, which simply fits a traditional pas de deux into the traditional

Italianate tunes of Gottschalk, and *Slaughter*, lifted from the 1936 Broadway show *On Your Toes*, these works take bits of Americana as little more than a pretext for classical ballets. They're like picture postcards: bow-legged cowboys and buxom dancehall girls, the flag-waving cheerleader and the cocky, too-short drum major, the gangland rubout and the hoofer with the heart of gold, the winking lights of the skyline and the clinch at the final curtain. These are hardly Balanchine's most profound or searching images, and collectively they reveal him as an outsider, a tourist, seeing the stereotypes and not so much making fun of them as finding fun in them.

Even *Ivesiana* enters gingerly into its music, takes a few searing glances at people who fail to make contact, and then withdraws from them, as if to peek at them any longer would invite trouble. The fragmentation and dissonance of Ives, his rhythmic unpredictability and his general thorniness, perhaps his most distinctive and American qualities, seem disconcerting to Balanchine, who responds to them with formalism or stasis. Though not necessarily better ballets, the four other Ives works on the festival were all unusual and less formal than *Ivesiana*, and were less extreme in their reaction to the music.

Peter Martins's *Calcium Light Night*, his first ballet, is offhand, grimly playful, sparing of its material. Jerome Robbins's *Ives, Songs*, his most recent work though not a festival premiere, indulges the sentimental, patriotic side of Ives, and perhaps of Robbins too, a ballet of childhood and family, of transcendental faith and chauvinistic courage. And Eliot Feld's *The Unanswered Question* contains almost no dancing and turns Ives's cryptic discontinuity into full-fledged dadaism, with weird machines and inventions and apparitions, all suggesting the curio cabinet world of Ives's youth in the late-nineteenth century. Paul Taylor's *Danbury Mix*, featuring his own modern dance company with NYCB soloist Peter Frame, made the clearest stylistic rapprochement with Ives, although it didn't even nod in the direction of classicism, except to suggest that waywardness and individualism can only submit just so long to regimentation before reasserting themselves.

The inclusion of Taylor as one of the guest choreographers on the festival tested the NYCB's long-standing aloofness from modern dance. The instances when the company used a modern dance choreographer are so few as to constitute special occasions in themselves. And though Martins invited Laura Dean as well as Taylor, together with the fusion choreographers Lar Lubovitch and William Forsythe, his attitude toward the maverick American form is still ambivalent, as evidenced by his own *Barber Violin Concerto*. In this didactic item, one of seven new works (nine if you count the trivia) Martins made for the festival, ballet dancers and modern dancers are shown as polar opposites, never to be reconciled except to their mutual detriment.

In the light of the festival's heaviest portents, I took *Barber Violin Concerto* as simply a polemic, with jocular overtones. Martins doesn't really expect to defend the bastion of classicism against a modern invasion. In fact, he seems to see fusion forms as the logical direction for the company style. Fusion dance borrows indiscriminately among vocabularies and tries to upgrade each of them with the most fetching aspects of the others. It doesn't give priority to any one discipline. The biggest drawback of fusion dance, I think, is this refusal to commit to any one point of view. As an aesthetic, fusion admits the choreographer's reluctance either to invent his own idiom or to penetrate deeply into an existing one. In its penchant for timeliness and spectacle, it admits that serving the audience is its primary motive. This might be a worthy democratic ideal except that its audience, in this country at least, is bourgeois and undiscriminating. Perhaps Peter Martins sees this escape into the present—jazzing up, smoothing out, or shaking apart the classical idiom with notions explored by modern dancers—as preferable to a sequestered life pursuing the Balanchinian ideal.

Since *Calcium*, Martins has made many classical ballets, but his modern ballets have been swinging away from pointe work, away from line and musicality, and toward a narrative sexuality that opposes the sublimated sexual content of classicism. His festival work *Tanzspiel* uses a classical vocabulary in conjunction with modern gestures and shapes to elaborate on and eventually transmute the first movement of *Ivesiana*. That is, while *Ivesiana* remains a formal enigma, *Tanzspiel* illustrates a contemporary news story. One ballet is an urban fear-fantasy; the other insists the fantasy is real. In both works, a woman and a man make their way through a crowd, searching for something but unaware of each other. Almost by accident, they meet, connect, part, meet again in a scene of cruelty. Then one of them leaves and the other continues as before. People spoke about *Tanzspiel* as if it were "about" the murder of Jennifer Levin, whose prep-school strangler had just been tried in New York. They didn't even notice it was a meltdown of *Ivesiana*, which, by the way, was tepidly received.

The audience's favorite ballet of the festival, *Behind the China Dogs*, was by William Forsythe, the hottest young choreographer around. Forsythe has been the *New York Times*' white knight for the past couple of years, and before the spring season was out, it hailed his Frankfurt Ballet as "a dance company for a young audience." Forsythe was a shrewd choice for NYCB in

Behind the China Dogs (Forsythe). Judith Fugate, New York City Ballet. Photo by Paul Kolnik, courtesy of New York City Ballet Archive and William Forsythe.

its urgent quest for that audience. *China dogs* turned out to be far less splashy than Forsythe's usual fare—it had no existentialist voice-overs, no stage devices to trap the dancers, and only a moderate degree of misogyny —but it was racy for the New York State Theater. Forsythe uses pointe-work skills, especially turning and balance, in equal parts with eroticism and alienation. Sequence, speed, and energy are compressed tightly while the body is stretched, skewed, twisted, and further distorted by expressionistic lighting effects. All his ballets seem to project dancers as moving, modern-istic objects in a series of decorative situations that make ironic reference to things the audience recognizes and often respects. Many choreogra-phers have given ballet dancers unballetic things to do, but when Forsythe dresses New York City Ballet dancers as punks and has the men throw Balanchine's divine women around, the audience gets a malicious thrill.

Peter Martins has been an apt pupil of this attitude, and at least three more of his ballets on the festival exploited it: *Black & White*, *The Waltz Project*, and *Ecstatic Orange*. His muse, Heather Watts, seems to have no tensile limits, and her frequent partner Jock Soto is just uncouth enough not to mind roughing her up. There seems to be a whole cadre of NYCB dancers adapting to these new choreographic demands, while another group is featured in the classical repertory. This division is not yet clear-cut or absolute, but one has to note that Kyra Nichols, Darci Kistler, Ib An-dersen, Merrill Ashley, Stephanie Saland, and Judith Fugate were rather pointedly underused by the "modern" choreographers in the festival, while the Watts/Soto wing dominated nearly every program.

The two ballets that I thought showed the best potential for bringing classical virtuosity and aestheticism into a contemporary mode received very little attention. Bart Cook's *Into the Hopper* didn't come off, mostly, I think, because the under-rehearsed dancers couldn't maneuver their way through a lavish production. Cook's idea of having modern paintings come to life and act out a detective story based on the legend of Orpheus was witty and ingenious, a collage of postmodern ironies and techniques. As more modest, downtown deconstructions during the season demon-strated, there's a lot to be explored in this genre, and a company with NYCB's resources can push it to the limit. However, the management seems to have written off Cook's experiment; it's not one of the nine festival creations scheduled for the fall season.

Laura Dean's *Space* is, however. Dean has been stalled lately in her own minimalist formulas, but in *Space* she gained some new perspectives. It's paradoxical that minimalism's best chance for development lies in get-ting bigger, but that's been the case with most of its avatars: Philip Glass,

Steve Reich, Lucinda Childs, Frank Stella. The State Theater's expansive stage and the disciplined enthusiasm of forty NYCB dancers spurred Dean into new ramifications of her striding, spinning dance designs. The clean, spare precision of Dean's style is not alien to classical dancers—Jerome Robbins tried it successfully a couple of years ago with *Glass Pieces*—and Dean has incorporated more ballet steps, leaps, and arm gestures than ever into her work. After so much writhing and anguishing in the rest of the festival, it was a pleasure to see a dance that had unusual floor patterns—crisscrossings, squarings-off, lines merging, splitting, cohering into diagonals, the stage filling with people, then thinning out. At its best Dean's work can be visually and spiritually satisfying, and *Space* is one of her best.

To my mind *Space* extends the both dancers' and the audience's range as nothing has done since the Jerome Robbins/Twyla Tharp collaboration *Brahms/Handel* five years ago. Interestingly, *Brahms/Handel* was dropped from the spring schedule due to that old villain "illness and injuries," and Tharp has still to make a ballet of her own for NYCB. To add to the irony, it looks as if she never will. As the spring season gave way to the hottest, most dreary European-imported ballet season in years, American Ballet Theater, NYCB's main rival for the past quarter century, announced that Tharp would become a resident choreographer and artistic associate. While the American Music Festival was on, Ballet Theater was quietly holding its best season in years across Lincoln Center Plaza at the Met, with a good-looking corps of dancers and an improving repertory that included large dollops of well-executed Balanchine. With Tharp on board and a new School of Classical Ballet launched over the summer, Ballet Theater could make a serious incursion into NYCB's turf. Add to that the Millicent Hodson reconstruction of Balanchine's long-lost and lamented *Cotillon* this fall by the Joffrey Ballet, which has lost its founder-leader in the past year and will consequently also be seeking new directions. Looks like we'll have an interesting 1988–1989 season, figuring out where's the best place to pick up the threads of new and old ballet.

 PATRICIA MCBRIDE'S FAREWELL
Christian Science Monitor, 16 June 1989

Patricia McBride's gala was more than a sentimental tribute to the well-loved ballerina who is retiring after an illustrious thirty-year career with the New York City Ballet. McBride went out in her own modest but memorable style, and the gala was thoughtfully arranged by company director Peter Martins to underscore how many ways this style could be employed.

When you picture a typical NYCB ballerina, you might think of the classic long, thin body; a vertical, open attitude; limbs that spear like daggers into space. Patricia McBride's image isn't anything like this. She looks angular in my mind's eye, with legs kicking up in high spirits, torso twisting, back deeply arched. Maybe one shoulder is cocked or her head is slightly askew with an arresting glance, and her arms are partly curled so that they hide her face or pull her away from stability. Most often, she seems to be in the act of flinging herself about in fun or flirtation. But at rare times she retreats inward, to enact some private subtext of what she's dancing.

The gala program on June 4 was an assemblage of excerpts from McBride's repertory, nearly all originally choreographed for her, by Peter Martins, Jerome Robbins, and George Balanchine. McBride danced five of the numbers, and her roles were taken in the others by younger principals in the company, so the performance not only celebrated the end of one extraordinary career, but affirmed a continuing tradition.

I hadn't seen anyone but McBride in some of the roles. Even the most lustrous of her successors not only looked different from her but had difficulties doing what she did. This isn't because they lack ability, but because McBride has a personal quality that all her choreographers have utilized and that she reinforced as she settled into new ballets.

The program opener, *Tarantella* (Balanchine), featured NYCB's newest bright light, Margaret Tracey, with Gen Horiuchi in the part created by Edward Villella. Tracey is young, eager, and technically brilliant. She easily mastered the steps of this bravura duet, and even added a few embellishments of her own. But Tracey's rhythmic sense, and Horiuchi's too, is almost dogmatically square to the beat, and this told me volumes about McBride. What made McBride so spectacular in a piece like this was her rhythmic flexibility, a musicality so secure that she could dance around the meter with great freedom, delaying and speeding up to make tiny expressive surprises, fresh ones at every performance.

The great Merrill Ashley took over McBride's luxuriant role in the Frülingsstimmen (Spring) section of Balanchine's *Vienna Waltzes*, and the occasion drew from her a degree of smiling circularity I've never seen. A somber section of Robbins's *The Goldberg Variations* featured the wonderful Darci Kistler, who, like McBride, has the ability to dance seriously without going blank.

Another of McBride's specialties was her daring. In Martins's *Valse Triste* she demonstrated an almost reckless impetuosity in hurling herself into Robert LaFosse's arms—backwards, upside down, off center, at terrific speeds and without the slightest hesitation. When Judith Fugate tried intricate things of this sort in the Intermezzo from Balanchine's *Brahms Schoenberg Quartet*, she couldn't undo her natural reserve and classical alignment enough to manage it smoothly, and Heather Watts just goofed her way through the technical and stylistic pitfalls of *Rubies*.

Kyra Nichols and Maria Calegari in Robbins's *Dances at a Gathering* and Valentina Kozlova in *Liebeslieder Waltzer* of Balanchine were more neutral in their approaches to McBride's duets, leaving the thought that new visions of these roles will always be possible again. One reinterpretation that has already appeared is Stephanie Saland as the Pearly Queen in the Costermonger Pas de Deux from Balanchine's *Union Jack*. Where McBride was a lady, or a would-be lady, in this music hall turn, Saland mugs it for maximum laughs and vulgarity.

Patricia McBride, in spite of her bravura and romantic roles, is by nature a soubrette, and *Coppélia*, which Balanchine and Alexandra Danilova revived for her, was one of her most successful. The third-act pas de deux, which she danced with Ib Andersen, was perhaps less memorable and less typical of her in this ballet. I would have preferred to see her as the doll-come-to-life who charms and then trumps Shaun O'Brien's Dr. Coppélius.

Besides this lovely comic scene, and *Tarantella* and *Rubies*, I think we'll most remember McBride for her introspective "The Man I Love" in Balanchine's *Who Cares*. In the gala performance, with LaFosse, she seemed more serene than she'd ever been. Her happiness and security seemed to build all evening, until the last dance, a solo variation from *Harlequinade*. This was a touching choice, since the dance ends with her blowing kisses to the audience, and she did it graciously. Her original partner in this and so many other ballets, Edward Villella, gave her flowers and kisses at the end.

All during the evening she was ecstatically cheered by a jam-packed audience. She got big bouquets from Robbins, Martins, and Mikhail Baryshnikov, and took final bows with her former partners, Bart Cook, Ib Andersen, and LaFosse, who had escorted her last dances, and Anthony Blum, Robert Weiss, Shaun O'Brien, Sean Lavery, and her husband, Jean Pierre Bonnefoux.

In the brief preliminary ceremony—she was hailed by Kitty Carlisle Hart, head of the New York State Council on the Arts, and Mayor Ed Koch—McBride thanked Peter Martins for making the tribute possible. "It was such a wonderful surprise," she said. "I just wanted to quietly sneak away, but he wouldn't let me." Neither would we.

Dance Ink, Fall 1992

Choreography is the most pressing issue in ballet: how to do it, what it should be about, whether it should support or subvert the status quo. The audience probably doesn't care much about it, but critics do. They're the ones who have to sit through nights and seasons of repertory, and if choreographic fare isn't extraordinary they demand that it be refreshed as often as possible. This spring New York's two biggest ballet companies faced a choreography crisis, real or self-induced, and came up with totally different solutions. If these efforts don't add substantially to either repertory in the long run, they at least gave us something to think about.

Loud yawns could be heard when critics received the first announcements of New York City Ballet's Diamond Project, and the names of the participating choreographers incurred a gamut of emotions from doubt to apathy. Could the New York City Ballet enhance its repertory, we wondered, by commissioning a whole crowd of ballets all at once, or was this merely to be another gimmicky spring tonic for the box office? Many of us still have dispiriting memories of the 1988 American Music Festival, whose thundering hoofbeats left hardly a trace on the repertory. Would the Diamond Project be any more of an inspiration to choreographers than acquiring ballets the old-fashioned way, one at a time? That was American Ballet Theater's plan this spring, but it didn't awaken much hope either, even if the roster of names was more catholic and better known. In the event, City Ballet turned in some surprises, while Ballet Theater's novelties could only be explained as flickering signs of an administrative and artistic confusion that is becoming alarmingly chronic.

The Diamond Project, like all such ventures, came packaged in high-minded rhetoric, some of it glib, some of it snobbish, some of it interesting. NYCB artistic director Peter Martins talked a lot about his insistence that all the choreographers use the classical vocabulary, "our" language, he called it. "You need to be educated in it—or at least grow up in the ballet idiom." It seems a little late for Martins to be trying to distinguish ballet from modern dance so precisely. He reminds me of that fuddy-duddy teacher in the car commercial, saying to a roomful of kids clutching crayons: "Stay within the lines, children. The lines are our friends."

Perhaps this is Martins's covert way of explaining why Twyla Tharp, the most creative and rigorous fusion choreographer of our time, was once again bypassed as a contributor. Actually, it wouldn't be so easy to determine on which side of the classical/modern tracks a good chunk of the NYCB repertory falls. Is Jerome Robbins a classical choreographer? What about Martins's first ballet, *Calcium Light Night*? Laura Dean had been choreographing pointe work for nearly a decade when Martins tapped her for the American Music Festival, and her *Space* was one of the most effective works of the tourney. But she's hardly a classical choreographer. Neither is Mark Morris, whose solo for Mikhail Baryshnikov, *Three Preludes*, was given as an outside-the-guidelines production two weeks after the Diamond Project. Except in jest, Morris has done only one dance on pointe, his most balletish ballet, *Drink to Me Only with Thine Eyes*, which Ballet Theater commissioned in 1988 and has regrettably mothballed.

As Peter Martins knows very well, classicism can always be bent or nudged aside when a big name or a trendy idea comes along. The New York City Ballet made its mark on the world because of the multiplex genius of George Balanchine, who could borrow, adapt, disguise himself in a hundred different dance styles without losing his identity as a classicist. Absent Balanchine's unfathomable ingenuity, classicism can be just another inert set of rules. Martins's characterization of the Project as a kind of workshop for developing choreographers acknowledged an acute Balanchine deprivation at NYCB. When Balanchine was alive the company never bothered about developing new choreographers. It didn't need to, except against the very fix it finds itself in now.

Apparently too, there were limitations on the amount of costuming for Diamond Project ballets, and a prohibition against decor. I wonder if this was, as claimed, simply a matter of economy, or if Martins had some subtle idea of pushing the choreographers toward the decorative austerity for which Balanchine was known.

But the instruction to make "classical" work was also a rather daring way of reasserting the City Ballet's artistic position. It forced both the choreographers and their audience to consider if there is a meaning to the aesthetic of classical ballet, and if that can be implemented as a working premise in the '90s. However noble or ignoble their motivation, these rules actually focused the Project, and by the end of the week I was quite impressed by both the range of possible interpretations and the elements that seemed consistent through all the works: clean dancing and visual patterns, good taste, music of integrity and/or imagination. Perhaps that constellation will define classicism in the '90s. One more thing. Just about all the ballets had the pas de deux form at their heart. Sometimes these duets had the usual romantic connotations and ramifications. But sometimes the choreographers seemed to be exploring alternative possibilities of partnering. This too is classical—and contemporary.

    ◠ Although the word "innovation" doesn't necessarily come into it, we want to see some retooling, some new insights when a choreographer works in a traditional form. Peter Martins's dexterity with composition, on which the company now so heavily depends, produces clever but mechanical ballets. I often felt, looking at a new Balanchine ballet, that he'd fallen hook, line, and sinker for some unsuspected vision and wasn't ashamed to dance after it, straight to the doors of hell if necessary. Martins never seems fired up that way. *Jeu de Cartes*, his Project piece, dealt out the Balanchine-modernist formula: circusy high spirits à la *Rubies*, athleticism à la *Symphony in Three Movements*, and sexy angularity à la *Stravinsky Violin Concerto*. Martins's MacGuffin was to have Darci Kistler, with minimal costume adjustments, play the Queen to three partners: Albert Evans, Damian Woetzel, and Nilas Martins. She tried and tried. They looked as if they were holding their breath. The corps ground on and on. The only wit came from the music. Before it was halfway through I felt the onset of claustrophobia.

One thing Balanchine ballet did for the audience was to educate us in the relationship of dancing to music. I don't ever expect to see his match in that, but I can't help being sensitized. Balanchine neither treated the music like clockwork nor ignored it. He followed it lovingly without ever making a carbon copy. His dance/music dialogue was like two great conversationalists on show. Maybe talk television has killed our capacity to even recognize great repartee, let alone create it.

Bart Cook's *Flötezart* was the most classical-looking ballet in the Project, but its pleasures for me were more visual than musical. Set to Mozart flute concerti (K.314 and part of K.315), it had a double female corps of five each, a male corps of four, two pairs of soloists, and two principals. The asymmetrical neatness reminded me of Balanchine. So did the way the solo dancers and the corps dancers often seemed to be working quite independently, and the poses that ended each movement, with the corps massed in different semicircular formations around the soloists. But I was also reminded of Twyla Tharp, specifically the second movement of *Push Comes to Shove*, when the corps goes calculatedly haywire in a dozen ways.

At the premiere of Cook's piece, mishaps occurred right away. Someone fell. Someone else left the stage and didn't return. I watched the rest of the performance wondering whether the blue corps was actually supposed to have one less dancer than the pink corps, or whether the four remaining blue dancers were courageously improvising throughout the whole ballet to cover a major gap. It turned out there had been an injury and the latter was the case. But there were also enough intentional quirks to save the ballet from being overneat. For instance, the ballerina, Maria Calegari, danced with the two secondary cavaliers and then with all the male corps members before, somewhere in the second movement, her prince (Erlends Zieminch) belatedly appeared.

Richard Tanner's *Ancient Airs and Dances* set out to work completely against the music by being arranged in a formal, classical style rather than going along with Respighi's scampery early-twentieth-century transcriptions of folk-derived baroque dances. Made for five couples and ten corps members, the piece seemed heavy and overblown to me.

Miriam Mahdaviani's *Images* (Debussy), for five women and five men, was much more clear-cut, or maybe too clear-cut. Of course we're all rooting for Mahdaviani, who's just about the only in-house female the NYCB has ever entrusted with creative work. In *Images* she takes the Balanchinian/ Robbinsian path of glossing ballet precedents, especially the "Grecian" nymphs-beset-by-satyrs convention of the early Diaghilev period. The nubile nymphs at their wafty dances are interrupted by males, whom they accept as partners right away in spite of their initial fear. Only in the claspings of their individual duets are there hints of pursuit and unwonted pleasure. The men dance alone in a competitive display, and after the women return there's an even more decorous ensemble. This is all done in a very refined and structured way, as if it's being recalled in a reverie later on, when the senses have returned to calm. I'm not sure whose memories it represents, though, or whether the incident left him or her dazed or simply mellow.

Lynne Taylor-Corbett and David Allan turned in energetic pieces. Taylor/ Corbett's *Mercury*, to Haydn, was more structured than anything I've seen her do, while Allan's *Reunions* to one of Ernest Bloch's concerti grossi more or less ignored the music's classical architecture. His fugue section, for instance, had one couple succeeding another instead of assembling into a group, which gave the stage a feeling of thinning out just when the music was getting denser. Toni Pimble's *Two's Company*, to part of a Dvorak string quartet, I remember mainly as quantities of blue people swimming by in shoals. At the second performance these were deleted, to reveal Stephanie Saland trying at great length to make up her mind between two almost identical suitors (Jeffrey Edwards and Peter Boal). Alexandre Proia's *Refrac-*

tions, to a John Adamsish score by Kamran Ince, had masses of moody people in somber-colored velvet bathing suits. Like the music, the piece was made of assorted components no one thought they had to fit together.

⤳ Surprisingly, it was the week's more modern ballets that interested me, from the standpoint of both music and of dancing, although none of the three was particularly strong on ensemble patterning. Robert LaFosse did attempt some structure in *I Have My Own Room*, while William Forsythe and John Alleyne took the easier way out, pretty much abandoning anything that looked like preplanned organization.

LaFosse began and ended with solos for himself. In between there were several apparently unrelated sections, each with a different main idea. What seemed like dozens of men and women squared off across a divided stage and later merged. There were duets—two men, two women, a man and a woman—each with a different quality. There was a section of individual overlapping solos—LaFosses said in an interview that the order was picked at random before each performance and entrances were timed fifteen seconds apart, so that this section of the dance would never be exactly the same twice.

Afterward, I was confused about this piece. In the initial solo LaFosse is curled up in the fetal position and seems to be embroiled in some kind of struggle or nightmare, Suddenly he "wakes up" when a bunch of rubber balls are tossed onto the stage from the wings and the other dancers swarm in. This all makes you think the dance is going to be about some kind of identity crisis. LaFosse has learned a lot from Twyla Tharp about imposing rigorous form on personal material, and it was the formal logic of his dance that kept it from looking juvenile. But in terms of personal logic, I didn't get how the solo figure was related to the bouncy, goofy crowd.

The Project's no-frills edict proved a great asset to William Forsythe's *Herman Schmerman*, I thought. For once, here was a Forsythe ballet with no dangerous objects for the dancers to maneuver around, no dismembering shafts of light, no shattering silences or blackouts. The five dancers (Kyra Nichols, Margaret Tracey, Wendy Whelan, Jeffrey Edwards, and Ethan Stiefel) didn't look like escaping convicts or mountain climbers in an avalanche. Forsythe concentrated on individuals rather than duets, for which I was also grateful. The whole ballet was spared the glare of misogynistic, violent sexuality that has hyped his work before, and for once I could see him working with form and body movement for their own sake.

Forsythe's dancers are in constant, jittery motion, reflecting Thom Willems's electronic score, a stream of explosive fragments built on a regular underlying pulse. There are precarious stretches while the body is balanced on one foot, body parts pulling in opposite directions, limbs snaking or slashing through space. The brief duets seem to be more about two individuals tugging apart than about their finding a way to unite or even accommodate. The dancer begins a phrase without pausing, taking a preparation from a bounce rather than a planted position. The phrase is arrhythmic, fragmented, breaks off abruptly, or gets flung away. And none of it seems to go into any memory bank of compositional motifs; everything looks newly made up. So instead of the ballet dancer's classical composure you see a kind of intense perpetual motion.

Forsythe's one semi-narrative convention is the theme of watching—poststructuralists call this "The Gaze." Performance as voyeuristic playground. There's a black flat placed upstage like a backyard fence. Dancers casually lean on it while watching the others. Or they lounge onstage when they finish their own solos, as the next person begins. The dancers may simply be checking out their colleagues while taking a breather, or acting as vestigial reminders of the courtiers and villagers in a nineteenth-century ballet, or even being surrogates for the audience, which is presumed to be getting a sexual charge out of these bodies on display.

Since there are only five dancers on the State Theater's huge stage, you notice what everyone is doing. You notice when they're dancing and not dancing. Although they seemed to be moving in quite individual ways, they often fell into chunks of unison. They oriented themselves toward any old part of the space rather than always toward the audience. And they took no particular care to look toes-first proper when they entered and left the stage. Forsythe could almost have been studying the staging conventions of Merce Cunningham.

Bet Ann's Dance, by John Alleyne, looked something like a Forsythe, but in several ways it observed the rules more respectfully. Alleyne also shows a small group of dancers in a nonhierarchical relationship, casual-looking but capable of stabbing pointe work and demonic multiple turns. However, Alleyne seems to be grounded in the classical vocabulary even when he's dismantling it. Most of his phrases start and end in one of the standard five positions, then skew out of line or get collaged unpredictably. Things that are normally seen with stretched legs are done in plié; a proper pirouette dribbles out into an upper-body spiral; the arms intended for one step are applied to another. In fact the whole dance is introduced and completed by Albert Evans with emphatically correct classical gestures.

Alleyne used interesting music by two Canadian composers. Jean Piché's "Steal the Thunder" combined percussion, including clappers and Chinese gongs, with electronic string and organ sounds. The live tympanist, William Moersch, was coyly placed half in the wings. I don't know why. Gary Kulesha's "Angels" had a marimba and electronic sounds—muffled voices, breaking glass—and a sinister feeling. I couldn't see whether Moersch was playing this live or not. The dance, however, did seem affected by the moods of the music, another difference from Forsythe's businesslike performing attitudes.

Classical ballet is a fuzzy term despite its magical connotations. Everyone uses it as if they know what it means, but it's hardly consistent when it translates into usable repertory. Essential classical ballet would be the nineteenth-century Russian classics, but I don't believe an American company today can draw primarily on this account. Even though the *Swan Lakes* and *Don Quixotes* go over big at the box office, they stunt the audience's artistic growth, and the dancers.' Diaghilev's classical-modernist ballets are the next great body of work, but most of the ones that appear today (*Schéhérazade, Carnaval*) are even more escapist than the nineteenth-century classics. The most avant-garde of them (*Parade, Le Train Bleu, La Chatte*) don't wear well. Like yesterday's extremist couture, they became dated very fast. I happen to love these antiques, but only certain companies can sustain them, usually in clusters, like the Joffrey Ballet's Nijinsky/Nijinska collection.

At New York City Ballet, classicism—if we could separate the style from the persona of Balanchine—has always meant a changing aesthetic. Balanchine himself knew this, which is why he kept fixing his ballets, and why the dancing style and even the look of his dancers didn't remain the same. We would probably think the original *Serenade* or *Concerto Barocco* were tintypes if we could have them back. It's a tricky maneuver, when there's no choreographic giant punching in a new program every day, to keep moving at the same time you stay the same. No one wants to see the Balanchine repertory frozen into a monument, but no one wants to see it disappear either. City Ballet dancers have to do this repertory, because it's the most demanding choreography that has yet been created for dancers. Nothing quite as challenging has been put to them in ten years. But the rethinking has to go on too, if only to keep the fires of inquiry lit.

Boston Phoenix, 18 May 2007

About the only question to ask about a new *Romeo and Juliet*, besides Why, is Why the New York City Ballet? Ever since its founding in 1948, the NYCB has cultivated an identity as a company that does pure-dance ballets. Even earlier, as George Balanchine was gaining a foothold in America, he affronted the Metropolitan Opera, where his dancers were installed as the resident ballet, by doing avant-garde ballet evenings. His 1937 program of the all-Stravinsky, all-but-plotless *Apollo, Jeu de Cartes,* and *Le Baiser de la Fée* was too unconventional, and the Met severed the relationship.

Myths and fairy tales weren't the red meat of ballet, Balanchine thought, but he was versatile, adaptable. Along with *Aida* and *Don Giovanni*, he'd been choreographing things like the Ziegfeld Follies, and he kept his dancers working in his shows and movies for the next ten years while the ballet company reconstituted itself for special purposes. Once established at New York City Center and then Lincoln Center, Balanchine's NYCB shunned the prefabricated story ballets except to embrace them as money-makers, like *Nutcracker*. His other adaptations of nineteenth-century stories were either stripped to the bone (*Coppélia, Swan Lake Act II*) or culled for their dance essence (*La Sylphide* as *Scotch Symphony*, for instance).

Now, twenty-four years after Balanchine's death, as the company celebrates the one hundredth birthday of its even more aesthetically minded cofounder, Lincoln Kirstein, New York City Ballet has mounted a full-evening *Romeo*, choreographed by its ballet master in chief Peter Martins. I don't know if this means the company will turn to more costume spectaculars, or if it's just another way-station in Martins's quest to supply the repertory with appealing items.

Martins initially got a lot of mileage out of his determination to cast students from the School of American Ballet for the leads. The ballet's doomed lovers should be the same age as Shakespeare's protagonists, he thought. This seemed like a pretty literal idea. Some of the iconic ballerina Juliets were created by Galina Ulanova at thirty in Leonid Lavrovsky's version, Margot Fonteyn at forty-six in Kenneth MacMillan's, and Alicia Markova at thirty-three in Antony Tudor's.

But the notion got a certain amount of press coverage for Martins and encouraged our expectations of a really new treatment, perhaps as trendy as his title for the ballet, *Romeo + Juliet*. As it turned out, the initial leading roles were played by NYCB solo dancer Sterling Hyltin and corps de ballet member Robert Fairchild. This couple were quite wonderful when I saw them in the flights of adolescent ecstasy that Martins choreographed.

The production was indeed stripped down compared with the scenic opulence and peripheral carryings-on of other versions. I think it was in MacMillan's version, or possibly John Cranko's, that the townspeople pitched into the first act Montague/Capulet skirmish, lobbing oranges or anything else they could get their hands on. Martins eliminated the civilians and staged the opening clash of the clans as a formal dance for the color-coded corps, backing up the first of several splendidly coached episodes of swordplay.

Martins introduces the story with a hearty trio for Romeo and his two pals, Mercutio (Daniel Ulbricht) and Benvolio (Antonio Carmena). Romeo seems a little bit dreamier than the other two, but the reason for this, his crush on Rosaline, isn't evident since the role of Rosaline has been deleted. With what might seem like a dispensable plot complication Shakespeare actually gave a finely observed dimension to Romeo's character—his youthful desire for romantic love. Juliet could be just another passing fancy, ennobled by the tragic workings of the plot. In Shakespeare it's the feud between the two families as much as the lovers' impetuosity that causes their deaths. Martins treats the social aspects of the tragedy as a side issue; he doesn't even bother to show the reconciliation of the clans after the deaths of their children.

Martins's story is scaled down so that it can be conveyed by formal dancing, with conventional miming to move the plot along. You don't get a sense of the lovers being surrounded by watchful relatives and busybody townspeople. As if to insist that dancing, not drama, is paramount, at every opportunity the bystanders gather into neat, audience-facing lines and do a ballet dance. Since there's no implication that the love affair is stiflingly public, you can't fully appreciate the secrecy with which so much of the plot unfolds.

A lot of this shift in theatrical values is shown in the way the main characters behave—the lovers are endlessly rapturous, the Capulet parents (there are no senior Montagues) are melodramatic monsters as danced by Darci Kistler and Jock Soto, the nurse is dithery and unsympathetic (Georgina Pazcoguin), the other young men are stock types—a pompous Paris (Jonathan Stafford), sassy Mercutio, faceless Benvolio, and a Tybalt (Joaquin De Luz) who seemed immobilized in his tubby, bright yellow doublet.

Martins resorts to violence occasionally. Lord Capulet slaps Juliet during one of her refusals to marry Paris. After mortally wounding Tybalt,

Romeo throws a cape over his head and stabs him five more times. These purple passages serve as energy boosters, a respite from the story, like the dueling and the dance set pieces.

What makes *Romeo + Juliet* look like a contemporary work is its casualness about dramatic consistency, its glossing over of the story's complexities and conflicts, the slapdash convertible set (by Per Kirkeby) that looks more like a rough granite minifortress than the streets and palazzos of Renaissance Verona. Martins's ballet rides along on its basic ingredients, Prokofiev's music and Shakespeare's play, rather than exploring them.

APOLLONIAN VENTURES

Boston Phoenix, 25 July 2003

Peter Boal has spent most of his career in the New York City Ballet, where he's admired as the purest of classical dancers, even though NYCB favors neo, modernist, and contemporary styles rather than traditional high classicism. Now thirty-eight, Boal is beginning an early transition from the supercharged mainstages to teaching and a longer but lower-key performing life. Perhaps taking a cue from Mikhail Baryshnikov, Boal has started commissioning solos from ballet colleagues and interesting choreographers working in postmodern modes. The newest Boal enterprise will be a company, to premiere next summer at Jacob's Pillow. This according to Richard Colton, codirector of Concord Academy Summer Stages, where Boal appeared Thursday night.

All three dances on Thursday's program had a wonderful calm and security, traits of Boal the dancer which his three choreographers obviously wanted to use. The pieces didn't present big contrasts or effects, but seeing one fine dancer modulating within a fairly small range turned out to be a rare and rewarding experience.

Boal first appeared as an almost-familiar prince or paragon, in *One Body*, by his fellow-NYCB principal Albert Evans. Wearing silken white tights and drapey, vaguely Grecian chiton, he swept around the space with expansive arm gestures, airy leaps, and pirouettes that were perfectly centered. Not a bump, not a hitch snagged the smooth flow of his line and direction. He seemed to be modeling his body to show it off to advantage, but not in any pushy, conceited way.

There were moments when I thought Evans was referring us to other ballets Boal has danced. The traveling jumps landing on one knee and sweeping through, from George Balanchine's Divertimento from *Le Baiser de la Fée*, for instance. But the whole piece had its own meditative quality, like the music that accompanied it, John Kennedy's "One Body" for orchestra and countertenor. The singer's words were so internalized they drifted just below the surface of meaning, but that in itself means something.

Wendy Perron's *The Man and the Echo* might have been an urban edition of the same sensibility. Boal wore a dark suit, sport shirt, and street shoes. His movements were more angular, asymmetrical, sometimes even broken, and tighter in to the body. His gestures were small, anxious—his fingers curled as if they remembered manipulating some complicated object, his arms circled around the back of his head. In a walking motif, very contemporary, almost jazzy, he sank comfortably into each hip, his upper body following in easy opposition. At times he seemed to be attending to the inner workings of his body, but then his focus would shift, as if he'd heard something outside somewhere.

At intervals, he'd be lying or sitting on the floor; instead of John Lurie's guitar riffs, we heard children's voices talking to their daddy. Boal had recorded them, and I read somewhere they were his own children. After these interludes he seemed increasingly agitated, tilting off center, shifting suddenly, gesturing across his body. He seemed even fearful at one point, but maintained his calm. The last we saw of him, the light was fading out on his profile, arms in a wide open stretch—one up and one down.

Selections from Lou Harrison's spiritual music ("The Elegiac Symphony") accompanied *Pola'a* by Molissa Fenley. Harrison's chordal string writing reinvested the classical sensibility in still another tone. The music even reminded me of Stravinsky and Balanchine's *Apollo* at times, as did certain moments in the dance. Fenley's title, in Hawaiian, refers to the ocean, and other viewers have seen the dancer's swirling, reversing eddies of turns, and later his agitated jumps and thrusts, as illustrative of the sea's motion.

I could see that, and how the characteristic Fenley motif of the dancer's body rocking from foot to foot with symmetrical bent-up arms could have evoked a small boat bobbing in a breeze. But what impressed me more about the dance was the serene continuum Boal made of his extended and changeable circling patterns, the crystalline clarity of his infrequent moments of stillness, the sense of a force, of work, that wasn't effortful. Through the whole eighteen minutes of the work, he seemed not only connected to the floor and the space but energized by it, as he changed directions, reframed his body with his arms, spun on and on.

At last he finished off a series of eccentrically shaped ballet moves with a contradictory pose, his upper body slightly twisted and his arms in an elegant wreath above his head. There was no way of knowing where the current would take him next.

VILLAGE OF DANCERS

Boston Phoenix, 16 June 2006

When you hear of a new ballet titled *Russian Seasons*, you visualize khovorods and trepaks danced in a simulated birch grove by peasants in earth-toned costumes. Fortunately, our expectations of banality can always be thwarted. Alexei Ratmansky's contribution to the New York City Ballet's showcase of new choreography, the Diamond Project, both utilized and overturned the stereotypes.

Ratmansky, not yet forty, is the artistic director of the Bolshoi Ballet in Moscow and has an impressive record as a choreographer, including a prize-winning *Anna Karenina* for the Royal Danish Ballet, *Le Carnaval des Animaux* for San Francisco Ballet, and *The Bright Stream*, shown in the United States two years ago by the Bolshoi. *Russian Seasons* has a fascinating score based on folk songs, set for strings, solo violin (Arturo Delmoni) and mezzo-soprano (Susana Poretsky), by the contemporary Ukrainian composer Leonid Desyatnikov. The music suggests the Stravinsky of *Les Noces* at times, and the earlier Stravinsky of *Petrouchka* at others. It can be more modern and dissonant, then even postmodern. The twelve dancers, principals, soloists, and corps members are grouped together quite democratically, but they all dance like stars.

What I noticed first, after getting over the initial shock of the stream-lined folkish costumes in pop-art colors, was how the movement was classical to the core. Without fudging the line, elevation, speed, "character" displacements of the upper body, articulation and mobility in the legs and feet—classical ballet's arsenal of technical resources—Ratmansky combined steps in new ways, gave his charged virtuosity spaces to breathe, and created a community through a constantly modulating stream of dancing.

You seldom see everyone dancing together. Instead the dancers come and go in small, variable units throughout the music's twelve sections. Sometimes these subgroups dance for themselves, rejoicing in their own physicality. They team up with partners for fast, airy duets. Sometimes they play games, not always cheerful ones, and sometimes they even seem to be

Russian Seasons (Ratmansky). Jenifer Ringer and men, New York City Ballet. Photo by Paul Kolnik, courtesy of New York City Ballet Archive.

going through some sort of ritual observance. Solo figures dance more individual feelings; the groups surround them, support them, offer them comfort.

Notes provided to the press, but not to the audience, explained the musical structure as a progression through the seasonal and liturgical calendar. We also got translations of the five sung texts, full of an intense love of the real world and shadowed with thoughts of death. The ballet reflected this cycle without literally describing any of it, but I wondered why the company denied the audience this other level of poetry.

If there was any narrative thread, I thought it was carried by the solo dancers. As the ballet went on, the somber thoughts seemed to overtake the happy ones. Albert Evans emerged from leading the men's group to serving as a father figure or priestly guide. Wendy Whelan, Sofiane Sylve, and Jennifer Ringer danced alone at different times, each shaken by some inner disturbance: Whelan by sorrow, Sylve by wildness, Ringer by mischief. Ringer seemed to become a kind of evil idea that pursued and possibly possessed Sylve. Whelan picked imaginary flowers desolately, as the others tried to console her and then passed by. The singer tells how her lover hasn't returned from the war.

After many encounters and dance inventions, Whelan is led off by Evans, both of them now in transfiguring white versions of the same costumes. The others embrace their partners and slowly lie down. Poretsky sings: "We need nothing, / Only six feet of earth / And four boards. / Alleluia, Alleluia."

Russian Seasons suggests *Les Noces*, Bronislava Nijinska's austere invocation of community. But like two great George Balanchine works I revisited over the weekend, *Divertimento No. 15* and *Donizetti Variations*, it also takes you on an absorbing journey into the pleasures of dancing itself.

CHRIS AND FRIENDS

Boston Phoenix, 26 October 2007

Starting an independent ballet company is no piece of cake, even if you can assemble a ton of talents to help you. Christopher Wheeldon's Morphoses made its New York debut last weekend after initial outings in London and Vail, Colorado, with two programs of dances mostly by the thirty-four-year-old English choreographer. If long-term stability could be secured by the warmth and affection that flowed from the City Center stage to the audience and back again, Morphoses would be all set.

The hype was huge, but Wheeldon seems to have a modest agenda. At an open rehearsal Friday afternoon he asked the audience not to think of Morphoses as a "fully formed company." He's collected significant start-up funding, tour bookings, and the assurance of performance bases at City Center and Sadler's Wells Theater in London. His idea is to build up some shows over the next two or three years—not necessarily with the same dancers—while gradually cultivating the much heftier resources needed to go permanent.

Wheeldon is even more reserved about his artistic vision for the company than he is about its prospects down the line. He describes the company's mission with an unobjectionable but vague optimism: "to broaden the scope of contemporary classical ballet by marrying dance, music, visual art and design." Just about anything could fill that frame, and these opening programs didn't clarify the picture.

Wheeldon has been choreographing for a decade as a prolific and successful freelance. He's held an important Resident Choreographer appointment at the New York City Ballet, and he was a principal guest choreographer in Boston in the late 1990s. Freelancing can give a choreographer great exposure, but it's more conducive to making miscellaneous, short-lived pieces than creating a durable repertory. Only a few of his ballets have made a lasting impact on our thinking, though I've often been impressed with his fidelity to the classical language, his musical good taste, and his gifts as a poet of theatrical dance.

Program building is one skill Wheeldon hasn't yet mastered. Each performance had six items, interspersed with bits of atmospheric rehearsal footage filmed by Michael Nunn and William Trevitt (of London's Ballet Boyz), who were also dancing with Morphoses. Choreographer friends were generous with their works; stellar dancers made appearances. Most of the music was played live by the Orchestra of St. Luke's conducted by Rob Fisher. Both performances I saw had the feeling of galas, when you relinquish any expection of a new masterwork as one special thing follows another, making only a momentary claim on your enthusiasm.

The season was heavy on duets, that contemporary kind where the woman gets hauled around by the man, and there were several selections boasting newly invented contortionist effects for two or three men at a time hauling the woman around. My tolerance for this kind of acrobatic sex play is much lower than what the rest of the audience appears to like. Wheeldon has an advantage over other purveyors of this trendy stuff because his dance is always grounded in the classical vocabulary. His movement doesn't look like poses randomly pieced together from here and there. Still, his most recent work, *Fool's Paradise*, merges with everything else on the program in my memory, with its duets, serial partnerships, and collective but deliberately not unison activity.

I barely got a grip on Wheeldon's twenty-three fine dancers, and only a few performances stood out for me as extraordinary. New York City Ballet's Wendy Whelan and Edwaard Liang performed William Forsythe's 2000 *Slingerland Pas de Deux*, one of that choreographer's less violent exercises in partnering. Whelan got to wear a stiff white tutulike affair, designed by Forsythe and likened by many critics to a potato chip. Ignoring this preposterous getup, Whelan invested her slinky circumnavigations and scramblings around Liang's torso with a sensual weightedness and a constantly surprising phrasing. In so many other items in this vein, on Morphoses's program and elsewhere, dancers do these moves with a flat, dispassionate attitude. Whelan made me feel she was doing more than waving her arms and legs decoratively. She made it okay, for once, that the women in these numbers don't really get to dance even if they're virtuosos.

City Ballet's expressive principal dancer Maria Kowroski circled tentatively around Tyler Angle in Liang's *Vicissitudes*. This duet seemed to refer to its music, from Franz Schubert's "Death and the Maiden" quartet, rather than to its naughty title, with both dancers in black and Angle enveloping her in his arms, lightly controlling her gestures, and she working up to submission as if she were a smaller, shyer girl.

NYCB principal Ashley Bouder did dance, in the funniest, fullest choreographic piece Wheeldon contributed to the season, *Dance of the Hours*, choreographed for the Metropolitan Opera's 2006 production of *La Gioconda*. Wheeldon begins with a double corps de ballet dressed (by Holly Hynes) in elaborate but abbreviated eighteenth-century gowns: four skinny, spacy ballerinas in gold and four tall, slightly klutzy ones in blue. The audience laughs on cue at the first campy notes of the theme (the Hello Mudda, Hello Fadda chorus).

The piece then goes on to scratch away at the conventions of the big-blast classical ballet finale, with the corps deployed asymmetrically behind the stars, Bouder and Gonzalo Garcia. There's a trickier-than-thou adagio duet backed up by the corps ladies, reclining on the floor and waving their arms. Bouder and Garcia do spectacular solo bits, the corps launches into a cancan, and at one thrilling point Bouder streaks in from nowhere and rips off a bubbly diagonal of turns and smiles. Finally she takes a classic Mercury pose and Garcia slings her upside down over his shoulder. The corps is staunchly revolving around them as the curtain falls.

Dance of the Hours reminded me of the sly but well-bred way Balanchine

There Where She Loved (Wheeldon). Tyler Angle, Leanne Benjamin, and Adrian Danchig-Waring, with singer Shelley Waite, Morphoses/ The Wheeldon Company. Photo by Erin Baiano.

used to poke fun at the clichés of the ballet trade while at the same time giving dancers the opportunity to show their mastery of its demands—*Stars and Stripes*, *Donizetti Variations*, for instance. I thought Wheeldon's dancers underplayed the humor of the situation, but probably that was better than outright farce.

Wheeldon channeled Balanchine's modern ballets in *Morphoses*, to the String Quartet no. 1, subtitled "Metamorphoses Nocturnes," of Gyorgy Ligeti, played by the FLUX Quartet. Wendy Whelan with Craig Hall and Sterling Hyltin with Edwaard Liang were the two couples in this 2002 ballet. To the knotty, atonal music, they extrapolated on the themes that begin *Four Temperaments*, the inversions and distortions that pull up short into classical poses throughout *Agon*.

A couple of Wheeldon's ballets had unorthodox musical settings. *There Where She Loved* (2000) alternated songs by Chopin and Kurt Weill (sung by soprano Kate Vetter Cain and mezzo Shelley Waite, accompanied by Cameron Grant). Vetter Cain's Russian romanticism was trumped by Waite's super-tragic interpretations of Weill songs that are better known through the rueful cynicism of Lotte Lenya. Wheeldon's eleven dancers assembled in various temporary relationships: passionate duets quickly cooled, a stud embraced, then discarded three women in turn, a male quartet manipulated a pliant Anastasia Yatsenko.

Mesmerics (2003) was set to selections by Philip Glass for eight cellos, seated in a row behind and slightly above the stage, and a string quartet in the pit. The seven dancers once again explored partnering in duets and trios, with acrobatic somersaults, flying women, and a few break-dance moves sewn in.

By the end of the second program Wheeldon seemed a less distinguished talent than I'd thought. You can't fault him for the overlong programs, the excessive trivia, and repetitious themes. Scheduling, rehearsing, and paying for your dream programming is so much more problematic if you work with a pickup company, but still. Let's see what Morphoses comes up with next time.

4 Balanchine Diaspora

MOZART VIOLIN CONCERTO

Christian Science Monitor, 14 November 1988

Reconstruction in dance means more than bricks and mortar. The largest part of the job, of course, is unearthing and learning the thousands of steps in a ballet that's been long out of the repertory or one that has belonged to different dancers. On top of that you have to make the ballet look right—by finding present-day equivalents of the original costumes and sets, by creating space designs that approximate the original, often with different numbers of dancers and types of stages. And perhaps the greatest challenge is to recreate the ballet's visual images, illusions, and metaphors.

Tulsa Ballet and Argentinean ballerina Esmeralda Agoglia have succeeded wonderfully, as far as I can tell, with their staging of George Balanchine's 1942 *Mozart Violin Concerto* (No. 5). The year-old production had its first New York performances in mid-October at Brooklyn College. Although the work was in almost continuous repertory for twenty years in Latin America, and has also been seen in Europe, it might as well have come from a pre-Columbian dig for all we knew of it here in the States. The best thing about the Tulsa revival is that it actually conveys an inner life that matches credibly with other things we know Balanchine was doing at the time.

The war years were tough ones for Balanchine. With the New York City Ballet not yet in existence, he struggled to keep his own dancers together while choreographing other people's musicals, movies, operas, and pièces d'occasion, in addition to ballets here and there. Yet he managed to produce the masterpieces *Ballet Imperial* and *Concerto Barocco*, and the first versions of the *Stravinsky Violin Concerto* (*Balustrade*) and *Danses Concertantes*. A 1941 goodwill tour sponsored by Nelson Rockefeller sent him to South America with Lincoln Kirstein's American Ballet Caravan, and a year later he created the *Mozart* during a residency with the Ballet of the Teatro Colón in Buenos Aires.

Working with unfamiliar dancers, Balanchine opted for a limited step vocabulary, a minimum of bravura solo work, and clear, readable group patterns. But the appearance of simplicity is deceptive. Within a perfectly formal, open structure, he implanted elements of drama, musical wit, and a surprising abundance of texture. The ballet introduces the female ensemble in groups of three with one foursome, thus allowing for both symmetricality and asymmetricality in the stage designs of succeeding passages. The uneven numbers also provide the corps with an odd-woman-out who can become a second lead dancer and insinuate dramatic possibilities where you'd expect only "pure dancing."

Balanchine's ability to transport you from the strict language of steps into a heightened realm of expression is constantly at work in *Mozart Violin Concerto*. In the slow second movement, at one point the ballerina floats in a balance on pointe, then falls back from the man's supporting arm. Members of the corps step behind both of them and gently propel them together again, as if they've detected some emotional trouble between them that must be quickly mended.

In this movement, essentially a long adagio pas de deux, the corps is always present, sometimes as witness, posing in lines and semicircles around the principal couple, and sometimes, strangely, forming little subgroups that seem engaged in their own private colloquies. Then, toward the end, the women become almost an abstraction, coming forward in a straight line so that they discreetly mask the solo man and woman just as she's fallen into his embrace.

In the lively third movement the proceedings get a little mad, picking up on Mozart's changes of mood. The music begins with a minuet, which Balanchine choreographs like a mazurka. The whirling "Turkish" section of the music he sets as a sort of tarantella. Various props are carried in and used by the dancers—soundless tambourines, lighted candelabras, long trumpets. It's as if the dancers are caught up in the musical hints of masquerade, but are too decorous ever to break ranks with their reveling comrades. But the props also remind us of other, much more conventional ballets, and the dancers might even be celebrating their release from the tedium of the standard repertory.

Mozart Violin Concerto was danced originally by one ballerina, though Balanchine apparently had hoped to find different dancers for the three stylistically different movements. Three dancers were scheduled for the Tulsa performances, although at the one I saw, Kimberly Smiley did the first two while Lisa Slagle sparkled in the demi-caractère finale. Smiley seemed less secure in the first movement, but she was unruffled and beautifully unmannered in the adagio. She was partnered by Matthew Bridwell for the first movement and Roman L. Jasinski for the second. Both men escorted Slagle in the finale, another example of Balanchine's originality.

Christian Science Monitor, 2 November 1988

The dance world has an almost primal ambivalence about its past, and the Joffrey Ballet revival of George Balanchine's famous lost ballet, *Cotillon*, is the latest subject of controversy. Even more than the Joffrey's *Le Sacre du Printemps*, revived last year by the same team, dance historian Millicent Hodson and art historian Kenneth Archer, *Cotillon* touched a lot of people's nostalgia nerve. Can a ballet that people remember with such affection ever be revived successfully? Some people think it's as hopeless as trying to bring back youth itself. On the other hand, if we let all the choreographic gems slip through the nets of time, the role models for the future can only be as good as the present crop, hardly a stimulating prospect.

Choreographed in 1932, *Cotillon* stayed in repertory until the mid-1940s, and people going to see ballet today can still remember it. This alone makes it more vulnerable than a work like the short-lived 1913 *Sacre*, which has few living eyewitnesses. The *Cotillon* that people saw in the '30s and '40s remains in mind untarnished by the subtle modifications that creep into ballets when they remain in active repertory. It's often attached to the most poignant impressions of their own youth, the discovery of beauty and glamour, and the poetry of expectation. That, in fact, is what *Cotillon* itself is about.

After the death of Serge Diaghilev in 1929 and the collapse of his innovative Ballets Russes, his prodigious collaborators scattered in search of working venues and audiences receptive to modernism. Balanchine tried out several situations before coming to rest in America in 1934, and *Cotillon* was created during his short-lived tenure as ballet master for René Blum's post-Diaghilev Ballets Russes de Monte Carlo. The ballet is loaded with portents and harbingers of Balanchine's later career, and even of its own eclipse.

Balanchine's inspiration for the work was the presence of three extraordinary teenage dancers he had discovered, Tamara Toumanova, Irina Baronova and Tatiana Riabouchinska. These girls became the first of Balanchine's "baby ballerinas" and the source of his well-known penchant for giving the most surprising new roles to the youngest of his dancers. Not only did *Cotillon* exploit the technical abilities of the three ingénues, it captured the tremulous quality of their adolescence—and perhaps also the fevered, transitional state of the world between the wars.

The ballet was a huge success, with its drifty, dreamy costumes by the painter Christian Bérard and its effervescent Chabrier music, tartly orchestrated by Vittorio Rieti. It became a mainstay of the company long after Balanchine departed. It finally expired with the decline of the Monte Carlo itself, and Balanchine never added it to the repertory of the New York City Ballet, claiming it was too intimately tied to the extreme naiveté and freshness of its original dancers.

Robert Joffrey, always looking to preserve the choicest examples of choreographic history, decided that Hodson and Archer could recapture *Cotillon* after their successful reconstruction of *Le Sacre*, and they settled their plans before he died last March. For the past year the team, based in London, has been commuting between hemispheres to interview surviving members of the succeeding generations of casts. Each ballerina added what she could remember, often demonstrating the steps to the recorded music. Aside from two films taken in performances, neither one complete, and a large file of clippings and photographs, there were no documents of the ballet. Hodson had to assemble the steps and floor patterns for the twenty-five dancers and six sections of the ballet, then stage it all in a replica of the original sets and costumes supervised by Archer. Hodson has said that in a way, the reconstruction of *Cotillon* was harder than *Sacre* because so many people did know it, and the versions they performed through the years were different.

Never having seen *Cotillon* in any form, I found the return of the work a momentous event. Any hitherto unknown Balanchine that's brought into the light is bound to be interesting, and the Joffrey dancers seem to have caught some of the spirit that the work's supposed to have. But seeing it now, I understand why it's a tricky enterprise.

The ballet is a clear choreographic bridge between the lush, narrative Diaghilev era ballets and the neoclassic austerity of the latter-day Balanchine. It does, however, represent a strain of romanticism and fantasy that the choreographer kept to the end of his life. It's not typical Balanchine. In fact, one of the older ballerinas told Hodson the present New York City Ballet style of dancing would be all wrong for it. I think Balanchine in 1932 was not only trying to be original, he was trying to evade the formula party-ballets that lured audiences. Being Balanchine even then, he used the formula, only to thwart it at every turn. *Cotillon* is a young girl's debut party, with obligatory virtuoso variations, love duet, ensemble designs, funny characters—choreographic building blocks that had been put together for years, especially by Balanchine's rival Léonide Massine, who, ironically, replaced Balanchine as ballet master at the Monte Carlo when the 1932 season was scarcely cold.

What Balanchine did so daringly was to eliminate story line and non-dancing characters, and let the ballet slide, almost unconsciously, into near-sinister intimations of heartbreak, scary portents of adult responsibility, and maybe even a fatalistic glimpse of the end of an era. Its hold on the imagination comes from many layers of glamour and insinuation.

The debutante and her best friend find themselves rivals for the same young man, a triangle that has its formal echo in the corps groupings of two women partnered by a man. There are scraps of high jinks—a harlequin dance, a jockey dance. In the midst of a Spanish dance the young girl strums a guitar, and her friend plucks at the strings from behind her, embracing and at the same time entrapping her.

Suddenly all the guests are gone and one man we haven't seen before finds himself dancing with a woman in a black dress with golden stars on it: the celebrated Hand of Fate duet. She twines her long black gloves around him, slithers voluptuously along his back, drapes herself in his arms. He hides his eyes in enchantment, or terror. When the guests come back, the heroine reads palms lightheartedly, until she finds something awful in one girl's hand. She draws away from the celebrants, has disturbing visions, clings to a momentarily sympathetic Mistress of Ceremonies, rushes through a ritualistic double line of friends, and finally vanishes behind some screens. Balanchine doesn't explain the girl's upset or her untroubled reappearance a few minutes later, as if it were all a party trick.

Just when you think order and gaiety have been restored, the guests rollick away in a farandole and the girl is left alone. She starts spinning, one leg whipping out like a hand warding off danger, and she's still whirling when everyone comes snake-dancing back. The last thing you see is her turning, turning, arms flung up, in the center of a turbulent spiral of tulle.

Tina LeBlanc was wonderful as the Young Girl, looking small and young, and also strong enough to survive more than adolescent trauma. Beatrice Rodriguez as the Hand of Fate and Glenn Edgerton as her cavalier suddenly made flirtation a grown-up game. Others in the excellent first cast were Carol Valleskey as the friend, Edward Stierle as the fickle young man, and Jerel Hilding and Leslie Carothers as the Master and Mistress of Ceremonies.

FABLE IN A LUCITE LANDSCAPE

Ballet Review, Fall 1991

Only seven years after the creation of *La Chatte*, George Balanchine told the English ballet critic Arnold Haskell that the ballet was "quite impossible now." *Chatte* (1927) and *Barabau* (1925), said the choreographer, "were made in another time. I have seen them both since their creation. They seemed very dull indeed. So many things have happened since."[1] This potent remark is an early sign of Balanchine's lifelong focus on the present and his disdain for his past creations, especially when they fell into the hands of others. Balanchine's prolific output, minus certain works he judged unsuitable, did serve for thirty-five years as equity in the New York City Ballet repertory, and I think we would be foolish to take his lifelong eagerness to burn his bridges and advance his own learning process as a definition of what is a dull or an interesting ballet.

In his view, his ballets were connected to the time, the place and the circumstances in which they were made. To revive the most site-specific of them at a later time, in different circumstances, not only didn't interest him, it could seem a negative way to represent someone whose energies were always moving forward. While he was alive, we could move on with him to the next phase, but now that his exploratory process has ceased, every work of his reveals something, fills in the puzzle of his creativity. Among the disinherited, for example, *Cotillon*, *Bourrée Fantasque*, and the original version of *Square Dance*, reconstituted outside the NYCB, even managed to hold their own in modern times.

Les Grands Ballets Canadiens' commitment to restoring *La Chatte* seemed clouded by a too-literal adherence to Balanchinian ahistoricism. The project was assigned to the meticulous researchers Millicent Hodson and Kenneth Archer, and the original Naum Gabo/Anton Pevsner constructivist sets and costumes were smartly copied under scenic coordinator Gilbert Grondin. It should have been a major event in the dance world. But the company did little to promote or place the reconstruction as anything more than one component of a five-performance bill that included *Serenade* and *The Green Table*. The program, titled "Les Années Folles" (the English alternative was "Glamour Years"), absurdly proposed that ballets from France in 1927, Germany in 1932, and America in 1935 could have come out of a single cultural milieu. *La Chatte* is not on Les Grands' schedule for next season, which leaves it hanging once more over the cliff of oblivion.

One reason, I think, for the company's ambivalence about it is that it's not perceived as a "dance ballet," and indeed it falls into the lint-encrusted cracks between the character and ritualistic one-acters of the prewar Diaghilev years and the new vistas opened up by Balanchine once he landed in America. *La Chatte* was born in the fertile decade between Balanchine's exit from Russia in 1924 and his arrival in the United States. During that time he worked wherever he found opportunity and sponsorship. In the

La Chatte (Balanchine). Serge Lifar and Olga Spessivtseva, Diaghilev's Ballets Russes. The Howard D. Rothschild Collection, The Harvard Theatre Collection, Houghton Library, © The George Balanchine Trust.

years following *Chatte* he choreographed nearly three dozen operas, a film, and four shows; restaged several early-Diaghilev ballets for the Danes; explored surrealism and Greek myth; and made *Le Bal*, *Cotillon*, the first *Mozartiana*, *Apollo*, *Prodigal Son*, and a clutch of lesser items. He was figuring out what modes of dance were going to be most productive for him, discarding overt narrative and scenic spectacle as primary vehicles. He was devising his own dance lexicon and symbol systems. It's natural that in 1934 he would dismiss what must have seemed a very minor experiment. Granted that *La Chatte* is not all dancing, that it's "dated" (a term that removes its subject arbitrarily to the rubbish heap of history). These aspects of Balanchine are fascinating precisely because they've been suppressed, and the renewal of a ballet like *La Chatte* allows us to examine them for the first time in sixty years.

La Chatte first of all is a story ballet on its way to abstraction. Boris Kochno devised the scenario based on the fable of a young man in love with a cat. Aphrodite turns her into a woman but then sends a mouse to test her. She reverts to her feline nature, eludes her lover's restraining embrace, and runs off after the mouse. The young man dies of a broken heart. Cyril Beaumont points out that in the original fable the cat begs to be transformed because of her love for the young man, and only then does her temptation and relapse make moral sense.[2]

This cavalier subversion of text in the service of stage expedience is not unusual, and it's not the only aspect of the ballet that doesn't make sense. But the lapses in strict logic might also be seen as analogous to the cubist and constructivist processes that Diaghilev was so eager to commandeer for dancing, in order to attract an audience of art lovers. Like a splintered guitar in a Picasso still life, *La Chatte*'s movement, its story, and its stage environment contain the outlines of real antecedents, but the outlines aren't complete shapes and they're embedded in unrelated patterns. They form themselves just long enough to shadow the dance with imagery but not long enough to take over and divert attention from the dance. The soft, fugitive references to romanticism in *Serenade* show Balanchine working with this device at its peak of refinement.

The movement sources of *La Chatte* are eclectic: mime and animal imitation of course, the attitudes of Greek athletes and Riviera beach boys, circus acrobatics, ballet classicism straight and skewed. None of these categories was new to the ballet stage in 1927. One of the most interesting things about seeing the ballet in the flesh was discovering how it linked together Balanchine's past and future experiences. Its nearest relations seem to be *Apollo* and *Prodigal Son*, and, more distantly, *Serenade*. But it also has absorbed the fervid chic of the '20s Ballets Russes, the severe modernism of Nijinsky, ideas from the Soviet progressives, and, most surprising of all, a nostalgic essence of *The Sleeping Beauty*.

It seems to me that the problem for all ballet producers in the '20s was to discover new ways to represent dancing and the dancer. Nineteenth-century emperors and empresses with their courts and their fairy-tale familiars were no longer suitable to the modern world of technology, science, and urbanism. Who then was the dancer to impersonate? Other ballets of the period featured scenes from life à la mode (*Les Biches, Le Train Bleu, Skating Rink, Within the Quota*). There were machine ballets (*Le Pas d'Acier*), and modernist collages (*La Création du Monde, Relâche, Ode*). In *La Chatte* Balanchine seems to have been trying for a dance image that wouldn't be overtaken by literal models from either art or life. He made a synthesis of three popular modes of representation: the Greek athlete as idealized human being, the animal as sensual and possibly magical being, and the technological being shaped by the gloss and dynamism of a machine-made environment. Although there are glimpses of "everyday" behavior—this is, after all, only three years after the sporty frolics of *Le Train Bleu*—Balanchine never really reverts to this particular formula of modernity.

The Young Man's six Companions in *Chatte*, though dressed in trunks and given to flexing their biceps, are simultaneously an Olympian guard of honor. Their job is to glorify the hero by creating a frieze of noble poses behind him, and by forming a chariot, pyramids, and finally a funeral cortège on which to bear him aloft. Instead of making traditionally decorative formations, they climb on each other's thighs and lock arms to create geometric structures in the manner of Goleizovsky's *Afternoon of a Faun*. Some of their unison movements recall the mechanistic exercises of Foregger and the other Soviet experimenters who attracted Balanchine's interest before he emigrated to Europe. In *La Chatte* Balanchine was trying out the idea of a male corps de ballet, without borrowing the courtly mannerisms of a classical corps. They leap and turn, but they moderate their rhythms, flatten out space into scroll-like pathways, show their upper bodies in profile. Strength, masculinity, and beauty of physique mark this corps as contemporary. Two years later Balanchine transformed it into a pack of grotesque hooligans in *Prodigal Son*.

The hero of *La Chatte* also dresses like a sunburned god, but his athletic interactions with the companions are only an introduction to a more fully worked out character. Balanchine gives him an expressive solo of slow, continuous poses, beginning on the floor and escalating into large jumps and stretches, as he discovers and yearns after the cat who's peeking through a porthole in the Plexiglas scenery. His later duet with the cat in woman's form upsets the classical stereotype of the male partner as a cipher who holds up the woman almost invisibly in order to show her off to the audience. In *La Chatte* the duet is physically intimate, even erotic. The cat coils and lounges around the young man's body and he seems less to be supporting her than embracing her, stroking her, making his body a cushion for her to repose on. This young man is certainly a prototype for *Apollo*, and the resemblance becomes more obvious when we remember that Serge Lifar originated both roles.

Olga Spessivtseva created the cat in Monte Carlo but became injured before the Paris premiere a month later, and the role was taken over by Alice Nikitina, who also danced the first Terpsichore in *Apollo*. Possibly the internal politics of the Ballets Russes, and Lifar's gift for self-promotion, gave him the principal spotlight in *La Chatte*. But the cat herself is a creature of great charm, and she was marvelously realized in one of the Montreal casts by Yvonne Cutaran. The other cat, Anik Bissonnette, and the two young men, Kenneth Larson and David Michael Cohen, were exemplary '90s dancers, technically clean, likable—and without personality. But Cutaran really worked the role, and showed me a kind of stylishness that must have contributed greatly to the ballet's initial success.

Perhaps she would be considered too "feminine" today, but the Ballets Russes's late audiences loved adorable women of the stage—Josephine Baker, Adele Astaire, Mistinguette, Danilova in Massine's character ballets. For the *Chatte* Balanchine found ingenious ways to combine cat gestures, well established since *Sleeping Beauty*, with kittenish gestures of flirtatious modern women and capers from social dances like the Charleston—the asymmetrical body line, lifted shoulder, tilted head, poking elbows, tucked in knees with flicked out toes. His cat is mysteriously neither a real girl nor a pretend animal, she could only be a danced persona.

This dream-person, in her clear plastic tutu with gunmetal headdress that suggests both Irene Castle's Dutch cap and the ears of a cat, seems perfectly at home in the ramps and spheres of Gabo and Pevsner's set. When the young man goes in search of her, he seems to be traversing a forest in miniature. He sees her first, just a few feet away, as if from a huge distance, and they touch with a circle of Lucite between them, as if looking into a double-sided mirror. I thought this was a contemporary version of *Sleeping Beauty*'s vision scene.

Another machine-age reference to the Petipa classic was the statue of

Aphrodite. Enthroned high above the rest of the set, the goddess is made of discs and cylindrical plastic, an elusive deus ex machina. Somehow I never caught the moment when the young man appealed to this presence. I didn't see her first acquiescence to his wishes or her later malicious decision to send in the mouse. I was interested to learn that some viewers of the original production had the same confusion. In fact Aphrodite is little more in this production than a statue. Perhaps Balanchine was willing to leave her mostly to the imagination, and in mine she doubled as the Lilac Fairy, except of course that she turned out to be far from benevolent in the end.

Perhaps it's reaching too far, but I want to suggest that in this transparent, sculptural object Balanchine was able to fix the image of the Lilac Fairy, and to let layers of meaning accumulate around her. Aphrodite, the goddess of love, the commanding, otherworldly mother figure, can reverse fate, can give the gifts of love and humanity, and can also take them away. Later Balanchine set this character in motion again and again, in ballets as diverse as *Serenade*, *Ballet Imperial*, and *Rubies*.

La Chatte belongs to its time, a jazz-age ballet, a precursor of neoclassicism in movement and musicality. With its lightweight score by Henri Sauguet, its deco environment, it also belongs to its place, the intimate theaters of Paris, London, and Monte Carlo. Montreal's vast Salle Wilfrid-Pelletier was a particularly inauspicious place for its rebirth. Marooned in aisleless rows of some 120 seats, seemingly miles from the stage, the audience converses idly through overtures, clings for dear life to its acquaintances, needs stupendous effects to work up its excitement. And the dancers, especially the dispirited-looking Olympian companions, must have felt they didn't have enough to do to fill that huge cavern. *La Chatte* in this setting seemed a miniaturized edition of a big ballet, instead of a little gem.

Nevertheless, I found it an invigorating experience. In a way, I was grateful that there hadn't been much advance publicity. I was unable to get to Montreal for any of Hodson's pre-performance talks, which only happened on the first of the two weekends. Besides, I found very little had been written about the ballet originally. These lapses allowed me to see it almost as if it was new, but more than new, because its accretions of historical precedent and progeny were just waiting to be uncovered. I would need to see it more times, and to know more about Hodson's research, to decide about its "authenticity." I hope, through the work of Hodson and other reconstructors, we're learning that even with some of the information missing, getting these archival works on the stage is important. Spectators and former participants, when they have a chance to look at a lost ballet, may be able to add more about steps, patterns, style. Only in performance can dancers discover how to "wear" them. We know where Balanchine had been and what must have influenced him at the time he made *La Chatte*. Hodson knew this, and she had concrete though fragmentary information from several sources. One of my biggest questions was whether the connections I saw were in the original, or whether they were devised by Hodson, astutely figuring out how Balanchine might have worked. Maybe it doesn't matter. I'm willing to say this *La Chatte* illuminates ballet history, whoever did it.

MIAMI CITY BALLET

Christian Science Monitor, 3 February 1989

Miami City Ballet has a lot of civic and critical hype behind it. But three years is too short a time to prove either the staying power or the creative and interpretive drive that marks a major ballet institution. It may be that the local fervor on the company's behalf is more of an investment in the city's renaissance as a cultural mecca, and the critical acclaim might not be quite so extravagant if the ballet world weren't suffering the loss of all its classical leaders at the moment. Opening a weekend of performances at Bailey Concert Hall on the Broward Community College campus, the company was maintaining the high technical standard we saw when they made a touring appearance in New York last year. This in itself is a good sign. Dancers are easily changed into conceited monsters by exaggerated reviews, but so far these heads have not been turned.

Artistic director Edward Villella has made it a high priority to challenge the dancers with George Balanchine's ballets, and the latest addition to Miami City's repertory is *Divertimento No. 15*. This work calls for a sweetness and delicate clarity to match its Mozart score. Although there's a modest little ensemble of eight women, the charm of *Divertimento* is soloistic. Five women are partnered by three men in a series of solos and duets, and it's like listening to a fairy tale told by several different narrators. No one has to carry the whole burden of the plot, but each contributes another embellishment to the adventure that's unfolding. The storytellers, all entertaining and evenly matched, were Kathleen Smith, Elizabeth Dretzin, Maribel Modrono, Marcia Sussman, David Palmer, Marielena Mencia, Paulo Manso de Sousa, and Brooks White.

The eighteenth-century style of *Divertimento* suits these dancers, and they looked even more engaging, I thought, in Daniel Levans's *Cothen Suite*. Levans says this ballet was "inspired" by Eliot Feld's *Meadowlark*. It seems rather to contain large chunks of Feld's rarely performed 1968 work, including the youthful good spirits that I remember fondly about Feld's first dancers. Levans wisely didn't borrow some of the more oafish jokes in the original, but preserved the light, formal style.

Besides the steady development of a classical style, Villella is working on the crucial problem of repertory. He himself seems to have no great choreographic ambitions, which can be an advantage in providing the dancers and audience with stylistic diversity. Besides commissioning ballets from visiting artists like Levans and dipping into the non-Balanchine repertory for revivals, Villella is cultivating a young Peruvian dancer/choreographer, Jimmy Gamonet de los Heros.

Gamonet had two new works on the Bailey Hall performances, bringing his contribution to a total of eight ballets. This is a lot for any choreographer to manage in three years, and in a rather touching recent interview, Gamonet admitted he was being pushed to create at a tremendous rate. He knew he had a lot to learn and was eager for the opportunity. From the new works and *Transtangos*, which the company brought to New York last year, he seems to have a good sense for formal patterns and vocabulary, but although he can adopt various surface styles, they don't integrate with the steps to make a metaphor.

Reus, to a percussion score by contemporary Hungarian composer Istvan Marta, was one of those showpieces that ballet companies seem compelled to put on in order to prove the virility of their male dancers. Seven barechested men ran, spun, jumped, and modeled their bodies in a dramatically lit space. Sometimes they sat sternly in chairs—those trademark props of European modernism. Yanis Pikieris and Paulo Manso de Sousa danced separately from the corps of five, and the program explained this as "the drama of Jury, Judge, and the Accused."

Caplet, to music by Andre Caplet, was either based on Edgar Allan Poe's "Masque of the Red Death," or it was not. Conflicting messages were given both in the program and on the stage. This ballet too had a strong ensemble section—perhaps a ballroom scene—that seemed to have nothing to do with the four soloists. Franklin Gamero slumped in a shadowy throne much of the time. Twin attendants, Mabel and Maribel Modrono, seemed to be urging him to cheer up, or leave the country.

A hooded figure appeared and frightened the party guests away. Gamero danced distractedly, and when the apparition reappeared he pulled off its cloak and revealed Iliana Lopez in a flesh-colored leotard. They danced a duet in which it was difficult to tell whether she was supposed to be alive or dead, whether they were in love or hypnotized, or even sharing the same state of consciousness. At the climax, he kissed her passionately, left her to expire on the floor, and returned to his throne.

 ## UR-TEXTS

Boston Phoenix, 12 June 1998

Since the death of George Balanchine, fifteen years ago now, the choreographer's work occupies less and less of the ballet repertory, and his whole enterprise descends into the murk of mythology. Saturday night's recital program of the Massachusetts Youth Ballet, at Robsham Theater, Boston College, offered an intelligent case for classical ballet, and especially for the vitality of Balanchine as danced by an eager and devotedly trained new generation of dancers.

Massachusetts Youth Ballet is a preprofessional group out of the Ballet Workshop of New England, directed by Jacqueline Cronsberg. To say that this is a student company isn't to imply you shouldn't expect fine dancing. The most poignant aspect of the performance was that so many of the participants looked technically accomplished and hungry to be tested in the fires of regular performing life—but they can expect few opportunities as challenging as the work they've just completed.

Ballet isn't just dancing on the toes, or hurling oneself around with passionate gestures. Saturday night's program demonstrated a fine continuum of discipline, from the nineteenth-century Russian classics to the reformer Michel Fokine to Balanchine, the master choreographer of our time. Having absorbed the glitter and virtuosity of Marius Petipa (represented Saturday night by the Kingdom of the Shades scene from *La Bayadère*), and the distillations of Fokine (as in the Waltz from *Les Sylphides*, transparent as an 1840 lithograph), Balanchine made a life work of re-orchestrating a lexicon of steps and theatrical conventions. Somehow, he never ran out of ways to do this, or of dancers who would go along with his game as far as he wanted to entice them.

One of those willing conspirators, Gloria Govrin, was on hand Saturday to talk about dancing and taking class with Balanchine. In the 1960s and 1970s, the big, powerful Govrin demolished the stereotype of the Balan-

Serenade (Balanchine). Larissa Ponomarenko and Roman Rykine,
Boston Ballet. Photo by Sabi Varga, © The George Balanchine Trust.

chine dancer as small, delicate, and submissive. At the New York City
Ballet I loved her authority and sensuality in classical roles, especially the
important "extra woman" who leads so many Balanchine ensembles.

Govrin was entertaining at the Robsham, but it was the ballets that
spoke most eloquently of what choreography can do for dancers, and what
worlds it can open for us. *Serenade* (1935) was the first thing Balanchine
choreographed in America, for the first dancers in his school. Placed on
the program after the grand illusion of the twenty-four Shades majestically
sweeping down a ramp, and the ethereal waltzing Sylphides, the sixteen
women in *Serenade* look plain and prim at the beginning, as they carve
their arms through the air, snap their feet into first position. But out of
these first classroom moves they build the most unimaginable and un-
equalled drama of patterns and designs.

The company omitted the mysterious and somber last movement of
Serenade, perhaps because it requires five men and male students are in
short supply at the Ballet Workshop. It was strange to see the piece end as
one of the soloists (Emily Waters) falls and all her companions leave. Yet it
left me with a strong impression of heartbreak; as if she'd suddenly realized
how wonderful it was to be young, and she'd remember the innocent and

harmonious friends, the waltzing with her first partner, the absolute joy of mastering one's body in a perfect pirouette. This image might not have struck me except that the dancers really were that young and expectant.

With tiny variations from two other ballets and a complete Divertimento from *Le Baiser de la Fée*, the company probed the remarkable range of Balanchine's thought. He could tackle Stravinsky's acerbic and syncopated modernisms (*Agon*) or the most engaging popular song ("Embraceable You" from *Who Cares?*). He could clean most of the story out of a Russian fairy tale (*Baiser*) and still show us a troubled love affair and a separation that turns into a final farewell. He could do this with classical steps and music and very little else, except his monumental creativity, of course.

For me the most enlightening part of Gloria Govrin's presentation was her discussion of Balanchine technique. Dancer Sophie Forman-Flack demonstrated a whole series of steps and combinations in both the "old Russian" style and the Balanchine revisions. Never has it been so clear what gives his dancing its attack, its directness and speed.

IN SEARCH OF REPERTORY

Boston Phoenix, 2 April 1999

While Boston Ballet was finishing up its "Balanchine!" programs at the Wang Center, another Balanchine work was being presented by Hartford Ballet down at Bushnell Auditorium. Getting to see *Serenade, Divertimento No. 15, The Four Temperaments*, and *Rubies* all in one week is a rare treat. But rarity is exactly the problem. An occasional crack at a master choreographer doesn't allow dancers to push past the terrifying challenge into a more assured interpretation. For the audience, Balanchine becomes just another novelty, one that lacks the obvious, audience-friendly tricks in more modern pieces.

One of the many singular aspects of dance as a performing art is that its repertory, whether old or new, doesn't "exist" in the way a play or an opera does. Productions of old works are often called "reconstructions," meaning that before they can be learned, rehearsed, and staged, they have to be re-created. Sometimes there's a film or a written score from a past production that gives a pretty complete account of the choreography, but revivals often follow a scenario embedded in the memory of a dancer. And no ordinary dancer, but one with a comprehensive grasp of all the steps done by the whole cast, not just the part she may have danced herself. Victoria

Simon, who staged the Boston and Hartford revivals, is one of the most trusted Balanchine repetiteurs, yet the Hartford and Boston recons differed, mainly in the matter of style.

One of the distinctions of Balanchine ballet is the stylistic imprint his dancers acquired. Some people call it American, some call it contemporary, but Balanchine dancing has a jazzy ease, a sharp attack, a musical assurance. Balanchine dancing, of course, doesn't "exist" either, except as a composite of wonderful things seen, remembered, and newly animated. The dancers may be doing the hardest step combinations in the world, but they can take minor liberties with the beat, lengthen or quicken the phrase, so that the performance radiates a joy that has nothing to do with smiling all the time.

Sometimes, individual moments of expression like this can illuminate a whole sequence. *Serenade* (1935) revisits the sighs and vapors of the Romantic ballet. Without a literal plot, Balanchine suggests the temporal and the supernatural worlds where courage and betrayal, love and death, co-existed on the Romantic stage. The totemic nineteenth-century ballet, *Giselle*, comes to mind in *Serenade* at the odd beginning of the last movement, where a ballerina lies on the floor and is solemnly approached by a man with another woman clinging to his back and covering his eyes.

But much earlier, implanted in the formal choreography, another woman falls in the same position. One night in Boston Pollyana Ribeiro anticipated that fall with a slight intake of breath, then got up with a dismissive glance. It was like the moment early in *Giselle* when the heroine has a dizzy spell while dancing, then recovers and shrugs it off. Her weakness will be fatal, and tragic. Ribeiro's fall brought all of that back and imposed the spirit of *Giselle* onto *Serenade* from that moment on.

It goes without saying that Balanchine dancers have to be technical virtuosos, even the corps de ballet. His total output constitutes probably the most exacting use of the classical ballet vocabulary that has ever been made, and I think it's for this reason that it needs to be performed. Balanchine isn't just another different-looking item in a repertory but an extreme test of what dancers can do. A Balanchine ballet may also be pretty, fast, spiky, sexy, or spectacular, but so are other ballets. It's the steps—their complexity, visual design, and resonance—that make these ballets so rich.

The steps can be simplified, and we in the audience might not consciously notice if the dancers do four foot beats instead of six, throw their leg in the air instead of placing it, or make a straight leg gesture instead of a circular one. But the dance won't look extraordinary. Of the Boston dancers, Ribeiro, Jennifer Gelfand, Adriana Suárez, and Aleksandra Koltun seemed consistently in command of the vocabulary and able to make those idiomatic decisions that brought it alive.

The others got through it with varying degrees of suavity. One bland performance of *Divertimento* made me understand why audiences sometimes consider Balanchine just so much boring technique. You could say Balanchine is nothing but steps, but those steps are like a story, full of events and reflections. Dancers don't always trust their own ability to make steps into narrative. In *The Four Temperaments* (1946) some of the opening-night cast, including up-and-coming American Ballet Theatre star Giuseppe Picone, mistook the musical titles for acting indications. I think for Balanchine the connection was so remote it was almost subliminal. In any case, Picone in the Melancholic variation and Gianni Di Marco in the Phlegmatic couldn't let the kinky classicism tell their story but dramatized what was already distorted.

Incidentally, the company made the peculiar decision to list Kurt Seligmann as the designer of *The Four Temperaments* without explaining that his designs are gone. Balanchine started stripping off the excessive decorations as soon as he saw these elaborate affairs, and by 1951 *Four T's* was down to the practice clothes in which it's danced now.

Balanchine's late Stravinsky ballets push the idea of distortion to the zenith. Instead of a pure upright vertical body line, the dancers often tilt off center. Their gestures may be broken up or angular or rotated outward with extra torque. The Hartford dancers really got into the extremity of *Rubies*, pushing their pelvises forward and crooking up their elbows, and doing the picky footwork as if it were some arcane form of tap dancing. The audience was underwhelmed.

But after Kathryn Posin's men-women-and-selves ballet, *Stepping Stones*, they cheered a lot. Posin's piece, created in 1993 for the Milwaukee Ballet, is one solution to the problem of repertory and also shows how choreographers can keep working when it's too expensive to have their own companies. Posin, a modern dancer, has been freelancing for a while. She uses pointe work, but only in a simple way. Balanchine is the most convincing argument that ballet is more than standing on the pointes and doing various acrobatic feats with a partner. Well, maybe the audience does want the acrobatics and fake love scenes right now instead of the intricacies of high-style classicism.

Stepping Stones has six women in short tunics and pointe shoes, six barefoot women in bodysuits, six men in trunks, and six graduated platforms with funny tilted bits of railings on the upstage side. The tunic women do something like barre exercises on the platforms. The other women loll on the floor a lot. The men hurl macho moves around and finally hurl the women around. One man and one woman separate from the others and help each other step from one platform to the next. These are placed far enough apart that the dancers have to stretch and twist each other to reach them. Aside from the opportunity to look at their bodies working so hard, I could see no reason why they weren't allowed to step on the floor. In a final section all eighteen dancers were stretching and lolling without taking advantage of the unifying structure of Joan Tower's piano-and-percussion score. The program told about this work's "exploring the relationships of women, their strengths and weaknesses, and their ability to reach out to each other for support and affirmation," but with a little wit the piece could have been a takeoff on the competitiveness and sexual deprivation of dance company life.

Seriousness and high moral tone were amply provided in the Hartford's last piece, *Acts of Light*, by Martha Graham. This late work, the most extended and to me the least engaging of several classroom ballets Graham made, *Light* is a kind of bare-bones recapitulation of earlier Graham duets and rituals, ending with an extended demonstration of Graham technique for a large ensemble. It has a lush orchestral score by Carl Nielsen. (All the music on this program was taped and played too loud, as if excessive volume would make us feel there was a live orchestra. It actually makes the music sound more artificial.)

GUARDING THE LEGACY

Boston Phoenix, 22 September 2000

The most important thing you can do for great works of art is to preserve them—but it's a vexing paradox of dance that preservation doesn't mean packing the work in tissue paper and sealing it in a vault. Dance has no complacent final option; you can't look it up and find it any time, safely on display in a good museum, or dust it off and expect it to perform with the turn of a key. There have to be dancers who love the strangeness of a past idiom and who have the unaccustomed skills to perform it. And coaches who can legislate stylistic essentials, fend off extravagance, reconstitute what's disintegrated since the last outing. You have to have institutions that honor the work and will accept its cost. You have to have audiences that care.

So though we all take George Balanchine for granted as the towering giant of twentieth-century choreography, his actual work is known to fewer and fewer people now that he's been gone almost two decades. Which is why the Kennedy Center's Balanchine Celebration was such a gift to the nation. The festival brought together five American ballet companies and one from Russia, for four different programs, fourteen ballets, choreographed during half a century. The unprecedented event, three years in the making, was dreamed up by Charles and Stephanie Reinhart, the Kennedy Center's artistic directors for dance, with the collaboration of the Balanchine Trust and financial and artistic help from too many sources to mention.

I saw the event as a confirmation of the Balanchine diaspora, an acknowledgment that the center for his work may already be shifting from his home company, New York City Ballet, to a diffuse network of interpreters. The choreography of the first two programs was quite varied, asking to be taken both on its own terms and as an arena for differing sensibilities. I tried to project myself a few more years into the future, when no one will have seen any performances Balanchine himself directed, when there's no little nagging voice inside us that misses Patricia McBride's wit or Gloria Govrin's statuesque développé or the long history of dancers who are imprinted on favorite roles. There's no doubt in my mind that his ballets will stand up then, and also that they will have escaped the restrictive stylistic notions we may have about them now. This won't be a good thing or a bad thing; it will happen, and I'd rather have different tones of Balanchine than no Balanchine at all.

The six companies came by their Balanchine inheritance in a wide variety of ways. New York City Ballet, his most direct heir, developed with him in a symbiotic fifty-year artistic inquiry. City Ballet didn't participate in the Celebration because of its prohibitive musician-union contracts, but three of the companies that did are direct spin-offs, with a heavy emphasis on Balanchine in their repertories. The directors of Miami City Ballet (Edward Villella), San Francisco Ballet (Helgi Tomasson), and Suzanne Farrell Ballet were all notable NYCB dancers, and very different Balanchine dancers— Villella the virtuosic extrovert; Tomasson the reserved, impeccable aristocrat; Farrell the expressive feminine muse—but all of them were superb classicists. The Joffrey, the Bolshoi, and the Pennsylvania Ballets maintain their Balanchine connections within more eclectic agendas. The four companies I saw last week did seem to have distinctive ideas about Balanchine. Perhaps it's only another reflection of Balanchine's remarkable range that he can supply many different directorial objectives.

Miami City Ballet dominated last week's programs, with four major ballets that showcased the company's energetic, personable dancing. *Rubies*

Rubies (Balanchine). Jennifer Kronenberg and dancers, Miami
City Ballet. Photo by Joe Gato, © The George Balanchine Trust.

(Stravinsky) was choreographed in 1967 on Edward Villella and still has the
spirited flamboyance I remember from its early days: the strutting, circusy
promenades; the galloping chases; the daredevil movement feats; the pas
de deux with the unexpected balances, sudden falls, and tricky, almost
accidental embracings. There's even a moment of mystery, like a suspense-
ful magic act, when the secondary woman stands still and lets four men
steer her around into a web of intricate positions.

Stars and Stripes (1958) also features Balanchine the showman, but his
references here were Busby Berkeley and the American marching band. In
three of the five sections, squads of twelve women or men with their leaders simply parade on into a wedge shape and go through various formations, mostly in unison. The leaders all have special tricks—baton twirling,
pointe work, complicated turns—building up to the principal man and
woman, who get the stage all to themselves and have the flashiest moves.
All the squads return at the end for a big chorus and a dramatic presentation of the flag. This ballet was made as an outright audience pleaser;
Balanchine never apologized for his appropriations of popular culture.

The big, unfolding symphonic ballet form, which *Stars and Stripes* typifies despite its glitz, actually solidified in the 1940s, before New York City Ballet was permanently established. *Four Temperaments* (1946) predated NYCB's official debut by two years. You could say it's the first modern restatement of his big-ballet format. Again, it has four sections with entirely different casts that lead into an ensemble finale. But here the soloists are the main subject and the corps is reduced to a scant fourteen. For additional variety he introduced the whole process with three couples who illustrate the structure of the music, Paul Hindemith's *Theme with Four Variations*, for piano and strings. *Agon* (1957) explores the corps-and-solo form even more adventurously, according to Stravinsky's sparse, atonal score, with angular movements and quickly shifting linkages among the twelve dancers. *Agon* has the same tightrope riskiness as *Rubies*, though one dance is high art and one is show biz.

It was great to see how eagerly the Miami City Ballet dancers worked at conquering these truly difficult ballets, almost as if they were creating something new. The Joffrey performances were smoother and maybe more accomplished, but the ballets it chose were admitted crowd pleasers. Balanchine was no slouch at producing an old-time, hit-'em-between-the-eyes pas de deux (*Tarantella*, 1964) when he needed one for the repertory. And it's astonishing to realize that the same year as the groundbreaking *Agon*, he made *Square Dance*, with its self-conscious nod to American folk traditions.

The Joffrey Ballet revived *Square Dance* in 1971, complete with its original square-dance caller urging on the dancers and reminding the audience to watch their feet go wickety-wack. When New York City Ballet took the work back into the repertory five years later, it was probably no longer necessary to point out the relationship between square dancing and ballet dancing; the caller was dropped and we simply saw seven sets of partners dancing balletic squares and contras to the Baroque composers Arcangelo Corelli and Antonio Vivaldi. The Joffrey Ballet in the 1970s made its fortune as a trendy company geared to young, unsophisticated audiences, but now the caller seems a bit condescending. His insistent patter distracted me from the surprising ways in which Balanchine connects the hoedown with its refined European ancestors.

Seven dancers from the famed Bolshoi Ballet of Moscow offered the dark and fateful *Mozartiana*. I thought the exacting footwork and rhythms were beyond ballerina Nina Ananiashvili that night, but the two male dancers, Dmitri Belogolovtsev and Sergei Filin, managed well. Balanchine reworked Tchaikovsky's tribute to Mozart four times, and this final one (1981) is an old man's reverie—nostalgic, intense, almost randomly dazzling.

It was in *Divertimento No. 15* (Mozart) that I saw the closest thing to my ideal Balanchine dancing. The choreography, like parts of almost every Balanchine ballet, elaborates on graciousness and civility, showing you how harmony can be worked out among even an unsymmetrical group. Performed by Suzanne Farrell's company, the work had the long, languid phrasing, the certainty of balance, the commitment to risk that characterized NYCB in Balanchine's last years. Farrell has gathered together a small ensemble of young dancers and soloists from other companies—Philip Neal of NYCB and Christina Fagundes, formerly of American Ballet Theatre, were the principals. The greatest pleasure to me in this performance of this wonderful ballet was how unassuming the dancers were, their familiarity with it. They didn't dramatize the choreography's dramatic implications—it's largely about how individuals can work together in different kinds of pairings—or try to impress the audience with its difficulty. As with NYCB in its glory days, this was what they did, and they were superbly going about doing it.

Farrell is obviously a fine teacher and coach—she staged several other works on the Celebration programs as well. I don't know whether Suzanne Farrell Ballet is an ongoing company or just a pick-up group. There have been other appearances, and the group seems to be taking on some kind of continuing role. Farrell doesn't push her own superstar status, except as it furthers the project of keeping Balanchine's work alive. The ensemble she's directing seems to understand his most profound lessons.

DANCES UNDER GLASS

Boston Phoenix, 13 August 1999

We often think of dance as irredeemably temporal—a momentary and elusive pleasure. But, as shown in two exhibitions this summer, dance can yield many byproducts that have deeper reverberations—that is, if the particular dance is important enough. Or maybe it's the existence of those durable byproducts that confer importance.

The expansive but short-lived "Dance for a City," at the New York Historical Society, curated by dance historian Lynn Garafola and historian of American culture Eric Foner, celebrates the New York City Ballet's fiftieth anniversary as a municipal institution. "The Art of Léon Bakst," at Harvard's Pusey Library, displays thirty-one drawings and other items from Harvard's holdings related to the flamboyant designer for the early Diaghilev Ballets Russes. The shows are vastly different in scope and intent, but they both provoke reflection about ballets and dancers we once knew, or never imagined.

Serge Diaghilev's terrific success in pre-World War I Paris and London depended on an inspired reinvention of the classical ballet that had reached its apex in Russia. You could almost say Diaghilev's modernism was defined by compression. Into a single act, less than an hour long, choreographer Michel Fokine fitted all the essentials of plot, action, and spectacle that used to consume whole evenings in the old story ballets. With the establishment of the one-act ballet, Fokine traded the leisurely narratives of the nineteenth century for an entertainment that was efficient, stylistically chic, and scaled for subtle thrills.

Léon Bakst's scenery and costumes for this compact classicism replaced chandeliers and dusty draperies with fantastic blasts of color and line. Bakst wasn't reproducing naturalistic scenes, like the nostalgic Alexandre Benois, another early designer for Diaghilev, nor was he nosing into abstraction like the protoconstructivist Natalia Goncharova. I think of him as an illustrator of fairy tales in the aesthetic style of his contemporaries Arthur Rackham, Kay Nielson, and Edmund Dulac. All of them worked in indulgent color, fine-lined detail, and sensuous exaggeration.

When the curtain went up on a Bakst ballet, the audience looked at a page from a storybook, a whole atmosphere, not just a generic palace or marketplace. *Daphnis and Chloe* was set in an impressionistic painted antiquity, with attenuated trees and purposely flat waterfalls and the landscape rolling away in Chinese perspective. The harem girls in *Schéhérazade* reclined on voluptuous orange cushions under a billowing tent of saturated green silk. And in the Biedermeier miniature *Le Spectre de la Rose*, the romantic young girl's boudoir was furnished in meticulous, tasteful detail.

Probably Bakst is best known today for his erotic costume designs. When he drew the human body, he went all out. No actual dancers could have had such elongated torsos, bulbous thighs and breasts, tiny exotic heads. They couldn't have danced in the auras of veils and feathers and beads that swirl around them on paper. But photographs, and an occasional reconstruction, show how that graphic sexiness did translate to the stage, in the flowing but revealing lines, the cutouts in suggestive spots, the elegant fabrics and decorations. Other artists then tried to capture these apparitions in paint, bronze, porcelain figurines, and caricature.

The culmination of all Bakst's decorative gifts was probably the 1921 *Sleeping Beauty*, a great financial disaster for Diaghilev and to some critics his greatest artistic achievement. By that time, the nineteenth century was still old hat, but exposed bodies and barbaric behavior were no longer novel enough to intrigue the audience. New modernisms were invading the theater. George Balanchine arrived from Russia in 1924 and by the time Diaghilev died in 1929, *La Chatte, Apollo, Prodigal Son,* and *Le Bal* had pointed ballet to the next phase.

It was nearly twenty years before Balanchine acquired a permanent company in America. By then he had tried out more styles and venues, created more masterpieces (*Serenade, Concerto Barocco, Theme and Variations*), and, through the extraordinary energies of Lincoln Kirstein, connected to the structures of power and money that make big culture happen. "Dance for a City" documents the many facets of New York City Ballet's career since 1948. It's striking to realize how few American dance organizations have even existed that long, let alone become a fixture in the great cultural center of a world metropolis.

It would take more than one museum show to tell this story, and Garafola and Foner don't try to do that. In a more or less chronological sequence from room to room, they do summarize the early days—Balanchine and Kirstein's School of American Ballet and the successive companies that evolved into the New York City Ballet—and the NYCB's trajectory from the City Center to Lincoln Center, from a "people's ballet" to the establishment that has survived its founders and now plays five months in New York and a month at its summer home, the Saratoga Performing Arts Center, and only has to tour under the most prestigious circumstances.

The success story here has two nearly independent but mutually essential ingredients: the creative genius of Balanchine and the strategic supporting maneuvers of Kirstein. The ballets are represented in photographs, designs, costumes, and video clips and musical selections that run continuously. The Kirstein component is less conspicuous. I don't remember seeing any evidence of Kirstein's extensive writing, in which, directly and indirectly, he implanted an aesthetic and a credibility for Balanchine's work over the years. But there is memorabilia about the buildings he patiently schemed for—Mecca Temple (City Center) on 55th Street, the first home of City Ballet; and the New York State Theater at Lincoln Center, which opened in 1964—and a subtext hinting at the support system Kirstein coaxed along, beginning with his wealthy, art-loving friends at Harvard and extending to politicians, funders, critical arbiters, and even subscribers.

There are onstage and offstage pictures of dancers and teachers, rehearsals and performances, the parties for the audience that the company knew so well how to throw, and the designers, composers, and techies who got the ballets on the stage. There's a good amount of attention given to Jerome Robbins's big contribution to the repertory, and to other noted choreographers who passed through. The myth of no-costumes-no-scenery is thoroughly debunked with evidence of production numbers like *Union Jack* and *The Nutcracker*, and forgotten surrealist escapades like Dorothea Tanning's fantastic designs for *Night Shadow*.

There's a 1960 letter from Eugenie Ouroussow, head of the School of American Ballet, offering a scholarship to Mrs. Ficker's daughter, soon to become Suzanne Farrell. And a 1954 page from the score for the Dance of the Little Swans, the first ballet to be written in Labanotation, by Ann Hutchinson. There are copies of mass magazines with ballerinas on the cover, and arty posed shots of the principals by fashion photographers.

I'm not sure the show really establishes the New York City Ballet as the dance for a city, as Garafola and Foner must have intended. Perhaps no one dance style or company could do that, now or ever. But the exhibition does range much further than the usual portrayals of NYCB as a neoclassical, streamlined platform for whizbang "pure" dancing.

Even more deconstructive is the handsome companion book, published by Columbia University Press.[3] This is less a catalogue of the show than a rather offbeat collection of essays by Garafola and several cultural commentators, meditating freely around the subject. If the book has a point of view, it's that New York City Ballet was never the single-minded, exclusive ballet enclave that's usually pictured by elitist critics. I'm not sure modern dance had as big an impact on ballet as dance historian Sally Banes asserts, but her thoughtful essay brings up a lot of things the purists don't consider, Merce Cunningham's early relations with the company, for instance. Homoeroticism is still a pretty taboo subject around ballet, so art historian Jonathan Weinberg's discussion of the photos of George Platt Lynes lets in a lot of fresh air. Thomas Bender and Richard Sennett talk about ballet's connections with the New York intellectuals of the '50s and '60s. There's a fine photo section and chronology devoted to the NYCB's real populist, Jerome Robbins. And Garafola's own essay situates Balanchine and Kirstein's enterprise alongside the ongoing cultural politics of New York City.

"Dance for a City," the book and the show, proposes a healthy revisionism, a more balanced way to look at the company's history and its public than what we read elsewhere. Perhaps the NYCB, after losing all its prime movers, is a shade of its former self as the aesthetes are complaining, but "Dance for a City" makes us think differently about what its former self was, and about what kind of a future this unique organization might create for itself.

BALLET, BIG TIME

Boston Phoenix, 31 October 2003

Twenty years after his death, George Balanchine is still considered the master choreographer of our times. This is no idle hype. The two works on Boston Ballet's fall program last week opened up once again the terrific possibilities of the classical enterprise. Audiences and dancers need Balanchine, not because he's history but because he's so far out.

Stars and Stripes (1958) and the fourth version of *Mozartiana* (1981) are worlds apart in style. *S & S* came at the peak of the New York City Ballet's pre–Lincoln Center years, when Balanchine could use Sousa marches and popular culture as confidently as he tackled the angular modernism of Stravinsky, Ives, and Webern. His last rethinking of *Mozartiana* came near the end of his life, when he was probably meditating on his own death. One ballet was big, formal, and extroverted. The other began with a prayer but assured us that ballet life would go on.

Mozartiana takes its title from the music, Tchaikovsky's gloss on themes of Mozart, so the idea of continuity is embedded in the ballet from the start. It begins somberly, with a ballerina and four teenage dancers, all in black tutus. Balanchine loved playing games with scale, and even without a tall ballerina (originally Suzanne Farrell), the effect when the curtain goes up jars you out of any monolithic ideas you might have about what ballet dancers are supposed to look like. The contrast plays out a little later, when the girls have "grown up" into four women. At the end of the ballet the two generations combine into a miniature corps de ballet.

Besides making the point about how ballet survives, *Mozartiana* showcases three entirely different solo dancers. The implication is that among their particular accomplishments they comprise classicism's range of decorum, wit, and mastery. The ballerina walks through the space, with prayerful gestures and gracious acknowledgment of her young companions, to the opening Preghiera (based on the hymn "Ave Verum Corpus"). When they leave, a young man in black, a sort of jester (Jared Redick in the first cast), dances a Gigue, with fast, rhythmically complicated steps that seem to ripple close to the ground except when he springs unexpectedly into the air.

After the four women dance a Menuet there's a phenomenal string of alternating variations for the ballerina and a partner. Guest artist Ethan Stiefel seemed to use the music like a trampoline for a whole variety of leaps and turning steps. Larissa Ponomarenko's variations expanded the pointe work of the Preghiera into a refined virtuosity. They do a supported adagio after this, and then are joined by the other man and the corps for a courtly finale.

Mozartiana celebrates what a ballet company can do on a small scale. *Stars and Stripes* is grand spectacle: three contingents of twelve dancers, each with its own leader, plus another solo couple. The fun is seeing how many ways Balanchine can turn the routines of a marching band into classical ballet behavior. Squadrons not only march in exact unison, they do massed entrechats, double tours, sexy battements, and a circle of grands jetés. It's kitschy, all those guys in the military uniforms and the girls looking like drum majorettes with white gloves and feathers on their pill-box hats. But you can enjoy the takeoff while you marvel at the regiments' inventive maneuvers. The corps at the Wang weren't always precise in their unison; Balanchine's New York City Ballet wasn't either, always, but he dared them to be.

The scale suddenly shrinks for the Fourth Campaign (Liberty Bell and El Capitan), a vaudeville pas de deux. Saturday afternoon Ethan Stiefel strutted and showed off brilliantly, sparking Sarah Lamb to do the same. In the first cast, Pollyana Ribeiro slid through some of the military affectations as if afraid to overdo them. But she and newcomer Nelson Madrigal seemed on the way to an affable partnership.

Balanchine knew the difference between reverential seriousness and serious comedy. David Dawson's ballet *The Grey Area* comes from the post–Forsythe school of European glitzy fatalism. The five dancers dressed in powder-blue bottoms and filmy, virtually topless tops seem lost in an immense space with a white void on one side, pitch blackness on the other. Lights fade partly in, then mostly out. The "sound design" (by Niels Lanz) consists of sustained discords and thunder. The dancers run and yearn and wrap around each other. They splay their legs wide, they swivel like broken compasses, the picture of directionless angst.

BALANCHINE AT HARVARD

Boston Phoenix, 23 April 2004

Everyone in the dance professions develops an acute sense of time as a flexible, almost palpable substance. Performing careers are short and must be cultivated for all they're worth. Unexpected moments on the stage can be inscribed in memory for years. The unwritten rules that determine how long a dance should be—or a performance, an intermission, the life of a dance work or a dance company—are constantly shifting. Last week we got to contemplate some of the longer intervals of dance time.

First, the Harvard Theater Collection celebrated George Balanchine's centennial with three public events, an all-day symposium, a talk by Balanchine's iconic ballerina Suzanne Farrell, and an exhibition from the Collection's diverse holdings related to the great choreographer. The show, arranged by curator Frederic Woodbridge Wilson and dance writer Iris M. Fanger, will be up at the Pusey Library through 28 May.

More than one speaker on Thursday acknowledged that the choreographer, who died in 1983, remains a continuing presence in their lives. I realize he's never far from my thinking either, as a reference point for the dance I see and study. I didn't know him personally, but I knew his repertory the way other people know books or music. When music historian Charles M. Joseph started his talk at the symposium by playing an unnamed Stravinsky passage on the piano, I saw Calliope's little running steps on pointe, saw her arms sweeping up in those dramatic gestures that identify her as the muse of poetry. Maybe we can't expect the whole educated world to know *Apollo* as well as it knows Hamlet, but how about the ballet audience?

Balanchine created scores of works during his lifetime; he was generous about allowing them to be performed by companies besides his New York City Ballet. After his death the body of work that's out there was bound to shrink, despite the efforts of the Balanchine Trust to keep the ballets alive. When a choreographic repertory is no longer being created it shifts onto the plane of history, where it requires a different kind of effort to be brought to the public. Not only do retention and recovery of a ballet become more problematic, but it has to compete onstage with new, hipper dances that look more familiar to the audience. According to symposium presenter Toni Bentley, author and former New York City Ballet dancer, Balanchine saw no need for preservation of his works, and to Bentley's mind film and videotaped ballets are only good for providing examples in lectures.

Fortunately the rest of the world is not ready to leave Balanchine in the limbo of nostalgia. Boston Ballet has just announced two Balanchine revivals, *Rubies* and *Divertimento No. 15*, for its fall season opener, and Farrell will bring back his legendary *Don Quixote* for her Kennedy Center–based company in June of 2005. But no one on the Harvard program was really willing to talk about the future of Balanchine. Asked by an audience member whether she worried about changes that could creep into the choreography when it's handed down to new generations of dancers, Farrell said Balanchine often left the dancers some expressive choices. But this doesn't account for changes that Balanchine didn't authorize, like wholesale misunderstandings or revisions of style, small dancers cast in what were big dancers' roles, liberties taken with steps, tempi, costuming. These things are happening. Some of them still give us credible Balanchine. But where do the keepers of the flame draw the line? When does the evolving DNA of a ballet produce a different ballet?

Only Farrell's interviewer, *New Yorker* dance critic Joan Acocella, was willing to look at the hereafter, a generation already into its third decade. Acocella finds the closest imitators of Balanchine the least interesting. The line will be carried on by the individuals who find their own voice, after absorbing his lessons about order, seriousness, music, and the use of stage space. Acocella named Karole Armitage, Twyla Tharp, and Mark Morris as current inheritors.

Harvard's symposium, perhaps understandably, concentrated on the more manageable questions of musicological research and documentary information. Perhaps inevitably, now that the firsthand spectators have diminished, there will be deconstructive takes on the work, revelations about it, critical assessments and prescriptions. Photographer Costas had wonderfully refreshing observations about the choreography he'd been capturing for thirty years at the New York City Ballet.

Most of all, the future of Balanchine will lie with those dancers who teach and perform his ballets. Suzanne Farrell is gradually building a base for them with her company. In her conversation with Acocella she seemed delightfully un-neurotic about her mentor, mindful of his voice but concerned to apply it in her own way to young dancers. She coached her former student Katie Daines, now a Harvard senior, in a variation from *Divertimento No. 15,* pointing out how the dancer's small rhythmic adjustments and spatial generosity could subtly make the difference between blandness and genius.

 ## LINKS TO A LEGACY

Boston Phoenix, 14 July 2006

In a postperformance talk at Jacob's Pillow last weekend, Suzanne Farrell was asked what she expects of the young dancers who are reviving George Balanchine's ballets under her direction. Farrell says she teaches the steps of the ballets and all the other information she gathered as a

Tzigane (Balanchine). Kyra Strasberg and Philip Neal, Suzanne Farrell Company. Photo by Tom Brazil, © The George Balanchine Trust.

principal at the New York City Ballet during Balanchine's golden age. But then, she said, she wants the dancers to find their own way into the works rather than copy the dancers who came before them. "I rehearse the possibilities, not an opinion."

As represented by the Susanne Farrell Ballet's programs at the Pillow, Balanchine's repertory carries the usual problems of recovery and authentication, plus an added burden. We haven't got the advantage of historical distance. The dancers who created the ballets are still here to teach them; the original performances live on in the audience's memory or on film. This can be daunting for young recruits. Balanchine's ballets are not in need of interpretation according to Farrell: "The steps and how you do them are the character." But the truth is, great dancers co-create the steps, imprint them with style. I think Balanchine wanted that, no matter how loudly he spoke the gospel of neutrality.

Natalia Magnicaballi took over *Tzigane*, one of Farrell's most celebrated roles, without trying to be Farrell. In the process she revealed something Farrell's own performances overshadowed. *Tzigane*, to Ravel's symphonized gypsy music, is an interesting choreographic progression, not just a flamboyant star opportunity. It begins with a long violin solo. The ballerina dances and mimes a whole series of melodramatic encounters with an imaginary partner, or perhaps she's telling fortunes. When the orchestra enters, along with her real partner (Runqiao Du), they dance a steamy duet, but he seems to tame her a little. Eight other dancers arrive, and the passion is restrained even more, and whole thing becomes a formal dance—gypsy steps conventionalized into a classical ballet. I purposely haven't looked at Farrell's performance with Peter Martins (preserved on a Nonesuch DVD of two New York City Ballet programs for Dance in America) but I see it clearly anyway, in memory.

Saturday afternoon it was Elisabeth Holowchuk, in *Clarinade*, who conveyed that sexy, mischievous side of Farrell. *Clarinade* was one of the first things Balanchine made for Farrell, with Anthony Blum, when she was a teenaged newcomer to the company in 1964. It was part of a larger Morton Gould ballet d'occasion that inaugurated City Ballet's tenure in the new New York State Theater at Lincoln Center. Farrell has retrieved the Contrapuntal Blues pas de deux, minus its additional two couples, from some archival film. Holowchuk, partnered by Benjamin Lester, brings back that jazzy, brazen creature with the extraordinary legs, flexible back, sassy hips, slouchy shoulders, sly glances, and the complicity in lifts that were one girlish flip away from debauchery.

These wanton females, adolescent or mature, hardly define all of Suzanne Farrell's possibilities, any more than Farrell in all her guises could have fully populated Balanchine's creative universe. She's smart to have chosen some ballets for her company that aren't identified with her own performances. Balanchine used Delibes's music from *Sylvia* and *La Source* several times, first for Maria Tallchief, then for Melissa Hayden, but the indelible *La Source* for me, and the one reconstructed by Farrell, was done in 1968 with Violette Verdy and John Prinz. Big, plush Shannon Parsley had enough of Verdy's feminine épaulement, her assertive footwork, to suggest the ballet's French flavor, but no one else I ever saw had Verdy's ballon and wit. The Mozart *Divertimento No. 15* reached its final form in 1956 headed by an all-star cast of five drastically different ballerinas. Just watching Farrell's young dancers take on the challenging variations, duets, and lively ensemble work, is an education in ballet's tremendous expressive range, its headiest demands.

Boston Phoenix, 26 July 2002

The Kirov Ballet of St. Petersburg looked like a completely different company in George Balanchine's dazzling evening-length *Jewels*, which ended the Russians' two-week Lincoln Center Festival appearance at the Metropolitan Opera House. They were the same dancers who'd done the nineteenth-century heavyweights *Swan Lake*, *La Bayadère*, and *Don Quixote* earlier in the run, but dancing this choreography, in the city where it was born, seemed to transform them.

Critical opinion frowns on New York City Ballet right now as having lost its Balanchine touch while trying to refashion itself without him. The Russians may not look like the Balanchine dancers of thirty-five years ago, but they don't market the hard-edge sexiness of Peter Martins's NYCB either. What was so moving about the performance of *Jewels* I saw Saturday night was the stretch the Kirov made from Petipa to Petipa's modern descendant. It was like watching ballet history jump the centuries.

Jewels was created in 1967 for a New York City Ballet riding to the crest of its greatest success. It had moved into its grand new home at Lincoln Center, the New York State Theater, and was enjoying long seasons, big subscription audiences, and generous public funding. Balanchine made an evening of ballets that showed off the facets of classical ballet in three different modes and styles while confirming the terrific dancer resources at the company's disposal. The slightly rococo French romanticism of *Emeralds* (led by Violette Verdy and Mimi Paul) was followed by the rough-and-tumble vaudevillian Americana of *Rubies* (Patricia McBride, Edward Villella, and Patricia Neary) and the imperial but tragic Russian expansiveness of *Diamonds* (Suzanne Farrell and Jacques d'Amboise).

The Kirov might never repair the scars left on our hearts by those originals, but in stepping into this choreography of Balanchine's, its members seemed to be learning a different way to dance. You could almost see them discovering an eagerness to grab the music, an appetite for space beyond their reach, and a pleasure at being cogs in a wonderful group machine. The ballerinas, especially Zhanna Ayupova in *Emeralds*, filled out the musical phrase instead of insisting on dragged-out tempos to make an impression. The male partners found they had to turn and jump instead of just being good leaning posts and porteurs. The corps members seemed to live in the music rather than waiting for it to move them.

I saw *Emeralds* through some tears, partly because of Ayupova's musicality, but mostly because of Balanchine's affecting journey through

Emeralds (Balanchine). Karin von Aroldingen and Sean Lavery, New York City Ballet. Photo by Costas, © The George Balanchine Trust.

Gabriel Fauré's theater music (Shylock and Pelléas et Mélisande). This is a ballet with all the usual forces and situations tumbled out differently from what's expected: an almost whimsical first couple; a somber, almost ritualistic second couple; a trio for a man and two women who leap joyously in tandem; and a corps de ballet that vanishes after the first section and comes back only at the end.

One misstep the Kirov made, or the Balanchine delegates who coached it (Karin von Aroldingen, Sara Leland, Elyse Borne, and Sean Lavery), was to omit the coda that Balanchine added in 1976. In an extended, virtually danceless leave-taking, all seven solo dancers have brief encounters with one another and the women exit, leaving the three men to gaze after them. These second thoughts may have been Balanchine anticipating his own death, but they also pulled the ballet back from the conventional, celebratory finale to a more serious conclusion, one that had been anticipated by a disquieting horn phrase during the initial festivities.

Rubies, set to Stravinsky's Capriccio for Piano and Orchestra, opens with the male and female ensemble standing rock-steady on their toes in a semicircle, clasping upraised hands. Then it splatters into a succession of shameless tricks and diversions from American popular stages: struts, shimmies and cakewalking, jokes, chases, and a pas de deux of deliberate feints and grabs. The dancers didn't quite capture the colloquial attitude of these carryings-on. The ballerina, Irina Golub, grinned all the time, unnecessarily, but her partner, Viacheslav Samodurov, made witty monster steps in the background and caught her nonchalantly when she suddenly let herself topple backward. Daria Pavlenko played the Amazonian third woman.

I thought Sofia Gumerova and Danila Korsuntsev were splendid in *Diamonds* (the last four movements of Tchaikovsky's Third Symphony), which could be one of many riffs Balanchine made on *Swan Lake*. The relationship was clearer than ever because I'd seen the Kirov's *Swan Lake* the same afternoon. You wouldn't want to discard one for the other, but Balanchine's economy, his capturing, even honoring, of high Imperial ballet's emotional and theatrical core without its pomposity, seems to me miraculous.

BALANCHINIAN BAUBLES

Boston Phoenix, 28 August 2006

George Balanchine's *Jewels* got a lukewarm critical reception when it premiered in 1967, although the public loved it right off for its triple-threat bravado. New York City Ballet wanted to create a festive work for its new home in Lincoln Center: the great choreographer disporting himself in three balletic modes. *Jewels* has proven to be a durable masterpiece.

The Paris Opera Ballet's new DVD, "Joyaux," produced by Opus Arte and distributed here by Naxos, is probably the first complete recording of *Jewels* to enter general release, and for that alone Balanchine fans should be grateful. POB acquired *Rubies* (sometimes called *Capriccio*) in 1974 from one of its original leading dancers, Patricia Neary. Later on Karin von Aroldingen and Sara Leland taught *Emeralds* and *Diamonds*, and the whole spectacle was first performed in Paris in 2000. Christian Lacroix designed new costumes, which look a lot sleeker and less glitzy than Mme. Karinska's originals.

These French dancers have the technical chops to do Balanchine, and the musicality besides. The video shows off their whizbang turns and assured balances, the clarity of their intricate step sequences, the expansive lifts and leaps, and the precise, demanding corps work. Their style, which is to say their interpretation of Balanchine's challenge, is very objective, with an overlay of generic emoting. The corps grins all the way through *Rubies*, to show you they're having a good time. The romantic couple in *Diamonds* gaze at each other soulfully, and in *Emeralds* there's an air of open-mouthed intoxication.

On a documentary by filmmaker Reiner Moritz that's part of the package, dancers and POB artistic director Brigitte Lefèvre offer some vivid but not necessarily definitive insights. *Rubies*, for instance, is obviously based on Broadway musicals, they think. Maybe Balanchine got jazzed from his Broadway work in the '30s, but he absorbed a lot of other Americanisms in his lifetime. I've always thought *Rubies* was more about circuses and musical hall entertainments. Pat Neary and its other first principals, Patricia McBride and Edward Villella, were earthy, not above lowbrow escapades. I'm sure that's why Balanchine chose them for this piece. In fact, all the ballet's original stars, including Violette Verdy, Mimi Paul, Suzanne Farrell, and Jacques d'Amboise, expressed NYCB's diversity at the time. NYCB has become more standardized now; perhaps it's an international trend.

When the ballet is intimate, like *Emeralds*, or compact and punchy, like *Rubies*, TV director Pierre Cavassilas brings the viewer into a welcome proximity, with medium-distance shots and close-ups. When the choreography expands, though, he resorts to a variety of reductive alternatives and hyperactive interventions, like filming one-half of a symmetrical pattern, zeroing in on the center of a large group and eliminating the sides, switching from one partial-view camera position to another, and tracking a cluster of dancers as they move through groups of other dancers.

I've never understood this thinking. While these choreography-resistant techniques bring our attention to selected dancers and their expressive gloss, the ballet's grand designs, its larger implications, slip away. In *Diamonds*, for instance, we get a good account of the pas de deux (Agnès Letetsu and Jean-Guillaume Bart) and of some small-ensemble sections. We taste how Balanchine used Tchaikovsky's Third Symphony to evoke the composer's other ballets *Swan Lake* and *Sleeping Beauty*. In the opening shots, we glimpse the diamond-shaped floor pattern that serves as a motif for the corps de ballet.

On stage, though, the ballet plays with scale, the interlocking possibilities of specialized units within the large cast of twenty-four corps members, eight demi-soloists, and two principals. Balanchine could miraculously expand and contract the panorama, and at the same time transform the female ensemble from twelve swanlike creatures to a regal, celebratory assemblage. Maybe television just isn't up to that.

WHAT BODIES ARE FOR

Boston Phoenix, 29 October 2004

Distant Flight, the new ballet for Boston Ballet by Peter Martins, premiered between two George Balanchine hits Thursday night at the Wang Theater. The program could have been read as a two-sided mission statement: ballet needs classicism to survive, as well as artistic sex.

Martins used one movement of a violin concerto by the contemporary Latvian composer Peteris Vasks, music suggesting the stretched-out dissonances of Arvo Pärt as well as the imagistic gestures of John Adams. As the ballet begins, Lorna Feijóo writhes invitingly on the floor in a glittering swimsuit, to the high-pitched wailing of the strings. Three men in sleek Tarzan costumes enter one by one (Yury Yanowsky, Roman Rykine, and Nelson Madrigal), and over the next many minutes they dance with Feijóo, pulling her up onto her pointes or twisting her into extreme shapes, tossing her in one-handed or no-handed lifts, spinning her dizzily. She leans on them, wraps herself around them, colludes in their every kinky design.

At first the men seem slightly different in the ways they handle Feijóo, and perhaps she's trying to choose among them. Or are they trying to choose who gets her? As each man takes his turn, another man appears and watches from a distance. Sometimes all three men watch Feijóo soloing. Eventually they dance amongst themselves in a challenge of equals. But after many visitations and departures, she remains alone, crumpling and unfurling on the floor.

Assuming Martins means more than just a catalogue of erotic moves, Feijóo might be taken as a dreamer, imagining, remembering, and replaying the men in her life. She doesn't make a choice because to solve the problem would end the dream she seems to enjoy. But this malleable and available woman could also be the object of a male fantasy, with the three men as stand-ins for the choreographer, who told the *Boston Globe*: "There is no story for women, unless there's men." Unquestioning, the happy voyeurs in the audience screamed their approval.

If ballet were only about how many alluring shapes a ballerina can achieve by twisting and stretching her body, it would just be legitimized porn. Fortunately, it often comes with the saving gift of choreography. George Balanchine displayed and adored the female body too, but the pleasure in his ballets comes from much more than that. There's an interlude in *Rubies* (1967) when four men manipulate one of the two featured women (Melanie Atkins), sharing her, turning her in arabesque so that the audience can see her extended body from every angle.

But this episode is part of a bigger, more interesting plan, a ballet about the flamboyance of ballet dancers. Balanchine pictures the dancers here as circus performers or vaudevillians, who happen to have extraordinary powers of rhythm, timing, wit, strength, daring, and yes, technique. *Rubies* offers continual new revelations along with its flash and jokes, provided we follow its dance narrative.

Seeing it this time I thought how generously Balanchine provided the dancers with character gambits. They aren't just jazzy technicians, but persons with roles to play. There's the ensemble of perfectionists whose job is to make a glamorous frame for the soloists. And then, Yury Yanowsky and Romi Beppu played the leading couple as an oafish but strong and phenomenally nimble escort with a ballerina who delights in the versatility of her own feet.

Melanie Atkins didn't seize the possibilities of Balanchine's "other woman," a role he inserted in several plotless ballets to give his dancers more visibility. This figure is never a rival for the man's affections, as she would be in a more pedestrian choreographer's domain. Rather, she can be a queen, a benevolent or foreboding fairy, a warrior. In *Rubies*, she can allow the men their game of showing her off because, in the rest of the ballet, she's the pivotal, powerful leader of the twelve-member ensemble, taking orders from Stravinsky and no one else.

The company looked a little ragged in the first performance of *Rubies*, but *Divertimento No. 15*, which opened the evening, was clean and delicate as the fins of a mushroom. *Divertimento*, choreographed in 1956, needs no character shading to enrich its movement throughline. It simply rearranges traditional ballet resources (three male and five female soloists and a small corps of eight women) to complement Mozart's music. Each component is featured in its own special ways, and just when you think they've shown you everything, they regroup for another invention.

If you want steps, there's a string of solos introduced by two of the men. The women and the principal male play with this movement theme six more ways. In duets relieved of desire, all five women are partnered in turn by the men, and each little pas de deux picks up an idea from the one before. You get to see the corps in a virtuosic display of its own. Starting with just walking on pointe, it rearranges itself into lines, circles, squares, its movement getting more complicated until the pattern yields its own duets.

The corps women looked confident and smart, and it was fine to see the variations so well danced. Balanchine is an acquired taste for the audience, and an acquired skill for dancers. Even when they aren't quite up to it, I'm sure every one of these revivals is a learning experience for them.

Boston Phoenix, 11 May 2007

You could say all three George Balanchine revivals performed last week by Boston Ballet were about destiny: the fulfilled reign of a queen (*Ballo della Regina*), the raw materials of human aspiration (*Four Tempera-ments*), and the lure of certain death (*La Valse*). Balanchine isn't supposed to be "about" anything except dancing, but it's a mistake to peg him as nothing but a brilliant formalist.

Ballo della Regina (music from Verdi's *Don Carlos*) looks like the glossi-est classical exercise, with masses of well-schooled women (a corps of twelve and its four leaders) celebrating the queen and her escort. Staged by Merrill Ashley, on whom Balanchine made the principal role in 1978, the ballet looked grand on the Wang stage in a very Balanchinian way. No fancy costumes or simulated courtly behavior, no perfunctory posing and forma-tions, just a choice lexicon of steps that unfolds to reveal all the partici-pants in escalating degrees of accomplishment.

What you come away with is an idea of symmetry, of complementarity, and the satisfaction of seeing that the monarch deserves her status through her phenomenal skill if nothing else. The four demi-soloists (Rie Ichikawa, Lia Cirio, Melanie Atkins, and Heather Myers on opening night) succes-sively command the stage with expansive traveling variations, and the corps women also get to show off in prancing appearances and two-by-two leap-ing vignettes.

Erica Cornejo made an impressive debut in one of the most technically outrageous roles ever invented for a ballerina. Though smaller and less grounded than Ashley, she had the daring to try Ashley's off-center turns, fast hops on pointe, and intricate footwork. She showed us with clarity how an arabesque could spurt out of a series of spins, how picky traveling steps could match a jaunty little figure in the music, how it would be fun to change from one supporting leg to the other while turning. Partnered in adagio by an elegant and thoughtful James Whiteside, she cut loose from him with exuberant little jumps and inventions.

Cornejo got a little out of control toward the end, as the technical ante rose, and she flashed an open-mouthed, million-dollar smile to signal completion of some difficult maneuver. From the outset I thought she was playing the role like a breathless debutante, more like Aurora in *Sleeping Beauty* than a regal empress of all she surveyed. The Boston Ballet dancers sometimes resort to generic performing devices when they're tackling un-familiar works. You can't blame them, when they get so few chances to try

Four Temperaments (Balanchine). Phlegmatic. Pavel Gurevich and women, Boston Ballet. Photo by Sabi Varga, © The George Balanchine Trust.

out new repertory on the audience and learn the depths of these roles for themselves. These three "Classic Balanchine" ballets were done only six times, with multiple casts.

The Four Temperaments doesn't benefit from standard smiles and literally acted-out emotionality either, despite its quasi-expressionist pretext. We can't know what Balanchine really intended for his ballet based on the medieval humors, melancholic, sanguinic, phlegmatic, and choleric. But if he was doing anything other than augmenting the compositional framework of Paul Hindemith's Theme with Four Variations (According to the Four Temperaments) for piano and strings, he must have assumed that the movement would convey whatever the audience needed in the way of emotional guidelines.

The choreography builds from three small, pristine duets, each based on one of three musical themes, and then introduces four sets of soloists with their small entourages. The whole cast assembles at the end to combine their movement signatures into a towering affirmation—of human chemistry or human hope, or just the power of classical form, we can only speculate. I thought John Lam, pressing forward and faltering back, against six implacable female sentinels in Melancholic, and Carlos Molina, a weather-vane in a quandary of indecision in Phlegmatic, were excellent.

The affectionately named *Four T's* was a more or less permanent fixture in the New York City Ballet repertory following its premiere in 1946. Balanchine revived and adapted it for a PBS Dance in America special in 1977. That production is now available on VHS and DVD from Nonesuch, with Bart Cook dancing the Melancholic variation. It's Cook who set the work for Boston Ballet and he's kept the 1977 version. Merrill Ashley is also associated with that production. She danced the Sanguinic variation, imprinting her virtuosity and wit on the role. Opening night in Boston, Larissa Ponomarenko and Nelson Madrigal danced Sanguinic. I thought they didn't really have the pyrotechnical flair that can make Sanguinic such a wonderful contrast with the men's variations that bracket it: the slow plastique of Melancholic and the jazzy waywardness of Phlegmatic.

Like the other variations the Choleric begins with a solo (Kathleen Breen Combes), very brief, fast, and rhythmically intricate, punctuated with unexpected vertical jumps and whole-body collapses. Almost before you can realize what she's doing, the soloist is surrounded by the other principals, her wild energy is gradually tamed by their stretched-out adagio and partnering patterns. With a smoothing-out gesture, she slips away and the great architectural coda begins.

Balanchine could make overtly dramatic ballets on occasion, and *La Valse* (1951) is one of the creepiest. Set to sumptuous but acid orchestrated waltzes of Maurice Ravel, *La Valse* portrays a ballroom that's scented with doom from the very beginning. Ballroom ballets were a standard item in the repertory, and Balanchine had made a few contrary ones early in his career, including *Le Bal* (1929), with its masked intimations of death, and *Cotillon* (1932), where ominous figures infiltrate a young people's party. Perhaps the choreographer was implying Viennese decadence in *La Valse*, or perhaps he was subtly undermining the prettiness and romance of the whole ballroom convention, while drawing the audience deeper and deeper into his own glamorous death trap.

Three women in evening gowns and long white gloves, their hair pulled back in ponytails, dance side by side with strange, angular gestures and sidelong glances. Men and women run in and out, pursuing partners, and eventually they dance together, abandoning themselves to the music. Against a background of sparkly chandeliers draped in black, a woman in a white ball gown (Karine Seneca) appears. After introductory formalities, she dances with a young man (Pavel Gurevich). The other dancers swirl in and out.

Suddenly, another man appears (Carlos Molina), just standing still and staring at the girl. He does nothing elaborate to court her but she feels irresistibly attracted to him. With growing uneasiness she allows him to dress her in a gaudy necklace, a black net cloak. She plunges one arm, then the other, into the long black gloves he holds out for her. She sees herself in a mirror, clothed for a funeral, and realizes who he is, and who she's become. She accepts his bouquet of black flowers, and at the moment she moves into his arms, she dies.

La Valse (staged by Francia Russell) is filled with extravagant dancing and melodramatic gestures. I thought Karine Seneca wanted to act them all out. So did the other dancers. They all looked more like the innocent romantics that inhabit standard ballroom ballets, instead of adults experienced enough to sense a danger among them. A smile in *La Valse*, it seems to me, never occurs without misgivings.

DECODING BALANCHINE

Boston Phoenix, 9 May 2008

Nancy Goldner's diminutive new book about George Balanchine's choreography, *Balanchine Variations*, is deceptively readable. Goldner, who's reviewed dance regularly for the *Christian Science Monitor*, the *Nation*, and the *Philadelphia Inquirer*, writes in an almost conversational voice that makes Balanchine seem transparent, easy to understand. But the simple appearance of the text belies an astute and highly sophisticated observer.[4]

Goldner is a lifelong New Yorker, a devotee of the New York City Ballet. Her gem of a book on the NYCB's 1972 Stravinsky Festival serves as both memento and sourcebook for that remarkable event. *Balanchine Variations* revisits some of the Stravinsky successes of 1972, along with eighteen other ballets, from the 1928 *Apollo* to *Ballo della Regina* of 1978. The essays are based on a series of lectures Goldner gave over the last decade, along with former NYCB principal dancer Merrill Ashley, under the auspices of the Balanchine Trust and the Balanchine Foundation.

Preserving their original intent as a kind of primer for balletgoers, the essays also constitute a lesson in how many ways there are to write about ballet. None of the chapters adopts a "critique" or review format, yet almost every ballet summons a different treatment, suggests a different focus. This demonstrates the versatility of Balanchine, but also the ingenuity of Goldner.

Sometimes her approach is historical. She traces the evolution of *Sere-*

nade, Balanchine's first ballet in America, with a capsule history of changes and revisions in the choreography over nearly seventy-five years. A committed balletomane, she amuses herself by looking at a video of *Concerto Barocco* several times to see if she can catch Balanchine in "a sag, or error in judgment," and concludes that the ballet is perfect.

She asks questions, sees mysteries, speculates about things that don't reveal themselves on the surface in the strange, semi-narrative *La Sonnambula*. She explores Balanchine's brand of Americana in *Western Symphony*, then decides that attitudes and gestures, like the cowboys doffing their hats, aren't what really define the choreographer's Americanism. Instead, *Concerto Barocco*, *Four Temperaments*, and the Stravinsky ballets are better indicators of his affinity for jazz, "the one uniquely American thing to which Balanchine was drawn."

In a casual remark long ago, Nancy Goldner taught me a profound lesson. "Ballet is about steps after all," she said, as if any numbskull would know that. Of course, most of the world still doesn't, and the audience gets very little exposure to this resource from today's trendy repertory. To Goldner, Balanchine's games with footwork supply enduring pleasure.

It's easy to think about *Agon* as a precursor of the sexy athletics of modern choreography. Goldner ignores this cliché and explores the 1957 classic in terms of the many ways Balanchine employed the canon and the tension this simple repeat-after-me trope can create, in the stage action and the viewer. She doesn't like *Donizetti Variations* all that much, but she appreciates the "number play" with which Balanchine parsed his eleven dancers.

Because it identifies a particular group of works from the choreographer's enormous output, *Balanchine Variations* has canonical overtones, as a "best of Mr. B" list. The book will no doubt be read as a key to the master's genius. But Goldner didn't make these reductive choices. Her lectures were arranged to supplement revivals of Balanchine works around the country, a gradually shrinking repertory of audience favorites like *Serenade* and *Rubies*. Goldner does expand sideways a little, by glancing at related works, but you could easily add another twenty brilliant ballets that deserve her analysis. Dare we hope for a bigger, deeper book?

5 Ballet in Transit

FORSYTHE'S ARTIFACT

Christian Science Monitor, 10 August 1987

William Forsythe's evening-length *Artifact* is a shrewd amalgam of the trendiest European avant-garde ideas, from Apollinaire and Gertrude Stein to Robert Wilson and Pina Bausch, salted with a few Americanisms and dressed in opera house taste, form, and largesse. Forsythe, an expatriate New Yorker, now heads the Frankfurt Ballet, and his highly touted works for this company have been part of the PepsiCo Summerfare at the State University of New York in Purchase.

Whether one thinks Forsythe is the future standard-bearer of classical ballet, as some critics do, or just the latest hotshot to tackle the rehabilitation of a feeble tradition, the theatricality of his work can't be denied. *Artifact* begins while the audience is still entering the theater. The curtain goes up on an expressionistically limelit and shadowed stage. Very slowly, Amanda Miller, a woman in a leotard with slicked back, mannish white hair, walks across the space, making obscure gestures with her hands. The audience calms down, and the expectant mood holds for the next five minutes or so, as the woman crosses and recrosses in different patterns of illumination, until the houselights finally go down and the lobby doors are closed.

By this time we know the piece is going to be about the nature of the dancer and her relationship to the audience. Two hours later we don't know much more, except that Forsythe has projected us into a state where we must question that nature and that relationship for ourselves, and extend whatever we thought were their limits.

He certainly doesn't offer us a conventional ballet, or draw our attention to dancers in the usual ways. In fact, the featured performers are not dancers at all. In addition to the androgynous, mysterious Miller, there's Kathleen Fitzgerald, dressed like an operatic diva, who recites a series of words with indefinite and endlessly interchangeable meanings. "She went inside and thought. He came outside and forgot. They'll always forget when. You were inside there." With shafts of light slanting up into the pitch-dark stage from the rim of the orchestra pit, Fitzgerald approaches a glowing trap in the floor. Hands (Miller's, it turns out) reach up from inside it and make what might be the right gestures for the cryptic monologue. Meanwhile, Nicholas Champion trudges around carrying a microphone and a bullhorn, sometimes answering Fitzgerald's litany and sometimes making subverbal sounds.

Dancers glide through the gloom, and for twenty minutes there isn't even enough light to make out their bodies fully, let alone their faces. They function like a chorus of opera singers, moving in mass formations, creating a backdrop or a commentary, or reflecting the actors' metaphysical angst. Occasionally they comprise the main action, but it's always as a group that we see them, never as individuals. Even the three solo couples are merely The Couples, since the pace is too fast and dense to distinguish them.

The movement itself, except where it's deliberately academic, seems to pit the body against itself. One part is thrown or twisted so far that it requires some extreme countermovement to prevent the dancer from falling. In the duets the men, strong as stevedores, propel and anchor the women, who often have to spread their limbs rakishly and spin in wide arcs to a dead stop. Their tempo seldom sinks below a sprint.

Forsythe seems to see the stage as a painter's canvas, and the dancers as moving compositional motifs. The dances are built for general dazzle but not for specific virtuosity, so he can chop them up, rearrange them, overlap dissimilar phrases, to create his effects. One section starts out with the women in a classroom lineup doing increasingly deranged arm progressions and tendus. Suddenly, shockingly, the curtain begins to fall, faster and faster. It hits the floor with a sickening thud. The music (the Chaconne for solo violin from Bach's Partita in D Minor) continues, and soon the curtain rises on a different formal dance pattern, crashes down, rises—six or seven times. The viewer is forced to give up being engrossed in the movement, and to consider dancing as infinitely capable of pleasing transformations. Who gets the credit isn't the dancers, but the designer/ choreographer.

Artifact is a succession of coups de théâtre, each one using the dancers but not featuring what they do. After an intermission the classical order gives way to postmodern chaos. Fitzgerald recycles her text once again, working up from a tone of loud accusation to a screaming tantrum—"And every time I step outside I forget what I never see!"—while Champion grunts into his megaphone and music blares and dancers jiggle and thrash in front of white flats painted with neat graffiti. Later they reassemble in another species of order.

I never lost interest in *Artifact*, and I never liked its pretension, its imitativeness, or its complete depersonalization of the dancers. If this is the future of ballet, it's going to be a beautiful but desolate scenario.

DE KEERSMAEKER'S *ELENA'S ARIA*

Christian Science Monitor, 7 January 1988

Six years ago, when she was studying at New York University and showing pieces on small dance concerts, Anne Teresa De Keersmaeker was pushing the overworked genre of minimalism into new strata of physical endurance and expressive power. Back in her native Belgium, De Keersmaeker established an all-female company, Rosas, which gained immediate acclaim and has now made two appearances on the Brooklyn Academy Next Wave series. Oddly, for this season at BAM the company brought a 1984 piece, *Elena's Aria*, instead of a more recent work, so we still don't know quite where the twenty-seven-year-old choreographer is now. With *Elena's Aria*, though, she seems to have retreated toward the maudlin precincts of European Tanztheater.

Elena's Aria uses the lexicon of Pina Bausch et al. to create a gloomy atmosphere of feminine loss and alienation. A long row of leatherette-upholstered side chairs is placed across the back of the space, surrounded by the dusty jumble of an unused stage—equipment, ladders, furniture shoved into the corners, curtains hoisted out of the way. This setting, sacred not only to Bausch but to the earlier master of choreographed spectacles, Maurice Béjart, exposes dancers watching not only other dancers but the audience, and signifies that both we and they are on display. De Keersmaeker's five women (Michele Anne De Mey, Nadine Ganase, Roxane Huilmand, Fumiyo Ikeda, and herself) are wearing unbecoming sheath dresses, black high-heeled shoes, and hairdos that get scraggly and limp when they begin to move: Tanztheater code for Women Oppressed by their Sexuality.

After a sort of prologue during which Ikeda reads a passage from Tolstoy in halting English, the curtain rises on three women seated, in a very dim light. Suddenly two of the women get up, grip the backs of their chairs. Spasmodically, almost angrily, they wheel around behind the chairs, their momentum sending them one chair further down the row, while the third woman shrinks out of their way and ends up sprawled across her seat, halfway to the floor.

This intricate but purposeless movement sequence provides the core material for the whole dance. Initially derived from naturalistic actions—

sitting, waiting, pivoting on the instep, walking—the movement accumulates detail, and at the same time grows less ordinary. Simple sitting suggests crossed legs, the problem of what to do with the hands is temporarily solved by gripping the sides of the chair or wrapping one arm around the waist or absent-minded primping. But this seemingly personal material is embedded in the movement phrase, where it can be manipulated by the conventional means of dance making. The gesture gets repeated, exaggerated, transferred to another part of the body, multiplied on two or three or all five women. In other words, what has obvious roots as expressive gesture is turned into abstract dance progressions before our eyes.

In doing this, De Keersmaeker dismantles the social meaning of moves and mannerisms associated with preliberation females. We continue to see these images in '50s movies—the provocative outward thrust of women's hips as they walk, the coy tweak at the hemline, the bent knee drawing our eye to a silken ankle. In De Keersmaeker's dance, these become large and often unwieldy movements, sequences that build into tumbling, running, crawling, and teetering tiptoe journeys. The "deconstruction" process is underscored by a short silent film of demolition projects where they blow up a building so it collapses neatly into its own basement.

De Keersmaeker also links her archaic and hobbling gestures with thwarted romance. Women sit at the side of the stage and read in different languages. The texts all seem to be about women having a trying time with their men. But the self-absorbed dancers don't relate to each other personally, except when individuals momentarily react to the rest of the group as a threat or a compelling power.

De Keersmaeker's craftsmanship is ingenious and beautifully wrought, but I don't understand why a young woman today does a dance like this. Is she trying to teach us a lesson? Surely it's one the wildly cheering Brooklyn audience had already learned. Perhaps she's reminding us of women's history as sex objects in order to gain sympathy for the difficult lives they lead when they choose independence.

MAGUY MARIN'S *BABEL BABEL*

Christian Science Monitor, 6 April 1988

Since introducing Pina Bausch's Wuppertal Dance Theater and the concept of German Tanztheater to America in 1985, Brooklyn Academy of Music has served the audience's taste for that neoexpressionistic genre by importing a steady stream of its European practitioners. This year's Next

Wave offered a French group, Compagnie Maguy Marin and the Belgian Rosas. Tanztheater mixes lavish spectacle with ritualized, often violent movement based on the behavior of alienated contemporary men and women. The Europeans like it because of its air of social critique, but I suspect Americans are more excited by its combination of theatricality and self-pity, its relentless, often dangerous movement that never verges on technically polished dance forms. Maguy Marin's *Babel Babel* projects the choreographer's views of sexual oppression through large and heavily moralistic theatrical visions. You watch it with a mixture of pleasure, excitement, and guilt.

Babel Babel begins with a dimly lit procession of naked people, laboring across an empty plain to the funereal third movement of Gustav Mahler's first symphony. The figures, though stripped to their natural selves, walk with artfully pointed feet, puffed-out chests. They begin to roll across the turf-covered floor. They encounter other bodies, embrace, fall apart. All this is done to the plodding beat of the music. After the men exit, the women, about six of them, dance together in a deliberately naive style.

Throughout these "primitive" sections of the piece, the movement looks calculated, a ballet dancer's notion of how nondancers move. The body is carefully molded, the timing is plotted for effect. This is as incongruous as Mahler's sardonic orchestration of "Frère Jacques," and recalls the earnest '60s, when group rituals were derived organically from simple breathing, stepping, and stamping motions.

The pilgrims return, now wearing plain pants and dresses, to the sound of crickets. Calling out to each other in a made-up language, they begin a series of work motions that build into a kind of rhythmic chorus. People hammer on metal plates in the floor. They bang with shovels, yank at chains. The women seem to be in charge. They all dance around a circle of lanterns, becoming more and more raucous and abandoned.

All of a sudden the lights go down and a village of tents appears. The villagers crawl inside, and for a long time there's silence, broken by occasional squeals and giggles. We begin to hear the sound of surf, and the village turns into a beach resort. Sunbathers tumble out of the tents, and soon the stage is bursting with hot, noisy fun. A rock combo and a pink-wigged singer in a prom dress blast out a song about a "tout petit bikini" followed by a deafening repertory of pseudo-Latin and pseudo–Middle Eastern pop numbers.

The music rouses the beachgoers to more and more rowdy diversions. Men and women pair up, squabble. In the melee, aprons get tied over the women's bathing suits, rubber babies appear by the dozens, some of them draped hand-in-hand around the women's waists like hula skirts. Couples begin to fight with other couples. Men behave like infants. Women punch each other. The music gets louder and louder.

When the orgy reaches a pitch of visual and aural pandemonium, the singer (Marin) strips off her fluffy gown. Underneath she's a sultry nightclub singer in chic black rags and leather. She flounces down into the audience, bawling and screeching into a mike she's holding two inches from her face: "This is a maaaan's world—but it wouldn't be nothin' without a woman."

The next time we notice the stage, the tents and party things have all been swept away. The turf is littered with scraps of plastic and paper, and babies, and people. The people squirm out of their bathing suits, and now the music is Mahler's Kindertotenlieder—Songs on the Death of Children. The people struggle to rise, making ghastly expressionistic shapes copied from Edvard Munch. Some of them fasten themselves together and try to walk. One woman suckles at another woman's breast. Couples slam into contorted embraces.

One woman dances a beautiful and horrible dance around the vanished campfire. Seemingly sightless, she scuffles round and round, sometimes bent over, sometimes erect and searching. She twirls with arms flung out, like a child, but without a child's joy or animation. Finally, to Mahler's consoling last song, the people continue their plodding journey across the space and away.

Maguy Marin's work, like much contemporary opera house performance, owes a considerable debt to the '60s inventors of new dance and theater, and to the turn-of-the-century European artists who were groping their way to an acceptance of the terrors of the modern world. Marin has a remarkable skill in orchestrating these familiar devices and images. But if there's a new message in her work, it barely shows through the spectacle.

FORSYTHE AND MARIN

Christian Science Monitor, 19 July 1988

It was after 11 P.M. and half the audience had gone home when the Paris Opera Ballet's second program at the Metropolitan Opera House staggered to its apogee, William Forsythe's *in the middle, somewhat elevated*. The work was created a year ago for the company and was having its first U.S. performances on this tour. The Forsythe devotees screamed en masse, but the best I can say for the piece is that it has a lot of dancing and a refreshing lack of theatrical diversions.

Forsythe is being touted by some critics as the crown prince of classical ballet, and excoriated by others as its fiend incarnate. He consolidated both positions this spring with *Behind the China Dogs* for the New York City Ballet's American Music Festival, a week at City Center with his own Frankfurt Ballet, and now *in the middle . . .* Forsythe's dance values are featured in the simple production—he designed his own cutout leotards and the characteristic strong white lighting that glares directly downward so it obliterates the dancers' faces.

Forsythe's movement is based on strong pointes and extreme flexibility for the women, muscular arms and torsos for the men, and everyone's ability to spin like mad. Detail is found in the shape of the gesture, not in the intricacy of the step. There's virtually no phrasing and hardly any repetition or development. The dancers burst into whirlwind motion, then leave off and stand around watching each other temperamentally, while Thom Willems's unvarying pulse music mutates from one set of synthesized chirps and thuds to another.

The ballet is a workout. The audience's excitement comes from its constant dynamism, and from the way stopped, often precarious poses suddenly interrupt the streaking momentum. This kind of virtuosity has been around for at least twenty years. Forsythe seems new, I suppose, because he pushes dancers faster than anyone has before.

The evening's program began at the other extreme of European opera house ballet, where dancing takes a backseat to theatricality. Maguy Marin's forty-five-minute spectacle, *Leçons de ténèbres* (François Couperin), gave the prevalent woman-as-victim genre a saintly gloss, as ten identically clad women in turn underwent various trials and rituals preparatory to martyrdom at the hands of thirteen male priestlings.

At first the stage is occupied by an enormous golden throne or altar where a golden saint is enshrined. A procession of noblemen prostrate themselves before the statue, each pulling off a piece of her raiment as he leaves. Stripped down to a white shift, she slumps, vulnerable and human, and the scourging can start. As in a Martha Graham epic (I'm reminded especially of her Joan of Arc dance, *Seraphic Dialogue*), each of the female dancers represents an aspect of the same woman, perhaps the spirit of the fallen city of Jerusalem referred to in Couperin's text, the Lamentations of Jeremiah.

She's anointed and then immersed in a tub of black liquid. She's dragged across the stage on long sheets of cloth. She's flung about and threatened and carried upside down by the men. She dumps dirt onto the floor from her skirt—a nod to the mistress of Tanztheater, Pina Bausch, who coincidentally was shoveling dirt on a grand scale the same week at Brooklyn Academy.

Intermittently the martyr figure emotes and anguishes, while the men stalk her. Marin's choreography looks like warmed-over early Martha Graham with aesthetic overtones, and it hardly showed up amid the decor, which included thirteen lighted six-foot-high candles at the back of the stage, and huge mirrored panels overhead that reflected dramatic lighting projections on the floor and distorted the action nightmarishly. At the end, after she has her hair shorn off, the last woman is laid out and wafted to heaven by means of wires and a harness inside her dress.

What was exalted about the ballet was the music, sublimely sung by Noémi Rime and Véronique Gens and conducted by William Christie, who also accompanied on the organ.

TETLEY'S *LA RONDE*

Christian Science Monitor, 2 August 1988

People don't make ballets based on other texts these days, except to deconstruct them. Glen Tetley's *La Ronde*, which opened the National Ballet of Canada's one-week engagement at the Metropolitan Opera House, could be a textbook example of a genre gone out of style.

La Ronde can be seen stylistically as somewhere in the middle of the Euro-American audience's obsession with couple ballets that began twenty years ago when John Cranko was transforming great works of literature into monumental duets. (Cranko's first big success, the 1965 *Onegin*, constituted the other bill on the Canadians' New York program.) Gradually, plot and production details got dispensed with, until they disappeared entirely in the contemporary works of William Forsythe and a million others. Who needs the complications of story, place, or period, when all we really want to see is superb young men and women grappling in lustful athleticism.

Arthur Schnitzler's *La Ronde* was no literary masterpiece, but rather a brilliant piece of social satire. As his characters made their way from bed to bed, the haut and demimondes of turn-of-the century Vienna merged in a great circling dance of hypocrisy and eroticism. Each character abandons his or her lover for someone new until we meet the first one again, and

Glen Tetley appropriates this dramatic device as a pretext for a string of duets, with an occasional brief solo thrown in.

Evidently he means these dances to reveal some psychological dimension of each relationship, but they consist largely of different varieties of writhings and simulated passion. Everyone acts very hot-blooded, and in every scene one of the partners throws his or her loins onto the prone body of the other after tearing off a discreet quantity of clothing. Other than the whims of the moment, they seem to have no particular reasons for being attracted to each other. Tetley doesn't make even a modest stab at establishing reasons why The Soldier meets The Parlourmaid, for instance, or why The Sweet Young Thing is abandoned by The Husband and discovered by The Poet.

Tetley's *Ronde* lacks any sense of place, despite John MacFarlane's airy structures suggesting doorways, sketchy street vistas, a crumbling baroque ceiling. The program note tells us who the characters are, but there's nothing in how they behave that identifies their status in society, which for the Viennese of 1900 was all-important. In fact, psychosexual behaviors were probably less responsible for the public's condemnation of Schnitzler than his dissection of the Viennese class system, which was being preserved in an elaborate web of social protocols while it was violated behind boudoir doors.

The ten peripatetic lovers were danced with high intensity. But the choreography offered little to convey the difference between fevered emotions and satire. The audience liked Canadian ballerina Karen Kain as The Actress, who got the most emoting to do. Erich Wolfgang Korngold's lush, post-Straussian Sinfonietta Opus 5 was written about ten years after Schnizler's play and suggests some of the decadence we don't see on the stage. Instead, Tetley's choreography brings out a triviality and extravagance in the score, showing you why Korngold later became a successful Hollywood composer.

Robert Desrosiers's *Blue Snake*, which shared the evening with *La Ronde*, takes the attitude that dancers don't even have to be lovers, all they have to do is jump around a lot. In fact, since Desrosiers seems to think the audience is about twelve years old, the less sex and the more action, comic-strip costumes, and funny objects (balloons, five-foot dunce caps), the better. Desrosiers seems heavily influenced by Japanese pop performance, and since the dancers obviously realized how little the niceties of technique counted in this spectacle, I couldn't tell at all whether he can choreograph. *Blue Snake* was one of the silliest expensive ballets I've seen in a long time, but designer Jerrald Smith's gigantic, man-eating puppet, which turned into a great fanged snake that spewed out a blacklit snake-dragon, was a triumph.

MORRIS'S *DRINK TO ME*

Christian Science Monitor, 5 July 1988

Mark Morris is the latest of a long line of modern dance choreographers invited to spice up the repertory of a traditional ballet company. His *Drink to Me Only with Thine Eyes* for American Ballet Theater surprised everyone by not being pretentiously avant-gardish. Morris's own company is so determinedly trendy, so emphatically antiheroic, I wondered how he could use ballet dancers at all, let alone stars like Mikhail Baryshnikov and Martine van Hamel.

Drink, as it's already been nicknamed by insiders, turns out to be Morris's least self-conscious, most attractive work in any medium. It's as if he'd had a latent affinity for ballet all along, and finally found himself in a position where he could use it legitimately. I'm not talking about Morris's ability to choreograph, which has never been in question, but about subtler matters of taste, attitude, and style.

What distinguishes Morris's work above all is his formalism. His dances are always based on whatever musical structures accompany them, and are primarily expositions of a predetermined vocabulary. For his own dancers he imposes odd gestures or poses that suggest an iconography of some kind, onto an earthbound, turned-in lower body, the chest and arms so unstressed as to seem habitually inexpressive. Often I've felt the vocabulary isn't interesting enough to bear the repetition, variation, and other compositional changes to which he subjects it, and his dances end up looking bombastic. Or they stick so literally to the music that they seem hermetic, precious.

Drink to Me Only is as formal as Morris's other work, but somehow it seems freer, airier, and altogether more gracious. Its score, Virgil Thomson's Etudes for Piano, is a terrific asset, because it's lean, modern, and hasn't been heard a million times. Michael Boriskin is seated center stage at the piano, and plays the first of the thirteen etudes almost all the way through before any dancer appears. At the last minute a man walks across with a woman lying athwart his upraised arms. Just before he reaches the other side, he lowers her to the level of his waist, and she shifts too in some small way.

The whole ballet is surprising that way. It doesn't fix itself in big presentational blocks—so many dancers per musical number—the way most ballet-ballets do, or set the stars apart from lesser lights with ballet's usual fanfare. In one section five or six of the twelve men and women come out in turn and do big circling leaping variations, all different, all spectacular and all just a few measures long. To a South American rhythm, Baryshnikov starts one number, spinning and stopping on a dime in quasi-Spanish poses. Long before the music runs out, other dancers enter to share it with him.

The dancers dash in and out so quickly and unpredictably that you hardly have time to identify them, let alone thrill to their antics, before they're replaced by others. In fact, *Drink* reminded me of Harald Lander's *Etudes*, which ABT was supposed to revive this spring but didn't. It's an antidote to that kind of obvious, virtuosic showpiece, simultaneously demolishing and honoring the stodgy stand-there-and-dance-till-you-slay-'em formula.

Morris accomplishes this not only by constantly shuffling the dancers and denying them the usual privileges of rank. Their traveling steps are often runs or skips in irregular rhythms that seem quite natural and unaffected. There's almost no unison dancing in the ballet, but at times the rhythm seems to sweep all the subpatterns into one large action, like the moment when they're suddenly all running in a big circle around the piano. The whole ballet has an air of playfulness that comes not from playful business or mugging, but from a rhythmic freedom and exuberance Morris seldom has shown before.

In fact, with the ballet dancers' elevation and their spacious arm gestures as resources, his whole vocabulary seems more expansive. It also seems more feelingful. Like his other work, *Drink* is deliberately unisex, avoiding most of the conventional role displays of ballet. He's often insisted on treating men and women alike, and in the process has eliminated emotional involvements altogether.

But at the end of *Drink to Me Only*, there's a final etude that sounds sentimental, like a descant to the title song, although the melody is never actually heard. Morris's dancers flock and disperse softly one last time, leaving four couples in a close, almost tender clinch. Then they too exit, and the curtain falls on one man sitting and one woman lying prone on the floor. This is the only moment of stillness in the ballet, and it's poignant, meditative, rare.

STRANGERS IN THE PALACE

Hudson Review, Autumn 1989

Twyla Tharp's debut as an artistic associate and resident choreographer at American Ballet Theater broke over New York in full force during the summer season at the Met. Tharp's daring move—disbanding her own company and throwing her potent choreographic gifts into ABT's arms—might turn out to be the nudge ballet needs to send it into the '90s. Or it might prove just another aborted mission in the costly game of ballet politics.*

Tharp has had her share of raves, but she seems to have peaked in critical favor several years ago. Nowadays she isn't mentioned when pundits read the tea leaves for classical ballet, though she has probably contributed more to the development of classical style than any contemporary choreographer. In a remarkable recent assessment of Tharp's public reception, *Newsweek* dance critic Laura Shapiro examined why this protean artist always seems to arouse suspicion, while critics and audiences are willing to indulge far lesser talents. Tharp, Shapiro thought, "is essentially and invariably avant garde." Shapiro quoted longtime Tharp dancer Sara Rudner's definition of avant garde as "not how weird your work is, but the integrity with which you go about doing the next thing."[1]

Twyla Tharp's embracing of ABT commits her to a world that has little precedent for judging and appreciating her, and even this ratifies her status as an experimentalist. But it is what ABT has committed to Tharp that provokes controversy. While she clearly intends to continue her maverick ways, Ballet Theater sees itself as an institution responsible for the preservation of classical ballet. In taking Tharp into its ranks it has entrusted her with something more than just making novelties.

American ballet for some years has been in creative decline. While George Balanchine was alive, we could ignore the fact that virtually no outstanding new voices were emerging in a younger generation of classical choreographers. During most of the '80s, American ballet companies have been casting about for material, in the historical repertory—*Swan Lake* still sells big—and in the International styles that fuse classical and modern techniques into something that looks contemporary but doesn't tax the mind or the emotions. Forays into the world of postmodern dance seemed invigorating at first, but after several commissions and a couple of com-

---

*At this writing, in late June, ABT artistic director Mikhail Baryshnikov has just announced his resignation, to take effect at the end of the 1990 season. This move will inevitably affect Twyla Tharp's future at Ballet Theater.

petitive funding projects aimed at linkups between the post-Judson formalist experimenters and the pointe-shoes-and-champagne crowd, no style or lasting repertory has resulted. Instead of inspiration, postmodernism added just one more novel ingredient to the ballet stage. As the '80s draw to a close, classical companies have turned to Tanztheater and other politicized European forms that actually denigrate classicism as a language and as a social phenomenon. Producers and critics are deeply ambivalent about the nature of ballet's future evolution. For so long that evolution was defined as wherever Balanchine took it, but now where do we go? Too much innovation may carry the form away from its particular mission, and too little may fix it in a lifeless mode of Balanchine replications.

One of the principal contenders for the saving of classical ballet is William Forsythe, the American director of the Frankfurt Ballet, whose *Behind the China Dogs* was the hit of last year's American Music Festival at the New York City Ballet. Forsythe's modernism resides in his deconstructive techniques. He uses classical vocabulary—extends it, according to his chief supporter, Anna Kisselgoff of the *New York Times*—as one of many texts, to be chopped up, distorted, layered with other material, in violently theatrical dances. His posture is quasi-intellectual; his dancers are like demonic acrobats, ready to test the limits of human flexibility and endurance. Provocative and gripping though Forsythe's ballets may be, only one or two of them have remained in anyone's repertory for more than a season. Forsythe isn't interested in the development of classicism but its opposite. He may use the classical language but his evident purpose is to exploit and devalue it rather than ensure its continuing health. Even Anna Kisselgoff has expressed disappointment that "he has settled into a formula for creating dances rather than a true esthetic."[2]

The other darling of the critics at the moment is Mark Morris, who, despite his great musicality and compositional skill, has not yet been seen by anyone as inheriting the leadership of classical ballet. Morris is a modern dancer, his dances nonballetic or antiballetic. Though capable of movement invention to suit a variety of periods and styles, his preferred look is an earthbound, deliberately graceless solidity and a mimetic rather than a decorative use of the upper body. Always an exhibitionist and provocateur, Morris has invited even more notoriety in the past year since he took over the Théâtre de la Monnaie in Brussels, former home of that other great antiballetic showman-modernist, Maurice Béjart. His most balletic work to date was composed for the 1988 season of Ballet Theater. *Drink to Me Only with Thine Eyes* was praised by *New Yorker* guest critic Alastair Macaulay for its "casual grace and unforced wit," which Macaulay saw as Tharpian.[3]

It would take another whole study to catalogue the critical displacement and qualified praise for Tharp. Though she's influenced a whole generation of dancers and choreographers, something about what she's doing herself is always troubling critics. They think she's too slick, too angry, they think she makes fun of classical dancing, they think she makes fun of dancers. The single most unsettling thing about Tharp is her refusal to stand still. She disregards the canons, even those she herself created five minutes ago. This leaves critics in the risky position of having to evaluate everything she does with brand new eyes.

She has been stylistically consistent—the Tharp "look" originated twenty years ago, from her body and those of her first dancers, especially Sara Rudner. Yet she has drastically changed subjects, modes, media. In addition to her own company, which underwent many turnovers of personnel, she has choreographed for ballet companies, ice skaters, basketball players, actors. Wherever she goes, she leaves behind a new perception of the body, new ways to see the choreographic process, dances that give enjoyment years after they're made. But the attraction to new venues, new sources, which counts in Mark Morris's favor, in Tharp is considered a disadvantage. Her three new works for Ballet Theater illustrate this unpredictability. Not only are the dances in three totally different styles, they propose three totally different ways to use and present dancers. I think each one is a small miracle of stagecraft and choreography.

Everlast is a pocket-sized musical comedy, with songs by Jerome Kern, a love triangle that works out for the best, a chorus line that fills up chinks in the rickety plot, and several extraneous but amusing characters Tharp created to give roles to dancers she couldn't use in the leads. It's set in a Gatsby-esque 1919, where two American mythic types, the fortune-hunting debutante and the parvenu prizefighter, submit to a brief, disinterested engagement that terminates when each of them falls for an unlikely substitute, a parlor maid masquerading as a sparring partner and a real sparring partner masquerading as Léonide Massine's Peruvian dandy in *Gaîté Parisienne.*

There's no more choreography in the piece than is good for it, but what there is is an anthology of balleticized social dance styles from the period. There are lovely in-jokes referring to the ballet repertory, like the moment when the debutante, played by Susan Jaffe or Cynthia Harvey, arrives for her wedding. The entire cast lines up on the diagonal, with the Champ, Kevin O'Day, waiting at the downstage end. When the bride appears, all in white, the moment evokes the lore of ballet weddings, beginning with *The Sleeping Beauty.*

So *Everlast* is a thoroughly entertaining show, with everything unnecessary left out including dialogue, and everything else in the formula neatly fabricated. It's also a good-humored comment on the clichés of the old Broadway musical and the old spectacle ballet, the crassness of their producers, and the way ballet companies are now eyeing show business in their quest for successful new material. It shouldn't be forgotten either that dancers, including Tharp and ABT director Mikhail Baryshnikov, aren't immune to the glamour of Broadway. No one is better than Tharp at taking a hard look at dancing and dancers with an attitude that is simultaneously serious and sardonic. The audience can swallow one side of this but not both, as was shown by its failure to appreciate Balanchine doing the same thing in *Bourrée Fantasque* when ABT performed it. Today, you have to be either trashing ballet, as Forsythe does, or treating it with deadly solemnity.

Tharp went deeper into farce with *Bum's Rush,* a work almost no one approved of and everyone enjoyed to some extent. Here Tharp was not only irreverent toward the conventions of dancing, she mixed her signals to the point of incoherence. *Bum's Rush* has three sets of dancers, who remain isolated most of the time. There are classical ballet dancers, Gil Boggs, Elaine Kudo, and Ashley Tuttle, plus Sandra Brown, who appears as a pair of pointe shoes inside a huge rubber tire. Richard Colton and Shelley Washington are a pair of characters almost recognizable as that goofy couple down the street. Kevin O'Day, Jamie Bishton, and Daniel Sanchez form a trio whose finely calibrated moves are either harmonious or belligerent. In a preview performance at the Guggenheim Museum in April, Tharp identified this last group with her sister and twin brothers, who talked in code which only she could understand, and who were always fighting. If you didn't know this or the other clues Tharp passed on about the piece, you could see its humor as related to the comic violence of Saturday morning kids' cartoons.

Bum's Rush seems to be an homage to Tharp's pop-ridden childhood. It creates a world where the literature was made of celluloid (her parents ran a drive-in movie), where language echoed radio advertising jingles, where cruelty was a way of showing affection, and where people yelled in order to be heard above a roar of competing egos. I infer all this from things Tharp has said and dances she has made over the years. In fact, I think *Bum's* is a kind of successor to her semi-autobiographical *When We Were Very Young* and *The Catherine Wheel,* both of which pitted abrasive family members against each other.

Collage techniques are certainly not new, but people didn't know what to make of *Bum's Rush.* It was too unflattering, too fragmented. The new postmodernists usually find ways to make their heterogeneous choices more accessible. Martha Clarke covers the same period or locale from different points of view; John Kelly follows a single narrative thread in contrasting "languages." But Tharp's dance has no apparent story, no stylistic reconciliation. The action splats all over the stage, the beautiful (a great duet of leaping in two styles, by ABT's Gil Boggs and Tharp's Richard Colton, also ballet trained) intercut with the dreadful (rude noises, pratfalls, collisions, hysterical laughter). *Bum's Rush* is violent, it's fast, it's graphic, literal, mundane, but it doesn't make sense. The dancers are phenomenal, but you can't love them. For these reasons, it strikes me as the most advanced postmodern piece I've seen this year, the one that truly reflects our culture.

I've always found Twyla Tharp's closeness to the real world admirable. What the audience wants, I think, is some sign of mercy, and this, so far, is not within Tharp's capacity. She is the most unsentimental of choreographers, the most hardened to the effects of passion. Her third new ballet, *Quartet,* is a virtuosic exercise for four of the company's high-powered technicians. (I saw Cynthia Gregory, Cynthia Harvey, Ricardo Bustamante, and Jeremy Collins.) To a minimalist string quartet, G Song, by Terry Riley, the ballet simply explores a vocabulary with the most sophisticated compositional manipulations: counterpoint, canon, inversion, mirroring. The movement is extremely smooth and fast, with almost no pauses or stressed transitions between steps. I love its dryness, its assertion that we need attend to nothing except the spectacle of Tharp working at her craft. By the end of the season, when Gregory was beginning to get more free with the piece, more rhythmically flexible, it seemed like a bonus.

There's always room for compassion, eroticism, personality in Tharp's work. Dancers can illuminate and transform her work, and that is also a mark of a great classical ballet. One of Tharp's gifts is the ability to visualize the best in dancers, and over the years nearly every member of her company became an individual presence through some choreographic opportunity she provided. Whether she'll be able to do this for dancers at ABT is a question. That she can inspire them, galvanize them to action that is rich and invigorating, has never been in doubt. But can she hold their attention? At ABT she'll always be competing for rehearsal time, for dancers. She'll need extra coaching sessions to help them gain her special skills— speed, fluidity, intricate timing, an articulateness of the whole body—and the nonchalance, wit, and surprise that make her style unique.

Another serious question I have is what will happen to the dancers she brought into ABT with her. Of course they'll do her dances; except for

Quartet they're featured in all the Tharp works now on view. But so far they haven't appeared much in any other repertory. Kevin O'Day mimed the Major Domo in *Swan Lake*, and at one performance of that ballet Daniel Sanchez was pouring wine. Will Elaine Kudo be reinstated in the roles she had when she left ABT a few years ago to join Tharp? The formation of a Tharp cadre within ABT might be efficient, but it would also demean their talents to relegate them to servant roles in the larger rep.

Even if Tharp gets what she needs from ABT for herself and her dancers, I wonder if she'll want to stay. She can certainly see her work showcased there. In addition to the three new pieces and two erstwhile Tharp Company dances (*The Fugue* and *In the Upper Room*) in the spring 1989 schedule, she has created a number of other ballets at ABT over the years: *Push Comes to Shove, The Little Ballet, Sinatra Suite,* and *Bach Partita.* And there are other Tharp ballets and prepointe dances that I'd love to see ABT do. I wonder, though, if she will be content with simply maintaining her repertory and making new works. She's always said that's what she wants, and the reason for joining ABT in the first place was to achieve some stability without the necessity of raising the money for it. But Tharp is a contrary animal. Just when her fairy godmother hands over her third wish and you think she'll turn into a princess, she's quite likely to kick the stardust away and ask for something else. I'm not betting on Tharp in the role of Cinderella.

TOO BRIEF A FLING

Christian Science Monitor, 30 May 1990

The ballet audience may be gullible but it always knows. American Ballet Theater was beginning its two-month residency at the Metropolitan Opera House—the season had officially opened the night before with a reprise of January's commemorative gala. Primed by advance publicity celebrating ABT's fiftieth birthday, curious about its future under a new management, prepared to be blown away by the company's biggest guns, the audience wasn't sure what to do. Throughout the first three ballets, tentative spatters of applause erupted in the wrong places, major stunts fell on unseeing eyes, dutiful ovations rewarded tepid star turns.

Then, scarcely five minutes into Twyla Tharp's new ballet, *Brief Fling*, all the doubt and suspense started to shake loose in little exhalations of laughter, gasps of surprise, stifled roars of appreciation, and the house exploded in a final outburst that called the company back again and again.

Whatever Ballet Theater may think about the audience's supposed love of tradition, Tharp demonstrated, not for the first time, that dancers can look both wonderful and contemporary, and that the audience will understand.

Brief Fling is a bird's eye view of Tharp's collaboration with Ballet Theater. The title makes ironic reference to her attempted assimilation of her own modern dancers into the ABT organization during the year or so she spent as artistic associate/resident choreographer. When her mentor, Mikhail Baryshnikov, announced his intention to leave last summer, Tharp's idyll came to an end. Now she isn't listed anywhere on the company roster although several of her ballets remain in the repertory, and her future there is uncertain. You'd never know *Brief Fling* was born of such a disappointing experience. The ballet is joyful, virtuosic, and brave. The dancers look totally energized and invested in the movement, as if devising new ways to make the audience see is what they do every day of the week.

Tharp sorted her ensemble of eighteen dancers into four cadres, each with stylistically different music and movement, and mismatching odd costumes (by Isaac Mizrahi). The four groups dance on and off in unpredictable but not clashing sequence, the music switches without blinking an eye from drumrolls to Percy Grainger to expressionistic atonality. The piece is almost a catalogue of ballet styles: Romantic (a quartet in red plaid, suggesting *La Sylphide*), classical (Cheryl Yaeger in a ballerina's tutu and navy blue tights, with Julio Bocca), modern (four couples in bold white plaid and ponytails), and Tharp dance (Keith Roberts and Tharp Company alumni Shelley Washington, Kevin O'Day, and Jamie Bishton, half-dressed in practice garb and green kilts).

The action moves so fast you can't see it all in one viewing. Yet, in the moment, everything seems clear and immediate and witty. One pleasure turns into another without pause for appreciation. Bocca flies through multiple pirouettes, then steps out of them to give Yaeger the floor. Washington spends much of the ballet lounging in the air, carried by her three partners. Bishton storms through a solo of huge leaps and rough but soft gestures.

Each group leads into the next, blends or accommodates with the others, until a big fugue where they all dance together in a formal pattern that still allows each group to keep its stylistic integrity. After that, they drift away to an almost-sweet string melody. The last thing you see is the corps in white beginning to strut on, hands on hips, shoulders leading, like the stalwarts in *A Chorus Line*. When the curtain comes down, you feel reconciliation is still possible, though you know it's just a wish.

Ballet Theater threw its full arsenal of bedazzlement into this program, but aside from the Tharp it all looked ornate and archaic. Frederick Ashton's *Birthday Offering* (1956) is a grandiose exercise in Russian-style classicism. Seven couples dressed to the teeth in awful ballet regalia—long, glittering tutus shaped like lampshades, tiaras, puffed-sleeve tunics—perform ensembles and variations that show off their elegant technique. Ashton's choreography landed square on Glazunov's beat, and the dancers looked very correct.

Next, Cynthia Harvey and guest artist Fernando Bujones waded through the Black Swan Pas de Deux. After the blandness or fake hauteur that ABT dancers affect in the classics, it was a pleasure to see Carla Fracci's rapturous acting style in Antony Tudor's 1936 *Jardin aux Lilas* (Lilac Garden). Fracci, a Ballet Theater favorite back in the '60s and early '70s, returned to dance one of her most famous roles. Technically she's no longer on top of Tudor's demanding choreography, which might make the audience think Tudor was only about "expressive" dance, but Martine Van Hamel, as the proud Other Woman, revealed Tudor's genius for steps with the passion built into them. *Jardin*, languishing in tragic longings, guilty secrets and loveless marriages, seems quaint and a little farfetched today. But Tudor's nostalgic vapors, along with the pomp of Imperial classicism, are apparently going to be a mainstay as ABT strides backwards into the next decade.

 RESURFACING

Hudson Review, Autumn 1991

Each of New York's big ballet companies is always struggling to create a separate identity for what it does, while maintaining its links with something bigger and even more unnameable called "ballet." In the past year, as the dance and culture worlds staggered under the triple handicap of AIDS, funding cuts, and the new puritanism, American Ballet Theater and the New York City Ballet resolutely cast their nets for the new support they must attract. Both companies have been through nearly a decade of wavering popularity and are searching for clear new artistic policies. Both companies have undergone major shifts in management and are attempting to conjure a working premise for themselves out of their past successes —and also project some vistas for ballet in the future. Above all, they both need a formula for filling those expensive and all-important seats, three thousand of them a night in the New York State Theater and four thousand at the Metropolitan Opera House. In their nearly concurrent spring seasons, neither one of them fared very well at the box office. More and more, I wonder whether big ballet is simply becoming obsolete.

Ballet Theater has made dramatic changes since Jane Hermann took over the company last year. She now lists herself, with longtime ABT chieftain Oliver Smith, as Director, and has purged potentially unfriendly voices from both administrative and artistic departments. Hermann's stated objective when she came in was to lower the deficit, and she seems to feel the best way to do this is to return to Ballet Theater's past incarnations as a purveyor of lavish classical ballets and romances, with world-famous stars in the leading roles. This isn't any more frugal than what the company was doing before Hermann arrived.

In the arts, the equation between income and product can be about as predictable as roulette. What costs big bucks to put on a stage may not bring in paying customers, while a comparatively modest attraction can be a hit. Ballet Theater's ostentatious three-year-old Christian Lacroix *Gaîté Parisienne* looks as dated and silly today as a 1988 Lacroix party dress would in the audience. New costumes and sets make very little difference in the quality of *Coppélia*; do they really draw enough patrons to justify their cost? The audience for one kind of spectacle may be indifferent to the next. Ballet companies have always had to find a balance between novelty seekers and loyal, long-term fans, and their most serious problem is finding and nurturing choreographic talent that the audience will be willing to follow. Ballet Theater has none of this at the moment. It's not even making feeble gestures at giving its own dancers a chance to choreograph.

Two-thirds of the 1991 ABT New York season was devoted to four full-length nineteenth-century ballets (*Coppélia*, *Don Quixote*, *La Bayadère*, and *Giselle*) and a twentieth-century facsimile, Kenneth MacMillan's *Romeo and Juliet*. The remaining twenty-six performances featured mixed bills of fifteen one-act ballets and two other nineteenth-century excerpts. Only five of the shorter works could remotely be called contemporary, four by Twyla Tharp and one by Mark Morris. Of the rest, Jiri Kylian's *Sinfonietta* is going on fifteen years old, and the others dodder back from there into antiquity. Gone are the postmodern choreographies commissioned by Mikhail Baryshnikov during his nine-year reign as artistic director. Gone too are Baryshnikov's imaginative efforts to modernize and diversify the company. Only two years ago ABT was performing dances by Merce Cunningham, Martha Graham, George Balanchine, Clark Tippett. Most of that has been phased out, and it seems Tharp will soon withdraw two or three more of her remaining ballets. Everything, in fact, that might have reminded the audience that it and the dancers have a contemporary existence in common has been banished. The fiftieth anniversary souvenir program book with the soft-porn Annie Leibovitz photographs of all the company bigwigs in perfume-ad poses and the middle-rank dancers in peekaboo déshabille is now a collector's item, replaced by a brochure featuring synopses of the fairy tales and dreary head shots of the dancers.

All this proclaims Ballet Theater's determination to be known as a classical company in the most regressive sense. Though Hermann would be the last to acknowledge her predecessor's contribution to this conservative agenda, Baryshnikov's persistent attention to the training of the corps de ballet turned it into a scrupulously technical instrument, indispensable to the credible execution of the classics. By the end of the 1991 season, what with the guest and resident stars dragging acquiescent conductors through any sort of tempi they desired while hogging all the bravos, the corps was once more disintegrating into a ragged, lackadaisical crew.

The classics according to Hermann are fancy platters heaped with dancing, garnished here and there with plot. If these ballets were ever really unified choreographed entities in the first place, they've now become icons, displaying certain incantatory scenes, gestures, atmospheres. *Giselle* must have its peasants and wilis, its mad scene and its repentant playboy aristocrat. *La Bayadère* is synonymous with its twenty-four Shades descending the ramp, then posing and balancing in perfect celestial accord. Beyond those signature elements a classic is anybody's ballgame. Its choreography will have been so thoroughly distressed by time that no one feels the slightest hesitation about inserting new bits, rechoreographing from memory, shifting scenes around, throwing out steps they don't feel like doing, and substituting what they like better.

I think George Balanchine's scorn for the creaky old potboilers was what led him throughout his lifetime to seek concise, gripping alternatives. New York City Ballet's *Sleeping Beauty* has been in the discussion stage for years: Balanchine himself set the Garland Dance, for sixteen children and sixteen couples from the corps, in 1981, but who knows if he ever would have reconstructed the entire ballet? Peter Martins, now sole head of City Ballet following the retirements of Jerome Robbins and Lincoln Kirstein, wanted to rehabilitate *Beauty* without losing its character, to somehow make a Balanchinian all-dance work out of it. What resulted was a curious and unsettling mixture. When the curtain rose on the Prologue's sumptuous court scene (called Act I, The Christening in this version), I felt an almost overwhelming dismay at the sight of this most original of ballet companies dealing in the mundane currency of nineteenth-century repertory.

Balanchine did revert to the classics on occasion—his *Nutcracker*, of course, is pure nostalgia. But he was more likely to renovate them in his own eccentric ways. He made a cleaned-up, nontraditional *Coppélia*, turned *Don Quixote* into a gothic nightmare, and staged four or five brilliant *Raymonda* one-acts as well as glosses on *Swan Lake*, *La Sylphide*, and others. I think Peter Martins was going for a similar revisionism in *Sleeping Beauty*. He made a virtue of what was termed streamlining. This meant nonstop dancing and elimination of the dramatics and other passages that, according to Balanchine doctrine, slow down the old ballets without adding anything. In the event, however, the tempi were pressured and the dancing looked less like Balanchinian panache than undue haste.

One reason for the survival of *Sleeping Beauty* is its tremendous variety and scale. It has peasant dances and court dances and a classical corps de ballet and eighteenth-century social dances. The omission of the latter, in the hunting scene, was Martins's most regrettable economy. The traditional *Sleeping Beauty* has virtuosity and magic, civility and charm, spectacular stage business and tiny, detailed solo dancing. Martins seemed to be trying to even out the stylistic disparities in the ballet, to make it a more unified exposé of classical style. The headlong pace piled one number on top of another without a break, so that the audience couldn't catch its breath and savor what it had seen. Without the texture and stage illusions, this seemed like a longer than ordinary evening of dancing. Some people liked the use of slide projections successively approaching the palace or showing the vines grow up around it. I thought this technological gimmick conflicted with the nineteenth-century aesthetic underlying a reconstruction.

Sleeping Beauty, of course, provides new challenges for the dancers, and the two Auroras I saw, Kyra Nichols and Judith Fugate, were as good as I expected them to be. Helene Alexopoulos surprised me, though, as a commanding, serene Lilac Fairy; and Merrill Ashley revealed a splendid gift for character in the mime role of Carabosse, the evil fairy. Propelled by their successes in *Beauty*, Fugate and Alexopoulos seemed to soar through the rest of the season with new confidence and technical assurance.

Dancing is really what the New York City Ballet is all about, and Balanchine's legacy of choreographies continues to inspire sublime performances. But this season, only a little more than half the ballets in the seven weeks following *Beauty* were by Balanchine, the rest coming from Martins, Robbins, and John Taras. As the Balanchine component of the NYCB repertory diminishes, not only do the demands on the dancers and the audience ease up, the company itself gradually changes. Today there are fewer dancers who can do Balanchine superbly; the Balanchine rep is slightly less convincing.

Martins continued his choreographic investigations into a speeded-up modernism with *Ash*, to yet another gratuitous score of repetitious but arrhythmic declamatory bytes by Michael Torke. In Europe, where all dance is seen as ideology, classical ballet signifies an imperialistic oppression, and the contemporary choreographer's job is to exact reparations. The gaunt, fast, grapplings distilled from the classical pas de deux, the harsh, distorted shapes, the reduction of phrasing to its propulsive usefulness have also been adopted by Peter Martins in his leotard ballets. Martins, though, combines classicism with anticlassicism. *Ash* is almost obsessively designed in space and uses a vocabulary of big jumps and multiple turns that don't stop for breath. You see the expansion, the speed, the physicality that Balanchine exploited throughout his career, but finesse, wit and virtuosity are replaced by an organized eroticism.

Wendy Whelan and Nilas Martins, who led the ensemble of four couples, represent the second generation of an evolving new look in NYCB dancers. Whelan physically resembles the prototype of Martins's dry, elastic modern ballerinas, Heather Watts, though she's younger and stronger technically. At the end of the season she was rewarded with a promotion to principal dancer. Nilas Martins was moving up into major roles all during the season. In looks he resembles his gorgeous father, but he lacks the intensity and the grounded sense of weight that made Peter Martins simultaneously authoritative and sexy as a dancer.

The younger Martins made a surprisingly decent debut in *Apollo*, the mere thought of which outraged some Balanchinians. Obviously he had been well coached in one of his father's most famous roles, but he was unable to rouse himself from his habitual impassivity, even when Darci Kistler, his Terpsichore, smirked and flirted with him like a prom queen. Kistler seems frozen now into a perpetual elation; she seems to be working at looking glorious and unable to tone it down and let her dancing speak for itself.

The search for an accommodation between classicism and modernity, decorum and flamboyance, is a central preoccupation at both NYCB and ABT. In the absence of choreographic inspiration, style is the hot issue. Both companies have a good supply of classical dancers now, and the Balanchine works show them off. But ABT's one "new" piece of the season was a pedantic rehash of bits from the third act of *Raymonda* by Fernando Bujones. And then there was Enrique Martinez's tired-looking touch-up of

Coppélia, and Vladimir Vasiliev's chaotic restaging of *Don Quixote*. No wonder the company called on personalities to sell its season.

Sylvie Guillem, one of the season's visiting box office attractions, wore what must have been her own, entirely mismatching costume, and adjusted *Don Quixote* to suit her surefire if somewhat limited technical tricks. Guillem played the Spanish innkeeper's daughter as an all-purpose, willful peasant girl. She could have stepped into *Coppélia* or *La Fille Mal Gardée* without any trouble. Guillem's performances sold well, as most of the other season attractions did not, and the kind of success she had not only encouraged the sensation-hungry audience. It helped reinstitutionalize star behavior as a role model for the dancers.

Ballet Theater has developed a few big stars from its own ranks, Cynthia Gregory and Fernando Bujones among them. I didn't see Bujones in the few performances he did before he was injured, but Gregory was carrying on her usual love affair with the audience, capped by a sold-out farewell performance of the second act of *Swan Lake*. Gregory has been known for her superstrong, smooth technique. She made the act of balancing on one toe an endurance contest, always capped by a triumphant knowing smile. In the 1991 season this trick was adopted by women at every opportunity.

Dancers in principal roles were encouraged not only to show off but to indulge in temperament. Julio Bocca, the young Argentinian phenomenon, is allowed an apparently free rein. Backstage scuttlebutt is full of his refusals to dance—Tharp's *Brief Fling,* for instance, was made on him last year, but now he thinks it's bad for his form. Onstage, his form in *Romeo* the night I saw him do it consisted of passionate tossings of the head and a minimum of dancing power. Another night, in *La Bayadére*, he insisted on twirling Cynthia Harvey for a few extra pirouettes that made the conductor wait a couple of beats each time before finishing the phrase. Twice, later on in the same performance, he gestured and hissed audibly from the stage to get the conductor to speed up his tempi.

It's a mystery to me that, although both ABT and NYCB have ballets in a range of periods and styles, neither company seems to prepare dancers stylistically or dramatically in an organized way. Dancers, left to their own devices, imitate what they've seen other dancers do successfully with a role, but we seldom see an interpretation that looks carefully thought out. When a dancer seizes a role, as Merrill Ashley did with Carabosse, not only is a new facet of that dancer revealed, the role's familiarity gets wiped away and we can see new things in it. Kevin O'Day, one of the Twyla Tharp dancers who joined Ballet Theater during the ill-fated ABT-Tharp merger, has worked his way into a number of character roles in the repertory. His rendition of the Friend who rescues Hagar from spinsterhood in *Pillar of Fire* was just such a revelation. O'Day stressed the dancing elements in what is usually done as a mimed role, and made me feel for the first time ever that his interest in Hagar was more than platonic.

And throughout the season Victor Barbee reanimated stereotyped character roles with loving specificity. As the High Brahmin in *Bayadère* he gave no hint of the pompous lecher we usually see; instead he seemed dismayed and tortured by the conflict between his spirituality and his unrequited love for Nikiya. His Doctor Coppélius was dotty and irascible enough not to be cute. Barbee greatly enlivened the second act by actually dancing the duets with the doll he thought had come to life. His physicality made the irony of Swanilda's trick even more poignant. His Gamache in *Don Quixote* was not just a fop but a nouveau riche who hadn't succeeded in covering up his gutter origins. And as Tybalt in *Romeo and Juliet* he was arrogant, spoiled, aggressive. If I could see all the characters in these old ballets danced and acted with such care, I might appreciate them more.

SURVIVAL SKILLS

Hudson Review, Autumn 1995

What big dance does these days is mostly marketing, institutional promotion rather than *la danse pour la danse*. Even dance performance itself seems to be concerned with selling the audience on what they came for. The traditional sequence seems reversed: instead of buying a ticket because you like dance, and then supporting the institution when you're satisfied, you enter the theater as an investor and if you get repaid by the performance, then the dance has gained a fan. Big dance isn't only the ballet companies, which have huge budgets to meet, but small- and medium-size modern dance companies trying to work on a more or less year-round basis.

American Ballet Theater's spring New York season arrived on a campaign blitz that included a high-gloss program book, the hyped return of Twyla Tharp to the fold, and the release—first in a theater, later on public TV—of Frederick Wiseman's film "Ballet." All these events could have held artistic interest, but all of them also resembled public service announcements for the company, which appeared to be in a relatively healthy phase of its chronic fiscal indisposition.

The Wiseman film, a seemingly disinterested look at the company, "chronicles the reality of American Ballet Theater," according to a Channel

13 press release. The respected documentary filmmaker had not yet turned his camera on a dance subject, and the three-hour film received major support from several public broadcast media and the National Endowment for the Arts. Too bad they couldn't have funded some dancing instead. The deeper I got into the film, the more depressed I became at the banality of Wiseman's vision. Not a shot, not a scene in the movie reveals anything that hasn't been said about ballet before. Wiseman yielded to every clichéd enthusiasm of the novice balletgoer: the sweaty body parts, the silk-shod feet, the tense backstage faces, the relentless teachers, the repetitive, grinding exercises.

There's almost no talking in the film. Most of that happens in offices. Cowering applicants are told they didn't make the cut, former company director Jane Hermann harasses presenters over the phone, ballet master David Richardson is interviewed by the late dance writer Otis Stuart. Terse dialogue in rehearsal scenes fades in and out, overheard but not understood. Hours into the movie, the company goes on tour to Greece, then to Copenhagen. The dancers—kids on holiday—sun themselves in between run-throughs, ride the rides in Tivoli. As a grand finale, after sketchy bits of performances, we get company stars Alessandra Ferri and Julio Bocca flinging passionately through two scenes from Kenneth MacMillan's *Romeo and Juliet.*

So Wiseman's picture of Ballet is not only trite but condescending. None of the speakers, teachers, choreographers, dancers, or anyone else is identified, either in the film or in end-credits. Grown-ups do the talking. Dancers don't talk, they go to amusement parks, take care of their stressed bodies, and think about clothes. They don't even dance ballets, not in full performance views. Wiseman's camera zooms in on them from strange angles, cuts away to the audience, stops when it gets bored.

If the film is a disappointment, the fact that it was made at all props up the company, and the enterprise of ballet itself. Wiseman studies the arts and has noticed that ballet people are dedicated. In canned interviews released by NET, he remarks on the "unmistakable force and sincerity in their approach." Yet he adds a disclaimer: "I have no more interest in making a statement about the importance of artists than I do about the importance of teachers or police officers." I don't know what to make of this extraordinary disclosure. Maybe it represents some new kind of objectivity in the arts, where the signifier is more important than the signified. It seems to be shared by choreographers. Tharp's new works, and the other two premieres I saw, seemed detached, even insincere, designed to prop up the idea of ballet in a society that's trashing art in a big way. All of them told you over and over what a moving, beautiful, exciting thing ballet is and how physical excess means moral perfection.

There was Lar Lubovitch's *A Brahms Symphony* (No. 3), most of which he had choreographed ten years ago for his own company. This spring he expanded the ensemble to nineteen and added the last movement for ABT. Four solo dancers in saturated colors were counterpointed against the black-clad corps, which swirled and surged across the stage in massive waves. Lubovitch's movement has little to do with virtuosity but everything to do with flow. Bodies alone, in couples, in groups, fling out in sculptural curves when the music is fast, stretch languidly when it's slow. The soloists seemed to represent something, but I didn't know what. Lubovitch's work is impressive without making any demands on the audience. Probably his effects are similar to those of Léonide Massine's imposing symphonic allegories in the 1940s, except that in those days the audience wanted to be astounded by ballet dancers' technical feats; those are a dime a dozen today.

States of Grace, by James Kudelka, drew on another musical classic, Paul Hindemith's Mathis der Maler symphony. This was knottier but in the end no more lucid than the Lubovitch. Three female soloists were hoisted and manipulated by various men in tricky designs that indicated suffering and religiosity. I thought the ballet might have had some reference to the source of the music, medieval painter Matthias Grünewald's Isenheim altarpiece, but I didn't read any promotional or critical confirmation of this, and I don't think the audience cared.

Tharp's *How Near Heaven* (to the Benjamin Britten Variations on a Theme of Frank Bridge) also aspired to cosmic meaning, by the choreographer's own admission. Before the season, Tharp said some pretty pompous things to the Sunday *New York Times*, which headlined a page-one-plus-full-page-inside interview "Twyla Tharp's Metaphysical Muse." I have to admit that I become nervous about Tharp when she talks most earnestly about her work. Here, two female soloists, Susan Jaffe and Kathleen Moore, are supposed to represent subjectivity and objectivity, while a featured couple (Cynthia Harvey and Charles Askegard) is more stable or complete ("intact" was Tharp's word). Heavy stuff.

Again the audience was treated to masses of perpetual motion and the sight of star dancers doing important things. Like her choice of music, Tharp's choreographic scheme was imaginative, but somehow the ballet looked eccentric rather than original. It didn't seem to hang together. Moore and Jaffe had some nice duets, dancing close together in an intimate way rather than showing off. Jaffe was partnered by two men (Gil

Boggs and Guillaume Graffin), while Harvey and Askegard hardly danced at all, wafting through every once in a while and gazing sedately at the audience.

What really surprised me about the ballet was how little relationship there seemed to be between these principals and an ensemble of twelve men and women, who were a very noticeable presence but whose movement didn't match theirs. Their rhythms and body shapes seemed to come from an alien source, rather than a complementary one. On one program *How Near Heaven* and *A Brahms Symphony* were programmed with George Balanchine's *Theme and Variations*, and then the virtues of classicism became totally clear. *Theme*, a glorious textbook case, shows you everything about the range of relationships that are possible between dancers, between steps, between categories of movement, between music and dancing. *Theme*, by the way, was choreographed for Ballet Theater in 1947, when Balanchine hadn't yet stabilized a company of his own and freelanced every chance he got.

For months I had been looking forward to the gala that celebrated Tharp's return to ABT after five years. Three new ballets by Tharp on one evening. What I didn't learn until the night of the performance was that only one of the premieres, the Britten, was going into repertory. The other two were throwaways. Now Tharp's throwaways can be better than most people's major work, but not in this case. *Americans We* and *Jump Start* showed Tharp in her patriotic guise, which often makes her revert to stereotyping and automatism. *Americans We* was set to nineteenth-century parlor songs like "I Dream of Jeannie with the Light Brown Hair" and reminded me of too many other ballets to be pleasant. *Jump Start* had live music by Wynton Marsalis and his orchestra, and presented stage renditions of assorted social dances—lindy, mambo, bebop, and so forth.

Ironically, at the moment when she is finally being celebrated by the establishment as a master choreographer, Tharp seems to be floundering creatively. Throughout her career Tharp has formed deep and productive attachments to dancers, and their devotion to her has given credence to her originality. Even if the public didn't understand her, the dancers did. Freelancing the past few years, she's worked with some distinctive modern and ballet dancers—Jamie Bishton, Kevin O'Day, Jodi Melnick, Shawn Stevens, Stacy Caddell—independents who risked safer careers in order to join her, and brought a feisty confidence to her dances. Though she has a cadre in Ballet Theater that she trusts to interpret her work (Moore, Boggs, Jaffe, others), her dance now seems impersonal, almost circumspect. Tharp's old fans miss the articulation, the sensuality of her early movement style, which she seems to have traded in for an escalating virtuosity in speed and turning, and the poised, vertical body to support it. The choreography is emphatic, orderly, with nothing thrown away. There are no hidden nuances, no jokes but the obvious ones, no numbers that suddenly reveal a treasure in a dancer you'd taken for granted.

I have great faith in Tharp's ability to galvanize the ballet stage, in "pure" ways as well as entertaining ones. *Bach Partita* (1983), *Quartet* (1989), and *Brief Fling* (1989) are examples of rigorous but ingenious things she's done for ABT that have disappeared. Perhaps she's decided her reformist efforts aren't appreciated there, so she needn't waste them. The company's faint-hearted New York repertory this spring was packed with full-length ballets: forty-four of the sixty-four performances were either *Giselle*, *La Bayadére*, *Romeo and Juliet*, or *Don Quixote*. Reconstituted from the past or newly invented, these productions give the audience what it wants: beautiful ballerinas, romantic suitors who can jump like grasshoppers, neat rows of chorus girls in filmy dresses, lush symphonic music, and fantasy plots enacted with plenty of authentic local color. Tharp's previous efforts to renovate this formula have sometimes been fabulously successful (*Push Comes to Shove,* 1976), sometimes unclassifiable (*Everlast,* 1989), but ABT backed off from keeping the borderline ones around long enough to gain a following. I sometimes think even *Push* would have evaporated without the magnetic attraction of Mikhail Baryshnikov in its first few years.

Ballet Theater has never claimed to be an experimental company, but it seems to me our definition of what is good dance is beginning to merge with what is safe, and innovation—or even minimal challenge—isn't a choreographer's most compelling goal. This idea occurred to me while looking at David Parsons's modern dance company during its two-week run at the Joyce Theater. Parsons, who danced for nine years with Paul Taylor, has a mordant wit, a plush sense of movement, and a shrewd intelligence about dance making in the '90s. His successful ten-member company performs a varied repertory, all by Parsons. In the phenomenally balanced program I saw, there was a formal piece to classical music (*Bachiana*), a dark and demonic piece (*Touched by Time*), a trick piece (*Caught*, in which a solo dancer, usually Parsons, operates a strobe light while running and jumping, to create the illusion of levitation), and a jazz piece with live music (*Step into My Dream*, with the Billy Taylor trio).

The dancing was good, the choreography well made. In some ways *Step into My Dream* ventured beyond Tharp's similarly conceived Marsalis piece, allowing sections of actual improvisation between dancers and musicians, and offering invented movement in place of conventional jazz transcriptions. I was enjoying myself, even as I was thinking the program offered little besides diversion. Maybe this is what theater dance should be—the kind of success choreographers have always secretly longed for while proclaiming themselves devoted to higher things. Today, to get an audience that comes because they like you and they like dancing, maybe you can't ask them to do anything.

David Parsons has also taken to the screen as a medium for reaching far beyond the theater. One night, channel surfing, I landed on a dance video that I soon determined was by Parsons. It didn't look like choreography, and it didn't look like drama. Later I tracked it down with the help of Parsons's company staff. Called *Fine Dining*, it's part of a 1992 video made in Denmark and directed by Thomas Grimm. The whole video is another eclectic program, including the comradely acrobatic duet for Parsons and Daniel Ezralow, *Brothers*, and *Reflections of Four*, a dance for women ankle-deep in water.

Fine Dining is a kind of danced counterpart to music video, with its look of a narrative gone haywire, its nonlinear editing and camera work. It starts in the everyday world, as Parsons and the dancers plod through a cafeteria line. Then it spaces out to a world of fantasy. Parsons is the headwaiter in a restaurant with a decidedly odd clientele and an elegant Old World Doppelgänger. The dining and dancing behavior of both sets of patrons, the demented moderns and the impeccable Continentals, is neatly choreographed, and so is some bizarre activity in the kitchen. *Fine Dining* owes as much to Charlie Chaplin as to David Byrne, and Grimm's zany camera work, which drives me nuts in his films of conventional ballets, is an asset here.

Maybe Parsons's approach is one answer for the millennium. The way things are going, the tab for art will have to be picked up by ticket buyers, either the aging conservatives who want to be comfortable with *Giselle*, or the generation that watches MTV and Steven Spielberg. Dance may not be able to survive at all if it has to depend on re-educating the audience every time, on convincing the public of its worthiness and high intent. Twyla Tharp was way ahead of everyone when she realized this twenty-five years ago. I hate to see her impersonating a middle-aged Rotarian now, but that alternative may lead to some kind of survival.

PLANET OF COOL

Boston Phoenix, 9 October 1998

Official dance lore has it that the modern dance lives on through the influence of Martha Graham. But ballet today owes far more to Graham's ideological foe, Merce Cunningham. The typical contemporary dance universe, constructed for us by the visiting Les Ballets de Monte-Carlo last weekend, is populated by an egalitarian tribe of highly mobile, dispassionate beings. Their ostensible subject may be sex, but their minds and hearts are on dancing. They can use the movement vocabulary of any academy almost indiscriminately, from the jetés of classicism to the squats and reaches of Limón, to the violent embraces of Tanztheater. And their choreographers seem interested in these languages for no particular reason other than to signify some situation or atmosphere. It astonishes me that the audience no longer seems to expect anything more.

Les Ballets de Monte-Carlo offered four pieces in this vein. They may have more range; I'm told their Boston repertory was scaled to fit the pocket-size stage at the Copley Theater. (Boston is probably the only big American city that hasn't built a good theater for dance performance in recent years, despite its perpetual rehabilitation and public works projects.)

The program opened with *Na Floresta*, by one of Europe's current hotshot choreographers Nacho Duato. This big eclecticism relied more on modern dance weightiness and expansive gesture than anything else, but the movement was set in predictable compositional lumps: a women's dance was followed by a men's dance, then the women singled out one of their group to be the partner in a love duet. There was a quasicompetitive men's duet, a trio where two men lugged a woman around, a woman's solo, and finally a duet sequence that ended with all five couples clustering downstage and gesturing away from the audience.

The solo woman in all these numbers might have been the same dancer, but in the dim lighting of this performance all the women looked identical to me—sleek and wire-thin, with glossy tight hairdos and inscrutable faces—and only now, writing down the sequence, did I think some narrative theme might have been intended. A poetic program note asked us to think of the Amazonian rainforest, but it didn't help.

Company choreographer/director Jean-Christophe Maillot contributed a duet (*Duo d'Anges*) where the tallest, most sleek, wire-thin, and glossy woman (Bernice Coppeiters) tangled with one of the good-looking men (Chris Roelandt). They molded to each other's bodies and stretched away for quite a long time until he kissed her. He immediately seemed ashamed and she jittered away. This brought on a quick resolution of sorts: she went into a spasm and fell on her back. He tenderly touched her face and blew a kiss—into the air. The emotional meaning of this encounter was no more evident than the reason for her pointe shoes.

Maillot is so confident of his ability to design dances that he didn't appear to have a qualm about using Paul Hindemith's Theme and Four Variations, which was commissioned by George Balanchine for what became one of the towering masterpieces of twentieth-century choreography, *Four Temperaments*. I found it impossible not to see and feel Balanchine's work while Maillot's banal creation slid before my eyes.

Ignoring both the loaded subtitles (Melancholic, Sanguinic, Phlegmatic, and Choleric) and the compositional architecture of the music, Maillot once again treated us to couples, four of them. During the initial presentation of the musical themes, the men were droopy and the women fierce, implying a reversal of gender roles. As the score proceeded, each couple demonstrated a different shade of incompatibility. By the time Hindemith and Balanchine soared to a magnificent climax, one woman was compulsively throwing herself against a man's out-thrusted arm, attempting to be caught in an embrace, but instead he gave way and swiveled around, forcing her to charge past him and try again.

Strangely enough, the post-Cunningham choreographer Lucinda Childs made the most extensive use of the ballet vocabulary on this program, in a short piece called *Concerto*, to harpsichord and string music written for it by Henryk Gorecki. Childs lets us appreciate the company's fine technique, without the bother of a pseudo-sexy pretext. The seven dancers traveled in lively linear patterns, with low jumps, chassés, pas de chat, chaîné turns, and other ballet steps, but instead of the traditional ballet dancer's stop-and-go, they propelled themselves continuously through space, making their preparations and arm placements visible only at strategic and satisfying stopping points.

MIND MATTERS

Boston Phoenix, 11 December 1998

It would take as long to read and digest all the supplementary material provided by Ballett Frankfurt for its production of William Forsythe's *Eidos:Telos* (last week at the Brooklyn Academy Opera House) as the ballet itself lasted. Forsythe wants to be known as an intellectual, a ballet insider, and an avant-gardist. This combination always whacks a certain segment of the public into submission, but it sends my skepticism into high gear. If you have to read a ballet's rationale to "get it," something's wrong. And if what you "get" doesn't actually mesh with the reading assignment, things are even more amiss.

I didn't read all of the philosophical/psychological/mythic argument for *Eidos:Telos*. I got bogged down in the first paragraph: "Eidos—[Greek eidos: something; form; akin to]: The formal content of a culture, encompassing its system of ideas, criteria for interpreting experience, etc. Form, Plato's term, the permanent reality that makes a thing what it is, in contrast to the particulars that are finite and subject to change." The program and press kit went on like this for pages. After the performance, before I slept, I went through the ballet several times and figured out some way its theatrically doctored chaos could have made a larger point, but I'm sure this interpretation won't resemble Forsythe's apologia.

Eidos:Telos is a big work, and not just because of its intellectual pretensions and its full-length duration. The stage is opened up to the bare walls and ceiling grids, miked for gargantuan effects, and goosed to higher levels of shock by coups de théâtre like the entrance, late in the first part, of three trombone players in black blaring atonally at megadecibels. This dadaistic universe is densely populated a great deal of the time with dancers in independent, uncoordinated action. It begins to seem like a speeded-up earthquake scene filmed from the top of the Eiffel Tower.

Forsythe, as if Merce Cunningham had never existed, claims to have discovered how to make movement by activating isolated body parts in unexpected relationships and sequences. When all twenty-two dancers are scramming around in the last act, they seem to be competing for our attention, ignoring one another. If two occasionally encounter each other they don't create a partnership; they elude each other's grasp, fail to accommodate, push each other's limbs into new positions that an instant later will be negated.

In part one, six dancers show us this distorted movement vocabulary, pushing hard at the inverted elbow and wrist joints, the scrunched-back shoulders, and spastic torsos. At moments they poke into balletic elongations. The four women especially draw our attention to these conventional poses, as if reminding us that balletic bodies are there only to be visually devoured.

The heart of the ballet is a poetic, disjointed monologue about the female life force, the anima, source of nurturing, sensuality, passion, and regeneration. Forsythe doesn't mention Carl Jung as one of his authorities, but Dana Caspersen, the woman who speaks, embodies all these sex-specific attributes, which were exploited long ago, in a different way, by Martha Graham. Caspersen first takes the voice of a spider, burrowing into the earth, merging with nature, surging with desire and menace. She's also identified with Persephone, the mythic bringer of spring to the earth, but I missed that part of her discourse. Bare-breasted and wearing a long filmy orange skirt with bustle to emphasize her underparts, she rages through a mysterious forest of slanted overhead cables and gnarls of equipment—lighting instruments, TV monitors, microphones.

After a long time, another person appears, dressed the same way except with her breast covered. She moves in big sweeping spirals to a waltz rhythm, then suddenly wrenches out of shape and croaks the verse to "Luck Be a Lady Tonight." Without any further enlightenment, she's joined by twenty identical creatures, all waltzing in the ghostly, wired forest. I thought of *Giselle* and the other tarnished relics of romantic ballet that the Europeans can't completely eliminate from their history. The moonlit burying grounds where jilted girls, now possessed by vengeful spirits, dance in filmy white dresses to entrap male passersby.

After this haunting image, the dance returns to chaos theory, and as the mobs are rushing around, striving, panting, freezing in strange, half-completed actions, the spider woman re-emerges. The dancers are running, competing, the trombones are blasting frantically, and the spider, now completely naked but lugging her cumbersome skirt behind her, squats and heaves and yells, demonically, triumphantly laying her eggs.

LOVELYLAND

Boston Phoenix, 20 November 1998

Everything was beautiful at the ballet last weekend when American Ballet Theater visited the Wang Theater. Beautiful and bland. ABT has preserved a varied repertory over the past five decades, and even caused a large cache of new works to be created. But, in common with Boston Ballet and other big classical institutions, it has been programming the softest, safest items for public consumption in recent seasons. The economics of big ballet require conservative business tactics, and the companies would say they're responding to public taste, putting on what will sell the most tickets. In doing this, though, they may also be cultivating a taste for more soft, safe ballet.

The most interesting and modern work in the show at the Wang was Jerome Robbins's first ballet, *Fancy Free* (1944). In other words, *Fancy Free* was modern in its time but it's a period piece now, and forget about whatever may have happened to ballet, or to us, in the meantime. Two of the other selections, Clark Tippett's *Bruch Violin Concerto No. 1* and the balcony scene from Kenneth MacMillan's *Romeo and Juliet*, were actually choreographed in the 1980s. But in style and content they looked back to the nineteenth century, from which two iconic examples were also on display, the act-three (Black Swan) pas de deux from *Swan Lake*, and the pirate-and-the-slave-girl pas de deux from *Le Corsaire*.

I'm not sure why Tippett's ballet is a repertory staple. Featuring four principal couples and eight subordinate couples, it's a formal, not very adventurous look at the art of partnering. Each principal couple (Van Chen and Marcello Gomes, Paloma Herrera and Maxim Beloserkovsky, Julie Kent and Robert Hill, and Ashley Tuttle and Joaquin De Luz) has a slightly different character, with steps to match. The corps is pastel—faceless, symmetrical and nearly always arranged in pairs and in unison to frame the principals or create a backdrop for them when they're not there.

The ballet opens with Van Chen high in the air, carried on in a graceful lift by Gomes. It seemed to me nothing much changed after that. I mean the dancers appeared chronically airborne or jet propelled, either hoisted by someone else or lofting past in huge jumps. Ashley Tuttle did a brief solo that showed off her clean, fast footwork, but that was the only real allegro work in the ballet.

Love, or sublimated love, is the subject of *Bruch Violin Concerto*, and it was the subject of everything else on the program. Amanda McKerrow tried to look cruel and seductive as the Black Swan, and Ethan Stiefel seemed uncomfortable as the confused prince. Angel Corella, the pirate, expressed his passion for Herrera when she wasn't on the stage, with a galvanic progression of leaps and a spin sequence that speeded up at the end like a skater's. Herrera later achieved some visibility with single and double fouettés that finished with a triple pirouette. The Romeo and Juliet, Guillaume Graffin and Julie Kent, looked right but they seemed temperamentally ill-matched. She didn't know what to make of him at first, then swooned as if that's what she thought young girls were supposed to do with their first crush. He couldn't have had an adolescent bone in his body.

Excerpted pas de deux have many assets for touring companies. They put lots of star dancers on display without requiring the company to bring along the elaborate sets and hordes of dancers needed for the full ballets. Besides these economizing advantages the nineteenth-century pas de deux are a proving ground for dancers, who must marshal their highest technical abilities, their most effective acting, stage projection, and partnering synchronicity, in the shortest amount of time. Zappo, either you stun the audience or they'll summon up dutiful cheers, with no second acts to make amends. On Friday's opening night, only Angel Corella went over the top.

As for *Fancy Free*, the Jerome Robbins / Leonard Bernstein combination made history. Maybe it's too much to expect dancers today to move like sailors and girls out bar-hopping during World War II. Joaquin De Luz, Ethan Stiefel and John Selya, in raucous pursuit of Sandra Brown and Amanda McKerrow, look more like contemporary singles. The particular ways Robbins had them bond and compete, show off and make passes, belong to another time. Without its edgy, pre-countercultural wit, *Fancy Free* becomes generic war romance.

⌒ BUILDING BLOCKS

Boston Phoenix, 9 March 2007

New ballets must be one of the world's most expensive consumable products. Choreographers keep hustling up new ways of moving and arranging bodies to serve this market, but what's new isn't necessarily contemporary, and what's contemporary doesn't necessarily reflect anything about life today.

Last week's performances brought up the riddle of how dance communicates—as distinct from how it looks. Nacho Duato's Compañía Nacional de Danza 2 from Madrid seems to think of itself as up to date, but for its two Boston performances the Danza 2 offered a three-part remix of Ailey/constructivist/fusion dancing with serious but invisible themes. Across the street, Boston Ballet's "New Visions" program showed that the classical tradition hasn't lost its power to speak.

Sponsored by Celebrity Series at the Shubert last week, Compañía Nacional de Danza 2 reprised works they've shown at Jacob's Pillow, all choreographed in the 1990s by Duato. Director of both Danza 2 and the main Compañía Nacional de Danza, Nacho Duato has gained a big reputation in Europe as a guest choreographer. His training began in the 1970s at the Ballet Rambert School, after that company had transitioned into modern dance, and he continued his studies with Maurice Béjart's Mudra school and the Ailey school in New York. He's among the best known of the generation of European contemporary dance makers now in mid-career.

Gradually since the 1960s a lot of theater dance has taken on an almost ideological resistance to identifying itself with either modern dance or ballet. At the same time, it relies heavily on both supposedly outmoded genres to supply the movement vocabulary. Duato's dances seen in Boston exemplified the clean, uncontroversial, eclectic gloss of "contemporary dance." I realized that one reason all three dances looked alike despite their thematic differences was that they had no physical point of view, only a determination to make the body move in unusual, preferably thrilling ways.

Remansos, to piano pieces of Enrique Granados, was mostly angular, quirky duets and trios, with the women manipulated into crotchy, upside down lifts, and with assorted novel shapes, leaps, bends, and pirouettes strewn into the fast-paced comings and goings. It seemed as if there was a jutting limb, a wiggling shoulder, a wide step, or some other embellishment for every note and frill of the music.

Halfway through *Coming Together*, set to an imposing postminimalist score by Frederic Rzweski, there was some dramatic business with a red rose that had been implanted in the floor downstage center as the ballet began and ignored by the dancers until that moment. The insertion of a prop into an otherwise propless, plotless ballet guarantees drama of some kind, or at least mystery.

A woman snatched the rose. She may have handed it off to one of the other dancers, but eventually a woman in possession of the flower crept behind a large white panel, her arm slinking after her, until the rose coyly disappeared. The only significance to this that I could tell was that it introduced a new part of the dance, featuring three men in successive solos and groupings. But the overall drive to keep moving and creating new and remarkable gyrations didn't change.

I couldn't tell why there were several sets of costumes and footwear in this piece, or why two dancers brought spotlights onto the stage and shone them onto two other dancers, or why a curtain rose to reveal backstage paraphernalia just as the dance was coming to an end. Rzewski's score included a loud voice reciting a text two or three words at a time, but the orchestration often drowned him out so you might not have been meant to follow his drift.

The program notes for *Coming Together*, and for the following work, *Rassemblement*, told of urban dynamics and human rights. Set to some Haitian folk songs arranged by Toto Bissainthe, *Rassemblement* apparently concerned slavery and liberation and Voodoo in Haiti. It wasn't any more specifically expressive than the other two dances.

Brake the Eyes, Jorma Elo's new piece for Boston Ballet, also applied sensational effects against otherwise formal movement patterns. Elo is another compulsive inventor of movement, but in this work, and in the two other ballets on the program, Christopher Wheeldon's *Polyphonia* (2001) and Val Caniparoli's *Sonata for Two Pianos and Percussion* (2004), classical ballet technique was the ground bass or palette from which a rationale or an argument could be proposed. In other words, we didn't get novelty or diversity for its own sake.

Brake the Eyes is in a way two ballets. A corps of nine dancers create formal but often spectacular displays, patterns for large groups and duets. Larissa Ponomarenko has her own dance, emerging first from the depths of the Wang stage, a tiny, tutu-clad woman with a menacing T-shaped grid of lights looming over her like an airplane taking off. In a silence broken by some groaning chordal sounds, she dances a progression of balletic postures and dislocations. She glances at herself, at the near space around her, as if she's checking where she is or what she might try, or judging whether a given move produces the right effect.

I was thinking she might represent the choreographer's mind. Later, when the ensemble were working through their duets, I thought Elo was especially concerned with what to do about partnering, how to make the women look new. Curiously, the men always looked classical in this work, even when they were stretching balletic presumptions, but the women often looked awkward.

Elo's in-your-face musical and staging ideas seem to have been influenced by William Forsythe. The lighting equipment, usually concealed, bore down on the dancers with harsh beams and shifting locations. The musical collage blurted out selected, sometimes looped phrases and segments of Mozart, then broke off. The sudden exclamations in Russian, the irrelevant laughter, the occasional effortful breathing, that were coming from the body-miked Pomomarenko, injected a touching and disturbing human counterpoint.

After many events, nothing lasting very long, and people coming and going when you least expected, Ponomarenko collected the group into a line and led them in some chorus maneuvers, and then the ballet ended abruptly, like an early morning dream.

POETS LOST AND FOUND

Boston Phoenix, 12 March 1999

Poetry isn't something we find very much in dance performance now. We live in pragmatic times. We're busy with life; we don't have time to reflect on it. Maybe that's why Christopher Wheeldon's new work for Boston Ballet was so unexpected and so touching.

Corybantic Ecstasies is a suite of dances to the 1954 Serenade after Plato's Symposium by Leonard Bernstein. The composer denied any programmatic intent, but allowed that the music is "a series of related statements in praise of love," according to one of his biographers, Joan Peyser. Wheeldon centers each of the five sections of the music on a different set of mythical characters: Eros (Patrick Armand in the first cast), Echo and Narcissus (Tara Hench, Simon Ball, and Zachary Hench), Hermes (Pollyana Ribeiro and Carlos Santos), Eros and Psyche (Armand and Larissa Ponomarenko), and Dionysia (led by Adriana Suárez and Yury Yanowsky).

Wheeldon has made a completely classical and formally structured ballet that nevertheless evokes the diverse human experience so enduringly symbolized by the Greek myths. The work has texture, virtuosity, and poetic resonance, and it doesn't give away all its gifts immediately. It's a wonderful addition to the repertory.

In the first movement, Eros dances with a complement of four couples. No roly-poly infant Cupid here, the God of Love is powerful. His leaps and confident revolutions provide a focal point for a fruitful series of dance designs by the attendants. I was reminded of George Balanchine's *Apollo* and, often throughout the piece, of the inventive and captivating way Balanchine could arrange small ensembles to feature their expertise within a symmetrical or alternating pattern. In other words, Wheeldon, now a soloist in the New York City Ballet, has inherited Balanchine's idea of making a ballet constantly interesting but never letting it spread out into aimless spectacle.

In the second movement, Wheeldon tells the story of the nymph deprived of original speech, who can only echo the words spoken to her. Echo first imitates three other women in an innovative three-against-one canon. Then she begins to follow Narcissus. The story of how he falls in love with his own reflection instead is shown economically and beautifully in a mirror dance, with the Narcissus in the water draped in simple cellophane strips. The men carry Echo on their backs, as if she's swimming. She dances between them but can't break their fatal attraction to each other. She sinks to the floor as if melting into the landscape. The gods turned Echo into a mountain spirit and Narcissus into a flower, but we don't need to see this in order to feel the poignancy of their encounter.

In a quick, brilliant duet, Hermes the messenger is doubled, male and female. Ribeiro and Santos dance in tandem except for supported punctuations, like the moment when she spins down almost to the floor and rises again without breaking her tempo. Wheeldon gives them a small circle of flashing leaps so we can see the golden wings on their heels. (The handsome costumes for the ballet were by Gary Lisz.)

With the lightest, smoothest bourrées, Ponomarenko sketches the adventures of the unfortunate Psyche, who provoked the jealous curses of Venus by being too beautiful. Armand holds her as she seems to languish, then revive. We might think of the daunting tasks Psyche had to undergo, and the faithful love Cupid kept for her through all her trials.

Finally the principals and the almost-forgotten original quartet of attendants, now joined by another couple, dance a wild and sometimes jazzy but still always formal Dionysian orgy led by Suárez and Yanowsky. With Bernstein in a Stravinskian mode, the dance takes on some of the exuberance of Balanchine's *Rubies*. By now Eros has disappeared into the revels, but the transformed dancers circle around the empty space where he first ruled.

Poetry of an entirely different sort was implied but not quite brought off in Roland Petit's *Le Jeune Homme et la Mort* (*The Young Man and Death*). Dramatic ballets are out of style if they come from the twentieth century, but unfamiliarity is no reason to eliminate an interesting period piece from the repertory. Revivals take extra care, though. On opening night this 1946 work seemed to be treading none too securely on the borderlines between renewing an old style, updating it out of existence, and producing a kitschy homage.

The Boston revival was staged on behalf of Roland Petit by Luigi Bonino. Created for the passionate French dancers Jean Babilée and Nathalie Phillipart, it had a libretto by Jean Cocteau and a kinky reputation from the start. It was choreographed to popular music and not paired with the real score, Bach's Passacaglia and Fugue in C Minor, until the dress rehearsal. The ballet has since served as a vehicle for several famous dancers, and a terrific film was made in the '60s by Rudolf Nureyev and Zizi Jeanmaire. None of this information was offered in the Boston program, and the audience seemed stunned but intrigued.

Le Jeune Homme comes from the existentialist Paris of the postwar period. Surrealistic and even lurid, it begins with a man alone in a seedy attic. A woman he's been waiting for arrives, but instead of making love, she teases him and finally goads him to suicide, returning with a death mask to lead him away over the rooftops, with the Eiffel Tower and a flashing Citroën sign in the distance.

We can ponder over the possible meanings of this seemingly pointless seduction, but on opening night it looked malicious rather than mysterious. Patrick Armand and Aleksandra Koltun seemed to be trying to imitate the two most famous bits of the ballet's iconography, the Nureyev film and a series of great noir images of the original production by the English photographer Baron. Koltun wore a yellow dress, black gloves, and a black

Dutch-boy wig, just like Phillipart. Armand even looks a little like the muscular Babilée. They both tried to simulate their dancer-predecessors without giving a sense of who they thought the characters were. The whole ballet seemed frozen in high intensity, technical precision, and twitchy mannerisms that had no psychological conviction.

Ballets were obsessed with the Meaning Of It All during the postwar years. Intellectuals and artists agonized over whether to act when one knew the act was futile, and whether suicide was an acceptable solution to despair. In the film, Nureyev was young and beautiful and tortured, perhaps with sexual ambivalence, though most critics and Cocteau himself portrayed him as a frustrated artist or poet. Jeanmaire, unlike the demonic Phillipart, smiled enigmatically and stayed cool throughout, a perfect antagonist for the increasingly enraged Nureyev. But, replicating their actions, Armand and Koltun showed no confusion, no ambiguity. They could have been depicting just one more tabloid story of sex and violence in the heartless city.

Also on the program was *Bachianas*, a new ballet by Daniel Pelzig. Set to selections from the Heitor Villa-Lobos Bachianas Brasilieras, the plotless work had five principals and six supporting dancers in tie-dyed leotards, and offered exacting and well-rehearsed choreography for all. The movement started out elaborating on a theme of circles, with cartwheel lifts, turns, and supported arabesques for Suárez and Paul Thrussell in the first part. Yury Yanowsky partnered various women and then walked back and forth through the moving group with a curious sliding, bent-over step and punchy fists. In a later section Jennifer Gelfand did a fast duet with Laszlo Berdo, and then, after a series of death-defying lifts, was thrown into the wings. By then the ballet was drifting from one idea to another. In the last section Gelfand and Suárez were both carried in the air by running partners. At one point they reached for each other. The other dancers assembled in trios and duos, lifting women and trading them off.

For the whole ballet the dancers seemed stuck on an emotional high, exulting in their physical prowess and unconcerned with anything more personal. Maybe I would have seen all this as more than a technical tour de force if I'd understood why the soprano (Maria Ferrante) was on the stage with them, singing passionately about something for two sections and retreating to the wings for the two instrumental numbers. The program supplied no lyrics or other guide to the music.

Given the sophistication and diverse origins of all ballet, the title for Boston Ballet's current series, "American Trilogy," seems simplistic. The pieces had almost nothing in common, but the rubric did invite us to reflect on George Balanchine's *Slaughter on Tenth Avenue* (1936, Richard Rodgers), Agnes de Mille's *Rodeo* (1942, Aaron Copland), and Christopher Wheeldon's *Corybantic Ecstasies* (1999, Leonard Bernstein) as artifacts of, for, or about American culture.

Slaughter on Tenth Avenue is a product of what any choreographer but Balanchine would consider a dry period in a career. Newly arrived in America, he had a school but no properly organized company. He took ballet commissions where he could get them, but mostly, during the late '30s and early '40s, he worked in show business, supplying dances for a long string of Broadway shows and movies. If he considered this a comedown, as many of his contemporaries did, he adapted to the situation with wit, style, and an astonishing lack of condescension. He even seemed to enjoy having fun with the ballet itself while he was going all out for entertainment values.

High art versus low art was a hot debate then, and *Slaughter* is one of several occasions where Balanchine depicted the argument in action. A modern jazz ballet, being presented by a snooty Russian ballet company, it actually furthered the plot instead of just decorating it, for perhaps the first time in a Broadway musical ("On Your Toes"). *Slaughter* can also be seen as a comment on Balanchine's muses. Choreographed on Tamara Geva, his first wife, from whom he was separated at the time, it was danced in the 1939 Warner Brothers movie by Vera Zorina, whom he'd just married. He revived it in 1968 at the New York City Ballet for the twenty-three-year-old Suzanne Farrell, with whom he was infatuated. A curious gift for these gorgeous ballerinas, because the heroine is a floozy—a stripper in a cheap underworld night club.

Aside from its possible insight into Balanchine's love life, *Slaughter* operates on several layers of representation and irony. A show within a show, it's the climax of a story involving a tap dancer who somehow finds himself working for an elitist impresario resembling Diaghilev. He's staged this jazz ballet starring himself and the ballerina he's in love with. The impresario and the hoofer's ballet-danseur rival connive to have him bumped off just when he's supposed to kill himself in the ballet. Mid-performance, he gets tipped off that the plot's been discovered and the cops are on the way. He signals the orchestra to keep playing choruses of his tap dance to delay the murder.

Well, it's all very silly, but the audience appreciates the corps de ballet's bumps and shimmies, the sexy allure of the ballerina-as-stripper, and the choreographer's digs at formulaic honky-tonk show numbers. Boston Ballet doesn't provide any program information that helps the audience see Balanchine commenting on the pomposity of the old Russian ballet style—which of course he intended to reform, but not by larding it with tap dance steps. He was also celebrating the integrity and courage of the down-to-earth vaudeville dancers and ridiculing the ubiquitous cops-and-robbers intrigues of stage, screen, and fiction.

What the audience here does see is an amusing cliché: leggy, hip-twitching chorus girls in sleazy, scanty costumes; an unlikely pair of lovers who seem doomed until Fate saves their romance; and the usual barroom characters—waiters, a pimpish manager, and dopey cops who arrive to the tune of "Three Blind Mice." The Boston cast, featuring April Ball as the stripper and Michael Johnson as the hoofer on opening night, looked okay on the surface, but they didn't succeed at being sincere, naughty, and knowing all at the same time.

Boston Ballet is not alone in having a low priority for characterization, but this was a real handicap in *Slaughter* and the other story ballet on the program, *Rodeo*. De Mille's work is thought to be a cornerstone of Americana, but to me it looks phony and hopelessly retrograde. The dancers didn't seem comfortable either, having to put across the story of a tomboy who discovers that she'd really rather wear a dress if it helps her get a man.

For *Rodeo* de Mille used a loosely classical vocabulary, together with vernacular American dance forms: waltzing, square dancing, and even a show-off tap dance with which one of the cowboys wins the girl. Taking a cue from her idol Martha Graham, she also used both literal and abstract gesture to modify steps and delineate character. The men mime horseback riding with splay-legged cantering and straight arms circling in the air with imaginary lariats. The pretty town girls affect preening hands and fluttery, gossipy chit-chat. The most naturalistic gestures, like the Cowgirl hitching up her pants or embarrassedly swatting an admirer in the solar plexus, looked the least casual. Frances Pérez-Ball and her eventual suitors, Simon Ball and Reagan Messer, all seemed to be working the surface of roles that needed utter conviction to save them from being tintypes.

Both the music and the choreography of *Corybantic Ecstasies* rebounded off the many Balanchine/Stravinsky collaborations, principally *Apollo* and the late, dissonant works like *Symphony in Three Movements*. Wheeldon created this fine, classical ballet for the Boston dancers and they still look well suited as its demigods of the passions. Paul Thrussell was a majestic Eros, with an ethereal Larissa Ponomarenko as Psyche, Tara Hench wafted in vain between Narcissus (Gaël Lambiotte) and his reflection (Patrick Thornberry clad in watery strips of silver), Pollyana Ribeiro and José Martin streaked through as a duo-Hermes, and Adriana Suárez and Yury Yanowsky led the Dionysian revels. They didn't have to emote or characterize, they just did the movement that was beautifully arranged in simple but elegant patterns by Wheeldon.

Across the street at the Shubert Theater, the Mark Morris Dance Group's weekend program displayed another brand of Americanism—a personal dancing style that can be humanistic, democratic, and free from external codes or aesthetics. Morris is a classicist to the core in his affinity with music and his sense of choreographic form. His new work, *V*, set to the Opus 44 piano quintet of Robert Schumann, was played, along with the rest of the program, by a group of New York chamber musicians known as the MMDG Music Ensemble.

The title *V* refers, I guess, to the seven-dancer floor formation we see at the beginning. After a grand, expansive welcome, a second group takes the place of the first and repeats their sequence. The dance embarks on a process of inventions and variations that seem inexhaustible but are repetitive enough to trigger off jokes, optical illusions, role reversals, and group exchanges that the audience can romp along with and savor. The patterns keep shifting right up to the last musical hurrah, but we know that everything is going to turn out all right in the end, just as there's never any doubt that Schumann's last chord will sound in the right key.

The dance often seemed hermetic to me, locked into depicting Schumann's music. But I realized two things I hadn't noticed before in Morris's work, and they showed up in the other group pieces on the program, *The Argument* (1999) and *The Office* (1994). One is how short his movement phrases are. In *V*, subgroups of the fourteen-member ensemble streak in and out, each making a miniature statement that's echoed or continued or overlaid by another small group. Sometimes a couple of people arrive just to show one pose or movement that will be enlarged upon by others. The effect of this is communal: no matter how effective some fragment is alone, it takes the whole ensemble to complete it, and because Morris crafts it all so firmly, it doesn't make us feel jittery.

The dancers are wonderfully accomplished, and they look extra animated in *V*, but they perform in a different way from ballet dancers. Morris's movement now can be quick and extended, but it isn't ballet movement. Nothing in a dance of his ever seems to happen without an expressive reason, and though the movement might turn awkward or goofy, they don't look apologetic about it.

Morris has remained a modern dancer despite the balletic tilt of so much other contemporary dance. His new solo, *Peccadillos*, to the toy-piano music of Erik Satie (played onstage by Ilan Rechtman), was a series of tiny portraits, a whole Coppélius's workshop of characters tumbling out to play when the shop is closed. He's a wooden soldier, a Petrouchka, a young girl at a dance, a yearning poet, a boulevardier, and a lot of other things his imagination seems to be conjuring up spontaneously. Never has a big man danced with such confident, elfin musicality.

EVOLUTION / DEVOLUTION

Boston Phoenix, 25 March 2005

Boston Ballet's "Falling Angels" repertory program last weekend summarized the state of the art: where it's going and where it's been. Everyone might not agree about which ballets represented which end of the timeline, but they all posed healthy challenges for the dancers.

Lucinda Childs is known as a postmodern choreographer, but when she started doing works for her own ensemble of eight or so dancers in the 1970s, her repertory looked more classical than anything being done on the postmodern scene at the time. After the dadaistic effusions of the 1960s, downtown dance in New York settled down to explore the basics, and Childs's early walking-jogging-sitting-rolling dances morphed into marathons of leaping, turning, and small, rhythmic step interjections. They looked like ballets in some ways, but ballets in a constant state of locomotion.

Childs has done crossover work for theater, opera, and ballet companies, but it was Mikhail Baryshnikov who made a convincing case in my mind for Childs as a choreographer of ballets. He'd included her in the PAST*forward* programs of postmodern dance reconstructions for his White Oak Dance Project; and in 2002 at Jacob's Pillow he presented her group work, *Chacony* (Benjamin Britten), and a solo, *Largo* (Arcangelo Corelli). Both of these were persuasive arguments for the success of postmodern reform, as ballet dancing—or dancing—that wasn't ornate or pretentious.

And the classical scores—as opposed to the purely propulsive minimalism that seemed to drive her former works—made me see Childs, at last, as more musical than didactic.

This history was embedded in *Ten Part Suite*, to violin sonatas by Corelli, for Lorna Feijóo and Roman Rykine, two demisoloist couples, and an ensemble of eight Boston Ballet dancers. Dressed in simple, simulated street wear of pale cream except for the principals in white (costumes by Charles Heightchew), the dancers looked as if surging leaps and lush unfolding legs were the most natural things in the world.

This impression of naturalness is created partly by the uncluttered way Childs projects the vocabulary. She favors expansive, space-covering steps and omits anything fussy. The arms may burst up irrepressibly in concert with leaps and soaring turns, but they often swing loosely by the dancer's side. This unfamiliar upper-body plainness has the effect of emphasizing the chest and shoulders. The dancers seem active, eager, and open.

As they travel, they sort themselves into precise squares and diagonals, staying the same distance apart from one another even when on the fly, so that you perceive the dance as a group enterprise, not a collection of individuals. Remarkably, these floor patterns never seem to settle into formula. The members of a quartet leave in the middle of a number and are replaced by another quartet, or they're joined at some point by two or six more dancers. This instability of design keeps replenishing our interest in how the stage looks, and conveys a sense of inexhaustible energy.

The Baroque dance forms of the music give the choreography a variety of pacing, from Feijóo and Rykine's slow sarabande duet to livelier gigues and gavottes. From the very beginning Child's ballet reminded me of two wonderful company works of George Balanchine, *Le Tombeau de Couperin* and *Square Dance*.

We get so few chances to see a dance work that its immediate context always influences how we receive it. After the Ballet's revival of *La Sylphide*, Child's piece had a feeling of Bournonville romanticism evolved into modern times, the joy of moving big with none of the portents and artifice. But what followed *Ten Part Suite* on the "Falling Angels" program could have been a vision of ballet's underside, the neuroses exposed and the flash emphasized. I wonder, if *Ten Part Suite* had ended the program, whether it would have looked more like the future of ballet, after psychotherapy had cured these excesses.

Jiri Kylián offered a doubleheader of gender angst with *Sarabande* (to a Bach teaser and assorted sound effects) and *Falling Angels* (to the first section of Steve Reich's Drumming). *Sarabande* is a shock'em-and-sock'em showcase for six barechested men. They make their appearance as a theatrical afterthought. First the audience sees six magnificent nineteenth-century ball gowns. We scarcely have time to realize that there are no models inside the gowns when the lights black out. When they come on again, the gowns are suspended in the air and beneath each one is an insectlike, spotlighted form that eventually turns into a man. The rest of the dance is a formal tantrum of gestures and body shapes suggesting frustration, anger, bravado, embarrassment, fury, and hysteria. Each move is underlined by a vocalist, breathing and emoting with electronic enhancement, and the floor is miked for maximum effect.

The eight women in *Falling Angels*, like the six men, are alienated from one another spatially but united in a lexicon of angry, aggressive moves. The audience screamed with pleasure after both assaults, but though I felt curiously admiring of the women's strength and commitment, the men's characters seemed kind of pathetic.

The only pointe ballet on the program, William Forsythe's *In the Middle, Somewhat Elevated*, is almost twenty years old now, but it still looks rebellious and deliberately distorted. The lighting (also by Forsythe) jolts out unpredictably from different angles and altitudes, blamming down harshly onto the dancers or smothering them in shadows. There's no music allowed, just Thom Willems's fantastically loud noises—rhythmic explosions, things boiling and scraping and whacking and thundering, while the dancers carry on their job.

Forsythe's choreographic plan is to make the work look as unchoreographed as possible. Dancers stroll into place and rip into tremendous bouts of turning or wildly improbable lifts. Then they walk away to watch the others or execute some other phenomenal thing off in a corner. It's as if they're giving a demonstration and only have to be "on" for their own parts.

The movement vocabulary is stressed and stretched, twisted and spun within an inch of its virtuosic life. The dancers, Romi Beppu, Yury Yanowdsky, Karine Seneca, Melanie Atkins, Jared Nelson, Heather Myers, Kelley Potter, John Lam, and Adriana Suárez on opening night, looked revved up yet matter-of-fact about it.

≈ DREAMING AND REMEMBRANCE

Boston Phoenix, 23 February 2007

Two momentous revivals in town showed us how big the category of classical ballet really is. Over the weekend George Balanchine's *A Midsummer Night's Dream* (1962) completed its nine-shot sojourn at Boston Ballet, and Antony Tudor's 1937 *Dark Elegies* was given four times at Boston Conservatory. Both works had multiple casts, so the dancers didn't get much time to experience their roles.

You might think role playing isn't the business of classical ballet. At least, that's what George Balanchine is said to have believed. Actually, when it served his purposes Balanchine was a wonderful storyteller and role creator; see his *Nutcracker, Don Quixote, Coppélia, Pulcinella,* or *Prodigal Son* for example.

Current critical and popular opinion favors Frederick Ashton's streamlined, one act *Dream*, but lately I appreciate the Balanchine version more and more. His expansive two act celebration of Shakespeare provides an antidote to the hyperactive, flavorless contemporary ballets we see everywhere. It invokes all the resources of a great ballet company—virtuosity, ensemble, acting, comedy, and the ability to create a poetic image. I thought the Boston Ballet dancers met this challenge admirably.

A Midsummer Night's Dream is one of Balanchine's variations on the traditional full-length ballet formula. He tells the whole of Shakespeare's complicated story in the first act, then gives us a second-act wedding celebration with a guest ensemble furnishing the entertainment. The music is all Mendelssohn: the descriptive, dramatic incidental music to the play for the first act, and symphonic selections for the divertissement. The lovers' contentiousness and mix-ups get resolved and then transformed into the pure classicism of the second act. Surrounding both the real world of the mortals and the idyllic formalism of the divertissement hovers the supernatural realm of the fairies.

At the heart of all this, and linking together the ditzy mortals, the credulous rustics, the butterflies, bugs, fairies, and aristocratic celebrants, is the idea of the duet. Six or seven different pas de deux are strewn throughout the ballet, not only to explore variations on a given form, but to convey character and states of mind. Never has the Balanchinian imagination been more tellingly deployed.

First off, after the introductory prologue, we get an extended pas de deux for Titania (Karine Seneca last Friday night) and a convenient Cavalier (Sabi Varga), accompanied by her retinue of fairies. They all seem to be running and leaping most of the time. There's no suggestion of romance in this duet, it's just an expression of joy and disinterested compatibility.

Taken to a higher level of perfection, the duet becomes an exquisite paradigm of harmony in the second act (Lorna Feijóo and Carlos Molina). Feijóo's tendency to emphasize placement and transitions worked against the melting, legato changes that can make this duet so poignant, but just to see the choreography, so serene after all the turmoil, was a pleasure.

Titania and her consort Oberon never dance together—they're absorbed in getting the better of each other—but when she wakes up, bewitched, and sees Bottom as a donkey (Gabor Kapin), she dances a duet with him that's a parody of the classical model, set to Mendelssohn's most ravishing love theme. The poor galumphing weaver-turned-beast is overwhelmed by this wondrous female who seems to be infatuated with him, but he tries to imitate the moves and supports she shows him. Balanchine's framing of this farcical scene in a dance form that's meant to symbolize ideal love puts another layer of feeling into the comedy.

The four hapless mortal lovers' merry chase is set against the intimate holding and balancing moves of the pas de deux—implicit partnerships broken apart by fate. When they're finally sorted out with the right partners, they celebrate their weddings with brief proper duets of their own, and then share a triple duo with the duke, Theseus (Bo Busby), and his bride, Hippolyta (Lia Cirio).

All of these duets avoid flashy virtuosity. This is reserved in ample supply for Oberon and Puck (Reyneris Reyes and Joel Prouty), and for the flittering, airborne butterflies, fairies, and bugs. Like the other paired characters, Oberon and Puck are at cross-purposes. Puck is overeager; Oberon impatient. In one stunning scene, they rush in and out in alternation with the fairy pack, each doing variations of tremendous elevation and allegro footwork. Reyes displayed impeccable beats and classical line; Prouty made his eccentric jumps and skidding stops seem part of a mischievous, bumbling personality.

This production was borrowed from Pacific Northwest Ballet, and to my eye it suffered from Martin Pakledinaz's designs, which are way fussier and gaudier than the originals by Karinska and David Hays. Maybe you rationalize these preferences after the fact, but the subdued colors and slim lines of Karinska's first act costumes, the mossy forest creatures and rustics, the quiet elegance of the second act, all allowed the three worlds of the story to seem compatible though different. Pakledinaz serves up spangly costumes in saturated colors and flowing fabric, obtrusive sets made of cabbage roses and glitterized vines, and cute billboard-size frogs and spiders. All ballet classics undergo rethinking and visual renovations as they migrate around the globe. Balanchine's work is no exception. But I think his Dream is more mature, in both serious and comic ways, than this production's Disneyfication leads us to believe.

~ Twenty-five years before Balanchine's *Midsummer*, the young English choreographer Antony Tudor was also rethinking the conventions of ballet. Unlike Balanchine, whose main choreographic interest was in form, Tudor was a social critic. His finest ballets are about communities and characters under stress. *Dark Elegies* is a lament, set to Gustav Mahler's Kindertotenlieder (Songs on the Death of Children). Rather than theatricalize the grief of the individual parents, like Balanchine's unhappy lovers dancing out their melancholy, confusion, and possessiveness, Tudor gives us a group of villagers acting out a somber ritual, feeling their way toward some kind of resignation.

They gather a few at a time in comfortless circles, enter and leave with lagging steps. They turn to each other momentarily, clasp hands or touch someone's shoulder, but there are no histrionics. Personal sorrow is contained by evolving patterns of stepping and circling. Even when someone ventures an individual statement, the vocabulary of the outcry is withheld, linear, as if giving way to the emotions would shatter the community itself. The solo women seem to rise on their pointes only to attenuate their stricken bodies. In the only male-female duet, she rushes blindly and he prevents her from going out of control, catching her in crooked poses and lifts.

I thought the Conservatory students danced with clarity and respect, but the Thursday night cast I saw didn't have the weightiness that conveys tragedy. In place of the original backcloths designed by Nadia Benois, there were some effective (uncredited) photographic projections of threatening clouds.

This program had interesting connections among three very different works. Tudor taught for many years at the Juilliard School, where Conservatory director of dance Yasuko Tokunaga studied with him and with José Limón, whose *Dances for Isadora* was revived. Fellow Juilliard alum Michael Uthoff created *Galleria*, a lively and demanding classical ballet piece, for the Conservatory students. Limón's flamboyant work, choreographed in 1971, contrasts with Tudor's study in restraint. Both draw on a deep humanistic tendency in twentieth-century dance.

A tribute to the mother of modern dance, *Dances* offers five solos, each evoking a different stage of Isadora Duncan's life. The dance gave the

Dark Elegies (Tudor). Autumn Hill and Philip Ingrassia, Boston
Conservatory Dance Company. Photo by Eric Antoniou.

students a crack at full-out dancing interpretations, and they seized the opportunity. Ae-Soon Kim was breathtaking as the ecstatic young Isadora (Primavera), and the others gave a moving account: Minah Oh (Maenad), Shelley Franklin (Niobe), Laurence Jacques (La Patrie), and Tiffany Spearman (Scarf Dance). Conservatory faculty member Jennifer Scanlon directed the revival; she danced in the original cast.

A CENTURY IN BRIEF

Hudson Review, Spring 2006

American Ballet Theater's three-week fall season at City Center comprised a pretty good scan of twentieth-century choreographic trends, and a few precursors and postludes to boot. Given the uncertainties of putting together a repertory, the company probably didn't plan a historical survey, but the nine ballets and assorted pas de deux had many links to the three-pronged commitment made by Ballet Theater's founders in 1940, to American, English, and Russian classical choreography. Curiously, only the two most recent ballets of this collection were actually created for ABT. The rest have been borrowed from New York City Ballet or retrieved from inactive repertories here and abroad.

ABT's two-season programming policy splits the company's New York presence into two distinct realms. At City Center you get smaller works, lower ticket prices, and a more contemporary, varied sensibility. For eight weeks beginning in late May at the Metropolitan Opera House, you pay higher prices for the "classics." In 2006 the Met schedule calls for an eight-performance bill of short works, with the remaining seven weeks devoted to evening-length story ballets in the grand style—costume spectacles that look comfortably old-fashioned even when they've been composed within living memory. The Met's vast stage and staging machinery can accommodate lavish productions, while City Center is friendly to chamber-size works. I suppose ABT's audience divides itself accordingly, though the dancers seem capable of handling both concepts. There's some logic to this dualism if you assume that a regressive audience is the mainstay of a ballet company's clientele and an adventurous one keeps it artistically honest. Maybe they're complementary.

The undoubted hit of City Center 2005 was the revival of Twyla Tharp's *In the Upper Room*. Created in 1986 for Tharp's own company, the *Upper Room* entered Ballet Theater's repertory two years later, when then-artistic director Mikhail Baryshnikov daringly invited Tharp to fold her own operations into ABT. That arrangement only lasted a year or so, but Tharp and ABT continued their productive if intermittent relationship, which began in 1976. Her last new work for the company, *Variations on a Theme by Haydn*, premiered in 2000. Tharp has concentrated on Broadway since then—the Billy Joel show *Movin' Out* closed in December after a three-year run, with a road company still touring and a new show based on Bob Dylan's music going into production in early 2006. Knowing Tharp's endless creativity, I don't want to assume she's through yet with either the ballet or the concert stage.

Tharp is sometimes called a fusion choreographer, but that's a gross simplification—most dances created today draw on eclectic movement sources and a solid classical technique. Tharp started her career with this premise but it wasn't only her ability to synthesize that made her so successful. She has a classicist's faith in form, an uncanny sense of the zeitgeist, and a way of treating every new assignment as if it required her to redefine all the parameters. Superficially *In the Upper Room* is a programmatic juxtaposition of ballet dancing and contemporary dancing. Half the people wear sneakers and lope around; the rest of the women are on pointe, with nimble male partners to steady them. Big deal—but no. What happens is neither a standoff between the two styles nor a compromise. Having established thematic differences, the two groups seem to move ever more densely and displace each other faster, until they reach accommodation with a sublimely escalating counterpoint.

Tharp commissioned the score from Philip Glass, who produced nine sections of his oddball chord progressions and arpeggios over chugging, pulsing motor-play. The music is recorded, which allows the volume to creep up insidiously until the final section, when a soprano levitates over the keyboards, trumpets, and strings, pulling the audience along with her toward some unimaginably euphoric climax.

This generation of ABT dancers took on the piece with some misgivings, I thought. Tharp's movement is packed and pressured. In small groups the dancers emerge and fade away into Jennifer Tipton's majestic floods of light and smoke. They rush on, execute steps that can be quite academic or improperly skewed, with vernacular punches and bounces spattering across the dance moves. Two sneaker-clad "Stomper" women lead the proceedings with a side-by-side litany of jogging and swinging, jabs and slides. They leave and return, patrolling the background like sentries. At one point they're partnered by two of the danseurs, and at another they join in a comradely sextet where three men and three women link together in an ingenious line dance, like a team of cheerleaders. The ballet types speed through extremes of partnering and pointe work. All the movement seems to demand a really grounded body attitude because it's so fast, precise, and detailed.

Keith Roberts, from the first ABT cast, staged the *Upper Room*, with additional coaching from the choreographer. In recent years Tharp seems to have placed her ballets more and more into the hands of the dancers. She likes dancers to inhabit her ballets, but they can sometimes exaggerate or overinterpret. The *Upper Room*'s hard-edged formalism is especially endangered as it passes from one generation to another. Ethan Stiefel seemed to be channeling Arnold Schwarzenegger or Superman as one of the Stomper men, and at one performance Michele Wiles threw herself around in giddy misalliance from her Stomper partner, Kristi Boone. Irina Dvorovenko's grand ballerina style appended a small irony to the Pointers' goings-on. Tipton's smoke became a big number instead of a supporting atmosphere. At all three performances I saw, the whole dance took place in a blurry mist. One night the stage was so socked-in that for the first two sections you couldn't see most of the dancers on the stage.

One thing *In the Upper Room* doesn't need is salesmanship. It succeeds as a "pure-dance" work for the ensemble, both a technical tour de force and a theatrical spectacle, without inherent characters or storyline. George Balanchine perfected this kind of display with *Theme and Variations*, created for ABT in 1947, and decades of stylistic reconfigurations. Tharp certainly doesn't imitate Balanchine, but *In the Upper Room* shares his conviction that dancing is all you need to make the biggest effect. Many choreographers subscribe to this maxim; very few have gone beyond conscientiously paying it homage.

Ballet Theater's big new work, *Kaleidoscope*, by the young Canadian Peter Quanz and set to the Piano Concerto no. 5 by Camille Saint Saëns, is a formal arrangement for two principal couples with a corps of twelve women and six men. It opens on the women of the corps, in handsome blue tutus by Holly Hynes, posing with flowery arms against a sparkle of sketched-in chandelier on the backdrop and mauve lighting. (Scenery was by Robert Perdziola and lighting by Brad Fields.) The audience broke into applause at this lovely picture, but then settled into good-natured acquiescence.

Instead of following through with a predictably formal exposition of classicism, Quanz introduces a hint of mystery by distributing the principal couples unevenly through the ballet. The first to appear (I saw Stiefel with Gillian Murphy at one performance, Herman Cornejo and Sarah Lane at another) leave after the first movement and don't come back until the finale. It's the second couple (Veronika Part and Maxim Beloserkovsky, Julie Kent and David Hallberg) who turn the ballet into a more dramatic affair. The women of the corps come between the lovers, but instead of claiming their sister for their own, they chase the man away. He doesn't dance at all until, after many group numbers, he reenters for the finale. By then his big leaps seem anticlimactic or perfunctory, since we've been given no reason to expect anything of him. Julie Kent played the jilted female with tragic intensity that was interesting but easily quenched by the automatic reconciliations of the finale.

Mark Morris's *Gong* pleased the audience but didn't provoke any curiosity at all for me. It was like looking at a beautifully woven piece of silk or a flower arrangement. Morris turned to composer Colin McPhee, one of the remarkable generation of North American artists and anthropologists who fell in love with Bali in the 1930s. Tabuh-Tabuhan (1936) is his ambitious attempt to transcribe the sonorities of the Balinese gamelan for a Western orchestra. I thought Morris's ballet, with its angular "Oriental" gestures and dressed-up tutus by Isaac Mizrahi, pointed out the exotic tilt of the music but didn't locate its depths of rhythm, texture, or cultural empathy.

Nineteenth-century ballet choreographers scavenged the ethnic universe for stories and signs that would pump novelty into a formulaic repertory. A few of these multi-act productions have descended into our times. The long, convoluted, and many times reconceived scenarios of *Le Corsaire* (Greek slaves, harem girls, pirates, and potentates) and *Paquita* (Spanish grandees, French noblemen, and gypsies) retain only the emblems of national difference, but they also yield short, showy excerpts for gala occasions and program fillers. The pas de deux, ten-minute packages of the most virtuosic dancing ballet stars know, constitute almost the only time we get to see the ultimate, the cream of the classical vocabulary, unencumbered by anything but the thrill of achievement: In *Le Corsaire*, Angel Corella's scissors kicks slashing across running leaps, his supersonic turns, his whirling descents on one leg into plié and back up to the vertical; and Xiomara Reyes's alternating single and double fouettés, exactly on the music. In *Paquita*, Jose Manuel Carreño's multiple turns with changing gestures of the leg, and Irina Dvorovenko's sudden balances, her hops on pointe while kicking out the working leg.

Much of the twentieth century's innovation arose from the desire to supplant such guilt-free exhibitionism with a more dignified presentation of dancing. Michel Fokine set out to reform classical ballet by scraping away all decadence and ornamentation. A ballet's movement and characters should harmonize with its story or locale, he decreed; everything should blend as one: music, décor, and the overall style of the performance. Virtuosity should never be flaunted for its own sake. Fokine's one-act fantasies and tone poems supplied the vehicles for the greatest dancers of his time—Nijinsky, Karsavina, Pavlova, Bolm. Seen in its final form during the 1909 premiere season of Diaghilev's Ballets Russes, Fokine's *Les Sylphides* simultaneously revealed Russian ballet to a twentieth-century audience and inaugurated the era of modern ballet that continues today.

Acknowledging the nineteenth century's intangible feminine allure, as personified in the corps de ballet of *Giselle* and *La Sylphide*, Fokine dispensed with any narrative attempt to explain these creatures. He thus effectively captured them and their mystery, in a series of Chopin waltzes, mazurkas, and other short pieces. A single man joins the women, to partner them and complement them with his own gentle variation, but no passion or tragedy stirs their spirits. It seems sufficient that they express the music alone. Iconic works like *Les Sylphides* have become tests of a company's stylishness and ensemble prowess. Sometimes the ABT dancers treat this work so solicitously it congeals into marble, but the cast I saw, Veronika Part, Maria Riccetto, Melanie Hamrick, and Maxim Beloserkovsky, and a sympathetic corps of sylphs, gave a persuasive account of romanticism.

If Fokine opened the Diaghilev era, George Balanchine closed it, emerging from Russia after 1924 to serve his choreographic apprenticeship and to forecast the next big change in ballet making. Committed, like Fokine, to demolishing excess and egotism, he went further in experimenting with themes, music, and unconventional dancing. Diaghilev, the master impresario, successively fostered the visions of both men. With *Apollo* (1928), Balanchine adapted Fokine's theories of clean, concise storytelling and dancing that arose naturally from a ballet's theme. His own sensibility, though, looked ahead, not back. *Apollo* isn't Greek the way Fokine's *Daphnis and Chloë* was; that is, it doesn't try to create a society or an atmosphere, or even to tell a story. It does capture an essence, like *Les Sylphides*, but Balanchine's essences have to do entirely with the possibilities of dancing and dance composition. Those possibilities could allow for the idealizations of Greek aesthetics, as well as the cosmopolitan speed, physicality, and wit that were emerging in Europe after the Great War.

Ballet Theater took on *Apollo* as early as 1943, and it's served over the years to show off the company's greatest male dancers: Eglevsky, Youskevitch, Baryshnikov. The work has been more or less continuously in the repertory of New York City Ballet. In 1979, Balanchine made some major changes to it, deleting the prologue that recounted, however sketchily, the birth of Apollo. Ballet Theater's version, staged this season by Richard Tanner, includes this scene as well as the original ending, in which Apollo leads the Muses up the slopes of an imagined Mt. Olympus.

Watching the deleted portions again situated the ballet for me in Balanchine's early years, when he hadn't entirely abandoned stories but was searching for economical ways to tell them. The birth scene takes place at the top of an impossibly steep staircase—the remnant of the original, more literal mountain indicated by a piece of scenery. Apollo suddenly emerges from under the staircase, his upper body bound tightly in strips of cloth. Two female attendants circle him, each holding one of the bands, to unwrap his body; then they wait while he undoes the last part himself by stepping in a circle.

Images of birth and infancy continue with Apollo's first dance, as he discovers how to play the lyre. These opening sequences humanize the god and prepare for his playful relationship with the three Muses: the contest for best performer, the games of follow-the-leader, the luxurious movements that could only have been invented after women began wearing bathing suits. Balanchine credited the neoclassical Stravinsky score with showing him how to economize and still convey his idea. In the performance I saw, Beloserkovsky and his Muses, Part, Wiles, and Hamrick, seemed to catch the sportive tone.

Jerome Robbins's *Afternoon of a Faun*, making its debut in the ABT repertory, provided another link to the Ballets Russes. Choreographed in 1953 just after Robbins left ABT for the New York City Ballet, *Faun* revisits the impressionistic miniature that was Vaslav Nijinsky's first choreography in 1912. Nijinsky might have succeeded Fokine—Diaghilev certainly encouraged his creative efforts—except for the personal and psychological trauma that caused his dismissal and ended his career. Robbins followed Nijinsky's scenario, substituting a modern boy and girl in a ballet studio for a Faun and the Grecian maidens who disturb his woodland reverie. The theme is the same. The Faun, alone with his thoughts, glimpses what he takes to be love. The nymphs shrink from him, then mock him and flee, leaving him to consummate his desire alone. The Mallarmé poem that inspired Debussy indulges in sensuous raptures, narcissism, the pleasurable exploration of identity without awareness. "Was I in love with a dream?" the poet asks.

Robbins made a brilliant transposition of this. Jean Rosenthal's gauze box-set with a barre along one wall and an invisible mirror across the proscenium establishes the dreamy atmosphere of a studio almost as private as a forest glade. The boy lies on the floor, doing slow stretches and leg

Afternoon of a Faun (Robbins). Allegra Kent and Francisco Moncion, New York City Ballet. Photo by Martha Swope, courtesy of The Robbins Rights Trust.

rotations. A girl comes in; intent on her own practice, she doesn't notice him until he moves in behind her at the barre. Without a word, they improvise a pas de deux, synchronizing poses, skin to skin, and studying themselves in the mirror. He kisses her on the cheek. She touches her face, reflects for a moment, and backs away. Alone, the boy sinks to the floor again and resumes exploring his body.

As staged by Jean-Pierre Frolich for Stella Abrera and David Hallberg, this *Faun* seemed realistic, even ordinary. Instead of observing themselves obsessively and exclusively in the mirror, the couple looked at each other, their touch was an invitation, their kiss a promise. Of course this is one way to interpret the ballet, but to me its real originality lies in its conviction that both parties aren't relating to each other but to their image in the mirror. It's not real sex they want, but creating the illusion of it.

Robbins's *Faun* has almost overshadowed its predecessor in the ballet repertory. The original is still performed, but the audience balks at Nijinsky's highly conventionalized movement, and waits for the hyped-in-advance final orgasm. It's risky to do a ballet today that trades in anti-naturalism. The audience hasn't enough of a grip on the practices of high art: abstraction, formal composition, and literary allusion. When the choreography rests on these premises, it's safer if the piece includes flashy dancing or hooks into current headlines. Ballet Theater took Kurt Jooss's 1932 expressionistic satire *The Green Table* into the repertory this season for the first time, perhaps because of its antiwar, antifascist reputation. Jooss left Germany with his company just ahead of the Nazi purges; he refused to fire his collaborator, composer Fritz Cohen, who was Jewish.

The dance is a series of scenes depicting a whole society cut down by an allegorical Death warrior—innocent girls and resistance fighters, gung-ho military recruits and the women they leave behind, and even a wily Profiteer. Two pianos play an acrid score of cheap barroom waltzes, sentimental tunes, a mechanistic march, and a tango. Jooss enclosed his Dance of Death within the parentheses of an endless diplomatic charade. It's the masked Gentlemen in Black who precipitate the war and escape its consequences, while all the willing combatants and fellow travelers are swept away. *The Green Table* and all of Jooss's surviving works are now under the supervision of his daughter, Anna Markard. She insists on absolute adherence to an established choreographic precedent, but this sometimes leaves the dancers without much breathing room. I thought Isaac Stappas gave a convincingly implacable performance as Death, but the rest of the cast looked a little frozen.

The Green Table was brought to America in 1967 by Robert Joffrey. It was the first major historic revival sponsored by the New York State Council on the Arts. Jooss was still alive to direct it, and the moment was right. I remember one Joffrey Ballet performance when what seemed like the entire audience left the theater and walked over to join a big peace demonstration in Times Square. What fervent days those were, for art and activism! The audience at ABT applauded *The Green Table* heartily, content to honor its protest as metaphor but not as a contemporary rallying cry.

Agnes de Mille's signature work *Rodeo* is a perfect example of how ballet can raise certain nationalistic images to the status of nonthreatening entertainment. Choreographed in 1942 for the Ballet Russe de Monte Carlo, during the early stages of our engagement in World War II, the ballet celebrated those American icons, the cowboys and their frilly girlfriends. It engaged ballet dancers in a vocabulary of made-up "frontier" movements and vernacular dances. There's very little classical display in this work; de Mille devised dance-mime gestures from riding, roping, and courting behaviors, and the choreography includes waltzes, polkas, a hoedown, a tap dancing face-off, and a square-dance running set. The ballet's greatest asset is its tremendous Americana score by Aaron Copland.

Ballet Theater took *Rodeo* into the repertory in 1950, and former Joffrey dancer Paul Sutherland staged this revival. Christine Sarry coached Erica Cornejo, who conveyed some of Sarry's explosive naiveté and charm, as the Cowgirl who realizes you can't catch a feller by trying to be one. Issac Stappas and Craig Salstein were the ranch hands who are smitten with Cornejo as soon as she puts on a party dress. I'm resistant to *Rodeo*'s stereotyping, but the piece entertains like a Broadway show. De Mille choreographed *Oklahoma!* right afterwards.

Agnes de Mille was a struggling young dancer in London when the English choreographer Antony Tudor saw that her talent didn't fit conventional definitions of classical ballet. Neither did his. He cast her in his lament *Dark Elegies* in 1937, and as soon as Ballet Theater got off the ground, she convinced the management to hire him. Tudor remained an elusive but revered presence in Ballet Theater for the rest of his life. He made relatively few more ballets, but *Dark Elegies* remains a unique statement. Set to Gustav Mahler's Kindertotenlieder, the choreography outlines a ritual of grief and catharsis. The company has preserved it and still performs it with respect bordering on piety.

A small community of bereaved parents gather on a hillside, overcome by grief and guilt. We don't know how the children died—an epidemic perhaps, or a sudden storm that caught them far from home or out in a boat. I've always thought of this place and these people as Nordic, not English or German. They're so pent-up and reserved. A baritone (Troy Cook) is seated on a bench and sings Mahler's laments, to poems of Rückert, with spare gestures, as detached from the dancers as they are from each other.

The costumes are shapeless, drab; the women wear tightly wrapped head scarves. The female soloists go on pointe, but only to draw themselves up in attenuated sorrow. The eight women and four men come and go, standing or sitting on the ground to witness their friends' heartbreak. People walk with dragging steps. Inside the circle their pathways are cut short; they turn and run up to the watchers; finding no comfort, they turn again to someone else. A woman bends and contracts in grief; a man lifts her awkwardly, ineffectually; they strain away from each other. Another man leaps straight up with narrow fury. At moments the whole group joins in a folk dance, chains and circles that bond them in their misfortune. The pitch of sorrow rises until the last man erupts in anger and the whole group runs in a frenzied circle. Finally the sky clears and the baritone assures us that the children are at rest. The parents leave in a formal procession, resigned but not yet restored.

Dark Elegies, almost seventy years old, is so perfectly made that it doesn't seem dated. Tudor's choreography expresses an idea of individual loss and community healing that will never be obsolete. We could take lessons from it in these days of hurricanes, exile, famine, and war.

ENIGMA IN THE MIDDLE

Hudson Review, Autumn 2008

Impressing the Czar, a twenty-year-old work by William Forsythe, staged by the Royal Ballet of Flanders, was the only dance entry in last summer's Lincoln Center Festival. Without revealing anything new about Forsythe, it confirmed the early emergence of the dance, theatrics, and inimitable stagecraft that have marked him as a major contemporary choreographer with his own company and a legion of followers.

Forsythe has been an enigma to me throughout his career. More than anything, his work is contradictory, not just contrarian. He could never be called ingratiating, and whatever is conciliatory on his stage will sooner or later get the shaft. Just when you start to perceive a pattern or a direction for the action, the lights go out, or the dancers drop what they're doing and walk offstage. He starts with rigorous, elegant ballet technique, then skews and accelerates it so that steps cede their importance to the unclassical thrills of danger, daring, and suspense. The dancers who make this happen may be virtuosos, but the choreographic design prevents them from being stars. They move on and offstage in brief appearances, their duets and solos often surrounded by other dancers doing movement in opposition. They dress alike; it's hard to pick them out of the streaming ensemble, hard to figure out who they are.

Yet they're devoted to their leader. Since movement improvisation is a component of Forsythe's choreographic process, they become partners in creating the dance. Instead of asking them to perform established steps or imitate steps he's made up, he frequently offers a movement sketch and asks the dancers to develop it. The results will be set and repeated in the finished stage work, with allowances for smaller variations in performance.

A gotta-dance person, Forsythe has been dancing since childhood, and at fifty-nine he's still a facile and inventive mover. In the studio he will spring into spontaneous action as fluent and as complex as verbal discourse. Complementing this intuitive, overwhelmingly physical talent is Forsythe's intellectual appetite—a brainy curiosity about art, culture, science, philosophy, technology, politics, realms of history that seem far removed from dancing. The signs and significances of these products of the real world inspire and often appear in his dances, though it can be an uncomfortable fit.

In an extraordinary scene from a 1996 documentary film "Just Dancing Around" (released in 2007 by Kultur), he struggles to reconstruct how he came up with a single phrase of movement. He's talking to a confused student.

> WF: "There's no way for you to enter into this."
> Student: "Enter into *what*?"
> WF: "Into this event. This is an event. It's very specific to me. This event has a significance, it has a meaning, it has an origin. It was a state. I can't quite find the scientific—I know how I got there. I got there through—at one point through geometry, for example? By following something—for example, I had this—what's it? bum-ba-bum [rotating his hands as if they were cradling a grapefruit] I had this curve here, observed it [left arm goes across his body]. And then traced it like that, with that part [right arm curves up from the elbow]. So then I put [tapping his chest with right hand] where I know my heart is, anatomy? Through that and I traced it where I assume to be my heart. General stuff like that [left hand at solar plexus and chest caved in].
>
> "And then there was an association at that point about [both arms winged out, hands clutching downward]—something with the space of the heart, or something with the heart—and I thought about my own kids, and I tried to figure out what height [right arm stretches out and curves down]—and the height of their heads, their height. So I end up in a state like this, and it goes to a kind of mechanics [lifts right leg rotated in, right hand grabs his knee] bum. Like that. And so on and so forth. So it keeps alternating between what is that other moment. What is the associative moment, for example? And the arbitrariness of this event. In other words, I don't know if they're really this tall. . . . I can make a sort of proprioceptive imitation."

Throughout this encounter, Forsythe is making small moves and adjustments, focusing inward as he gropes back over his tracks, then looking earnestly at the student to whom he's trying to relay the information. The camera only shows us the student once, in close-up, his face perplexed. We never see the original phrase that provoked the dialogue.

In an interview for the same film, Forsythe says, "Choreography is not about steps. It's about organization, of the body or the body with other bodies." I see his choreography as a product of his attempts to contain the massive data bank in his mind, of keeping that grapefruit between his hands. Other choreographers would edit their movement ideas severely, as Twyla Tharp does, or assign control for chunks of data to other people and to chance operations, like Merce Cunningham. Forsythe has developed a system of choreographic analysis, influenced by the German movement theorist Rudolf Laban. *Improvisation Technologies: A Tool for the Analytical Dance Eye* was first published in 2003 as a CD-ROM and later a book. I haven't made a study of this methodology as a determinant of any Forsythe dance, but in the middle of *Impressing the Czar*, I thought, Oh, he really can choreograph!

Impressing the Czar originated in a pure-dance work, *In the Middle, Somewhat Elevated*, commissioned in 1987 by Rudolf Nureyev who was then artistic director of the Paris Opera Ballet. This was Forsythe at his most severe: nine dancers in practice clothes, offering an exposition of rakish, speeded-up ballet, set to a single metronomic pulse with percussive elaborations, by Forsythe's frequent collaborator, composer Thom Willems. The dancers make use of a virtuosic ability to leap, turn, gesture with their feet while suspended in midair. They make ample use of the plié to give themselves a little spring off the ground, to effect a connection between steps and body gestures, and to minimize preparations and pauses. They look a little like joggers at times. The movement never really looks "everyday," but it looks casual, even at its most exacting. The upper bodies are very active, but the dancers don't push into those refined, stopped curves of the classroom. They swing their arms up to position, and their hands finish the trajectory without throwing away the curve entirely. Their whole torsos rebound off the thrust of the legs, torquing improbably away from the vertical in all directions.

In the Middle, Somewhat Elevated is a series of duets and solos, almost always witnessed by less prominent dancers. Featured dancers drift away, walking or running to the sides, as they're replaced by others. The choreography avoids exact repetition or symmetricality, and there's a sense of continuous, space-covering motion to the whole stage. You get urged along by the dance; you get denied the pleasure of stasis.

This choreography was made during a crucial period for Forsythe. After dancing with the Joffrey Ballet II and beginning his choreographic career in 1976 with the Stuttgart Ballet, he had joined Ballett Frankfurt in 1982, becoming artistic director two years later. During the late 1970s and early 1980s European opera houses were enjoying great success with new audiences by producing the lavish, antiestablishment spectacles of Tanztheater exponents, led by Pina Bausch and her Wuppertal Dance Theater. Forsythe shared Bausch's genius for seedy glamour, her critique of contemporary society, her preoccupation with male-female relationships, and her unerring theatricality. But instead of the pedestrian look cultivated by Bausch—sweaty social dances in thrift-shop clothes—he preserved the classical ballet as his main movement language. Even when he was forcibly reshaping the technique into expressive action or ripping into the conventions with harsh light and dire imagery, he was candidly presenting the audience with ballet's superhuman leaping, turning, and pointe work.

His bombshell ballet, *Artifact* (1984), established his credentials on the front line of ballet reformers in the wake of George Balanchine, who had had died in 1983. After its Paris premiere, *In the Middle* was taken into the Frankfurt repertory, bracketed by the melodramatic and unballetic *Potemkins Unterschrift* and *Bongo Bongo Nageela* with *Mr. Pnut Goes to the Big Top* to comprise the full-length *Impressing the Czar*. It seems typical of Forsythe's antic resistance to the obvious that he put the existing dance in between the new sections instead of at the end, where it might have constituted a reassuring antidote to the excess and chaos of the rest. The *Czar* was a great success in Europe, and Forsythe went on to an international career as a freelance choreographer, continuing to lead Ballett Frankfurt until it was dissolved in 2004.

Act 1 of *Impressing the Czar* is a montage of characters, activity, and cultural icons, a bewildering crowd scene that rushes past at high intensity for half an hour. Beethoven's Quartet no. 14, op. 131 plays intermittently, sometimes intact with all its romantic and classical resonances, and sometimes electronically bent out of shape or drowning in other sounds—a musical analogue to Forsythe's manipulation of ballet technique. A low platform with a floor laid out like a big chessboard occupies about a third of the extra-wide stage of the Rose Theater. People shout through microphones, evidently giving information or instructions. The amplification was up so high at the Rose that I understood little of this discourse and could seldom make out which of the many busy characters was speaking.

People in sumptuous period costumes sweep in and out. Other men and women are dressed in white shirts and black trousers or skirts. Still others are dancers in unitards. A man in a white flaring miniskirt poses with a bow and is later impaled with arrows. Large cloth curtains—or de-accessioned canvasses—are portentously held up and then whisked away to reveal tableaux behind them. Alone or in small clusters, people cross, enact pantomimic bits, fall down, do inscrutable things with props, leave, return. Some people seem to have twin companions, but the twins don't always behave in accord. Eventually the clashing entities begin to cohere into more or less readable characters or cadres. The people in the opulent gowns do old-fashioned court dances. Sometimes in counterpoint with them, the unitard group does feverish, Balanchinian modern ballet. A communication between an airplane pilot and a control tower drifts in and out—sometimes the pilot seems to be in distress or maybe about to crash; other times the flight goes smoothly. You can tell the props and costumes are beautifully crafted, but you're too far away in the audience to make out the details. Was that golden object the same bow wielded by the mini-skirted man? Or was it an astrological symbol? Or an oversized harmonica?

The curtain finally fell on this panorama as the crowd arranged itself in approximate ensemble order, to do a formal dance with disco flavoring. I didn't know anything more than when it began, except maybe that art is indistinguishable from noise. *In the Middle, Somewhat Elevated* cleared the mind and the eye. Then we were back in the maelstrom again with act 3, *La Maison de Mezzo-Prezzo*. Agnes, the woman in the white shirt, now played a motor-mouth auctioneer in a strapless evening gown, with a look-alike assistant who kept getting in her way. She was trying to sell off golden mannequins representing the Great Works of Western Art. Again, the words were largely obliterated by the over-miked sound system, so I failed to understand why Agnes was so frantic to unload these dubious treasures, and whether she succeeded or not. There was a box on her rostrum, and at intervals a door in the box would fly open to reveal a man's head stowed inside, a talking head. Agnes and the man yelled at each other over the raucous, milling-around mannequins. Periodically Agnes would shut the door on the man's face. She obviously didn't like him, and finally stabbed the box with an arrow.

Act 4/5 dispensed with most of the dadaistic clutter to assemble the entire company, dressed in white shirts, black schoolgirl skirts, shoes and kneesocks, and Louise Brooks wigs, for a huge tribal dance. In lines, clusters, and stage-covering circles, they tramp and stomp out patterns that are highly organized but not in precise unison. The man in the box, who was also the man with the golden bow, reappears, now called Mr. Pnut. Having been repeatedly martyred in the first act and imprisoned in the third act, he lies on the floor holding an arrow to his chest as the tribe celebrates around him in a goofy evocation of *Le Sacre du Printemps*. Resurrected, he leads them in more line dances as soloists emerge to challenge him. He seems to be successfully fending them off, by blowing into an unrolling paper party favor, when the curtain falls for the last time.

When you think about the meaning of *Impressing the Czar*, any thesis you might come up with is equally feasible. Forsythe told interviewers he didn't want anyone to worry about the elaborate symbols and references, they should just have fun watching the piece. This is his way of undermining the critics and empowering the audience, I guess. I certainly wouldn't venture any master narrative for the work, although I've no doubt Forsythe must have had some conceptual reason for gathering all this cultural paraphernalia under this politically provocative title. Maybe the "Czar" represented the outdated and overfunded imperial ballet traditions that were still enshrined in European opera houses, those traditions that he intended to demolish in 1988, along with their complacent patrons. In the end, the Opera House defeated him. The City of Frankfurt withdrew its funding and the Ballett closed. But like Mr. Pnut he picked himself up and began again. He enlisted many of the Ballett Frankfurt dancers and in 2005 formed The Forsythe Company, based in Dresden and Frankfurt.

It's early to tell what direction the new company will take. Forsythe's physical-theater proclivities seem to have dominated the antiwar piece *Three Atmospheric Studies* (2006), which toured to Brooklyn Academy and Berkeley. Forsythe maintains his presence as a prolific freelance choreographer, genre crosser, and networker. His dances, films, videos, and far-flung collaborations generate scads of verbiage, which in turn feeds his reputation as a thinker and innovator. He knows academic-speak, and his widespread interests make him a good conduit for what he calls a "greater permeability" between experts in the dance and nondance fields. Researchers comb through the scores, essays, learned program notes, and documentary materials generated by his many projects. A 2000 issue of the journal *Choreography and Dance*, edited by dancer/choreographer Senta Driver, was devoted to him, and critic Rosalyn Sulcas is writing a full biography.

Forsythe has spearheaded a long-term multidisciplinary study at Ohio State University, the Online Interactive Scores Project, which is based on an analysis of his 2006 film *One Flat Thing, Reproduced*. A cinematic adaptation of a 2001 dance, OFTR uses the idea that a group of people doing ordinary things in an incongruous setting can suggest meanings, metaphors, and relationships that transcend the place or the action alone. The dancers move through a grid of worktables lined up close together in a vast indoor space, an arena or a train shed. They don't actually dance, but as they slide among the tables, crouch underneath them, touch or retreat from one another, their actions take on dramatic overtones.

According to project codirector Norah Zuniga Shaw, a member of the OSU Dance Department faculty, Forsythe's choreography consisted of several phrase structures that were brought into play in performance as the dancers responded to an elaborate assortment of cues from their colleagues. These cues could be actual movements or other aspects of the interplay, like lines, curves, or changes of direction in space. As the phrases overlap, the dancers create patterns without falling into unison—a kind of counterpoint that the audience might not even perceive. Forsythe calls them "form-flow alignments." Computer graphics will replicate the design and evolution of these deep structures over time. The study, intentionally, won't consider the highly dramatic activity that dominates the surface of the dance. Zuniga Shaw sees the input of her colleagues in science, technology, design, and humanities as a way of facilitating an interface between dance and other fields. The resulting "research space," to be launched as an interactive Web site at OSU next spring, could serve as both a tool for creative work and an entree into a more sophisticated conversation about creativity.

As an assured dance maker and theater man, Forsythe has worked the borders between tradition and anarchy, making both sides of the cultural debate work for him. Historically, he comes out of the late twentieth-century turmoil in ballet, when the opera houses were looking for new ways to sustain their hold on high art. John Cranko in Stuttgart, along with Kenneth MacMillan and others, updated the nineteenth-century story ballet genre with modern movement and sexy plotlines. At the same time, picking up the threads of Balanchine's all-dance modernism, Cunningham, Tharp, and the Joffrey's Gerald Arpino developed formal structures with contemporary energies. Forsythe somehow partook of all these precursors to consolidate a singular view of dance. Now his dances serve as models when they're adopted into the repertories of other companies. His sensibility fuels a network of younger choreographers and legitimizes the current wave of new dances that feature demanding, offbeat movement and no particular concern for thematic unity.

The revival of *Impressing the Czar* was the idea of Royal Ballet of Flanders artistic director Kathryn Bennetts, who danced with Forsythe's Ballett Frankfurt. Helen Pickett, guesting with the company in the role of Agnes for the Lincoln Center Festival performances, is another Ballett Frankfurt alumna. Pickett made her choreographic debut in 2005, with *Etesian* for Boston Ballet. She's also worked as an actress and teacher with the Wooster Group in New York, where Forsythe has been a role model and collaborator. Pickett's new dance *Petal* was commissioned by the Aspen Santa Fe Ballet last winter. That company, led by Tom Mossbrucker, a Forsythe associate years ago at the Joffrey II, showed *Petal* on a program at Jacob's Pillow Dance Festival in August, along with Forsythe's 2000 duet *Slingerland* and contemporary dances by Jorma Elo and Itzik Galili. The program exemplified the success of contemporary dance, an audience-pleasing display of theatricality and movement.

If you spend any amount of time looking at ballet, it's hard to remember the extended crisis of authority the field went through after the death of its twentieth-century giants—George Balanchine, and then Robert Joffrey, Frederick Ashton, Jerome Robbins. Now you can see that these losses at the top of the field cleared the way for a whole new generation of choreographers, and, more than that, a new perception of classical ballet. The audience for Aspen Santa Fe Ballet, and even New York City Ballet and its establishment siblings, is learning to regard Balanchine's neoclassicism as a historical style, alongside the international fusion styles of Tanztheater, physical theater, and contemporary dance eclecticism. This modern audience may not even be able see examples of neoclassical masterpieces as they recede into the past and as dancers lose the skills to perform them well.

One thing that distinguishes Balanchine's ballets, even twenty-five years after he was alive to supervise them, is their fierce confidence in form as the vessel for dance ideas. William Forsythe's ballets emit this assurance. You sense that they're propelled by something besides generalized physicality or personal ambition. Maybe it's anger, or boredom, or simply a need to keep moving. Or maybe it's the tensions that bind his dances together: between the desire to hide and the desire to reveal; the need to explode and the need to hold back. As an artist he always seems to be dug into the present while at the same time peering into the future. Perhaps the ambiguity is what makes us interested in him, and what makes other artists follow his lead.

6 On with the Show

NO BIZ LIKE IT

Boston Phoenix, 13 February 2004

The relationship between Broadway and ballet has been tightening little by little for years. Ballet dancers have gotten more flashy and extroverted; show dancers have piled on more technique. Susan Stroman's new *Double Feature*, for the New York City Ballet, demonstrates that there's still a big difference between genres, and Stroman hasn't made a convincing fusion.

Stroman belongs to the recent generation of dance makers who've come to ballet from a successful Broadway career. Usually the traffic has gone in the other direction, as ballet choreographers ventured into show business. George Balanchine did masses of commercial work in the 1930s and 1940s, but for a lot of reasons it stayed on the back pages of his resume.

Balanchine often used commercial opportunities to have fun with classical conventions that would be taken more respectfully elsewhere. I'm thinking of his *Swan Lake* and *Schéhérazade* send-ups, and his idea of *Romeo and Juliet* as a ballet/tap tournament. These morsels can be seen in movies. Among the tantalizing but vanished treasures there's stuff like the 1942 *Ballet of the Elephants* (to Stravinsky's Circus Polka) and "The Ill-Tempered Clavichord" from the 1943 musical *What's Up?*

Balanchine's relish for these out-of-school antics spilled over into his popular ballets. In pieces like *Who Cares?* (Gershwin) and *Union Jack* (English music hall) he could set out a completely classical form, lightly disguised in thematic clothing, and make you see ballet as a broader playing field than you'd thought. The dancers didn't have to actually *do* jazz dancing or honky-tonk, only wink at it. Maybe Balanchine felt it would be undignified to use vernacular material literally, but popular ballets in his hands never turned out stodgy.

What Susan Stroman does in *Double Feature* is to apply a minimally skewed ballet vocabulary to a silent-movie pretext. The result, in her hands, is efficient, entertaining, and styleless. For the first act, "The Blue Necklace," Stroman and Glen Kelly dreamed up a melodrama about a baby-switch, a mean stepmother, and a happy ending where the ill-treated but cheerful heroine gets Prince Charming and is reunited with her real mother at a fairy-tale party.

"Makin' Whoopee," the second act on the bill, is based on Buster Keaton's 1925 movie *Seven Chances*, about a hapless hero who will inherit seven million dollars if only he can find someone to marry by 7:00 P.M. Although Keaton didn't like the script, he turned *Seven Chances* into an inspired updraft of wackiness. He scrambles out of one predicament only to land in something worse. As in a nightmare, he must outrun diminishing time and expanding space. The later it gets, the further he has to go to solve his problem. On screen these distortions become not only plausible but funny. Translated to Stroman's more pragmatic stage world, the plot dissolves into the figment that it is.

Tom Gold plays the Keaton character with inexhaustible wide-eyed bashfulness and marathon legs. When he fails to win several prospects, he advertises for a bride and then has to escape from a church full of thwarted applicants. Keaton's denouement may be the greatest chase in movie history, involving trolley cars, cops, beehives, taxicabs, construction equipment, barbed wire, rowboats, brickbats, and a football game, as the hundreds of would-be brides pursue him through town and over hill and dale, till they turn into an avalanche of marauding boulders. Stroman's horde looks like a pack of multigendered wilis.

In "The Blue Necklace" old stagey tropes are dressed up in glamorous pretechnicolor costumes by William Ivey Long. The baby bundles are left on the church steps. The stuck-up daughter wrangles with the virtuous foundling. Kyra Nichols, NYCB's still-gorgeous senior ballerina, played the awful mom with social-climbing gusto.

Stroman's choreography has no particular distinction, either as '20s-inflected ballet or subject for jazz-age satire. It serves as a vehicle for presenting pretty girls and romantic get-togethers, while the plot bumps along with the assistance of title cards projected on the backdrop. Dance after dance skimmed over the peppy Irving Berlin songs, played infectiously in Doug Besterman's orchestrations by the NYCB's fine big band. Rhythmic bounce and echoes of Fred and Ginger went unnoticed on the stage until the appearance of Damian Woetzel as the matinee idol our heroine has been dreaming about. Then he charmed the whole party with his generous turns and jumps, his dead-on portrayal of a bon vivant who's also a nice guy.

Boston Phoenix, 21 March 2003

The audience today loves dancing, no doubt about that. What it doesn't love is the aura of preciousness and affectation that clings to ballet. Classical ballet companies have yet to find convincing ways to erase these misconceptions and hook the permanent audience they need—and still preserve the idea of classicism. Last week at the Wang Theater the Eifman Ballet of St. Petersburg launched a massive U.S. tour of its evening-length spectacle *Who's Who*.

The company's informational verbiage touts the noble political and artistic intentions of director/choreographer Boris Eifman, and trumpets how successful the Eifman Ballet is all over the world. In two and a half pages of back-patting, the program managed only three sentences of "synopsis" for the sprawling pastiche of music, narrative, and high-energy hoofing we were to see. Two dancers were listed for each of the main parts, but the company didn't inform the audience who was actually dancing Saturday night. As the evening went on, and stereotype followed poorly digested cliché, I decided the ballet wasn't about individual dancers. Instead it was a cartoon of 1920s America as skimmed from old movies, maybe Russian movies.

Who's Who concerns two Russian ballet dancers who flee the revolution and seek the American Dream, to the tune of jazz, swing, and Rachmaninoff. Right away they annoy some gangsters and dress up in drag to disguise themselves. But they behave so outrageously you can spot them a mile off. One of them falls for a chorus girl who thinks he's just being motherly. The other gets engaged to a movie director resembling Cecil B. De Mille and isn't unwigged until their wedding. The plot is laced with improbabilities like the transformation of the chorus girl from a gawky waif to a ballerina simply by the application of toe shoes.

Although much of the plot takes place in Prohibition nightclubs and tawdry dressing rooms, the ballet is staged on a grand scale. All of the action is arranged and projected out to the audience bigger than life. Cubistic, machinelike scenery moves in and out to change the scale. Hanging where the moon should be is a huge metallic circle that seems made of bas reliefs of skyscrapers but sometimes spins like a windmill or winks on and off in the dark. Smoke hangs over most of the scenes, including a Hollywood beach. And there are ramps, venetian blinds, chandeliers, and enough costumes to stage a season of Boston ballets.

When the main characters give vent to their feelings, their solos are all very expressionistic—desperate, intense, and danced with open mouths to signify passion. In the duets, whether the characters are fighting or making love or both, they're either twisting and angling into grotesque shapes or stretching their arms and legs out as far as they can, sometimes in leaps, sometimes in high kicks. Then there are big unison choruses that always seem to end in rows facing the audience. All of the drag sequences and all of the chorus girl vamping and the gangster chases and beatings are performed as over-the-top burlesque.

The music—by Duke Ellington/Billy Strayhorn, Louis Prima, Count Basie, with some anachronistic jazzmen thrown in (Stan Kenton for instance), together with miscellaneous pop band tunes, klezmerish orchestral music by Kol Simcha, and bits of Rachmaninoff and Samuel Barber—bounces you from one specific stylistic impression to another. But the dances set to these selections either have a bland modern-balletic style or they slide off target. We see the chorus girlfriend noodling around on a table as if making up a tap dance, but she's faking it, with halting heel and toe steps and a few shuffles. The chorus lines are clumsy approximations of Broadway dancing and Broadway sex appeal.

When the lovelorn Alex finally tears off his wig and dress for good—I forget what happens to the shady nightclub boss who's after him—he acquires a magnificent ballet company all his own. We don't find out who bankrolled it. Max, his partner *en travesti*, heads back to the homeland after failing to marry the movie mogul. Maybe he'll become the next populist choreographer in Soviet ballet.

⌒ JEROME ROBBINS'S *BROADWAY*

Christian Science Monitor, 6 March 1989

Jerome Robbins's *Broadway* is a rarity, a successful musical that doesn't have a star. The long, lively compilation of numbers from twenty years of shows has no plot and only the thinnest of interlocutory narration. What holds it together is the ensemble dancing and clowning by a cast of sixty, directed and choreographed by the real star of the enterprise, who is, of course, Jerome Robbins.

Robbins has kept one foot firmly planted in show business and one in ballet since his first smash hit, *Fancy Free*, in 1944. The paint had scarcely dried on this ballet innovation when he redrafted it for Broadway as *On the Town*, by doing a completely different treatment of the same theme, three sailors on a one-day pass in New York.

Broadway is a wonderful anthology of Robbins's working process over the years. I kept seeing echoes of his ballets and being surprised at his ability to recycle ideas in fresh terms. Besides the more obvious connections, like the ethnic ties between *Fiddler on the Roof* (1964), *Les Noces* (1965), and *Dybbuk Variations* (1974), his South Bronx Romeo and Juliet, *West Side Story* (1957), had its first inklings in a short-lived modern-dress ballet with masks called *The Guests* in 1949.

The famous bathing beauty scene from *High Button Shoes* (1947), which I'd never seen before, escalates hilariously from Gay Nineties couples cavorting "On a Sunday by the Sea" to a Keystone Kops–and-robbers chase involving beachgoers and city folk, two sets of twins, a ghoulish clan of villains, and a gorilla. After this improbable crowd has charged in and out of a row of bathhouses, the pandemonium suddenly collects itself into a balletic pseudo-gypsy dance having nothing to do with anything that went before except its manic energy. Robbins's first piano ballet, *The Concert* (1956), works itself up into the same kind of headlong fantasy.

As in a ballet gala performance, each of the unrelated numbers in this show is electrifying or seductive in a different way. The audience's adoring response at one of the last previews reminded me how deeply attached we are as a culture to the songs and dances of our musicals. Even without any of the original story lines, these numbers make sense, have an emotional impact. At the stabbing of Riff, the Mercutio character in *West Side Story* (superbly danced and sung by Scott Wise), there was a horrified gasp, as if the audience had forgotten Shakespearean destiny and become totally involved in the life of the character. I've seldom seen that happen in the course of a forty-minute ballet.

Robbins has an uncanny ability to condense character, occasion, and interaction in the fevered compass of a Broadway number. His eye for behaviorisms that tell a story is legendary—in fact, many of them have become staples of the commercial stage, like the splayed, balls-of-the-feet crouch of *West Side Story*'s defensive teenagers. Robbins can engineer masterly sight gags like the byplay with three clownish Proteans who seem to have interchangeable body parts (*A Funny Thing Happened on the Way to the Forum*). He can make a corny trick like an actor flying on a wire (*Peter Pan*) truly magical again, through the exhilarated singing and soaring of Charlotte d'Amboise in the Mary Martin role.

Robbins has been fortunate in his musical and scripting partners, exacting in his production requirements. He's honored the original styles and stagings—no swoopy vocalizing or mumbled lyrics here, no misguided updatings of the choreography. The one big number that didn't engage me was "The Small House of Uncle Thomas" from *The King and I*. Beautifully costumed and performed, it's a delicate, would-be charming drama in "Siamese" style, and the Eliza is Susan Kikuchi, daughter of Yuriko, who played the original and helped restage the scene. To me it looked precious next to the bawdy, frenetic brashness of the rest.

Everything else was exciting in one way or another, even the "premiere" number, "Mr. Monotony," which had been cut from both *Miss Liberty* (1949) and *Call Me Madam* (1950). After Irving Berlin's song, delivered with nice innuendo by Debbie Shapiro, the dance that followed (Luis Perez, Jane Lanier, and Robert La Fosse) looked like any old triangle, except that the competing males mimed musical instruments. Robbins, by the way, was into sex triangles as early as his *Facsimile* in 1946. And he had dancers represent the theatrical qualities of musical instruments in the 1953 ballet *Fanfare*.

The cast of Broadway is so large and the numbers so rich that I didn't have a strong sense for individual performers. The ballet dancers looked weak and out of place, including Robert La Fosse, billed at the top with Jason Alexander, the versatile actor/singer/comedian who stepped into character and introduced each of the wildly diverse numbers. The company, assembled from Broadway, modern dance, and every other kind of professional dancing, worked with supercharged energy and split-second timing. When they all turned upstage in the finale to look at the backdrop, a collage of theater marquees with Robbins's shows in winking lights, the audience was satisfied. Dazzled, thrilled, and refreshed all evening long, we went out humming.

WHAT THEY DID FOR MICHAEL

American Theatre, March 1990

Denny Martin Flinn, *What They Did for Love: The Untold Story behind the Making of "A Chorus Line."* New York: Bantam, 1989.

Kevin Kelly, *One Singular Sensation: The Michael Bennett Story.* New York: Doubleday, 1989.

Ken Mandelbaum, *A Chorus Line and the Musicals of Michael Bennett.* New York: St. Martin's Press, 1989.

Strange things happen to the arts under the aegis of journalism. These books, on the life and works of the monomaniacal, creative ex-hoofer Michael Bennett, demonstrate the corrosive and transfiguring effect a journalistic mind can have on an admired career.

Michael Bennett's phenomenal success *A Chorus Line* is now in its fifteenth year on Broadway. A precedent breaker from its inception, the show originated in a couple of all-night bull sessions among Broadway chorus dancers that took place in the winter of 1974. The tapes of these cathartic, soul-wrenching marathons formed the basis for several months of workshops where a cast of characters and a style gradually emerged, together with a minimal plot about seventeen dancers auditioning for eight places in the chorus of a new show. An electrifying success at once, *A Chorus Line* sped from previews at the New York Shakespeare Festival's Public Theater to Broadway in three dizzying months. Since then it has spawned a whole industry in spin-offs, from two touring companies to coffee mugs and T-shirts.

Three new books now join that list, two focusing on Bennett's life and career, the third scanning the development of the musical as seen by its performing co-creators. In *What They Did for Love*, Denny Martin Flinn recounts the genesis of the show from the dancers' point of view. He describes the inspired, fevered, sometimes agonizing process by which the personal histories of Broadway gypsies got shaped into a moving, funny demystification of show business. In that process, the cast, all featured dancer-actors, became a family—bonded by the collective autobiography they were creating, and honed by Bennett to an excruciating vulnerability and strength that was to be the show's hallmark.

Flinn's own bio says he danced in a road show of *A Chorus Line* for two years in the '80s, but he selects and weaves together the original dancers' words to build the story with a professional writer's skill. He's particularly good at shaping the discontents and insecurities that erupted into disillusion once the show became a success. Flinn thinks the move to Broadway, ironically, glamorized the innocence out of the show. Suddenly the dancers thought big money and instant stardom would be theirs, but the show's whole point is to glorify those in the line who'll never get a shot at the big prize.

Bennett himself makes an appearance in *What They Did for Love* only through the other characters' accounts of how the brilliant, demonic director worked with them in rehearsals. In his introduction to *One Singular Sensation* Kevin Kelly, theater critic of the *Boston Globe*, admits that his long personal friendship with Michael Bennett didn't prepare him for the conflicting subtexts he uncovered in preparing his book. Rather than attempt to judge or psychoanalyze Bennett, Kelly says, "My decision was to present the memories exactly as they were given, the Bennett story filtered through the sometimes paradoxical sides of 'truth.' " The way Kelly

A Chorus Line (Bennett). The Line. Photo by Martha Swope.

selected and arranged the pieces of his story, however, results in a memorial that's honest, unvarnished, and ultimately scathing.

Ken Mandelbaum, who writes on musical theater for several New York
publications, takes a more detached view in *A Chorus Line and the Musicals
of Michael Bennett*. I don't think he knew Bennett, and although he spoke
to many of the same co-workers Kelly did, he chose to focus on Bennett's
work, eventually placing it in a pivotal position on the continuum from the
blockbuster postwar script musicals to the plotless, nearly wordless "concept shows" of Broadway's last two decades. Kelly's and Mandelbaum's
books ought to be complementary, but only if you need to see the artist in
his underwear to understand the art.

Michael Bennett's personal life was a mess, and Kevin Kelly examines every scuzzy corner. His narrative is acridly flavored throughout with
the grievances of Bennett's mother, Helen DiFiglia, who seems never to

have understood what happened to her family. With a mom like this, Kelly keeps reminding us, no wonder Bennett had problems with women, with his own identity. Kelly also ventilates the resentful demands of everyone who tried to get a piece of the fabulously successful *A Chorus Line*, the grudging retrospective allegiance of people Bennett betrayed or used, the long history of familial breakdown, and the details of Bennett's agonizing death from AIDS.

Kelly and Mandelbaum talked to many of the same informants (we don't know which interviewer got to them first; neither book is scrupulously documented as to sources), but where Mandelbaum is circumspect, skirting around drugs, booze, sexual bad behavior, and backstage deals, Kelly gets the gossipy side of every story. His Bennett is frenetic, frighteningly intimate, almost crippled by his inner contradictions. What's most disappointing about Kelly's book is that the actual theater work never gets discussed, only the scheming and bullying that set the work in motion.

Mandelbaum's star is a great collaborator, generous and loyal to his coworkers, a man of vision and unerring judgment for how to make a show work. What in Kelly comes off as immaturity, even regressiveness, Mandelbaum sees as a great asset: the ability to imagine as a child does. What both authors agree on is Bennett's need for control and the often conflicting need to give people around him a free hand.

In Mandelbaum's book Bennett's complex personality emerges through the story of his ten major productions, leading to and draining off of the great watershed that was *A Chorus Line*. Mandelbaum looks carefully at the musical theater during a period most people have written off as a colorless decline. Just the other day, for instance, I read in a dance publication that "Stephen Sondheim's work excepted, the Broadway musical stage has been a disaster area for the better part of two decades." Mandelbaum convincingly traces a series of small shifts that brought musicals into the modern sensibility; for better or worse, you can't say after reading his book that nothing has happened.

Michael Bennett came into the theater when the musical was changing to meet the technology, the nonlinearity, the anti-romanticism of the Vietnam period. He danced in *West Side Story*, arguably the last big book musical, and Jerome Robbins became his idol for life. As a director Robbins did more than choreograph steps. He put the whole show into motion, a feat Bennett was to emulate. After only a couple of years as a gypsy, Bennett began choreographing for stock companies, then for Broadway shows.

In Neil Simon's *Promises, Promises* he had his first big success and met some of his future collaborators, notably Donna McKechnie. Already, he was pulling off nondance-related stage coups that helped the overall show, and choreographing ensemble scenes that had the look of ordinary behavior but were plotted precisely for each individual performer.

Ken Mandelbaum cites *Company* (1970) as Bennett's first concept musical. Like its precursors, the 1948 Kurt Weill–Alan Jay Lerner *Love Life* and Joe Kander and Fred Ebb's 1966 *Cabaret*, it intercut the story line with nonrealistic numbers that explored the inner preoccupations of the characters. In *Company* Bennett found how to mend over the seams between stylistically different sections by choreographing the actors, making the movement personal, and creating variety in the show's pacing so that the action never came to a halt. *Company*, says Mandelbaum, was "a musical in which all the elements—book, songs, musical staging, and direction—were deployed in a truly integrated fashion and at the service of an overriding metaphor, the city as an embodiment of modern relationships." But it was still a show with a conventional plot, and Bennett was still only the choreographer, uncredited for his contributions to the larger scheme.

Bennett's skill as a choreographer is the one thing Mandelbaum fails to make a case for. He describes "numbers" in detail, but is ineffectual in evoking their particular movement idiom. The best he can do is mention that Bennett borrowed ballroom or other dance styles, which he "heightened for emotional effect." We can only imagine how this might have looked. I began to wonder how substantial Bennett's choreographic talent actually was, especially since he often delegated making the steps to assistants like Tommy Tune, Michael Peters, and his devoted friend and collaborator, Robert Avian. In any case, his theatrical imagination and his need for total control wouldn't have long been satisfied with the minor role of dance maker.

He was invited by Harold Prince and Stephen Sondheim, the creators of *Company*, to be co-director of *Follies*, and this became the first of his many shows about the life of people in show business. *A Chorus Line* was the supreme achievement in this genre. The show's unique power, Mandelbaum thinks, came from the overlap between theater and real life. Not only was the script devised from dancers' original stories, but Bennett managed (sometimes by standard directorial techniques, sometimes by trickery) to keep the cast spontaneous in their competitiveness, unified in their desperate need to dance in this show. Both Mandelbaum and Flinn evoke the familial interplay, with Bennett as inspiring, intimidating father figure, that sparked the memories, anger, trust, and compassion that the show needed. Flinn's description of the cast's suggestions, and Bennett's responsiveness to their personal shaping of dances, songs, dialogue, reminded me of the collaborative way many modern-dance companies work, rather than the didactic process of rehearsing a conventionally scripted show.

Mandelbaum is alert to the ironies of the smash finale, where these hopefuls, who have just bared their souls for the sake of the job, are transformed into the theater's most spectacular anonymity and banality, the applause-meter kick chorus. And he notes that "while the show celebrated and glorified the chorus dancer, those who played in the original cast, now that they had been allowed to act and sing onstage for the first time, became dissatisfied with being only a chorus dancer." Yet none of them achieved major status in show business afterward.

Nor did Bennett in the twelve remaining years of his life ever break the creative barrier that such a giant success represented. It's Flinn who reveals how much of Bennett's energy and time was consumed by the *Chorus Line* industry: the regenerating and recycling and constant rehearsing and revisiting casts on Broadway and on tour, as well as the oversight of a multimillion-dollar business and a celebrity career.

Mandelbaum calls *Dreamgirls* (1981) "his state-of-the-art show, a very advanced production that took musical theatre as far as it had ever gone in terms of continuous motion and speed . . . a show that pointed to the future." But even as he perfected his gifts, Bennett may have over-reached himself. The ingenious sets that made *Dreamgirls* as flexible as a movie came to dominate the production in some critics' eyes and had to be scrapped because they were unworkable on tour. Mandelbaum's conclusion seems to be that this "master conceptual artist" became enmeshed in delusions of grandiosity after *Chorus Line*, his demands for extravagant rehearsal time and production values making it harder and harder to create viable shows. The burdens of his psychological distress, drinking, and drug taking were soon compounded by illness, and his tragedy—and the theater's—is that he didn't live to find a way to surpass himself.

RAZZLE

Boston Phoenix, 4 February 2000

Broadway choreographer Bob Fosse made a career and a dance style out of his life. At least that's the message of *Fosse*, the award-winning revue, back in Boston till February 13 at the Colonial Theater. By now mythology has pretty well established Fosse as a famously demanding and insecure workaholic, sweet guy, and womanizer, who died a physical burnout in 1987 at the age of sixty. He told his own fictionalized story in the movie *All*

That Jazz, and since his death at least two full-scale biographies have been published. The *Fosse* show doesn't try to give a narrative or even a chronology of Fosse highlights, but it does riff extensively on Fosse's vaudeville background, his glittery stage successes, and his taste for sexy sleaze.

The show opens with a photo of Fosse's face projected on a scrim, gazing benignly down toward a dark stage. To one side, we see a proscenium lit all around with tiny white lights—a miniature of the Colonial's bigger proscenium frame. Reva Rice, in a black corset, silky black stockings, and heels, sings "Life Is Just a Bowl of Cherries" with torchy irony, and on the other side of the stage we can just make out a man's figure in a zigzag pose, in front of another miniproscenium. Terace Jones emerges in a spotlight, a Fosse-surrogate in bowler hat and tight black suit. He brings on the rest of the company and they show the Fosse dance lexicon in small groups, almost as if they were demonstrating a technique.

Fosse's dance style is instantly recognizable. It's a dance for the eye, a dance about maximizing the body's erotic attractions. The curve of the hips against the slope of a shoulder and the elongated neck. The arm and wrist joints crackling out to the splayed fingers. The hunched upper back opposed by the swinging or bumping pelvis. The sinuous walk that sinks into the floor. The florid gestures that stay tight in around the body, the feet that slide in curves along the floor instead of straight lines. And the provocative way the dancers project it all, full into the face of the audience or in sharp, angular profile.

People say Fosse developed the style as a defense or a facade to counter his self-consciousness about not being a perfectly turned out, noble, and body-beautiful dancer. Okay, but the more I looked at the numbers in Fosse, the more I thought his dance model must have been burlesque.

There is an outright burlesque number in the show, "Razzle Dazzle" from *Chicago*, with another Fosse-surrogate, Greg Reuter, and two women in the show's basic-black underwear costume. The women wave big white feathery fans as the song struts along. Later the lights go pink and seven women in white undies and tiaras parade to "Who's Sorry Now?" These references to Sally Rand and to the Follies girls of the 1920s point to Bob Fosse's professional roots. He was a song-and-dance man before he was out of grammar school. A tap duet by Reuter and Rick Faugno at the end of the show recalls Fosse's teenage partnership in showbiz with Charles Grass.

Together with these nods to Fosse's life story, and the actual numbers reprised from his shows ("Big Spender" from *Sweet Charity*, "Steam Heat" from *The Pajama Game*, "Mein Herr" from *Cabaret* and lots of lesser-known ones), the show includes transitional bits "inspired by" Fossiana that's lost, and numbers that recall his favorite music or movie stars. The performers get some leeway in interpreting the material, so it doesn't all sound like it's been reproduced from a soundtrack. Reva Rice carried most of the solo songs, often tapping into the luscious styles of contemporary black pop music, and Terace Jones mingled undulating torso and pushy muscularity with high balletic arabesques, split jumps, and turns à la seconde in "Percussion 4" from *Dancin.'*

The Fosse show is a team effort. Directors Richard Maltby Jr., Chet Walker, and Ann Reinking and artistic advisor Gwen Verdon, achieved the slick, driving momentum that audiences love. But when you look at a whole evening of Bob Fosse numbers, you realize that while his choreography had its unique look, it didn't have a lot of range. Stripped of the plots and sympathetic characters that inhabited the original shows, the numbers accumulate a kind of merciless detachment. However charming these dancers were trying to be, I couldn't escape feeling beset, as the evening progressed, by a gang of hoods and hookers.

CENTER STAGE

Boston Phoenix, 19 May 2000

Center Stage is a ballet fairy tale. Not the kind you see on the stage but the kind people imagine takes place backstage. The college-age aspirants get through puberty, adolescence, disillusion, and self-awareness during one winter at a prestigious ballet school. The black girl with attitude learns humility and discipline, and makes a hit as a stand-in at the school recital. The girl with bulimia trades in her pushy mom for a cute boyfriend and leaves ballet forever. The one with below-par turnout decides to turn down the stodgy ballet director's job offer so she can dance with the womanizing dancer/choreographer who's starting a troupe of his own. Oh, and only one of the boy dancers is gay.

The movie was handsomely shot around New York's Lincoln Center and the depths of Soho, where the rebels go to take (sshhh!) a jazz class. Director Nicholas Hytner gets surprisingly convincing performances out of the dancers (Amanda Schull, Zoë Saldana, Sascha Radetsky, and Ethan Stiefel are the featured ones).

But whenever there's any dancing, in a stage, a studio, or a salsa club, the film reverts to prehistoric techniques: incessant cuts to new camera angles, breakaway shots onto the rapt faces of onlookers, music that doesn't accompany what you see. So the choreography of Susan Stroman, Christopher Wheeldon, George Balanchine, Kenneth MacMillan, and Kirk Peterson stumbles by in disconnected passages of virtuosity and sublimated sex.

⤳ *BILLY ELLIOT*

Boston Phoenix, 13 October 2000

"And what do you like about ballet?" the stony-faced examiner at the Royal Ballet School asks eleven-year-old Billy Elliot, who's fought his way to an audition from the coal-smudged alleys of the north of England. Groping for a serious enough answer, he finally blurts out, "The dancing." And it's the dancing that transfigures Stephen Daldry's movie about being different in a world of sameness.

Although *Swan Lake* music is heard throughout the film, we don't see even a snippet of high ballet. Billy hasn't either, until his fateful audition. Instead, dancing serves as an outlet for his feelings and a connection to himself. Billy's life is bleak and comfortless, and the family—robbed of their mother at the beginning of the film—sinks into poverty as a miners' strike drags into the winter months. Everyone at home is isolated. Grandma (Jean Heywood) is halfway to dementia. Older brother Tony (Jamie Draven) and father (Gary Lewis), locked in silent machismo, get more and more furious at the union's impotence—and their own. Billy's secret dancing lessons become the target for their rage.

When Billy accidentally wanders into a local dancing class, taught by the bored and discouraged Mrs. Wilkinson (Julie Walters), it absorbs his preadolescent energy and anger better than a punching bag or a trampoline. Frustrated but with a mysterious determination to learn, he begins to conquer his body, and he understands how much this means. Every crisis in his struggle to keep his new identity is a dance. His boogie duet with his teacher, his first pirouette, his kicking slamming rage when his father finds out and forbids him to continue.

The dance of Billy's initiation into ballet is intercut with the mass violence of the miners' strike. Little girls in tutus twinkling their toes alternate with mobs of strikers hurling eggs at a bus full of scabs. Ballet is somehow all tangled up with sexuality too—all the men he knows think ballet dancers are poufs. Michael, his friend from school, likes to dress up in his mum's clothes. Debbie, the teacher's precocious daughter, offers to let him see her bum. Billy is confused about everything except that he wants to keep on dancing.

Jamie Bell, the thirteen-year-old star of the film, is no exquisite ballet boy. He doesn't miraculously achieve perfection. His dance is awkward, blustery, wildly flung all over the room, with everything he's ever seen thrown in—ballet, boogie, clogging—and it's also instinctively musical and expressive.

HOUSE ON HOLD

Dance on Camera Journal, March–April 2008

Dancer Josh Hilberman was working at a tap festival in Greece on September 5, 2007, when he got word from a friend that a water pipe connector had let go in his house just outside Boston, causing a major flood. He and his wife rushed back to the States, to find all their furniture on the lawn and the inside of the house soaked to the studs and floorboards. Their life was in limbo.

Everything got moved into Hilberman's studio in a separate building next to the house, and the couple moved to a temporary apartment in Chinatown. With the house stripped bare and the reconstruction ready to start, Hilberman negotiated with the insurance company and fretted. The trouble was, he was booked for a one-man tap show at Arlington's Regent Theater on the first of March. He couldn't use his studio because it was full of furniture, and he couldn't concentrate anyway, because of the hulking job to be done next door.

Hilberman is a sturdy, upbeat guy, a problem-solver with a loopy imagination. Since he couldn't work on his dance he decided to make a film, using his derelict house as the set. He took a slightly damp video camera and his tap shoes into the house and started filming himself. What resulted, the four and a half-minute *FloodHouseDance*, is neither a tap dance film nor a film with a tap story. Instead, with the ruined house and all its meanings resonating around him, Hilberman's dancing becomes a voice— a witness, a commentator, and in the end a kind of exorcist to a calamitous event.

First off, the fixed camera stares at a blank wall with an electric outlet in it, and a patch of floor. You hear some attention-getting raps coming from nowhere. Then you realize that at the side of the frame there's an empty bookcase, and on top of the bookcase is a pair of feet, shouting into the empty room.

Then, in a series of short takes, we tour the skeletal house. You hear syncopations echoing two rooms away. From behind a partition a leg reaches out, tentatively tests the floor. Big red, yellow, and blue tap shoes take over the screen, dancing insistently, shaking the floorboards. Behind some studs and electrical cables, a shadowy figure whistles and scours the gritty floor with a sand dance, stomps down a hall and up some stairs. A ghostly form is glimpsed running through spaces, leaping through doorways. He's stamping in circles two rooms away, the sunlight washing in behind him. He seems to be getting angry. His blurry figure throws pieces of lumber onto the floor.

Then the tapping gets quieter and we're looking at the culprit, a toilet on the second floor, covered with a crumpled sheet of plastic. There's a commotion behind the blueboard construction panels, and then one panel comes loose and slams to the floor. The dancer, who's pushed it over, stops his tapping and walks slowly toward the camera. Finally we see Hilberman's face, coming closer and closer, peering into the lens, until the screen goes black. We're left to ponder about empty houses, spaces filled with light and the sounds of frustration, disasters we live through.

FloodHouseDance was shot in two days and edited in Hilberman's new Apple computer in time to make its debut at the Regent. Hilberman is back in his house now and the mess is almost gone, except for some mold under the kitchen cabinets that may never get excised.

⌒ CRASH DANCING

American Theatre, July/August 1994

The set for *Stomp*, the British tap/body music/cabaret that captured the East Village this spring, looks like the aftermath of a manhole explosion. Entering the Orpheum Theater you peer down the aisle into a boxed stage. The sides are corrugated tin, with green plastic sheets, the kind they put up to reassure us we're not being sprayed by dangerous substances. The walls are festooned with metal and plastic objects that could have blasted up from anywhere over or under the littered pavements. In the foreground there are trash cans and brooms awaiting the hour of cleanup, or maybe left behind by a dispirited sanitation crew.

Stomp, an eight-person ensemble of frenetic movers, appropriates, celebrates, and eventually transcends this environmental chaos, using only their bodies, their wits, and a heavy dose of attitude. We've all experienced the cathartic effect of bashing things, from the time we did rhythm band in kindergarten, and grown-ups have found healthy ways to channel this innate desire to hit: gamelans, drumming, bang-on-a-can festivals, and all kinds of rhythm dancing from clogging to kathak. But *Stomp*'s sophisticated urban primitives shape the percussive urge into music, theater, even poetry. No words, no program notes. Just them and the junk.

Three or four guys with push brooms come in, suspicious, thin-skinned, making sure everyone knows they're not sissies with loud snuffles, grunts, and whoops. Like flocking birds, one broom wielder answers the others, and the call-response builds into a rhythm. More people arrive and soon all of them are sweeping and stamping and hawking in complex counterpoint. They upend their brooms and continue with a stick dance that eventually ends as a chorus line.

During the next ninety minutes these touchy types evoke an amazing range of images and energies, seemingly by just going along with what the objects suggest. Right after the broom dance, in complete contrast, four men are shaking matchboxes in close harmony, like a barbershop quartet. There's a park-bench number that begins with one character quietly doing a crossword puzzle and ends in a lunatic chorus of acting-out in response to what people read in their newspapers. Most of the papers get shredded in the process. There's a serenade in the dark with clicking Zippo lighters, and lots of satisfying, fast, loud clomping with flat feet in beat-up combat boots.

One reason *Stomp* is more than a suite of oddball dances is that, as the performers handle and transform ordinary objects into percussion instruments, they start to become a kind of community. At least, as much of a community as you ever find in a mean, decrepit city. Any day, people make eye contact when something funny happens on the subway. In the elevator neighbors complain about the weather. A crowd gathers around an accident. Out of wariness comes a momentary entente that plays out in group rage or rescue, and then dissipates, along with the group.

Luke Cresswell, *Stomp*'s leader, is a baby-faced, sturdy guy who pumps up his cohorts, gets peeved when they upstage him, and reestablishes his dominance by doubling the speed of whatever they're doing and by teaching the audience to do a two-clap cadence on cue. David Olrod plays the local nerd, a hollow-cheeked loner with glasses and a vaguely official demeanor. At one point he wanders in with a fire bucket—not the first reference in the show to the famous avant-garde ballet of the '20s, *Relâche*, where a fireman poured water from one bucket to another.

A beetle-browed guy with a ponytail (Fraser Morrison) does a furious solo that looks very much like flamenco. Nick Dwyer occasionally goes out of control, his riffs escalating into a full-scale tantrum, after which he seems to feel better. A small woman (Fiona Wilkes) hammers murderously on the biggest drums but also occasionally cracks a smile.

Rhythm keeps these angry roustabouts from antisocial behavior and bonds them momentarily into a collaborative unit. The cleanup images of the first part of the performance grow more and more extravagant, until three of the men waddle in like tribal warriors from the jungle, with kitchen sinks strapped to their chests. Scraping their rubber gloves on the drainboards, they thump utensils, pour out water, make gurgling sound effects, transformed into housewives in a crazed soap commercial. But junk and aggression win out over cleanliness, and the whole last section is a celebration: symphonic duels with garbage can lids, clanking on the wall decorations, and drumming themselves into trancelike ecstasies. At the end they've subdued cans, pans, pails, hubcaps, fire extinguishers, washtubs, beer kegs, and even their own two feet.

BRAVING THE ELEMENTS

Boston Phoenix, 2 July 1999

We often think of dancers as superhuman, more beautiful and accomplished than the rest of us. Their bodies are perfectly honed to execute tremendous feats that remain in their muscle-memory banks for years. They can make an instantaneous physical response to a visual or mental stimulus, and they can coordinate with their fellow movers, sometimes even without being able to see who's next to them. Despite these extraordinary attributes and skills, they always seem to be looking for ways to transcend what few limitations remain.

Dance Umbrella's final shows of the season, in mid-June at the Emerson Majestic, featured several varieties of "aerial dance." This is not a single form or technique but a shared quest for a range of movement that isn't defined by one's relationship to the ground. The eight companies seen on the first evening were working within two related aerial traditions: the aesthetics of circus and acrobatic athletes, and the arranged risk-taking of rock climbers, high-wire stuntmen, and Evel Knievel. Aerial dance isn't new to the theater or the experimental dance scene either. I thought most of the groups were working on refinements of very simple strategies tested around the late '60s and early '70s in Trisha Brown's equipment pieces (*Planes*, *Walking on the Wall*, *Man Walking Down the Side of a Building*). By now, aerial dance has become one component of a whole genre of spectacle ranging from Cirque du Soleil to Elizabeth Streb's Ringside.

Streb, by the way, has developed a portable set, called a box truss. Adapted from the structures used for rock concerts, it contains and supports the many flying, falling, diving, tumbling, multidimensional effects that constitute Streb's dance. In New York last week I heard a "tech talk" about that elaborate, environmental grid. It was being installed in the Winter Garden of the World Financial Center, where Streb and company are conducting a three-week, six-hour-a-day public rehearsal residency.

For all its diversity, the Dance Umbrella program seemed tame compared to Streb's drastic and demanding work. Of course it takes training and courage to strike beautiful poses and change your grip from hand to ankle to crook of the knee, while swinging or hanging upside down on a wire—I would not dream of doing it. But this seemed to be the extent of technical and aesthetic aspiration for many of the works, and finally, they began to look alike.

Pilar Cervera of Fura, based in Barcelona, used a red silk cloth that she tied into slings and knots to stand in and lean out of and sometimes drop from, as she melted from one shape to another. At various times she looked like a snake charmer, a Hindu goddess, and an exotic dancer. She finally fashioned the cloth and herself into a six-pointed star. This piece, *Catorze*, set an Orientalist tone of exquisite exhibitionism that carried over into several other things.

Axis Dance Company's *Descending Cords* (directed by Joanna Haigood) had two people on a revolving ladder going through a series of continuous, complementary, and possibly amorous shapes—I thought of Susan Marshall's 1987 *Kiss*, where the dancers floated apart and together harnessed to the ends of two cables. In another part of the Axis space, two other dancers wafted in tandem on two almost-invisible swivel chairs. And two men sensually partnered each other on a swing-trapeze in Bodyvox's *One*, choreographed by Eric Skinner, to romantic Songs of the Auvergne.

Only a few pieces emphasized movement as something more than the maneuvers required to create decorative or metaphoric effects. Jo Kreiter showcased her upper-body strength in *Test*, throwing herself at an upright pole, climbing it, winding around it, fastening herself perpendicular to it. The program closed with David Parsons's sensational solo *Caught*, danced by Jaime Martinez. Using a handheld switch, Martinez activated a strobe light every time he hit the peak of a jump, so that he made himself seem to be levitating. But the most physical and risky event of the evening was a pre-performance cliff-caper by four people from Project Bandaloop (based

Out West somewhere), who scaled down and rappelled off the side of the Castle at Park Plaza, stopping rush-hour traffic and collecting an awe-struck crowd on Arlington Street.

The week after that, I went to Washington, where I caught up with the Royal Swedish Ballet, touring to only two places in the United States with an amazing program of reconstructions from the celebrated but almost totally extinct Ballets Suédois. Avant-garde dance disappears fast. It either fades as soon as its novelty wears off or it serves, like Trisha Brown's early work, to open up new and increasingly sophisticated genres. The self-styled dance archeologists Millicent Hodson and Kenneth Archer have been bringing the dance history of the early twentieth century to life for more than a decade. Hodson researches and directs the choreography, and Archer recreates the designs. They've resurrected works by Nijinsky, Balanchine, and now the Ballets Suédois' Jean Börlin.

Seeing the program at the Kennedy Center (it was premiered last summer in Stockholm) was like entering a time machine. When they're performed at all, period pieces tend to get tucked in among more familiar fare, as if producing companies are afraid we'd forget what they really do. It was Robert Joffrey who sparked a serious interest in the choreographic heritage of ballet, but after his death in 1988, the 125-year archive he built up—including Hodson's monumental recreation of *Le Sacre du Printemps* and fourteen others from the period 1910–1940—quickly disappeared again.

Joffrey never got around to the Ballets Suédois, but he might have, after working his way through the choreographers of Diaghilev's Ballets Russes —Fokine, Massine, Nijinsky, Nijinska, and Balanchine—plus the German expressionist Kurt Jooss. A rival of the Ballets Russes though much less durable, the Ballets Suédois (1920–1925) was arguably more experimental, and democratic, than Diaghilev's enterprise. Bankrolled by its founder, Rolf de Maré, it didn't have to cultivate an audience as strenuously as the Ballets Russes. De Maré employed the modern painters and composers of the time, but all the choreography was done by Börlin, who had neither the physique, the virtuosic ability, nor the inclination to work in a neoclassical direction. This means that the Ballets Suédois didn't acquire either the elitist clientele or the long-term critical caché that the Russes did. With only one choreographer, who died five years after the demise of the company, the repertory didn't spread out beyond its original venue. Nothing but bits were filmed, and until now, nothing survived.

Hodson derived her stagings of *Within the Quota* (music by Cole Porter, designs by Gerald Murphy), *Dervishes* (Aleksandr Glazunov, Georges Mouveau), and *Skating Rink* (Arthur Honegger, Fernand Léger) from existing visual materials, musical scores, written accounts, interviews with surviving dancers, and a dancer/scholar's immersion in the sensibility of her subject. We can't know how authentically they replicate the originals, but probably they're the closest thing we'll ever get. They certainly tell us more about the Ballets Suédois' aesthetics than the other reconstruction on the program, Ivo Cramér's *El Greco,* which followed Börlin's scheme of animating famous paintings and connecting the tableaux into a story, but used an expressionistic movement and mime, and seemed more modern than 1920.

Within the Quota, where a Swedish immigrant lands on American soil and meets up with every stereotyped character a European would have recognized from movies and shows of the time, was interesting mainly for the simultaneous, clashing rhythms and keys of Cole Porter's score. *Dervishes* replicated what we still see in traditional Sufi ceremonies, with hints of personal relationships underlying the ritual patterns of the five dervishes and the five soldiers who pass by. The troops become intrigued and join in the whirling dances, but they finally capture the devout practitioners.

Hodson has spoken a lot about the cubist intentions of *Skating Rink.* Fernand Léger's geometric set and costume designs are set in motion by the large group of simulated roller skaters, who glide continuously in big and small circles and cut-up linear tracks, while various characters emerge to enact their stories. This is a big and interesting ballet, more than you can grasp at one viewing, and I hope the Royal Swedish will keep it in repertory.

Some of the things that struck me about the whole program were the range of thematic sources and the attempts to differentiate all the dancers. Even the twenty-four members of the corps de ballet in *Skating Rink* had titles designating their occupation, their class, and sometimes the color of their costumes, so the audience could pick them out. In these four ballets at least, we can see that the Ballets Suédois' idea of modernism was not limited to reformulating traditional ballet classicism with the same polarizing social setups. Class boundaries are much more permeable; people are recognized for what they do, not the status into which they were born. The subject matter could be ethnological, as in *Dervishes* and many other folk-dance ballets Börlin devised, and religious themes could be quite specific. The dancers looked more convinced about all this than many other performers in supposedly updated classical ballets.

HOOP TAMER

Boston Phoenix, 2 October 1998

One of Michael Moschen's most endearing exploits involves a small silver baton and a hoop about eighteen inches across. As he steps carefully across the stage, he points the stick at the twirling hoop, or strokes the circle's edge. The hoop obeys the stick, stopping, reversing direction, floating up and down in front of Moschen's body. Moschen doesn't seem to touch the hoop at all.

Postmodern juggler Moschen, who opened the Dance Umbrella season last weekend at the Emerson Majestic, is a wizard, a clown, a dancer, and an animator of Euclidean science. Other jugglers toss objects around. Moschen assumes objects have a life of their own and trains them to be beautiful. At the beginning of his show, the audience screamed at his feats. Fifteen minutes in, it was holding its breath.

Moschen gives titles to various sections of his program (*Triangle*, *Circles*, and so on), but the evening is basically a one-man display of unique virtuosity. There are some new effects and some well-loved old ones, like the opening, where he keeps a stack of eight crystal tennis balls in the palm of his hand, massaging them to life. One by one he releases the balls, continuing to keep the rest in motion. They creep around his hand, slide up his arm and across his chest, roll over one another like kittens. Although it isn't possible, he appears to be doing nothing more than providing the balls with a place to play.

Not satisfied with putting one set of inanimate creatures through their paces, Moschen extrapolates to bigger objects or new environments. Besides the palm-sized balls, he likes things in the shape of a circle or a snaky curve, and sometimes you can't tell whether something is a prop or a sculpture. At the end of the first long section, he sets one of the crystal balls inside a huge crescent moon sitting on the floor. The ball slides down the crescent and up the other side, gently rocking the moon. Later on, Moschen rolls the crescent and other outsize curves along his neck, shoulders, torso, as if they were giant hula hoops.

He uses a ten-foot triangle as a three-way handball court, bouncing balls off its inside surfaces to create different rhythms. Stepping inside the triangle, he tap-dances softly in a tennis-ball duet. Later on, he throws rhythms onto a doubly rebounding surface—a drumhead made of a lit-up disc, with a similar disc lowered over it. As the balls streak from his hands and ricochet off these surfaces, they seem to create their own geometric designs in space. But there are also designs for their own sake, like the big constructivist sphere made out of different-sized hoops that revolves on a wire and creates an infinite number of three-dimensional patterns.

Although Moschen is developing ideas choreographically with his collaborator Janis Brenner, he basically thinks like a circus performer. He's clowned with the greats—Lotte Goslar, Bill Irwin—and at the Emerson he silently enlisted an accomplice from the audience to help him juggle with an apple that had to be chomped on in exact timing.

 ## ZALOOMY TOONS

New York Press, 23 December 1988

Paul Zaloom is an enthusiast and a believer—the ideal consumer of American culture. He must have started out as a kid broadcasting imaginary baseball games and spinning records at parties. Maybe he sold encyclopedias to pay for his college education. And then he graduated to puppetry so he could not only present a product but create it too. The thing is, he gets to telling you how great your life will be once you buy his package, and then he fails to stop himself before he's also exposed you to its not-so-wonderful side effects.

In *The House of Horrors*, at Dance Theater Workshop, there's this all-American family out to buy their dream house. The house is a two-story cut-away doll's house, and Zaloom stands right in the middle where the stairs ought to be and introduces his puppet characters from there. They include Dad, a nice guy with a nervous chuckle who starts to sneeze the minute he walks into the synthetic-carpeted living room; Mom, who has a Southern accent and loves all the modern conveniences in the house; a baby that squawks for attention; twin loutish kids who alternately bash each other and flop in front of the TV set; and a sweet little old-country Grandma who takes up residence in the kitchen.

After showing them all the great features of the house—the climate control, the plastic wall coverings, the up-to-date bathroom now called a Cleansing Spa—the real estate agent offers the Smiths an afternoon's free trial on the house. By the time it's over, Mom's hair has fallen out, Grandma has turned into a split personality from sniffing the mushroom air purifier, the twins contract a lethal rash, Dad gets flattened by a ravenous rug, and the baby falls through an electrically controlled trapdoor into the cellar.

The story unreels at high speed, like a film gone haywire, with Zaloom standing center stage all the time and whisking puppets in and out of sight almost faster than you can keep track of them, and carrying on the dialogue in as many different voices and accents as there are characters. I forgot to mention the Developer, Mr. Brown, who has a limp and a lantern jaw and a von Stroheim air of authority—he not only will hold the mortgage, but he's the neighborhood dentist as well. All the puppets are made of horrible pink plastic, with mostly no bodies under their clothes, so that their heads, hands, and feet move with pinpoint precision but their torsos sway and jiggle and constantly go out of control.

Zaloom is the kind of performer who has aggressive and exhibitionistic instincts, but who's somehow more comfortable if the audience doesn't see him. And in fact, you almost don't see him. Sometimes even he loses track of the borderline between himself and his characters. He gets so involved with them, and they're zipping in and out of trouble so fast that sometimes he seems to forget they're puppets, and they talk in intimate asides to each other. I think he works with a very fast stream of consciousness, flashing whatever comes into his head right back out in the most immediate form. In one brilliant scene, the mother is waxing the floor with an aerosol spray when her hair straggles into her face. Absent-mindedly she uses the can for hairspray, then in rapid succession it serves as deodorant, bug killer, air freshener, toilet cleaner, and medication for the boys' rash.

This high-speed mental facility is what shapes the second part of the program, "Safety Begins Here," a lecture by an alleged public information officer from the Environmental Protection Agency about what you can do to protect yourself from toxic wastes. He points to slides of spill pillows for mopping up contaminated materials and panties with lead shields for keeping your gonads safe from radiation. We realize that this is just another commercial and Zaloom is once again a pitchman who can't distinguish between society's blessings and its poisonous effluents, between the copy writer's blurb and the awful truth. This confusion spreads to the audience, as he extols the beneficial uses of nuclear waste. Does Kerr-McGee really recycle radioactive cesium to make fertilizer, which proceeds through the food chain into our milk?

You can't help feeling Paul Zaloom is in love with objects. They're clearly more enchanting to him than people; sometimes he probably thinks they are people. And the charm of his theater is the faith he has that the audience will find them just as alluring and alive as he does. After "Safety Begins Here" two attendants clad in white coveralls and plastic shower caps set up for the third part, "YIKES!" It takes them a long time and they're very careful even though the set is basically a few rickety bridge tables piled with stuff under slightly used plastic garbage bags.

What follows is four skits entitled "Peace," "Justice," "Nature," and "Truth," in which objects represent characters or ideas and enact dramas of the twisted morality of our time. "Justice" is a courtroom drama—I forget who's on trial. The court stenographer and the bailiff are dummy hands. The opposing lawyers are a snake and a weasel fur piece. The jury is a box of eggs. The judge is an old-fashioned brass scale, and he decides the case by weighing the evidence (a magnifying glass) against a large wad of money supplied by the defendant's lawyer. You can guess who wins.

Zaloom's kind of cynicism is like a breath of fresh air—remember fresh air?—after a summer of ozone immersion. His approach to the modern world is to confront disaster head-on, confident that stink bombs are his best response to the other kind. I hope they put him on television before the election.

 ## LARGELY BILL IRWIN

New York Press, 5 May 1989

Largely New York is back in town, and everybody who never goes to a Broadway show ought to see it. So should everybody else. With some new bits added since it whisked in and out of City Center last spring, the show is still funny without being smart-ass, intelligent without being arcane, and contemporary in the best possible sense. Bill Irwin, who wrote and directed the show, appropriates styles freely, includes elements that don't usually belong together, and lets everything clash companionably. You could call him a postmodernist. What's so endearing about him is that, although he criticizes the society that dumped all this aesthetic trash on him, he never takes a superior attitude toward it. Knowing full well that he'll never be able to get the system to work, he keeps tinkering with it anyway.

In *Largely New York* he plays his familiar baggy-pants character, dressed up for the occasion in a top hat to replace his old squashed derby. The show is about his misadventures in electronic wonderland. A classic misfit, he's desperate to make a place for himself in the world. As the piece begins, he seems resigned to his chronic inability to communicate with other people, and he's trying to win approval as a Star. He appears with a remote-control device that makes the stage curtains open and close, the lights focus on him, and the music begin to play, "Tea for Two" on a Wurlitzer. He dances happily, floppily, for a second until things start going wrong. The music cuts off, and when he tries to click it back, the curtains close on him instead.

In attempting to retrieve control, he slides deeper and deeper into technological chaos, meeting a bunch of incongruous characters who may be able to help him, or may just as easily betray him. There are a couple of break-dancers (Leon Chesney, a tall black man wearing a stylish flattop haircut and red sweats, and Steve Clemente, a feisty little guy from the Bronx dressed in ornate denim and plaid). There's a modern dancer, Margaret Eginton, in svelte pink unitard, with whom Irwin is immediately smitten although she's so absorbed in her movement practice that she barely notices him. There's a group of people dressed in academic robes and mortarboards, led by a small, owlish man (Jeff Gordon), who swarm in and out and often loom behind our hero menacingly, although they never lay a hand on him. And there's a videographer and his assistant (Dennis Diamond and Debra Elise Miller), who know how to use the technology but may not be entirely benign either.

Irwin, refusing to trust his innate paranoia, keeps trying to make contact with all these people. He eagerly pursues Eginton, first trying to learn her dance and discovering that she only notices him as a convenient leaning post. Then, when he sees how interested she is in tapes of her own performance, he filches a video camera. They manage to make some kind of connection by means of the tube, and he enthusiastically videos himself so he can mouth "I LOVE YOU" while she's gazing at the screen. Unfortunately, he gets trapped inside, and it takes all the wacky ingenuity of Eginton and the breakers to get him out.

Irwin is always getting trapped. One of his running jokes is that a mysterious something gets hold of him from behind the scenes and starts pulling him offstage. Here the danger lurks behind the curtain. Irwin himself triggers it off by aiming his remote control at a member of the ensemble who has somehow fallen down and is cluttering up the floor. The remote signal works, and the body slides out of sight. Gloating over his success, Irwin gets too close to the curtain and, bingo, something grabs his leg and he starts to go. He manages to struggle back this time, but now that the thing is awake, it could snap him up without warning.

He keeps forgetting to be careful, though, because he's so anxious to make friends with all the other characters and experiment with the electronic toys. He does get through, temporarily, to the breakers. Chesney and Clemente are great clowns as well as dancers, with a finesse of timing to match Irwin's. When they first amble by, bopping to a giant portable they're lugging with them, Irwin is astonished. Chesney seems to be able to send a current through every part of his body, with bumps and jerks anyplace he chooses along the way. He can even separate his fingers, his lower left rib, his hairline. Clemente can twist his legs into a knot and untie them while spinning on a shoulder blade.

Undaunted by this virtuosity, Irwin tries to pick up their moves, sandwiching them into his own soft shoe. The two cool ones don't know what to make of him, but soon they dig his moves and teach him a few of theirs by zapping their energy to him through their snaky arms and necks. Eventually they're all hip-hopping and Charlestoning to "Tea for Two."

The genius of Bill Irwin, like that of Chaplin and his other predecessors in visual comedy, is that the very same images that are so hilarious can have profound meaning as references to the predicament of our civilization. *Largely New York* is of course about a lovable clown. It's also about magical, sinister forces, about ill-conceived envy and imitation and infatuation, about trust and mistrust. It's about dancing and dying and above all surviving, in the jumbled circuits of '80s culture.

CLOWNS IN FLIGHT

Boston Phoenix, 15 September 2006

Cirque du Soleil's newest production, *Corteo*, remixes the dazzling Cirque formula of virtuosic physicality, showbiz zaniness, and spectacle. Director Daniele Finzi Pasca came up with the concept and headed a team of fourteen creative masterminds. Premiered in Montreal in the spring of 2005 before starting a ten-year international tour, *Corteo* will be in the big blue and yellow tent at Suffolk Downs until October 15.

Corteo's pretext is the funeral of a clown (Mauro Mozzani). Surrounded by his circus companions and attended by a troupe of angels, he looks back on his life as a performer and anticipates an afterlife filled with even more splendid buffoonery, tricks, and marvels.

Female rope dancers dangle from crystal chandeliers in sumptuous gowns. The chandeliers start to spin. The women strip down to silken underwear and slither through the big ornaments, perch elegantly in midair, hang from one foot. The chandeliers are dipping and swaying dizzily all the time. In micro-timed pairs and quartets, gymnasts pinwheel in 360-degree arcs over the horizontal bars, avoiding collisions by inches. Trampoline acrobats don't just bounce off beds and seesaws, they do

Corteo. Helium. Valentyna Pahlevanyan and Pierre-Philippe Guay, Cirque du Soleil. Photo by Rob Finch / *The Oregonian*.

somersaults and half-gainers in the air. They bound across the space like kangaroos. They spring up and are caught by other people on high platforms and swung down into new corkscrew pathways.

A woman in a glittery red jumpsuit traverses a tightrope in pointe shoes, rides across on a unicycle, makes a barefoot transit while swiveling hula hoops around her torso. She has a safety wire attached to her waist, but there's an angel hovering nearby too, encouraging her as she walks up another tightrope fixed at a forty-degree angle. Who knows whether it's skill, engineering, or magic that keeps her steady.

The aerial work wafts further into fantasy with *Helium Dance*. The Dead Clown has captured the Clowness, an elfin Valentyna Pahlevanyan, in a rotating harness attached to six enormous balloons. She seems delighted to be up there, waving her arms and feet as if to enhance her flight. Finally Mozzani releases her and she sails free over the audience. When she drifts down, ecstatic spectators loft her up again by her tiny feet.

The show comes down to earth in *Teatro Intimo*, a boisterous toy-theater event. Valentyna and her partner, Grigor Pahlevanyan, attempt to enact Romeo and Giullietta but end up more like Punch and Judy, assisted by five or six self-important stage managers all crammed into the booth with them.

The skill and inventiveness in *Corteo* often seem about to spill over into excess, even surrealism. That's probably true of all good circuses; no wonder they fascinated twentieth-century intellectuals and artists. Cirque du Soleil is not unaware of its cultural lineage. In one of several processions the performers play quadruple-belled horns that resemble Cubo-Futurist noise machines. A line of disembodied shoes follows the procession. In one relatively quiet moment a clown walks across a tightrope upside down, carrying a lighted candelabra.

And did I mention the man who stilt-walked a two-legged ladder? And the glass harmonica with tuned bowls on a revolving stage? And the horse with high-heeled shoes?

WARM WITH SHOWERS

Boston Phoenix, 23 March 2007

Cirque Éloize's *Rain* culminates in an onstage downpour, but the audience knows that in advance. Instead of building up to this watery coup de théâtre, the show gets more and more low key, until it seems logical to see eleven grown people sloshing and sliding around in what's essentially a great big puddle.

The Montreal-based company, which visited the Cutler Majestic last week, seems devoted to downplaying the spectacular and the superhuman. The performers are very good at circus skills—juggling, acrobatics and tumbling, aerial work, and feats of strength. They're also singers, actors, musicians, and fakers. They want us to believe they're kind of improvising, slightly unprepared, maybe even self-conscious about going in front of an audience with nothing more impressive to show than balancing on one hand on the head of a man who's standing on the shoulders of three or four other people.

This disarming diffidence is an act, of course, an offhandedness that makes Cirque Éloize unique among new-circus shows. Early in the evening, a woman stands in a dogmatic downlight and asks, "What's with this new circus anyway? It's so cerebral . . . " Another woman wanders in and tries to explain: "New circus explores the unconscious." While they're debating aesthetics, an object that looks like a size fourteen sneaker falls out of the flies and thuds to the floor. Then another and another. "That's beautiful!" the young woman remarks in an aside, as the argument continues.

Stéphane Gentilini, a thin, bookish man, is the master of ceremonies. He's really too shy for the job, and women are always prompting him and correcting his pronunciation. He juggles with beer bottles and Indian clubs, and joins a team of precision pyramid-builders. He juggles apologetically with a suitcase and later supervises the job of packing Nadine Louis into another suitcase not much bigger than a carry-on.

For the finale of the first act, Teeterboard, the whole company scurries around setting up a large seesaw, along with a thick landing pad and a brightly colored but flimsy-looking lifeguard tower. Two men climb up the tower and another man stands opposite them on one end of the seesaw. Pianist Jocelyn Bigras announces that we're about to see a Double Back Scissors Flip with Degree of Difficulty 9.2.

The two guys on the tower link arms and jump down onto the high end of the teeterboard. Propelled skyward, the other man does two back flips in the air and lands on the pad. The tricks get trickier, the two helpers more nervous, and when it all goes terribly wrong there's a moment of consternation. Then they carry on.

Cirque Éloize's approach to spectacle is a little like competition ice skating. You can't just do one trick after another, no matter how fabulous, so you surround the tricks with other stuff to create a choreographic narrative—in their case, ineptitude, anxiety, covert rivalries.

The tricks are memorable too. Krin Maren Haglund and Jonas Woolverton spin, splayed out inside of six-foot hoops. Two women slowly share a trapeze in an erotic duet. Two musclemen maneuver each other into extreme, seemingly no-handed shapes. Five women slither and revolve high above the stage on swags of cloth.

But it's the scatty and lovable web of interplay that distinguishes Cirque Éloize. People move pianos in and out, they sing and dance and play in a motley marching band. They exchange wigs, they twirl around in pointe shoes. They do clowning bits—pratfalls, sleight-of-hand—as players who have too much to do and are gallantly coping. Eventually some of them sprout wings—possibly a sly allusion to their monster circus compatriot Cirque du Soleil, whose show *Corteo* was written and directed by the head of their own creative team, Daniele Finzi Pasca. Cirque du Soleil may be glamorous, but Cirque Éloize leaves you singing in the rain.

APPLE PIE

Boston Phoenix, 13 April 2007

We've had several visits from the elegant practitioners of New Circus (Cirque du Soleil, Cirque Éloize, Cavalia), those high-concept, highly theatrical shows that refashion the ancient circus techniques into spectacles worthy of being called high art. To bring us back to the basics, the Big Apple Circus has pitched its tent in City Hall Plaza till May 6.

Founded thirty years ago, the Big Apple Circus aims to preserve the idea of circus plain and simple, as a display of unusual skills and outlandish fun. This year's show is called *Step Right Up!* and it lightly references the midway attractions of the turn-of-the-twentieth-century World's Fairs. But the straw-hatted dandies and bathing beauties who entertain the audience during equipment changes are really only fringe benefits. The real theme of a Big Apple show is the circus's collective madness—the impossibly risky stunts, the zany props and prop wielders, the clowning misfits and grotesques—and the strangely symbiotic connection between this surreal community of mountebanks and the mundane world that's embodied by us, the audience.

We sit in a shallow amphitheater around a center ring, and the performers can get up close, entering down the aisles, perching at the edge of the ring to shake hands and recruit volunteers for their acts. The aerial acrobats could have landed right in our laps with the slightest slip of a toehold. At least one patron got sprayed with water last Wednesday night, and then got briskly toweled off. You could see the small details of their goofy wigs and makeup, the moments of tension as someone prepared to confront disaster, and the unrehearsed triumph as someone outsmarted it.

There were lots of kids in the audience. The emcee, Joel Jeske, and clowns Barry Lubin as a grandma with a couple of screws loose, and Francesco as a bumptious jack-of-all-toys, traded insults and pratfalls and hit each other with anything handy at every opportunity. There was a whole act devoted to how many different ways you can get somebody else and yourself wet, including kid favorites: spitting, peeing, and wallowing.

One Russian team did an adagio trapeze act and another pair bopped rubber balls off their foreheads while jumping rope. A troop of nine teenage acrobats from Zhengzhou, China, bounced in and out. They gyrated inside of hoops. They shinnied up twenty-foot swinging poles until they got going fast enough high over the ring to jump no-handed from one pole to another.

Perhaps because of its intimate scale, Big Apple Circus doesn't have huge wild animals, but Yasmine Smart commanded a team of six smart white horses, who paraded around the ring and trotted in unison. These beasts passed close enough to be slightly scary. Johnny Peers supervised his Muttville Comix, a menagerie of fourteen assorted dogs. The stiff-legged, grinning small ones did clever tricks like tightrope walking, and the floppy big ones mostly stood on the sidelines and barked encouragingly.

My favorite act was Justin Case, an Australian with a very credible French persona, who enlisted a man and a little girl from the audience to join him in calisthenics and balloon-play (another opportunity for kid-friendly stuff like bopping, snapping, and farting noises). Case's specialty is bikes. The sleek vehicle on which he makes his entrance soon begins to fall apart. He keeps on riding, without a seat, handlebars—eventually he's maneuvering around on one wheel. Later on he puts the pieces back together the wrong way but rides the contraption anyway.

Case is the ideal Big Apple performer—amusing, resourceful, slightly demented. His act is very straightforward, almost classical, as his witty fake-French character spins the bike idea into a long string of surprises. "In ze history of ze bicycle, I'm ze first one to do zis trick," he announces, as he pedals the upside-down wreckage. Then he winds up his act with one last absurdity, involving flames and a microscopic two-wheeler.

⟐ MULTICULT—THE SHOW

Hudson Review, Autumn 1996

Ethnicity plus stage spectacle equals a smash hit formula on Euro-American stages. It has for a couple of centuries now. Producers of both highbrow and lowbrow entertainments have understood the thrill of the exotic, especially when it's posed against the familiar. These fusions seem more plentiful than ever in recent years. As funding cutbacks reduce performance activity among indigenous music and dance makers, as the costs of high-art performing institutions continue to rise, spectacle becomes an increasingly viable staging ground for collaborations and even experiment. Unlike the perilous nonprofit arts, spectacle rests on the edge of commercial enterprise; its high costs can yield high revenues. For economic and other reasons, it is extremely user friendly, has great demographic appeal, and might be a major factor in keeping theater alive in these depleted times.

While still recovering from *Riverdance*, I realized that I'd seen half a dozen similar shows in the past few months. They all focused on a national or ethnic style, but they all reinvented tradition some way to suit modern agendas. The Balé Folclórico da Bahia fused European contemporary dance ideas about design and body shaping with traditional Brazilian dance and martial arts. Conjunto Folklorico Nacional de Cuba reconstructed folk and social dances in handsome period costumes, emphasizing a strife-free Afro-Hispanic cultural duality. The National Ballet of Spain's programming was devoted to stagy versions of folk and flamenco dancing, plus a local retelling of *Medea*, choreographed in a Grahamesque declamatory style with interpolations of flamenco.

Although ethnic shows may want us to believe we're seeing some "pure" essence of a people, we know that culture and cultural forms don't remain static. Tribal groups migrate and mix; their dances get suppressed or exploited; technology adds its enhancements. Politics often pays the piper and calls the tune. The touring Cubans acknowledged the bicultural background of their dances, but disguised history's contentious moments under a party atmosphere. Les Ballets Africains of Guinea, one of the oldest folkloric companies (it was founded in 1952, before Guinea became an independent nation), brought New York a collection of tribal dances from different regions and neighboring countries, folded into a two-act story ballet format with a Guinean legend as a theme. Les Ballets' purpose wasn't to exhibit archival dances as the Cubans did, but to dramatize cultural and moral lessons for the audience, using the dances, music, and storytelling as a didactic device. The American audience embraced this as a fast, flashy, exotic entertainment with definite racial appeal. The way the African dances blurred into a fairly generic style resembled the modern street dances influenced by jazz, tap, Brazilian capoeira, and MTV, that were spun together in the funky downtown hip-hop show, *Jam on the Groove*.

Riverdance so far exceeded these and other intercultural performances, in ambition, in scale, that it began to look like a whole new animal, not just a syncretic blend of known ingredients. Irish step dancing seems an unlikely premise on which to build an extravaganza. It's a tight, modest style focused on rapid footwork. You have to hear it in order to see it. But *Riverdance* sailed through New York after more than a year of packed audiences in Dublin and London. In five days at Radio City Music Hall (capacity 5,900), it played to what amounts to the population of a small American city. Then it toured several more Irish cities and returned to London. An American tour has been announced for the fall, starting with three weeks at Radio City. As a big commercial success, *Riverdance—The Show* has already hatched press kits, slick program books, a video, a CD, a tape cassette, and at least one scholarly paper. Not only did the public fame of the show escalate quickly, the show itself had gone through quite a bit of evolution by the time it reached New York. In a way, its career is a condensed version of the way culture itself adapts, expands, and reconfigures constantly over the course of time.

Like Pan-Africana and Hispanic shows, *Riverdance* doesn't pin down specific dances, dance forms, or even the identity of the performers in each number. Nothing in the extensive program book or press material tells us the specific social, spiritual, or entertainment origins of any number. The show proposes instead a new form of Irish dancing, an exteriorization of the genre's quiet expertise and its ability to assimilate outside influences. Rooted in an ancient Celtic past, Irish dancing hybridized with English country dancing and then evolved into the highly specialized routines of twentieth-century step-dance competitions. The current big resurgence of Irish dancing, both in Ireland and here in the States, partakes of all these precedents. The training puts an emphasis on intricate footwork—clogging in hard, loud shoes, and a more airborne style done in soft shoes. Nothing whatever is made of the upper body, the back stays ramrod straight, the arms pulled down at the sides. The body is carried in a single unit over the legs, the focus front. Everything, all at once, thrusts down into the ground or bounds up or pivots into a new direction. The basic rhythm is a string of fast, equal beats, like a locomotive chugging down a track, with embellishments of intermediate taps, brushes, clicks, stamps, flutters, and syncopations in superhuman abundance.

For all but a dedicated step-dance fan, though, the fascination of this might wear off quite soon. Irish dancing and its relatives, flamenco, kathak, clog, tap, and all other kinds of rhythm dancing, do well in close quarters, where the audience is watching and listening appreciatively. The bigger the venue, the more it seems the dance has to expand, to reach out, to make the flourishes more visible, and to introduce extra tricks. Volume, visibility, virtuosity. Perhaps these are some of the defining needs of spectacle. *Riverdance* flaunts them all.

The basic step dance gets amplified in several ways, most prominently by the effect of large numbers of dancers doing the intricate rhythms in unison. Microphones placed along the edges of the stage literally amplify the sound of their steps to a fusillade, shrouded in the electronic sibilance of a rock concert. The groups are usually arrayed in close ranks facing the audience, a chorus line effect that automatically sends our temperature up a few notches. Having locked onto this gambit, they add a few more standard come-ons from show business: the heads whipping to the side one by one precisely on the beat, the end poses in profile with the heads turned provocatively to the audience, and even a unison high kick or two. These are always understated, as if the dancers wouldn't know how to make a hard sell.

Step dancing has a natural elevation, or the potential for it, and *Riverdance* pushes the movement into the air with high, straight-up jumps. The jump can be decorated with heel clicks or cakewalk struts, but it keeps its vertical character. Step dancing has a lot in common with ballet, and the female soloist, Jean Butler, is tall, blond, and slim, with long legs. She looks a bit like Darci Kistler, and it's only a momentary surprise when she hops up onto the tips of her toes. Butler's exceptional elevation allows her to turn the mechanics of the step into big gestures, one leg hooking back hip-high or hitching across the other knee while she springs into the air. Toe-stands get interpolated by the other dancers too. Traveling while continuing the rhythm is another addition to the lexicon.

These innovations might be attributable to *Riverdance*'s original choreographer, the American Michael Flatley, although Flatley left the show before it came to New York and was listed among several other people in the choreographic credits. Colin Dunne, who replaced him as the male soloist, is a super dancer, but he shares the company's restrained performing style. It's only when you look at *Riverdance—The Video,* taped in 1995 at one of the early performances in Dublin's Point Theater, that you can understand what it was about the show that smote these audiences.

Flatley's dance is wildly eclectic. While his feet are reeling out some mind-boggling rhythmic puzzle, his upper body is beguiling us, telling us to forget about all that cognitive stuff and fall in love with him. His torso twists into the evasions of flamenco, then spreads to confront us with Broadway pizzazz. His arms, sprung from their prison at the sides, curl up around his head, jut in decorative angles, whip him around into extravagant finishing poses. All the while he grins at the audience, as if there's nothing to it.

Flatley has imparted some of this arsenal to the rest of the dancers, but what he really brought to the show was sex appeal and star appeal. The ensemble looks prim and preppy despite the women's long, crimped hair and modish miniskirts, the men's tight pants and flowing shirts. On the video Jean Butler offers Flatley some well-bred smiles in their chaste duets, but the only steamy seductions occur when he partners Maria Pagés, an exponent of fusion flamenco who was with the show from the beginning. Having seen the video after the New York run, I now think the whole show must have shifted in tone without Flatley's presence.

It also shifted, since the first Dublin season, in the cast of characters and perhaps in concept. *Riverdance* is built like a variety show, a series of specialty acts with the dance ensemble as a recurrent theme holding it together. In addition to Maria Pagés, Colin Dunne, Jean Butler, and the thirty-six-member Irish Dance Troupe, the New York show included the Anúna singers, an a cappella group specializing in modern arrangements of folk and ancient music; tap dancers Tarik Winston and Daniel B. Wooten, alumni of *Black and Blue,* TV, and other showy venues; youngsters from the New York school of Donny Golden, Jean Butler's teacher; six Moiseyev dancers constituting themselves as the Moscow Folk Ballet Company; and assorted solo singers and musicians. On the Dublin video there are three tap dancers and a gospel choir as well.

Some of this roster has stylistic cohesion. You can trace the connections between tap, flamenco, and Irish dancing way back. Perhaps the Russians were thought of as related to the Eastern European migrants who have influenced modern Irish culture, though what they did was mostly balleticized leaps and folky spins. The multiculturalism worked best in New York when the tappers challenged the male step dancers and after an escalating duel of rhythms, they combined styles. In a way, the show looks more Irish—albeit a synthesized, invented Irish—without Flatley.

The ensemble itself, with Dunne and Butler more equally blended in, became the show's visual center and, together with Bill Whelan's music, its rhythmic heart.

The score, yet another syncretic artifact, uses traditional Irish instruments in combination with other ethnic sounds, contemporary keyboards, and electrified strings. The same modern chordal progressions, perhaps constructed on an initial fiddle tune, recur throughout the show, especially during the big dance ensembles. They get modified rhythmically and reorchestrated, but their driving pulse begins to infiltrate your subconscious. Loaded through Radio City's massive sound system, the beat is irresistible, and by the end, when all the dancers advance to the footlights and the theme comes back, the audience can do nothing but produce an ovation. It's show biz magic. George Balanchine switched us on with the massed corps, the flag, and Sousa's famous march at the end of *Stars and Stripes*—invoking our patriotic reflexes. Bill Whelan manages to program the audience for a newly created Irish imagery.

Riverdance had other attractions. Virtuoso musicians played soprano saxophones, drums, Irish bagpipes, castanets, and Russian mandolins. Eileen Ivers, a manic American fiddler, finished every solo with hairs dislodged from her bow and lashing around like a horse's tail. For a change of pace, the Anúna singers interpolated songs of nostalgia and longing. There were scenic projections and stage mist. And there was even a kind of story that ran through the show, about the settling of the Irish homeland and the subsequent diaspora into North America. A poetic, unintelligible voice intoned it through a hundred loudspeakers like the Word of God.

What *Riverdance* is really about is Irish nationalism. The show was born as a seven-minute intermission number at the 1994 Eurovision song contest, and was built up from there. Glowing ads in the program encourage us to buy Irish recordings, whiskey, and other products, and to visit this strife-torn country that's trying to be an entity in the modern world. Tourism and political credibility are being promoted, as they are, I guess, in all multicultural performances. What's truly multicultural about the modern world is how much we share—computers and TV, traffic, loud music, jeans, and sneakers comprise the cultural style most kids grow up with, even in remote places. So national distinctions must be fabricated, partly out of old traditions, partly out of synthesized new aspirations.

Riverdance's fall Radio City run was announced with maximum splash—a two-page color ad in the Sunday Times Arts and Leisure—like an eager Oscar prospect. American connoisseurs will disdain this whole idea, the arts and Mammon having parted ways long ago, about the same time art supposedly swore off politics. But this and many other performance packages today evade those easy categories. They are by nature commercial and political, even when they are engaged in the reclamation of art. Nationalism may be a dictator's platform; it's also an emerging population's means of establishing community. Tourism may weaken the authenticity of art forms, but it also gives artists work.

It seems to me this genre must be taken seriously; it has the energy not only of enterprise but of discovery. Its creators don't yet know what contemporary art is for their cultures. The issue of what and how to perform isn't settled yet. Contemporary American dance on this level of visibility—from Peter Martins to Stephen Petronio—is predictable: technically accomplished, visually stunning, with a veneer of polished modernity, but its motivation seems automatic, self-sustaining. I don't get this feeling from most multicultural shows. To present their version of a culture in and to the world means something to these artists, and it's moving to catch them in the act. I've never been to Ireland, but it's hard to imagine I'd find a more authentic or enjoyable Irishness there than I did on the stage of *Riverdance*.

TOES ON THEIR FINGERS AND DRUMS IN THEIR HEART

The Second Annual New York City Festival of Percussive Dance at Symphony Space
New York Press, 21 April 1989

Waiting for the show to start, the woman behind me said to her friend: "Is this supposed to be a festival? It looks like a performance." Well, right. I don't know why it was called a festival either, except that it featured a multicultural array of dance styles, all originating in the inexhaustible human resource of rhythm. Put together by Ira Bernstein, the director of Ten Toe Percussion, the performance featured Bernstein's lickety-split clog/tap, Brenda Bufalino and the American Tap Dance Orchestra, and Keith Terry, who calls himself a body musician.

Bufalino is extending one of the traditional images of tap by applying techniques of modern dance composition. Drawing her dancing persona from the Fred Astaire–Honi Coles line of urbane smoothies, she wears white tie and tails, talks with the audience in an intimate, husky voice about how dancing came into her life, sings about regret and loss. She dances mostly to popular songs like "Bye Bye Blackbird" and rhythms like the samba, and although her style is solid and controlled, she can skim across the floor making a sound as soft and rapid as a tongue trill.

Bufalino counterpoints her solo dancing against a small combo led by pianist Aiki Steriopoulos, and later against a group of eight men and women, also clad in white tie and tails. When the group dances on, they inevitably recall Broadway tap chorus lines, movie numbers with Fred and his doubles. But Bufalino is trying for something more complex choreographically than a back-up group imitating a star. She sets different but complementary patterns of sound on groups of three or four dancers in the ensemble, like the collaborative rhythmic textures of jazz musicians or African drummers.

The idea of visual polyrhythm is extremely exciting. It could be like the electrifying mass chants of the Balinese Kecak, which we saw at City Center that same week. I thought Bufalino's tap orchestrations were heading in that direction but the deployment of the dancers' bodies in space wasn't as interesting as the weave of sound they created. Bodies in tap dancing, after all, are a minor asset; it's the feet that do everything. But for the audience it's hard to grasp what you're hearing as an intricate pattern if what you're seeing is just a couple of lines of people snaking back and forth.

In one number, "Flying Turtles," Bufalino had the dancers flapping their arms and swooping around the stage—she'd been talking about discovering that jazz isn't only an urban phenomenon when she moved to the country and heard the rhythms of the birds and the bugs. But the thing about a tap group that turns us on is still that moment when they all line up and belt out the time-step, releasing a fusillade of sound and simultaneity.

Ira Bernstein sensibly didn't try for anything fancy in his upper body. Wearing a colored T-shirt and a pair of pants and a pigtail, he was completely unassuming, not pushing his personality but letting his miraculous feet carry the act in eclectic blends of tap, clog and step dancing. Bernstein's dance reminded me that the original tappers, like their European clogging relatives, got their power and their articulation from a free-swinging hip and leg action. The nonchalant shoulder shrugs, fancy arms and hands, even the charm, came along later when audiences may have stopped appreciating rhythmic virtuosity for its own sake. Bernstein can carry on sonic designs while traveling across the stage, he can jump, syncopate, or soft-shoe in intricate patterns, and all the while looking natural and at ease, as if he were sauntering across the street.

Keith Terry's dance is an even more eclectic mixture of tap, juggling, body slapping, and way-out clownish imagination. Before I read that he worked with the Pickle Family Circus in San Francisco, I figured he must be a friend of Bill Irwin, another alumnus of that group. Terry's the kind of performer who'd do a funky, slouchy tap dance (choreographed by Kimi Okada) that winds up in a cascade of explosive slides along a strip of bubble wrap. His basic technique is an embellished walking step, refined further by patting all over his body, clapping his hands, snapping his fingers.

Sitting in a chair in one number, he starts bouncing a handball, accumulating a rhythm by adding slaps, clicks, foot stamps. To make it more complicated, he includes a leg, looping the ball over and under. By the end of the dance he's got two handballs, two legs, and just about everything else going in rhythm, but he's still sitting in the chair. I forgot to say he vocalizes too, punctuating the riff with grunts, chuckles, whoops, intakes of breath. The guy is a one-man band machine.

Terry has been influenced by percussion music of all kinds, and to him anything that so much as blips can go into his tune. At one point he dedicated a number to the "spring brides" in the audience by placing two open greeting cards on a music stand and retreating while their computer-chip wedding march played canonically into a microphone.

His zany grand finale was a stick dance, but what a stick dance! To a tape of Jay Clayton's "7/8," music for synthesizer, sax, and voice, he began innocently enough, twirling two eighteen-inch wooden batons, in rhythm with the music of course. The rhythm got more and more complicated to his own "Rembang," for recorded bamboo instruments and bells. He was hitting the sticks together and tapping and twirling, and then he was playing a big contraption made of about thirty more sticks upended on a wooden frame, like a vertical xylophone. I expected flames to come out of his head by the time he was through.

For an encore he did a little dance with four of those cans that have cows mooing inside of them. He whanged out body rhythm with those too. You'd have to see it to believe it.

⟳ TAPSTRAVAGANZA

Boston Phoenix, 13 May 2005

Critics like to complain that there aren't any great dancers today although there are many above-average ones. Savion Glover is one of the greats. Fifty years from now, people will remember his performances with awe and mistrust. Could anyone have danced for forty-five minutes non-stop with such a continuous flow of inspiration? Did he really do those

Classical Savion. Savion Glover. Photo by Tom Brazil.

remarkable feats of daring, intricacy, and stamina? Did he actually tap, sing, and carry on a sophisticated give-and-take with four musicians/ partners, all at the same time?

Savion Glover does do these things, and in the last few years he's been touring the country, generously, obsessively, so that audiences can see for themselves. We got four chances last weekend, when CRASHARTS brought his *Improvography II* to the Cutler Majestic. Glover is only thirty-two but he's already had a long career. He dances as if every night were his last, deserving of his best invention.

Friday night the show began with bassist Andy McCloud laying down and elaborating on a rhythm. After a while you heard clumping footsteps offstage and Glover kind of sneaked out, barely acknowledging the audience's welcome. He picked up McCloud's rhythm and kept it going with a long cadenza of interpolations and embellishments, establishing a baseline of extreme virtuosity right off.

The first thing you notice about Glover is his funky appearance: long and thin with a short black beard and his dreds tied up in a topknot, he wears an undershirt with another shirt over it flapping open, and some beads and a dangling ID card around his neck. Besides his offhand attitude toward the audience, he's a noticeably into-the-ground dancer. His steps seem to go down and down, hardly ever up, except when he hitches himself from the shoulders or hauls out of the floor from the hips and back. His legs compose tremendous volumes of taps, stamps, swipes, kicks, hops, skids, and vibrations, and as the surprises roll out you also notice that he doesn't do anything stylish to emphasize them. His arms just rappel off what his feet are doing, nothing pretty or picturesque. Sometimes he seems aggressive, insistent. The show is amplified to the point of distortion, but you get used to that.

After a long duet with McCloud, he finally turned and smiled to answer the audience's applause, before going on. Then he summoned solos from the other three musicians—Patience Higgins, saxophones and flute; Brian Grice, drums; and music director Tommy James, piano—accompanying them and sometimes dialoguing with them, but still keeping us in mind of that original bass rhythm. This was only the first number.

He stepped offstage to towel off, then was right back to sing a very upbeat "The Way You Look Tonight" with a kind of locomotive tap driving underneath. This melted into a new song, new exchanges with the band. He ended a chorus on one toe, spread-eagled and off balance, and he finished the set with a jump and two heel clicks in the air—known elsewhere as a brisé. Act 1 ended with another song where the audience got to sing "toot toot!" on cue and Glover brought out new stuff including grands ronds de jambe à terre, neatly set into the embroidery.

Savion Glover is very conscious of his place in tap history. Tap is defined by individuals and perpetuated by sharing and stealing, alliances of convenience and the bonding of pupil to master. Glover takes care to credit his mentors Gregory Hines and Jimmy Slyde, and he clearly wants to cultivate his own progeny. For the *Improvography* tour, he brought three young tap whizzes, Maurice Chestnut, Ashley Deforest, and Cartier A. Williams, to lead off the second act. Then he joined them and they all took turns in solo choruses.

There was another extraordinary duet with Higgins's sax. Glover started singing and dancing lines from "Nature Boy" in a mixture of bop, scat, and blues. Higgins imitated each phrase as Glover spiraled deeper and deeper into a stream-of-consciousness riff that was neither words, music, nor any kind of dancing you'd seen. Eventually all four guys in the band followed him phrase by phrase into Oz. The other dancers came back to wind up with "The Stars and Strips Forever, for Now," a huge tap, jazz, and Sousa jam that, if the title meant anything, suggested the best thing to do in these troubled times in America is to let out all the stops and wail.

Boston Phoenix, 21 October 2005

Much to Boston's good fortune, the Celebrity Series and CRASHARTS teamed up to bring Savion Glover back for the second time in six months. The fans who filled Symphony Hall Sunday afternoon for a blast called *Classical Savion* weren't there to see a concert in any orthodox musical sense, but they got a virtuoso performance just the same. For two intermissionless hours Glover and thirteen instrumentalists played the socks off of Vivaldi, Mozart, Dvorak, Bach, Bartok, Shostakovich, Mendelssohn, and Sousa. Who knew those composers were all tap dance kids?

Still in his early thirties, Glover has a twenty-year career behind him but he shows no sign of burnout. I don't know how he arrived at his new format of dancing the classics, but it isn't as incongruous as it might seem. The late Paul Draper, for one, rendered Bach and Couperin in a cool, graceful style he called ballet-tap. Glover's project isn't to make tap more classical; just the opposite. What he hears is the dancing inside the music. By percussion-izing what's already there in fifteen mostly up-tempo selections, Glover reminds us that Baroque music was often meant to accompany dance forms, and that the European romantics from Beethoven to the early twentieth century infused their symphonic compositions with the dance rhythms and melodies of folklore.

Glover has refined the *Classical* show since I saw it in New York last winter. Instead of relying on a conductor, the nine young classical players take their cues from each other, like a chamber ensemble or a jazz combo. Sometimes Glover lays down a few bars of rhythm to get them going, and he winds up each piece with a flourish or a pattering decrescendo. Now, instead of a separate jazz section, Glover's house band, The Otherz (Tommy James, piano; Brian Grice, percussion; Patience Higgins, flute and sax; Andy McCloud, double bass), almost stealthily infiltrate the strings.

With every note memorized, Glover sometimes underlines the musical score, adding a fifth voice to his expanded string quartet. He picks out inner rhythms by accenting or syncopating what's written as metrically regular. He does all the ornamentations in a Mozart Divertimento and makes up a few of his own. He makes his own witty comments, swooping into pirouettes as Mendelssohn makes musical roulades, raising a ruckus to the dissonances of Shostakovich. And when Patience Higgins began a Bach flute cadenza, with the orchestra playing continuo and Glover tapping an obbligato, you could see how classical music sprang out of the same improvisatory/collaborative impulse as jazz. Higgins eventually found his way back to the piece, and then, astonishingly, without stopping, the music changed key and segued into some exotic chords out of which a violin emerged, playing one of Bela Bartok's Romanian Folk Dances. My one reservation was that the amplification was set to overbalance Glover's dancing against the strings. Although the music was familiar, I kept losing the melodic structures and harmonies that were giving rise to his soloistic extrapolations.

For the last part of the program, starting with Andy McCloud's bass solo meditation on themes from "Nature Boy," Glover and all the instrumentalists played a long, joyous jam session together. As McCloud kept an unwavering anchor figure on the bass, the group played "Nature Boy" variations. Glover introduced the musicians in turn for their own improvised solos, which he responded to with complementary ideas, arguments, and images. Feeding off McCloud's steady basso ostinato, he changed the rhythm several times in interludes between their solos, and drummer Brian Grice shouldered the last variation into a conga rhythm.

Finally, Glover introduced the last number, a signature now although it's different at every performance. Glover merged into the ensemble and the tune itself dissolved into a drawn-out, barely discernible line on Higgins's sax. Vivaldi and Mendelssohn had morphed into a freewheeling, seemingly inexhaustible, moody improvisation on "The Stars and Stripes Forever."

HEARTS ON FIRE, FEET ON ICE

Dance on Camera Journal, May–June 2007

The name of Savion Glover doesn't appear in the top credits for *Happy Feet*. You can find him if you scroll down into the hundreds of artists and technicians who created the animated penguin movie. But Glover's "voice," aka the dancing abilities of Mumble the misfit Emperor penguin, is the crux of the story. His contribution is as essential to the movie's success as that of the actors and singers who dubbed the spoken lines and songs. Glover's exclusion from the featured ranks weirdly reflects the plot of the movie itself.

When the cute little Mumble was dropped as an egg, his DNA got discombobulated, and he became tone-deaf. He can't summon up the vocal Heartsong by which an Emperor finds its mate and gains its place in the community. Mumble expresses himself by dancing. (He speaks in the voice of Elijah Wood.) He doesn't know dancing is not an acceptable behavior, but it embarrasses his parents, exasperates his teachers, and earns him the disapproval of the Elders. Wandering off by himself, he falls through the ice, is chased by a leopard seal, and bounces to safety in the land of the Adelie penguins. These jovial birds aren't as straitlaced as the Emperors. They adopt Mumble as a super-cool dude, and take him to Lovelace, the Rockhopper guru, to see if there's an answer to Mumble's persistent curiosity about why the penguins' supply of fish is shrinking.

Returning to Emperor land without an answer, Mumble teaches his best friend, Gloria, and the young penguins to dance. When he refuses to silence his happy feet, he's banished by the superstitious Elders, who suspect his strange behavior might be causing the food shortage. He and the Adelie Amigos set off to find out why, really, the fish are disappearing. After that, the movie follows a classic fairy-tale plot. The hero journeys through strange lands, makes new friends, overcomes obstacles, slays dragons, uncovers secrets, debunks myths, and eventually returns to save the kingdom and claim his true love. Mumble's greatest asset along the way, besides a reckless courage and a beaky grin, is neither a sword nor a magic potion, but his gift for dancing.

Thanks to Savion Glover and motion capture, *Happy Feet* is a terrific tap movie. Wearing a sensor-laden suit, Glover danced for multiple cameras; his movement information was transferred digitally to a predesigned Mumble figure that "learned" the dance almost simultaneously on screen. Other dancers supplied the material for other characters, after learning to move like real penguins themselves. The group numbers were staged with intricate plotting by Kelley Abbey for seventeen dancers and the technological expertise of director George Miller's team. In some scenes the penguins celebrate in a chorus of thousands, carrying the Busby Berkeley spectacle to epic proportions.

Dancing animals are no strangers to animated films; they go back even further than the talented hippos borrowed from stars of the Ballet Russe in the 1940 Disney masterpiece *Fantasia*. On the surface *Happy Feet* looks like an adorable fairy tale, with its crinkly-eyed creatures who sweetly overcome ecological peril. But there's a modern sensibility here that only begins with the filmmakers' access to high-tech animation. For one thing, the characters are postmodern eclectics.

Glover's tap style in itself is a mix of historic references—Mumble shuffles on the ice like a sand dancer, his big solos are expressionistic monologues that sprawl through a free-ranging rhythmic unpredictability, and when he teaches his moves to other penguins, they work it out in classic call-and-response dialogues. The finale includes riffs from Zulu, gumboot,

Native American, and Samoan slap dancing, according to the movie's extensive production notes. (See happyfeetmovie.com) The score covers pop music from funk to Latin, pop, rap, and gospel, with opera and movie adventure music thrown in, and somehow the animators have made the tanker-truck shapes of the penguins elastic enough to wiggle and sway like pop singers.

There's a generous streak of subversion in the characters played by Robin Williams, who does his manic thing as the Mexican-accented Ramon. He's the leader of the Adelie Amigos, played by four well-known Latino comedians. Williams also plays the Rockhopper penguin Lovelace, a high-living bogus guru with the charisma of a black evangelical preacher and the Wizard of Oz combined. Lovelace sets a satirical tone for all the authority figures in the film: the windy Russian diva who can't teach Mumble to sing, the Calvinistic leader of the penguins with the dowager's hump and the heavy Scots accent, the gangster Skua who's humiliated in front of his predatory honchos when Mumble asks about the strange band on his leg. "Alien abduction," blusters the bird, played by "Without a Trace" TV detective Anthony LaPaglia. The dialogue rolls along on a stream of improvisational zaniness that must have been influenced by Williams. The kindergarten teacher asks, "What's the most important thing a penguin can learn?" and Mumble pipes up, "Don't eat yellow snow?"

Happy Feet is a very smart movie, not only because of its funny script. It skims nicely alongside today's universal doom-plots: alien abduction, overfishing, trash disposal, ecotourism, generational schism. The characters may look like Disney denizens but their souls belong to pop culture. Mumble's mother Norma Jean (Nicole Kidman) speaks in whispery Marilyn Monroe apologetics. Memphis, his father (Hugh Jackman) is a strong silent type who warns his peculiar offspring not to try "doing that" around the other penguins—he never can bring himself to utter the word "dance." Gloria, Mumble's girlfriend (Brittany Murphy), tries to deter him from his quixotic ways, but she stays true to him while he's gone, like the stalwart heroine of a World War II movie.

Besides the direct contributions of singers like Prince and Gia, and the smart interpolation of iconic pop songs, the action is underlined with musical double entendres. As Mumble and the Amigos waddle away into exile, the soundtrack breaks into a lament worthy of a Kansas lawman heading off across the prairie to find the outlaws, with guitars and the Adelies singing "They'll never forget him, the leader of the pack." Ramon does a Cyrano de Bergerac, serenading Gloria while hiding behind Mumble's back. The song is "My Way," in Ramon's hilarious Mex-Adelie accent, with additional reference to Debbie Reynolds dubbing for the vocally challenged Jean Hagen in "Singin' in the Rain." Strains from operas blend into the symphonic mix—Wagnerian heroics as Mumble chases the factory ship that's taking away the fish, Puccini as Mumble and Gloria glide through their last love duet. The Elders chant a malediction under the joyous dance of the penguin colony when Mumble returns to announce he's contacted the aliens.

Happy Feet is visually beautiful and astounding, even on DVD. When the adolescent Emperors, led by Mumble, take their first dip in the ocean, the Beach Boys are singing one of their surfing songs, and the delighted penguins streak through the water in formation like jets in an air show. Doing this exuberant water ballet, with Mumble and Gloria at the center of heart-shaped formations, they're also learning to catch fish. Members of the production crew went to Antarctica to film the landscape, which then became a panoramic moving canvas for the animated action. Just as human moves can be transposed onto graphically created animals by means of motion capture, these digitized landscapes can be magnified, zoomed in on, morphed into limitless frozen habitats. Mumble and the Amigos fall over a precipice and skateboard for miles down glacial chute-the-chutes, their blubbery bodies caroming off the walls.

The dangers of Mumble's journey are equally grand and graphic. There are mind-boggling contrasts of scale—the monster jaws of the leopard seal and the killer whales, the inert chunks of discarded machinery, the oncoming ships that are too big to fit into the frame. Mumble looks no bigger than a bug, clinging to the massive net full of fish being hauled out of the water. The penguin pilgrims slog through a blizzard, they become barely visible specks making their way across immense crags and plateaus of ice.

And then, after all this dramatic struggle, there's the inert, claustrophobic animal park where Mumble wakes up after his capture. The story has a happy ending, of course. Mumble figures out how to entertain the visitors to the park; he becomes a dancing celebrity and gets released with a telemetry pack on his back to guide his new friends to the penguin colony. The fantasy ends up in the hands of the real world. In black-and-white TV news clips, bureaucrats and pundits argue about what the penguins are telling them. They decide to ban all fishing, and the penguins celebrate with the most massive dance of all. The notion that penguin love will save the Antarctic from overfishing is pretty farfetched, but the Australian production crew seems to believe there's still hope that human intervention can save the planet.

Happy Feet the DVD includes a library of twenty-eight highlights, two music videos, and a deleted scene in which the late animal hunter Steve Irwin played a friendly albatross (Irwin also dubbed the giant elephant seal in the final cut). There's a 1936 Merrie Melodies cartoon about an owl chick with an irresistible urge to sing the one kind of music his music-teacher dad absolutely forbids, jazz. Besides all that, Savion Glover gives you a dance lesson—nothing to it, you just balance, toe-heel, shuffle, and after that it's all music!

7 Riffs and Translations

Dance traditions can cross borders as easily as the people who practice them. It's getting hard to know what's meant when a tradition is invoked. English choreographer Matthew Bourne's *Swan Lake* swerves way off the plot of the nineteenth-century classic, and it's been considered as a deconstruction, an interpretation, a new aesthetic. But it does use Tchaikovsky's music and it hinges on the familiar, magical premise of a prince fatally in love with a swan.

Bourne's *Swan Lake*, running at New York's Neil Simon Theater until mid-January, opened in London in 1995 and has been breaking box-office records and winning awards ever since. I guess everyone who's interested knows by now that the swans are men and the royal court is updated to somewhere in the recognizably recent Windsor dynasty. The production has inspired many games of critical ringtoss, because it's just near enough to the classical text, and just outlandishly far enough away, so that no one can make an authoritative interpretation. Is it a drag show? A morality play about a decadent monarchy? A new standard of aesthetic beauty?

To begin with, this *Swan Lake* isn't a traditional ballet. Choreographer/director Bourne and the international cast have eclectic backgrounds in contemporary dance, television, and shows, and the choreography isn't restricted to a classical movement idiom. Except for a spoofish entertainment in the first act, no one dances on pointe. This is a crucial departure but I suppose a logical way to present an ensemble of male swans. Pointe work, the province of women, always comes off as appropriation or send-up when men do it, and Bourne doesn't want his corps of swans to be seen solely as a voyeuristic play on sexuality.

The corps, barefoot and wearing white feathered plus fours, do fill the stage in neat group formations, but their movement contradicts the precision and impassivity that identifies traditional ballet swans. Instead, they flap and slash their arms, gesture awkwardly with broken wrists, swoop down with force and even ferocity. Bourne says he was thinking of the aggressive behavior of real swans, and the swans' scenes have a kind of sinister dynamism that at first seems at odds with the story, where the swans were helpless prisoners of an evil magician, waiting to be released by the power of love.

The production keeps revising the traditional scenario, while it also expects you to see it against the original conventions. The White Swan, who isn't even named as such in the program, does belong to this flock of angry creatures, but at the end of the ballet they turn on him for trying to remain with the Prince. *Swan Lake* is usually performed as a tragedy, in which the fairy-tale Prince is trapped between his idealistic, otherworldly love and his luxurious, lazy lifestyle. Bourne's *Swan Lake* begins in an exaggerated here-and-now. The Prince decides to cash in his pointless life before he meets the White Swan, but after that things only get worse.

As in the original story, the same dancer (Will Kemp in the cast I saw) plays the manipulative Black Swan. He appears at the Prince's birthday ball like a cat burglar, skittering in over a balcony, and proceeds to seduce not only the Prince but all the females in the place, including the Prince's nymphomaniac mother. This brazen conquest ignites the Prince's Oedipal fury, which has been smoldering beneath his protocol-blanketed personality for the entire ballet. The plotline falls apart in a menacing czardas where everyone eyes everyone else jealously, and somehow the Prince's lower-class girlfriend gets shot.

This disastrous Freudian denouement is only to be expected when an heir to the throne has been programmed to be a good little boy and bullied by a mother who taunts him with her lovers. But there are other, less reasonable new twists to the plot that seem to have been inserted only to supply spectacle and satire. As for the dancing, it's usually overshadowed by the burlesque acting style of the production.

The most interesting part to me was the gender-bending first encounter between the Prince (Scott Ambler) and the White Swan. To a very speedy rendition of the traditional second act pas de deux music, the two characters discover each other and fall in love. But Bourne abandons the fixed roles of Prince as pursuer and Swan as captured and eventually capitulating quarry. Each man desires and seduces the other; each man lifts nd caresses the other. Many choreographers are attempting to remove the sexist implications from ballet partnering, but they usually conclude that male-female equality can only be achieved through violence. In this ingenious pas de deux Matthew Bourne shows another alternative, but one that is doomed from the start. Ultimately both transgressors are destroyed by their own kind.

Boston Phoenix, 25 June 2004

The ballet world has a curious custom of remaking its oldest, best-preserved, and most cherished icons. Reasons for this ritual of inverse homage can be anything from the practical (costumes wear out and sets fade; new ones might as well be different) to the creative (for some, re-inventing history is an irresistible challenge). Still, the idea of updating a monument seems paradoxical. The key question is always: is it still *Swan Lake?*

What I liked so much about Pennsylvania Ballet's controversial *Swan Lake* by Christopher Wheeldon was its absolute trust in fantasy. Without waiving the ballet's technical demands, Wheeldon shifted the whole affair onto a different plane, forcing the audience to entertain a new concept of the plot and the characters. His *Swan Lake* is a sustained fiction. The tempi are variable but brisk; the story doesn't come to a full stop so the audience can demonstrate its approval.

This *Swan Lake* is almost intimate, theatrically involving. The three-walled set (by Adrianne Lobel) opens out to bigger spaces that are wonderfully lit (by Natasha Katz), to suggest not just an outer environment but places where the onstage action continues. The chorus of swans moves outside during the act 2 pas de deux, and you see them in the distance, shadowing their queen as she gradually yields to the prince. In act 3, the partygoers tumble out onto a terrace, making Odile and the Prince's duet a clandestine affair.

When the overture ends, on a series of apprehensive chords, what we hear as the curtain goes up, instead of bustling party preparations, is the modest little Valse Bluette, lifted from Tchaikovsky's last act and transcribed for piano. This shocking but brilliant departure tells us to forget all our expectations. The scene is a room, a dance studio or entryway, with a barre along the wall. Girls in knee-length tutus enter and pause in a string of poses taken from Edgar Degas paintings.

Then the wall goes up and we're in a bigger studio, with an enormous framed mirror and high French doors. The customary music resumes and the rest of the ballet continues musically much as we know it. The story begins with Degas' ballet girls, their teacher, a gentleman patron who's led to a chair with a good view of the girls, and a young man who could be the choreographer. Instead of a castle with a prince and his royal retinue, we see a sweaty dance rehearsal, and the ballet they're rehearsing is *Swan Lake.*

Wheeldon layers his new libretto on top of the old one. Intriguingly, the music and the steps reflect the familiar *Swan Lake*, but the Queen Mother is a bored supernumerary and the Prince's tutor is the ballet master. As the dancers put on bits of costume and run through the dances, you're drawn into the action. You go along with it, believing it as you do a dream. The rehearsal ends, the company goes home, but the young man stays behind, absorbed in his own imaginings—perhaps he's thinking about a new ballet —and discovers the swans.

Wheeldon's clever reworking doesn't always track the standard plot literally but the premise of a dream allows for implausible slippages and jump cuts. You can make up your own explanation when the rich playboy who visited the dance studio morphs into the vicious, tattered Rothbart with his captive harem of swans. In the third act the whole setting moves up a couple of decades from Degas' 1870s to Toulouse-Lautrec's 1890s. The dance studio is turned into a cabaret, with a new take on the divertissement dances: a seductive Spanish trio for a Jane Avril look-alike and two partners, a sleek Russian lady who does a decorous striptease, a bawdy non-Neapolitan cancan.

After the Black Swan's betrayal, the whole back of the set flies out. The stylish debauchery of the nightclub gives way to an expanse of churning water and threatening sky. The swans return and attack Rothbart. But neither their retaliation nor the Prince's remorse can undo his mistake. After Odette has apparently drifted away to die of a broken heart, he surfaces from his dream and finds himself back in the studio. At the final curtain he sees the very same girl among the coryphées returning to work in the studio.

Some critics have taken offense at the lowlife third act, and dismissed Wheeldon's thoroughgoing transformation of the work. For me the very fact that it simultaneously resembled and camouflaged the old familiar ballet made for a riveting experience. Philadelphia's Academy of Music, a beautiful theater in the form of a small European opera house, gave the modest scale of Wheeldon's concept an elegant frame.

TOE FROLIC

Boston Phoenix, 21 January 2000

One source of the Ballets Trockadero de Monte Carlo's appeal—for the audience and the performers—is its capacity for innocent pleasure. Grown men in this culture are supposed to take their fun as a serious

Swan Lake. Black Swan pas de deux. Robert Carter and Rafaelle Morra,
Les Ballets Trockadero de Monte Carlo. Photo by Sascha Vaughan.

matter, preferably with a tennis racket or a weapon in their hand. But the
dancers of the Trockadero grab at the movement with the eagerness of a
bunch of preteens. Travesti, or cross-dressing in current lingo, is a form of
disguise, a way of allowing you to escape the conventions of your time and
place as well as your gender. So it can be a source of comedy and commentary, not just titillation. Most contemporary drag is political, providing a
platform for asserting identities and demanding the expansion of social
boundaries. But the Trocks have been around for a quarter of a century;
their revolution has become almost a trend.

Last Friday's show at the Emerson Majestic began with the expected: an
over-the-top satire on *Swan Lake Act II*. There was a barrel-chested Odette
the Swan Queen (Margeaux Mundeyn), a simple-minded Prince (Mikolojus
Vatissnyem), and a hard-working Rothbart (Velour Pilleaux), who resorted

to hauling off his victims by force when his magic failed to work. The corps de ballet, with hairy armpits and costumes that needed laundering, embellished the traditional steps in their separate ways. The Prince's valet, Benno (The Artist formerly known as Prince Myshkin), made a comeback as a lifter and carrier of the ballerina, demonstrating why he has been obsolete for half a century. Not that Vatissnyem was any better at it.

Toward the tragic end of the act, Mme. Mundeyn and Vatissnyem managed to dance quite a lot of the original steps of their variations, but not without lengthy buildups and false starts. This production chose the "unhappy" ending option. Rothbart dragged Odette off to his castle. The Prince fainted. But Benno, after snapping his picture, stayed to console him.

In a sense, this kind of parody is old stuff that never loses its laugh. But when the Trocks get into their stride, and the audience has dealt with the transgender imagery, the takeoffs get more subtle and witty. Peter Anastos was one of the founders of the Trockadero. He became established in the straight ballet world as a choreographer and company director long ago, but his nom de guerre, Olga Tchikaboumskaya, is still being dropped as a token of the company's past glories. His *Go for Barocco* has been in the repertory since the '70s.

It's a fond and funny tribute to George Balanchine, based on *Concerto Barocco* but with wisps of *Serenade*, *Four Temperaments*, *Apollo*, and a few other Balanchine icons dribbling from its fingertips. Nadia Rombova and Iona Trailer are the principal ballerinas, supported by a relatively well-behaved corps of six dancers. The ballet is about dancing, and the ensemble dances so well that the jokes are only an added dividend. The arabesques get higher and more wavering the more they repeat, the daisy chains look charming before they turn into knots, the tricky coordinations of arm gestures with hops on point, and the traveling pas de chats in nearly perfect lineups are exhilarating, the precision power-walk exits seem perfectly logical.

We hardly ever get to see Merce Cunningham's work here, so it was great to have *Cross Currents* on this program. The audience laughed more at the musicians, Mikhail Mypansarov and Bertha Vinayshinski in male drag, who played John Cage riffs with an aerosol can, crinkling cellophane, bubble wrap, and assorted barks and meows. At one point the Carolyn Brown surrogate walked over and shushed them. Except for their wigs, the three dancers played it quite seriously. It was interesting to see how wrong they could go and still be doing choreography.

The variations in *Paquita* showed off the virtuosic if eccentric skills of the ensemble. Ballerina Svetlana Lofatkina had to stop to tie the ribbons on her toeshoes, but later redeemed herself by doing about twenty fouettés just off the music, for which she was effusively congratulated by her colleagues. When her partner, Igor Teupleze, ran out of changements halfway through his solo music, he vamped through the rest with vaudeville bits.

The program included an outrageous *Dying Swan* (Bertha Vinayshinski) who bourréed on in a cloud of molted feathers and whose prolonged and melodramatic fadeout was worthy of a 1930s gangster movie.

TROCKIN' ON

Boston Phoenix, 23 January 2004

Les Ballets Trockadero de Monte Carlo returned to Boston last weekend for another hilarious bout with dance history. The company, now thirty years old, has brought travesti dancing to new levels of technical excellence and sartorial bad taste. The three performances at the Cutler Majestic featured the classical branch of the Trockadero's extensive repertory, with numbers ranging from the Romantic period (*Pas de Quatre*) through Imperial Russia (*Swan Lake Act II* and a pastiche ripped from *Raymonda*) to the early twentieth century (*The Dying Swan*) and a contemporary throwback (*Tarantella*).

Drag performing isn't the shocker it was thirty years ago when the Monte Carlo split from its mother company, the Trockadero Gloxinia, but the sight of male ballerinas still has the same fascination. The Trocks deck themselves out in eyelashes and tacky wigs, but you're always aware they're men. These are by no means the jawlines and calf muscles of sylphs. In fact, the better their pointe work gets, the more disorienting we find their sturdy ribcages.

Ballet itself is an illusion, and the Trocks don't try to duplicate that. Instead, they reference it, expecting us to see both the ballet image and its inverse. This, of course, is the basis of parody. The Trocks do a lot of exaggerating and mugging, but their appeal goes deeper. Their dancing is neither light nor subtle, and things that female dancers can breeze through or make us think are easy become much clearer when worked at by these big bones. When one of the Trocks does a series of whipping fouettés with interpolated double tours, it seems more virtuosic than a ballerina cranking out thirty-two. You have to appreciate the skill of the klutzy jumps, skewed balances, and musical pratfalls, even as you're laughing at them.

The Trockadero's humor is a combination of all-out slapstick and sly commentary on the conventions and vanities of dance culture. All fourteen dancers have both male and female identities, with accompanying bios that make up a collective history of intrigue and injury, royal liaisons, fabulous successes, and political blunders. The company attitude assumes that dancing reveals and even inspires jealousies bordering on outright hatred. Grand playing up to the audience is permitted if not encouraged, and all performers must have an ability to cope with wavering spotlights, deteriorating costumes, and memory lapses by their colleagues. They must never lose their cool, even when being kicked by a rival—unless they can fit a return insult into the choreography.

The *Pas de Quatre* may have been the first ballet competition. Staged in 1845 by Jules Perrot, it brought together four star ballerinas, and in the hands of the Trockadero, Marie Taglioni, Carlotta Grisi, Fanny Cerrito, and Lucille Grahn show off their differing styles of upstaging one another as well as their dancing.

The best possible role for one of these divas, of course, is the solo. In an interpretation of Michel Fokine's cameo for Anna Pavlova, *The Dying Swan*, Ida Nevasayneva bourrées bravely through drifts of discarded feathers. After her touching demise she recalls another predecessor in the role, Maya Plisetskaya, by working the audience until the curtain call lasts as long as the dance.

The Trockadero is deeply committed to perpetuating the ballet mystique (ballet is unknowable; therefore we won't tell you everything). During a very long pre-performance announcement, many cast changes were read off, with copious transparent excuses for the failure of the original dancers to appear. The list included one dancer who did not subsequently dance and had apparently left the company before the program was printed.

The pas de deux *Tarantella* was inserted into the performance without any indication that the ballet had been choreographed by George Balanchine, in 1964, for Patricia McBride and Edward Villella. *Tarantella* is Balanchine's homage to Bournonville's homage to Italian street dancing. In fact, Sveltlana Lofatkina and one of the brothers Legupski—I didn't catch whether it was Marat or Vladimir—gave a quite credible representation of the work, except for that sudden lift when she turned him upside down.

For the big production of the evening, *Swan Lake*, Mme. Nevasayneva, in her alternate persona Velour Pilleaux, played the arch-villain Rothbart, terrorizing the corps of women-turned-swans with his flamboyant cape and orange wig. The Trocks' rendition of this classic brings back the forgotten character of Benno, the prince's confidant, played by the versatile

Igor Slowpokin, who, as Fifi Barkova, had also impersonated Taglioni, smirking aggressively at her companions, in the *Pas de Quatre*.

The Benno character was introduced by the choreographer, Lev Ivanov, to help an aged Pavel Gerdt in partnering Odette, the Swan Queen. Slowpokin, however, rushed in eagerly at all the wrong times and nearly dropped the imposing Odette (Olga Supphozova) when she hurled herself confidently backwards into his arms. The prince, Pavel Tord, tall, pale, and easily flustered, backed off and waited to see if they'd both be all right.

DECOMPOSING SUGAR PLUMS
AND ROBOT MICE

Ballet Review, Spring 1991

Nobody expected Mark Morris to do a "real" *Nutcracker*, did they? The new production at Brussels' Théâtre de la Monnaie—revealed, with characteristic Morris perversity, after Christmas—is actually quite authentic in a couple of respects. It uses the whole score, with an excellent orchestra and chorus. It also keeps the basic story line which prompted original collaborators Tchaikovsky, Petipa, and Ivanov and which underlies the touchstone American production at the New York City Ballet. Otherwise, beginning with its naughty title, *The Hard Nut*, Morris's work is a deconstruction. He's dismantled the ballet from the seams out and pieced it back together, with remnants and new bits of material, jeweled ornaments, and chachkes. The remade garment looks enough like its prototype to show us both how threadbare and how excellent the old one was.

Deconstruction is one of the most intellectually interesting of dance forms. Because it's not bound to the traditional unities of style or argument, it can open windows of political comment, historicity, and wit onto the normally hermetic surface of a dance work. What deconstruction excels at—always over the cries of outraged traditionalists—is the revitalization of an old, over-familiar text by refitting it as contemporary. This has been the aim of Peter Sellars's Mozart operas, which, I think, are a model for Morris. *The Hard Nut* begins with a fairly literal first act, reinterpreted for cartoon characters of the 1960s or early '70s. The Stahlbaum household is upper-middle class, with its chic, modernistic black-and-white decor, a black maid who's one of the family (played adorably by Kraig Patterson, in travesti and on pointe), and pampered children. (Clarice Marshall is Marie, Marianne Moore is Fritz, and Tina Fehlandt is Louise, a petulant adolescent who doesn't exist in either the Alexandre Dumas libretto Petipa followed or the E.T.A. Hoffmann original.) The party guests are a rowdy collection of hipsters, all dressed in mismatching bellbottoms, miniskirts, and caftans in assorted reds, greens, and black.

Events of the party proceed pretty conventionally, if you update all the behavior and drape it with raunchy trimmings. At the beginning the kids are kept out of the living room watching TV while the parents decorate the tree, and when everything is ready, someone switches on the Yule Log channel as a finishing touch. One of the first guests asks the way to the bathroom and rushes offstage fumbling at his fly. Drosselmeyer's dolls have evolved from a Columbine, Harlequin, and Toy Soldier, to a Barbie Doll and a gun-toting Robot operated by Fritz with a remote control. The party is very lively and amusing. Morris has given each dancer a character to play, including bits of comic business, ways of walking and moving. But some of his revisions strike deep at the heart of ballet protocol.

First of all, there are no other children present. Almost all other *Nutcracker*s recreate a gemuetlich Christmas seen through a child's eyes. Hoffmann's original story is divided into short episodes, presumably to be read at bedtime, and it has a happy ending to banish the scary evil forces that have charged across its pages. Marie marries the prince in a splendid dream wedding and reigns to this day over a kingdom where "the most wonderful and beautiful things of every kind . . . are to be seen—by those who have the eyes to see them."[1] Morris's Christmas is only an excuse for a boozy, semiorgiastic get-together of the parents' pals. The Stahlbaum kids seem to be allowed in only as tokens of parental pride and solicitude. Whenever they start demanding attention, more presents are shoved at them. The kids aren't shy about complaining when they're disappointed either. When the adults and the children interact, it's on a level of near-equals. In taking apart the traditional family, Morris eliminates one of *The Nutcracker*'s principal attractions, its sweetness and nostalgia.

The party in George Balanchine's *Nutcracker* isn't ever informal. Despite a rather realistically detailed mise-en-scène and action plot, the stage seldom looks random or naturalistically motivated. The movement of both the children and the adults, even when they aren't actually dancing, is dancelike—formalized gesture and groupings rhythmically contained by the music. Also dancelike is the way Balanchine preserves the divisions between children and adults. The children occasionally run to their parents for reassurance or submit to chastisement, but they interact mainly with their peers, boys with boys, girls with girls, parents with their spouses.

The world, inside its lace-doily frame, is hierarchical, comforting. Children and adults know their place. Servants too, of course. No one steps out of that place; everyone finds satisfactions and responsibilities within it. Marie and the Nutcracker/nephew remain children to the end of the ballet and we don't mind at all. The second act is totally credible as Marie's dream underneath the Christmas tree, a dream untroubled by psychosexual promptings.[2]

Many contemporary choreographers have objected to this pre-Freudian projection and developed Clara's dream according to various psychoanalytical interpretations. Nureyev suggests a transference: Clara's daughterly love for Drosselmeyer masks a latent sexuality that gets gratified when Drosselmeyer turns into the Prince. In Baryshnikov's version, Clara remains ambivalent: she longs to elope with the Prince but she's also threatened by male potency—the mice in her dream wear the distorted faces of the male guests at the party—and she feels safer as a little girl, cuddled and protected by her godfather. Mark Morris's version proposes a different set of circumstances and relationships. In depicting a very democratic party scene, he uproots the nineteenth-century vision of how adults and children can live in harmony.

Straight off, he also brings up the issue of gender roles. During the first of the party dances, men and women are strictly segregated. By accident Marie gets into the men's line and is firmly steered back with the women. But this point seems made only to signal its own subversion. As you look around the room, you see men playing women, women playing men, male couples dancing together, female couples likewise. Mrs. Stahlbaum (Peter Wing Healey) is a large booming maîtresse with a meek and prissy husband (Erin Matthiessen).

The children behave like children sometimes, like adults at other times. Marie is a big girl in a babydoll dress; Louise, the nymphet older sister, may represent the other half of Marie's borderline maturity. In fact, when Morris introduces the E.T.A. Hoffmann subplots in the second act, his most radical narrative departure, it's the precocious Louise, not the schoolgirlish Marie, who has to submit to the Mouse Queen's curse and be transformed; restored as a vamp in pink lamé, she rejects the Prince.

Drosselmeyer (Rob Besserer), far from being old and mysterious, is young and sexy; no wonder Marie finds him attractive. When the Prince appears (I saw William Wagner, but the role was also to have been danced by Baryshnikov), Morris underscores his resemblance to his elegant uncle by having them do a shadow dance with a scrim between them. Marie's attachment to Drosselmeyer isn't the only time Morris suggests incest either. More than once at the party you notice Louise in a clinch with papa.

But I think Morris is driving at something beyond a send-up of conventional social roles. I think he's trying to show how thoroughly gender pervades classical ballet itself, and to skewer it as a useless convention. Throughout the work he takes every opportunity to reverse or equalize sex roles. The one heterosexual match, Marie and the Prince in several pas de deux, looks touching and toylike and slightly absurd in this milieu.

Morris's critique isn't confined to the construction of romantic or family love in ballet. All of the dance sequences following the party have been shorn of their gender associations. His corps de ballet is a mix of men and women. This synthesis works stunningly in the Snowflakes scene, which Morris has set with great visual and musical effect. The twenty-two dancers stream in and out in phalanxes so that there seem to be at least twice as many of them. They wear black and silver tutus, bare midriffs, and white bodices. About half are barefoot and half wear black toeshoes. Instead of the usual simulated snowstorm, Morris borrows an effect from Japanese theater. The dancers throw up handfuls of confetti as they leap and pivot across the stage. He's found a surprising number of ways to do this, all growing out of the musical phrase. First they fling the confetti with a pas de chat on the flute roulades; they toss it high while leaping on clashing cymbals; toward the end they dribble it from their fingers as they bourrée in circles, surrounding themselves with sparkle. Each effect is prolonged by canonical strategies that coordinate the confetti bursts with the musical accents.

Nothing else in the ballet is as beautiful or as musically satisfying as this scene. What it manages to do is preserve the dance values without relying on the exploitation of the female body. Contemporary theorists attack the pointe shoe as symbolizing dependency, voyeurism, and the dematerialization of women. Mark Morris is not the first to concur choreographically with this view, but I think in his Snow scene he goes further than anyone in demonstrating what can happen when the pointe shoe isn't the sole property of women. Peter Anastos reportedly came in to coach the dancers in pointe work, and, for people without extensive ballet training, they can achieve quite a lot. I should note, however, that I think Balanchine's Snowflakes scene demonstrates just as strongly that women in classical ballet are not languishing creatures who need men to hold them up and who are compelled to cede virtuosic authority to males. Their pointe work alone, amid the accumulating debris of the fake snowstorm, proves them intrepid and powerful as well as creators of poetic imagery.

The Hard Nut (Morris). Snowflakes, Mark Morris Dance Group. Photo by Tom Brazil.

Besides deconstructing gender, Morris's unisex corps takes the calories out of Tchaikovsky. This music can seem syrupy, even maudlin, in the many *Nutcracker*s that dwell on the ballet's storybook aspects. Morris doesn't allow you to wallow in sentiment; he insists you hear the music with new ears. Modern choreographers have suffered endless conflicts about the issue of romanticism in ballet, and Morris represents the negative extreme, short of refusing to confront it altogether. He embraces both the story and the music, you can see that, even as you see him overturning them.

Balanchine, at the other extreme, went all the way with both the narrative and the score even though he managed to overcome his romantic streak in almost everything else he did. In the Snowflakes and Waltz of the Flowers, as well as the ballet's smaller numbers, he propels individual and group virtuosity to the limits that have defined the ballet ever afterward. Morris's downplayed movement vocabulary leaves the dancers with a kind of lumpen ecstasy unequal to Tchaikovsky's sweep and density. The soft runs and Duncanesque plastique of the Flowers, the skipping and stripped-down air work of the pas de deux, the epic kisses during the finale, aren't important enough images to stand up to the music, however daringly they may counter it.

Yuri Grigorovich's solution to the problem, as given at Brooklyn Academy by the odd company of Soviet students that the choreographer enlisted to tour the States, was a *Nutcracker* stripped of everything *but* virtuosic dancing. Balanchine triumphantly proved that ballet is its own spectacle, and doesn't need all the other trappings, but in Grigorovich, who excels only at mass maneuvers, impressive flamboyance, you see Balanchine's instincts without his genius. None of the Grigorovich ballets that I've seen offer any texture, musicality, detail, or naturalistic drama. Having eliminated mime altogether, he substitutes characteristic shape for character. A telling posture or gestural affectation not only distinguishes one dancer in a crowd from another, but the dancer is condemned to append that signature onto every kind of action—dancing, conversation, traveling. The people at the party are eighteenth-century tintypes who behave in just as constricted and artificial a way as the cardboard entertainers in the second act. There are hoards of children, all played by adult members of the corps. The Nutcracker him/herself is played first by a small female dancer, then by a male dancer, then by a floppy panda-size doll which is Marie's only consolation when she wakes up at the end of the dream.

Grigorovich's improvement on the supposedly creaky story line is to stage the whole post-party adventure as an extravagant magic trick by Drosselmeyer. At the end of the transformation scene, dancers run out from underneath the enlarged Christmas tree, like dolls come to life, and they later dance the divertissements. There is no Kingdom of the Sweets; the whole second act takes place at the top of the Christmas tree, the program note tells us, a featureless place that might be Marxist Heaven. All the divertissements are duets, and all are performed virtually in unison. This might be construed as a gender statement too, with the choreographer asserting that men and women are equals in dancing skills and hardly ever have to resort to sexist lifts or balances. Except that the choreography is so stilted as to dehumanize the dancers before their gender can become an issue. With everything in his *Nutcracker* the same scale and intensity, Grigorovich evades romanticism only to become trapped in militaristic formalism.[3]

All modernists have objected to the romantic escapism of the fairytale ballets, but the stage can only partly realize this anyway. Romanticism is an act of the imagination above all, and may work best in those forms that are least palpable, like poetry. Today, television is our most manipulatable escapist medium, and Pacific Northwest Ballet's film-turned-video *Nutcracker* is the ultimate ballet fantasy, successful in rousing the imagination through the idea of dancing.[4] Not, it must be said immediately, through dancing, since the editing chops bodies, steps, and phrases into slivers that cannot even be mentally pieced together into whole dance sequences.

This, however, isn't director Carroll Ballard's intention. *Nutcracker—The Motion Picture* stems from the concept of designer Maurice Sendak, and may even be a projection of that artist as personified by Drosselmeyer.[5] The film opens with a montage of toymaker images: clocks ticking and chiming with little peasant figures popping out of tiny doors, Drosselmeyer furiously sketching mechanical dolls, then carving them and lovingly putting them together. These turn out to be Drosselmeyer's presents to the Stahlbaum children. They live in a wonderful Moorish palace/dollhouse, which later becomes the setting for the second act. Transformed into a Turkish pasha, Drosselmeyer whisks the divertissements in and out like a series of magic tricks. The story even ends with a shot of Drosselmeyer asleep at his workbench after Marie and the Prince have drifted euphorically out of the dream palace. The dancers reenter in a processional coda under the credits.

The ballet isn't only Drosselmeyer's dream, though. Marie dreams the party as a memory of childhood; Julie Harris reads evocative lines in voice-over to establish this. For this and other scenes, double images create supernatural contrasts of scale, so that everything is real but nothing is. We see Marie and Fritz and the nephew as tiny figures with a giant film of Marie asleep behind them. The children peep into the dollhouse window to see the toy dolls dancing—and we seem to be inside with the dolls. Marie is a shy thirteen-year-old girl who adores her father and is a bit frightened of the strangely childlike, ingenious uncle who brings her magical gifts. When things get mixed up in the dream (the Mouse King wears Drosselmeyer's cloak, for instance), they're delightful or monstrous but unstable, never really threatening or real. If anything, the vestiges of the original ballet that have been preserved, like the Snowflakes, seem the most artificial and out of place.

The Hard Nut, in spite of its theatrical devices and surprises—a huge, lit-up, working clock, a map of the world with flashing lights to show you the homes of the divertissement dancers—is overwhelmingly anti-illusionistic. You don't get carried away into fantasy by it. You don't identify with the characters, nor do they ask you to. Instead you're reminded constantly that they're commenting on something, first of all on other versions of *The Nutcracker*. The subplots introduced in the second act, though they do come from Hoffmann, add nothing enlightening to what those other versions have told us. Morris makes them set pieces, tableaux almost. The maid who's supposed to be minding the infant Pirlipat somehow lets the wicked Mouse Queen get in and lay a curse on the baby by stomping on her in the carriage. The extra business with the clocks, the unsuccessful suitors, the gold nut, the additional transformations—all this is fun and theatrical but it doesn't improve on the traditional scenario.

By the time the dream is over and the children settle in front of the TV again, the *Nutcracker* ballet has been thoroughly demolished. Fritz and Louise see Marie and the Prince kissing passionately on the screen. They seem to recognize the lovers, but the maid drags them off to bed. It's all in there in the TV set, the romantic love, the power struggles, the patriarchy, the magic, the sensuous dancing, and the illusion of safety. And that's where Morris would like to keep it.

AFTER-DINNER NUTS

Boston Phoenix, 13 January 2006

The Christmas season careened to a finish Thursday night at Concord Academy with yet another *Nutcracker*, sort of, the first complete Boston performance of David Parker's *Nut/Cracked*. Parker and the Bang Group showed sections of the work-in-progress two years ago at Summer Stages, and it's now evolved into an hour-long extravaganza of dance diversions and visual one-liners with a distant relationship to the perennial ballet.

Parker dispenses with plot and characters, retaining only trace images of the ballet's most clichéd devices. What does touch off his imagination is Tchaikovsky's music, or rather, a few iconic portions of the music, played and replayed via soupy choral arrangements, Ellington, bebop, clickety-clack percussion, and handbells, as well as the symphonic real deal. Anyone saturated with the standard *Nutcracker* can visualize the dancing sugar plums, the Grand Pas de Deux, and the exotic divertissements as the Bang Group is dismantling them.

In one version of the Waltz of the Flowers, played by the Glenn Miller band, Kate Digby unrolls a scatter rug of bubble wrap and then skirts around its edges for a while, letting the audience savor the possibilities. Finally she throws herself onto it for one satisfying explosion, and then goes on to slam and stomp the life out of every bubble with a satisfying orchestration of pops. The same music, played straight, recurs later for an ensemble dance, with bouquets handed around and sneezes augmenting the musical climaxes.

Each of the twenty-two numbers comes with an incongruous prop or costume detail to start a trail of dancing jokes. Three women try to do a Chinese dance but are soon overshadowed by Parker, who appears with a takeout box and a long strand of noodle in his mouth. I can't tell you what the women did, but Parker managed to inhale the last noodle just as the music ended, and walked off chewing it. Later on, he upstaged the entire company, who were doing a finger-pointing, hip-swiveling dance to the Reed Flutes (Marzipan) music, by teetering across behind them on pointe. They continued dancing but switched their focus en masse, from brazen audience-beguiling smiles to inward gazes.

I think Parker's point here, and in the whole piece, is to demystify the conventions of ballet. The corps de ballet's job includes not only negotiating a set of carefully plotted steps but being able to fade into the background when the star appears. In the Grand Pas de Deux, Parker and Jeffrey Kazin parody the kinky mechanics that ballet partners try to conceal as they maneuver into graceful turns and poses, with an orgy of lascivious thumb-sucking.

What comes through Parker's antics is a deep affection for dancers and what they have to go through. The Bang bunch get choreographed into tricky positions and can't untangle themselves in time, so they dance gallantly on into the music like toads. They wrench into bizarre but artistic group formations. They forget which way to face but they keep doing the steps and hope they don't collide with anyone.

Kazin and Parker maintain a perpetual rivalry and attraction. Whenever they meet, they begin a codependent dance. It could be a side-by-side shuffling tap routine, or a cubist nightmare of interlocking shapes, or a turf war over a wineglass that ends in a falsetto chorale to the Snowflakes tune. They may need each other but they're an uneasy match: Parker, the primo, vain and lordly, capable of making a classically pure attitude pose amongst his klutzy pointe bourrées; Kazin, the second banana who nevertheless gets to show off his speedy pirouettes and windmill turns at every opportunity.

When the whole troupe finally comes out to fling themselves into a series of bows, the audience is in love with them all, Parker, Kazin, Digby, and Cristina Aguirre, Marissa Palley, Nic Petry, Amber Sloan, Emily Tschiffely, Zack Winokur, and Anne Zuemer. On the last note of the coda, they toss celebratory fistfuls of snow into the air.

NUREYEV'S *CINDERELLA*

Christian Science Monitor, 29 June 1987

Rudolf Nureyev's *Cinderella*, which his Paris Opera Ballet gave for a week at the Metropolitan Opera House, is too busy by far. In every scene there seem to be at least two sets of characters enacting simultaneous scenarios. Some of them come from the Cinderella story we all know, at times appearing in inexplicable disguises. Some belong to Nureyev's updated Hollywood-in-the-thirties story. (It looks more like the twenties but never mind.) And some are just miscellaneous extras, like the twenty nymphs and satyrs who might have strayed in from Jerome Robbins's *The Four Seasons* but who, the program says, are giving a fashion show.

Cinderella is not just another ostentatious reworking of a standard ballet. Composed by Prokofiev in 1945, it never had a definitive, classic version. In Nureyev's hands it becomes a "think ballet," psychological and cinematic. Nureyev sees thirties Hollywood as an escapist fantasy, easing the lot of Depression-battered Americans, and Cinderella's midnight retransformation from movie queen to downtrodden waif as a metaphor to explain the sybaritic life of movie stars. Time is short, we're all rushing toward our doom, he thinks, so we might as well enjoy every minute. Not that anyone in the ballet looks particularly amused, but this philosophy may explain their frenzied pace.

Nureyev's plot sounds fairly interesting on paper, but in staging it he has a peculiar gift for undermining his own ideas. Everything in the ballet is overplayed. A whole assortment of farcical movieland stereotypes is present in addition to the fairy tale's grotesques. Cinderella's stepsisters (Isabelle Guérin and Clotilde Vayer) stumble about and screw up their faces. Her stepmother (Georges Piletta in drag) has the shoulders of a football player, and frequently knocks people to the ground when she isn't furiously spinning on pointe.

The movie types include a fat director and his assistant, a dance instructor, and various camera crankers and scene setters, all of whom spend their time striding back and forth and gesturing in two-handed consternation. The producer (Nureyev) enters in a Groucho Marx moustache/nose/cigar disguise, and after a pallid Groucho imitation, he discards nose and moustache and spends the rest of the ballet chomping the cigar and gesturing in one-handed benevolence. See, he's also the Fairy Godmother, who discovers Cinderella and offers her a contract.

The most spectacular aspects of this production are the sets, designed by Petrika Ionesco. Like the action, the environment is eclectic, often without explanation. When they're filming a movie about Tahiti, I guess I can see how a proscenium-size gorilla puppet fits in—it's supposed to be fed one of the native girls as a sacrifice. But how did Cinderella's home, the kitchen of a decaying medieval castle with a skylit Parisian dance studio where the breakfast nook ought to be, get into the same country, let alone the same century, with the art-moderne movie studio? And that Constructivist clock, with its enormous, slowly revolving wheels and mechanistic superstructure—did they smuggle it out of revolutionary Russia just so it could strike midnight with a bang?

Amongst all this hullabaloo, the dancing doesn't show up very well. There's quite a lot of it, actually, but it has problems of scale, of pacing, of emphasis. Nureyev can't seem to estimate how to make his choreographic effects fully. Often he chooses to activate several small groups so that they interrupt one another, overlap, or just plain blur each other out. The ends of ensembles and solos often run into what follows, so the audience doesn't have time to assimilate what it's seen. The men's ensemble have some striking sequences in the last act as they leap back and forth across the stage in search of the owner of the plastic high-heeled slipper. They're led by Laurent Hilaire, the prince who's now an Acteur-Vedette (movie star). Hilaire is a fabulous high-jumper with the speed to carry off Nureyev's nonstop choreography.

The Cinderella, Elizabeth Platel, is a lyrical dancer with a lovely, soft line and an especially poignant way of making slow and expansive leg gestures. Most of her solos are expressive rather than purely virtuosic. By that I mean Nureyev uses classical steps conversationally, to show the rising and falling of emotions—hesitancy and longing, expectation and despair—rather than formally so as to show only the steps. In these solos, and similar pas de deux with Hilaire, Platel dances beautifully but she doesn't particularly act the role. Under the circumstances, it seems the wisest course.

GRIGOROVICH'S *THE GOLDEN AGE*
Christian Science Monitor, 8 July 1987

Yuri Grigorovich is one of the few choreographers to have successfully made thorough renovations on the classical ballet format, and his approach to modern ballets has been widely imitated. Grigorovich's agenda, on the face of it, doesn't look very different from that of George Balanchine. Both were interested in clearing away narrative and decorative clutter, in unifying the action by eliminating passages of mime and other stage business, and in extending the highest skills of academic dancing to all members of the ensemble and all parts of the performance. The results, however, couldn't have been more different.

The latest example of Grigorovich modernism, *The Golden Age* (Shostakovich), was on view in the early performances of the Bolshoi Ballet's Metropolitan Opera House engagement. Past visits of the Bolshoi and the Kirov have displayed several others, including his best-known work, *Spartacus*. Of them all, I like *The Golden Age* best, for its stylish appropriation of twentieth-century art, fashion, and pop culture. But the genre as a whole turns me off.

Grigorovich sees his ballets as a series of scenes illustrating aspects of the society or the characters in his story. The plots tend to be minimal or well known, so he devotes little time to presenting them. All character is established by signature gestures or body attitudes, often stereotyped and incorporated in the dancing, which never stops. So in *The Golden Age* the Good Guys are the honest workers and fishermen—hearty, virile, and proud. They bound through space with expanded chests and huge, high jumps, and open-handed, inspiring gestures. Their women are modest and soft, dressed in aprons and head kerchiefs, and dance with their arms folded like Russian peasants or their hands clasped guilelessly behind their backs.

The Bad Guys come in at least three varieties: decadents, capitalists, and petty criminals. The decadents have slick hair and dance the tango. There's a chorus line of flappers, who flounce from one cliché pose to another while launching sexy looks over their shoulders. The capitalists have stomachs that stick out, and they strut or waddle. The robbers run on tiptoe and hunch up when they jump. They gesture with a thumbs-up fist, like the thugs in *West Side Story*.

From time to time the action shutters down to a smaller group, and you get to see the soloists dance even more athletically, or lyrically, or decadently, than their massed confederates. There's a love story—Boris (Yuri Vasyuchenko), a fisherman, loves Rita (Alla Mikhalchenko), a dancer in a night club. For some reason their romance is complicated, and she's pursued by her dancing partner, Yashka (Aleksei Lazarev), who secretly heads a band of thieves. His girlfriend, Lyuska (Maria Bilova), gets stabbed in a jealous quarrel, and of course the workers overcome the thieves and the lovers are reunited at the end.

But the real story of the ballet is the triumph of the proletariat over evil, and the choreography is meant to illustrate this in the most schematic terms. All the movement for the groups and their leaders who are the principals in the story is consistent with their assigned character traits, and most of the time it's designed for large numbers in unison. So you get blasted for a long time with forty or fifty workers leaping in idyllic comradeship, then for another long time you look at twenty or thirty decadents living it up in the café. Each scene is paced the same all the way through, so the ballet feels like a series of long cadenzas in different moods or temperaments. The symphonic modulations and elaborations that make Balanchine so interesting to follow are of no importance to Grigorovich, nor is the singling out of individual qualities. Mikhalchenko is good because she's faster, stronger, and more yielding than the other women, Vasyuchenko can jump higher than the other men. But as special personalities they're not notable here.

I have the same reaction to Grigorovich's step vocabulary: it's virtuosic and expansive, but all the steps begin to look alike, differing only in force or numbers. For instance, in one scene Yashka the villain is plotting jobs for his gang. He crouches threateningly, kicks both legs in the air, hunches, and punches. The thugs arrive and they all continue the dance. Lyuska the flapper gun moll joins in. Then everyone leaves except Yashka. His scheming dance hasn't essentially changed, but it has gained in intensity from reinforcement.

The emphasis on spectacle, on high physical involvement, and on expressionistic gestural motifs allies Grigorovich to some of the early Soviet theatrical experimenters, like Foregger, Meyerhold, and Goleizovsky. Simon Virsaladze's constructivist designs underline this analogy, as does the twenties period of the ballet itself. But where the constructivists used fragmentation, distortion, grotesquerie, and non-naturalistic movement to explode the soothing effect of traditional theater, Grigorovich uses classical line and virtuosity, high visibility, and attractiveness to engage the audience and sell it the party line.

ANTI-BALLETICS
Boston Phoenix, 28 April 2000

Olga Spessivtseva, the highly fictionalized subject of Boris Eifman's *Red Giselle*, was one of the great Giselles of the twentieth century. Trained in the Imperial Russian school at St. Petersburg, she starred in the whole gamut of ballet classics, and resisted the innovations of Soviet avant-gardist Fyodor Lopukhov, as well as those of Serge Lifar at the Paris Opera and the young George Balanchine. After a touring career in Europe and

South America during the 1930s, she emigrated to the United States. She was institutionalized for twenty years after a mental breakdown in 1943, and then resided at Tolstoy Farm in New York State until her death in 1991.

What Eifman makes of this life is billed as a tribute, but it looks more like pure theatrics, laced with some confused polemic. To a pastiche of selections from Tchaikovsky, Bizet, and Schnittke, his Red Giselle gets involved with a Secret Police Agent and eventually flees Russia, but she comes unhinged from sexual tyranny, it seems, rather than political oppression. The Ballerina (Yelena Kuzmina in Friday night's premiere at the Wang Theater) first submits to the sadistic regimen of her ballet teacher (Sergei Basalaev), so it's no surprise that later she likes being dragged around by the leather-raincoated Soviet official (Albert Galichanin). After arriving in Paris she falls for a narcissistic ballet master (Igor Markov). His homosexuality is what finally pushes her over the edge.

Truckloads of big effects and hallucinations pad out this dubious plot. Any account I could offer here about the dance/politics in St. Petersburg would be as glossy as Eifman's rendition, but it appears that the real Spessivtseva had a stellar career during the early Soviet period, when the ballet classics were kept alive as populist entertainments despite their taint of imperialism. Boris Eifman had his own difficulties under the latter-day Soviet regime, and his depictions of mechanistic proletarian armies and refugees trudging up a gangplank must have appealed to the many Russian-Americans in the audience.

The first time the Soviet rabble marched into our faces, I flashed on many similar maneuvers in the ballets of Yuri Grigorovich, the last head of the Bolshoi Ballet under the Soviet regime. Eifman has adopted the spectacular choreographic tactics of his former antagonists, along with the glitzy homiletics of Maurice Béjart.

Eifman's Giselle in effect becomes yet another example of the Nijinsky stereotype. Naïve, dedicated, and filled with uncontrollable sexuality, the artist becomes a victim of the very society that adores her. To complete this phony moralizing, as the ballerina descends deeper into irrationality, all her male admirers are also punished. The ballet teacher collapses over her defection to the arms of a revolutionary; the KGB guy commits suicide after she splits; even the Paris partner suffers regret as the doors of her delusions shut him out.

What we don't get much of here is the art part. There's a lot of motion in Eifman's choreography but little to show us the dance Spessivtseva lived in, the dance she resisted, or the gifts that established her place in history. Embedded in the movement of large social groups, like the lumpen revolutionaries or the revelers in a jazz-age nightclub, or intimate encounters, like the duets and trios where the ballerina gets wrenched into submission by various men, or the serious exercise of classicism in a studio or a stage, the steps of classical ballet are just another part of the eclectic vocabulary that Eifman uses to create effects.

There are broad gestures and poses to identify character, distortions to signify emotional states, quotes from at least six or seven other ballets. When the ballerina reenacts her Doppelgänger, the betrayed and doomed heroine of the ballet *Giselle*, we get a fast precis of the first act and some even wispier nods to the second act, with signature steps but no sustained dancing at all.

I don't know if Kuzmina and company can dance classical ballet. That is not what Eifman requires of them. In their program bios they sneer at the clichés of ballet, and often speak of themselves as actors. Eifman seems to be making an alternative to the ballet stage, a medium that doesn't depend on classical ballet's conventions, its virtuosity, musicality, or formal structures. Although his productions are conceived on an operatic scale, the personal crises at the center have no comparable grandeur.

Well, it's a demanding enterprise, ballet. Eifman is not the first to unload its burdens, to forego its exacting discipline and its "elitist" rewards. Classical dancing is what elevates Giselle's story to tragedy. Without that, I find Eifman's account merely monotonous and melodramatic.

YO, JEWELS!

Boston Phoenix, 8 December 2000

Can hip-hop translate into a theatrical dance form? Directors and producers have been worrying at this question ever since hip-hop and its companion, break dancing, made their way out of the streets and into the face of a wider audience a couple decades ago. Hip-hop is a challenge dance form, a contest between the virtuosic inventions of its performers. Its dynamism became a driving engine for the technological escapism of MTV. But pressed into the confining frame of a theater, it usually adopts the revue format, where a series of loosely related numbers show off the dancers' specialties and the more complex issues of choreography, dramaturgy, and mise-en-scène don't have to be addressed.

Rennie Harris Puremovement has taken on this bigger task in *Rome & Jewels*. His gloss on Romeo and Juliet, as shown at the Emerson last weekend under the auspices of Dance Umbrella, was visually and verbally impressive, although Harris had higher aspirations—about love, spirituality, and life on the street—that the piece didn't clearly communicate to me.

Harris says he was led to Shakespeare through Jerome Robbins's *West Side Story*, and you can see how the feud of the Montagues and the Capulets, transmuted into racial gang wars under the highway ramps of 1957, would resonate for today's rappers. Sadly, this chapter of our urban history is still being written. Rap and break dancing, like martial arts and Shakespeare's poetry, can transform harsh reality into entertainment or art, into something more controlled, where the consequences aren't fatal and maybe can inspire hope.

Harris's take on the story is entirely modern, but one-sided, focused on the opposing gangs, the Monster Qs and the Caps, and on a few speaking characters, Rome, Ben V., Merc, Tibault, Iz-Action, and a Narrator. Like the world of rap, this is a male enclave. (Two token girl members of the Caps are quite irrelevant—one of them doesn't even get her name in the program.) There are three sides to every man, the Narrator tells us: the play side, the pimp side, and the hustle side. Not a peaceful prospect.

Basically what they do is fight, boast, trip out, and prey on each other. Rome falls in love with Jewel, an imaginary girl. This conceit doesn't really work as a plot device, but Shakespeare's fatal accidents of timing aren't all that credible either. Maybe Rome's love-ideal makes him a better boy, but like his namesake, he fails to prevent mayhem. Most of the characters are dead by the end of the piece, and there's not much sense that any reconciliation will ennoble the tragedy. The Narrator, who stays apart from the gang warfare and comments on it bitterly, kills Rome instead of resolving the feud and putting an end to the violence like his Shakespearean counterpart, the Duke of Verona.

As you might expect, dancing is the physical medium for this tale. It isn't much of a stretch to go from standup hip-hop numbers to crews of opposing street thugs mixing it up with spins, flips, and moonwalking arrogance. The dancing, especially in the climactic rumble, was spectacular. Three DJs, Mix, Cisum, and Evil Tracy, played their own virtuosic tricks in a wild turntable cantata. Blurry, busy black-and-white projections filled the backdrop, and the stage was almost always smoky or noisy or both.

The frenetic style of the production may have felt more like "Shakespeare in Love" than Romeo and Juliet, but the really original feature—and the thing that made the Bard connection best for me—was the language. Not that I could understand it most of the time. The slight story line was conveyed in a macaronic text written by Rennie Harris and several collaborators including Shakespeare. Gorgeous images from the play slammed up against vernacular patois and code words, dialect, profanity, quotes from popular songs, and parentheses addressed to the audience. The speaking dancers, especially the gifted Rome, Rodney Mason, in a tremendous, multiplex monologue, gave a fine account of the original poetry when they weren't being acoustically distorted beyond intelligibility.

Though I regretted not being able to understand the text, I finally accepted it as a sort of music, even a sort of subversion. Rappers, street dancers, and their oppressed ancestors throughout history have hidden their meanings in coded words and behaviors. I'd be interested in the response of a black audience to this piece. Rennie Harris is onto something; as he said in his pre-performance remarks, he feels he's moving away from the street, into a bigger universe. Ynowamsay?

A DREAM AWAKES

Boston Phoenix, 5 November 2004

Four years after George Balanchine choreographed *A Midsummer Night's Dream*—it was his first original full-length ballet—he joined with director Dan Ericksen in 1966 to film the work with a cast of wonderful young dancers he'd trained at the School of American Ballet. The fate of that film, still to be resolved, moved into another phase last Sunday night at the Walter Reade Theater. The Film Society of Lincoln Center gave a one-time screening of the most complete version of the movie known to exist, a converted-for-television, remastered and color-corrected, projected-in-a-theater adaptation of a video print.

Balanchine created the *Dream* to display the diverse resources of New York City Ballet at its peak of success. The film, made before anyone devoted much attention to translating art dance to the screen, looks a little primitive technically, and there are traces of Hollywood in it, from Balanchine's years making movie musicals in the 1930s. It's a document, a memory, a treasure. It also dampens a few myths about the Balanchine enterprise.

The twenty-one-year-old Suzanne Farrell is ravishing as Titania, not only in the worshipful glamour shots and close-ups. Dancing the pas de deux (partnered by NYCB stalwart Conrad Ludlow) she's a queen with authority. Lifts and falls that today would be considered submissive, she attacks with daring. Her competitive but affectionate Oberon, Edward Villella, who's now remembered mostly for his butch roles, in *Rubies* for instance, is an elegant danseur noble who masters the fastest, loftiest beats and leaps ever seen to this day.

For the second act divertissement, Balanchine made another stunning pas de deux, to Mendelssohn's little-known Symphony no. 9 for strings, one of several selections he added to the composer's incidental music for the play. It's danced in the film by Allegra Kent at her most refined, partnered by Jacques d'Amboise, who didn't have much classical line but could make a girl feel totally secure in his hands.

Balanchine supposedly rejected mime and expressive acting of all kinds, but following Shakespeare's lead, he superimposes a quartet of foolish mortal lovers onto the magical kingdom of Titania and Oberon. For the film, he trimmed the comic passages of mix-up and wrangling among the bewitched lovers. But Patricia McBride and Mimi Paul have great little dramatic dance scenes as Hermia and Helena, the jilted or too-sought-after Athenian girls.

Arthur Mitchell's Puck connects the two worlds, spinning a tangle of well-meaning but miscalculated sorcery. My favorite moment in the whole film was Mitchell's slow, cringing realization of his first mistake, which suspended the racing tempo of the whole first act with a funny, "uh-oh" pause.

Balanchine feared the constricting effect that cinematic framing would have on his work, so he replotted the *Dream* carefully to fit. The action of the fairies, mortals, and rustics is confined to shadowy little forest clearings; you can see how so many mistaken identities and blundering chases could occur. The space opens out, though, for the big formal dances of the second act.

The movie wasn't a great success in its initial showings—after all, at the time you could see the whole thing, with all its stellar personnel, on the living stage. When it got reformatted for television, the outside edges of its Panavision picture had to be cropped off, and Balanchine disliked it so much he pulled it from circulation. Then there was the question of who had the rights to screen it again in public. The newly spruced-up video shown on Sunday was the result of a five-year retrieval effort sparked by Patrick Bensard, director of the Cinemathèque de la Danse in Paris, who's still tracking down a usable film version.

Farrell, Villella, and Kent appeared on Sunday to add their comments to the odyssey. Neither Farrell nor Kent was in the ballet's first cast. "I wasn't the original but I was the original understudy," remarked the still-playful Kent. "I thought I was going to be Puck." Too bad this didn't happen at least once. Farrell went out and got her first cat when Balanchine advised her to rehearse with a pet for her spellbound love scenes with the donkey, a.k.a. Bottom the Weaver. According to Villella, when he saw his own solo before the soundtrack had been added, it was so fast he couldn't make sense of it.

None of them seemed nostalgic about their vanished youth, so superbly displayed in the film. Nothing to regret, they all said, just privileged to have been in on it. And so were we.

SEE IT LIVE

Boston Phoenix, 16 April 2004

Ballet's treasure-house of great works can be seen live by only a pathetically small audience. In most companies today ballets, new or old, get done in a home season or two; maybe they go on tour to a limited number of cities. Then that's it unless a revival gets put together down the line. Public television has played a primary role in resolving or at least alleviating this paradox. Since the mid-1970s the Great Performances and Dance in America series, under executive director Jac Venza, have brought repertory to a mass audience. These PBS productions have greatly enhanced our national dance awareness, and more than that, our literacy about specific ballets and modern dance works. The PBS production of Frederick Ashton's *The Dream* that premieres April 21 was filmed in performance at the Orange County Performing Arts Center last summer. American Ballet Theater revived this gem of a ballet a couple of years ago, and it's already disappeared from their repertory.

Ashton's one-act translation of Shakespeare's *A Midsummer Night's Dream*, set in a shadowy forest in the Victorian era, was choreographed in 1964, just two years after George Balanchine's much more extended and traditional version of the play. Ashton's ballet is marvelously English. It was made for young dancers who became legendary stars of the Royal Ballet, Antoinette Sibley and Anthony Dowell (who staged the ABT revival), and it's imprinted with English wit and charm—dithery lovers and hearty pantomime bumpkins, an imperious, possibly parodistic fairy nobility, and Mendelssohn's lilting music complete with treble voices crooning lullabies.

Trying to televise a live ballet performance has built-in drawbacks. As Venza admits in a contribution to the new dance-on-screen anthology *Envisioning Dance* (edited by Judy Mitoma, from Routledge, with illustrations on accompanying DVD), big ballets are expensive to transfer to a studio. Venza's teams have developed some wonderful repertory renditions in the controlled studio situation, but trying to capture *Swan Lake*, or *The Dream*, straight through a performance in a theater, is a challenge they haven't surmounted yet.

Matthew Diamond, the director of the *Dream* telecast, admits in another essay in the book that the live performance situation isn't ideal for the camera. He approaches the problem assuming, I guess, that in the flat and static plane of a television screen nothing moves by itself. His set-up for *The Dream* called for eight or so cameras positioned at various distances out front and to the sides of the stage. Constant cuts from one to another are meant to simulate movement by changing the viewer's perspective. In the PBS *Dream* this process disrupts the flow of the dance itself. Throughout the hour-long ballet, the dance phrase is chopped into small pictures. You'll be seeing the corps de ballet in full-stage view, then two measures later, half the corps, then one dancer close up, then another half of the corps from another angle. The video editing substitutes its own continuity for that of the choreography.

The solos, especially those of Ethan Stiefel as Oberon, suffer the least in this situation. Usually Stiefel is alone on stage, and just one or two cameras stay with him, keep his whole body in the frame, and allow us to appreciate his beautiful line and elevation. All the other dancing, including that of the Titania (Alessandra Ferri), Puck (Herman Cornejo), and Bottom (Julio Bragado-Young), comes across less distinctly.

Diamond handles the storytelling as if it were separate from the dancing, like a nineteenth-century ballet, and he cuts to whoever's "acting." But Ashton doesn't break up the story and dancing that way. The comedy and the choreographic line are often shared by the battling or reconciling couples. If you don't see them both, you lose reaction, you lose the dance phrase. Besides that, close-ups are unkind to ballet dancers performing for an audience. They reveal the dancers' effort, magnify their small movement adjustments, and make caricature out of acting designed to read in the back of a theater.

Diamond's cuts are unusually respectful of the music, but he makes them with a heavy hand. I mean that there's metric musicality and there's another, far lighter musical notion that Ashton was pursuing. *The Dream*, musically and dramatically, is just that, a fluid, confusing thing where stories overlap and identities keep changing. It's about concealment and desire, and tenderness that underlies petulance. Mortals and fairies forgive, and finally, they sleep. Ashton's *Dream* is all illusion. No wonder it succumbs to the realism of "live" TV.

WAKING SOMEWHERE ELSE

Dance on Camera Journal, January–February 2007

Jean Cocteau (1889–1963), the twentieth century's most famous aesthete, made art in many forms. He may never have danced himself, but he contributed to a surprising number of ballets and films that became landmarks of modernism. An intimate of both the Ballets Russes and the Ballets Suédois circles in the teens and twenties, he provided libretti, design ideas, and/or conceptual triggers for *Parade* (1917), considered the first Cubist ballet; for the collage-satire *Les Mariés de la Tour Eiffel* (1921); and for Bronislava Nijinska's beach ballet, *Le Train Bleu* (1924). Cocteau violated the conventions of the ballet stage by grafting avant-garde nonsense and illogic onto the rationality of everyday life. He had a hand in thirteen other ballets and produced a constant stream of writings, graphics, and lyrical films, including the psychological dreamscape *Le Sang d'un Poète* (1932) and the surrealist masterpiece *La Belle et la Bête* (1946).

Cocteau was an intellectual dandy. Film historian Gerald Mast called him a "cinematic amateur." Yet his poetic sensibility, his recurring themes of transformation, transcendence, and the interdependence of love and death, have inspired filmmakers to this day. *Opium*, screened at the 2007 Dance on Camera festival, was codirected by the Canadian writer Miles Lowry and dancer David Ferguson as an adaptation of their stage work about one of Cocteau's visits to a detoxification clinic. The film incorporates many of Cocteau's artistic symbols and gestures into an impressionistic narrative.

A young man (Ferguson) is taken to a sanitarium by a mysterious woman who never actually returns but whose power continues to haunt him. Imprisoned in his room, he hallucinates, tries to write, sees violent visions, and finally, reluctantly, readies himself for a return to life on the outside. The figments of Cocteau's imagination appear and fade: the candelabra and the smoking flesh from *La Belle et la Bête*, the white-faced nurses with their features outlined in black, the seductive noose, the woman who caresses and betrays again and again. When the young man finally seems to pull himself together, he gets dressed and sits at his desk, compelled to write but unconvinced that even writing matters. The scattered pages of his manuscript fly up from the floor into a neat but crumpled pile, next to his hand.

The film has a curious duality of viewpoint. It projects the addict's withdrawal fantasies, but at the same time it looks at him more objectively. Is the camera eye registering the young man's own druggy visions? Or does it represent the doctor and nurses who check on the patient through the keyhole of his room? The atmosphere is hermetic, the visions glamorous. In the young man's nightmares he's being restrained and at the same time sexually aroused: the sheets snake around him, he's embraced by black-gloved hands, threatened by his nurses, attacked by a Kabuki princess with a sword.

Although none of the characters in the film speak, voices drift in and out over the moody score by the Eclipse Quartet, with aphoristic lines from Cocteau's writings. Over the opening credits a voice announces, "Opium is for those who dream of waking somewhere else." The film suggests it wasn't only opium that seduced Cocteau into escapist transports, but art-making itself. He alternated between these two self-induced dream states throughout his life, and the film *Opium* suggests that during his repeated incarcerations he was seeking a creative refuge as much as a cure.

Cocteau's works illuminate and in a sense fix the type of the tormented, addicted artist. In *Le Jeune Homme et la Mort* the drive to create merges with the desire for oblivion. Death offers the artist a final release, and he accepts the solution. By 1946 Cocteau had formed a new creative alliance with choreographer Roland Petit, who was just beginning his long career as a leader of French postwar modernism. *Le Jeune Homme* is now considered Petit's ballet although Cocteau conceptualized it and directed all its details—"raconté" is the word used in the credits—Cocteau "explained" the dance, décor, and costumes to Petit, designer George Wakhevitch, and costumer Karinska. He surely would have choreographed it if he'd possessed a dance vocabulary, but he called it a "mimodrama," meaning a piece in which acting style became exaggerated to the point where it resembled dance. *Le Jeune Homme* premiered at the Théâtre des Champs-Elysées on 25 June 1946, immediately after the first showings of *La Belle et la Bête*, which Cocteau had worked on for the past year. In a way, the ballet is a kind of fairy tale, a transfer of Cocteau's cinematic mythos to a darker, more matter-of-fact stage reality. Underlying both works is Cocteau's belief that once embarked on the journey to illusion, the poet must follow his muse even if it leads to death.

Cocteau loved film for its ability to break up time, a property he extended in *La Belle* by using George Auric's score in an edited counterpoint with the filmed image. He'd already tried disconnecting score from image, to create what he called "accidental synchronization," in *Le Sang d'un Poète*. For *Le Jeune Homme et la Mort* he wanted an even more drastic rupture. The ballet was rehearsed to jazz piano and other classical music; the dancers devised their own counts for the movement. At the dress rehearsal Cocteau introduced J. S. Bach's Passacaglia in C Minor, which became the final accompaniment. Setting the modern-day Dance of Death to the tune of a Baroque masterpiece added a layer of sensationalism to *Le Jeune Homme*'s reputation.

The ballet was a shocker at the time, not only because of the musical misalliance. The theme—an artist's fevered progression from creative impasse to suicide—resembles that of *Le Sang d'un Poète*, but instead of the distancing effect of period costumes and cinematic fantasy, both the young man and his visitor are in modern dress; they behave almost like dramatic actors. He sprawls on his bed, crushes out a cigarette with his foot, checks his watch over and over. A film-noir hero waiting for a woman who's late. But when she arrives, she teases him with a series of come-ons and rebuffs, and then, having roused him to a frenzy of desire, she shows him a noose hanging from the rafters and runs out of the room. The artist has no choice but to seize it. The breakaway set turns the attic room into a neon-lit Parisian skyscape and the woman returns wearing long red gloves and a skull mask, to lead the young man away over the rooftops.

With its lurid sexuality, its pedestrian movement threaded with ballet steps, the work turned out to be an icon of danced existentialism and a theatrical hit that served generations of great male ballet stars. It's been filmed with its original dancers, Jean Babilée and Nathalie Philippart, and with Rudolf Nureyev, Patrick Dupond, and Mikhail Baryshnikov. Petit abridged the sixteen-minute ballet to half its length for Baryshnikov as the opening scene of the Hollywood film *White Nights*. The complete ballet has now become one of several additions to the ballet DVD library by the Paris Opéra Ballet that are being distributed here by Naxos. Recorded in a 2005 Paris performance with étoile dancers Nicolas Le Riche and Marie-Agnès Gillot, the ballet is paired with Roland Petit's *Carmen*, also starring Le Riche, and the disc includes interviews in French with the choreographer, the dancers, and Paris Opéra director Brigitte Lefèvre. Nureyev's benchmark film, with Zizi Jeanmaire as Death, was made in 1968 for French television. Released in sixteen-millimeter format, it's widely known and gives a fine account of the sharply contrasting performances—Nureyev's feverish young man and the enigmatic, alluring Jeanmaire. Pursuing this essay, I was sure I'd seen a film of the original cast long ago and I wanted to compare interpretations. A search in the Lincoln Center Library's Dance Collection turned up only clips from it on various documentaries. But these few moments of black-and-white footage showed me why Jean Babilée's performance was extraordinary.

All the other dancers in the role of the young man that I've seen, live and on screen, have made much of the technical possibilities of the role. Nicolas Le Riche rips off soaring brisés, double assemblés, barrel jumps, multiple tours en l'air, strings of perfect pirouettes where he negotiates transitionless switches from one leg to the other. From these ballet feats he slips effortlessly into slow Graham shoulder falls and furious acrobatics with the furniture. Le Riche exemplifies the superb technical level of today's Paris Opéra dancers. Gillot displays fabulous extensions and wraps herself around her victim in what's mainly a nondance role.

But those snatches of Jean Babilée recalled a naturalism that was very much a part of both the ballet and modern dance aesthetics after the war. No one dances like this now, but we see it in films of French, English, and American dancers from the 1940s and 1950s. Babilée moves like an ordinary man—weighty, self-absorbed, impulsive—not like a dancer playing an ordinary man. His spins and leaps and slow, slow falls arise as if spontaneously out of the young man's mundane dilemma. What starts like a recognizable situation turns sinister, then incredible. I think Cocteau must have intended this insidious transformation. No one we know of since has pulled it off. The dancerly displays and pretend realism of all the ballet's later interpreters seem expected, banal. "Morbid beauty and unhealthy fascination," wrote one of the ballet's first critics. Cocteau would probably have approved that reaction.

WAYWARD DANCING

The Dial, April 1982

For most of his twenty-five-year choreographing career, Paul Taylor has eluded definition. Trained as a modern dancer, with a classical instinct for form, he is nevertheless a committed breaker of images, a disrupter of accepted order. His dances take place in an atmosphere of extreme gravity even when they are playful or raunchily comic. His movement—and he is one of the last modern dancers to have developed an individual movement style—seems to cling to the ground through its most extravagant attempts to get airborne. Taylor's work gives me an acute sense of dislocation. It begins to seem that the primal systems of life have failed and that the dancers must be sustaining motion by means of some other laws I never suspected. *Le Sacre du Printemps* (*The Rehearsal*) and *Arden Court*, the works on public television's April 12 Dance in America show, "Two Landmark Dances" lead us deeper into the world of antic seriousness that we glimpsed earlier this year on his "Three Modern Classics" (*Aureole*, *Three Epitaphs*, and *Big Bertha*).

Perhaps no dance work of the twentieth century is more talked about and less known than *Le Sacre du Printemps*. Critics have labeled Nijinsky's contribution everything from "a wretched scrap of choreography" to a masterpiece. It had been so difficult for the dancers to learn that it was never revived after its first season. Stravinsky, ever solicitous for the survival of his own work, arranged the first concert performance of *Le Sacre* less than a year after its theater premiere. He further ensured that it would be heard by transcribing it for two pianos. This reduction, which thins out and clarifies the immense web of the orchestral score, is the only version of *Le Sacre* that veteran Stravinsky interpreter George Balanchine has ever considered choreographing, and it is the one Paul Taylor uses in his 1980 version. The choice is more than practical. Because it's so unlike the rich, raging sound that's become a cornerstone of twentieth-century music, the two-piano *Sacre* is relieved of many past associations. We can almost see it fresh, free from notoriety, partisanship, and conjecture. I think that's what Taylor intends.

He's set the dance as a kind of silent movie cops-and-robbers comedy with a subtext about a dance company—perhaps his own—rehearsing a new work. Through this plot, no more unlikely than that of a Hollywood thriller, he propels us from conspiracy to narrow escape to furtive romance. We don't get much idea why these events are happening or how they're connected, but they have a crazy kind of fascination. Like all pop art, the characters and events appear familiar, but we can look at them without guilt or sentiment. We can, in a sense, look *through* them to see the dancing. Instead of sympathetic characters or tragic plots, we perceive a spectacle of fractured, distorted movement that reflects the few remaining photographs of Nijinsky's *Sacre*.

Holding their bodies flat and precisely angled, the dancers seem to move from some newly discovered inner mechanism, a force more explosive and less refined than foot power. Fingers curled onto themselves, feet and knees flexed, arms bent stiffly away from the body, they scurry across the floor in straight, short bursts. Every move has the clarity and the largeness of semaphore. You see the beginning of a move and the end, but not the transition. Someone planted on the floor one instant is perched atop someone else's shoulder the next. Christopher Gillis grips the bars of his jail cell, and then he's free, but we don't really notice *how* he escapes. In the climax of the chase, instead of a lifelike bloody massacre, all the characters line up and, one by one, stab one another by inserting a dagger under the opponent's arm.

Nowhere in the dance do we find traces of the original scenario, about sacrificial spring rites of ancient pagan Russia, except in Ruth Andrien's final solo, a controlled orgy of grief at the loss of her baby, who has fallen victim to the mob wars. Taylor does add a sly analogy to *Le Sacre*'s star-studded history in the role of the Rehearsal Mistress, played by Bettie de Jong, a reference to the stern matriarchs of modern dance like Martha Graham, with whom Taylor danced before forming his own company. Graham played the Chosen Maiden in the first American production (1930) of *Le Sacre*, with choreography by Léonide Massine.

Probably the most significant thing about Stravinsky and Nijinsky's ballet was not the discordance and harshness but the overriding fact of organization, of control. At first you may hear only shards of melody, unpredictably shifting accents, polyrhythms, sections of the orchestra braying at one another in different keys, volcanic crescendos unbearably prolonged. What horrifies the unsuspecting listener is that this sensory chaos, this "ugliness," is not only premeditated but arranged with definite forms and effects to fulfill. Nor are there "expressive" concessions—neither song nor smile—from the performers to soften the impact. Perhaps this is what shocks us about any really revolutionary art: not that it does something unheard of but that it deals so drastically and so intentionally with what we know and love. As a critic of the original *Sacre* remarked, no one would have complained if they'd been told the dance was about the Maori.

Arden Court (1981) is, in a sense, about the Maori: a pure-dance work celebrating that special tribe of people called dancers, who don't resemble us at all but who merely entertain and delight us and keep their secrets to themselves. This dance represents Taylor at his most sunny and attractive. A direct descendant of his first overtly balletic piece, *Aureole* (1962), *Arden Court* is a strikingly successful approach to virtuosity in the modern dance idiom. Without resorting to the classical ballet vocabulary, Taylor accelerates and elaborates his own movement language until it acquires the same self-evident meaning as the feats known in ballet as steps. If *Le Sacre* makes no concessions to beauty or softness, *Arden Court* is ingratiating, open, easy to like.

Set to the symphonies—really concerti grossi—of the Baroque English composer William Boyce, *Arden Court* is a series of small divertissements connected ingeniously by their movement plots. For example, in the first of several duets Carolyn Adams circles with triplet rhythm around Elie Chaib, who's moving legato one beat to every three of hers. Next Lila York follows at David Parsons's heels as he does suspended foot gestures and jumps with dotted rhythms. Then York begins doing slow rising poses while Robert Kahn skips and runs around her. The logical line of the dances is linked to the music but doesn't illustrate it. To the several concurrent ideas of a musical fugue three couples blithely consolidate in a unison dance. There's a minuet for Susan McGuire and Thomas Evert that borrows its tempo and its rising steps from the real thing but looks like something tall dancers do naturally, instead of the decorous ornamental recreation of a drawing room.

Paul Taylor takes great pleasure in these contrary games. Even when he can suppress the macabre streak that colors *Le Sacre du Printemps*, his dance insists on the awkwardness of dancers. He seems long ago to have accepted that weight and inertia are insurmountable circumstances, that the joints aren't made of rubber, the toes will refuse to twinkle, and the elbows look like knobs, not flowers. He is determined to make bodies dance anyway, to find, in fact, that knobbiness is a neglected attribute.

PRIVATE DOMAIN

Washington Post Book World, 23 December 1984

Like the dance it's named for, Paul Taylor's autobiography, *Private Domain*, depicts a tribe of people he's created.[6] Absorbed in their own and each other's physicality, they're seductive and not very nice—and probably in disguise. The life Taylor portrays isn't exactly fictionalized, it's theatricalized. For someone who's been posing as an inarticulate person all his life, his performance as a writer is unexpectedly virtuosic—controlled, textured, funny, and at all times fascinating. It's one of the best dance books I've ever read.

After a rather ramshackle childhood with a too-distant family and a proto-Beatnik adolescence in the '40s, he is more or less mindlessly making his way through college as a swimmer and art major when, on page 25, he discovers his real calling is dance, and after that there's nothing else. Recruited as a partner by a college girlfriend, he proceeds to the American Dance Festival and Juilliard, acquiring the basics of technique. He spends years with Martha Graham, learning what he doesn't want to do, and a short time with Merce Cunningham, on the frontiers of modern art. He makes his own dances almost from the beginning, with cohorts who be-come the nucleus of his company, and they traverse the modern dancers' classic route from grimy lofts to out-of-the-way theaters to the big time, from the wilds of iconoclasm to the tricky heights of success.

Curiously, though, the book has very little in it about the act of dancing itself—the agonies and epiphanies of life at the barre and in the limelight. Although he says dancing is his life, he writes more about touring in haz-ardous circumstances, functioning in persistent poverty, and the fantasies that feed his creativity. There are, fortunately, accounts of choreograph-ing, some fragmentary, some more extensive: the successful early *Aureole*, which he sometimes eyes ruefully, like a faithful but clingy old flame; the patriotic satire *From Sea to Shining Sea*, made almost entirely from "found" movements and pop-art icons; the convoluted, metaphorical *American Genesis*, the dance that felled him as a performer.

Taylor is most interested in the people with whom he dances—his teach-ers, his company members, and the many familiars and alter egos who are aspects of his own personality. Most of all, the book is about Taylor's inad-vertent and often harrowing metamorphosis from novice to dancer, rebel, young choreographer, star, artist, while his role among his co-workers is changing, unchoreographed, from pal and ringleader to director and pater-nal overseer of several people's souls and livelihoods.

As a literary device, he writes in an imaginary mentor/father figure, Dr. George Tacet, who has accompanied him since his lonely boyhood, as both Id and Superego to Taylor's never-very-successful straight man. Tacet is the prissy aesthete who sometimes designs costumes with too many frills on them. He's also the libidinous companion on Taylor's sexual escapades—his flowery language obscuring the names of the innocent and other em-barrassing details. Tacet can express the unpresentable and, as an artistic muse, help Taylor process his hunches and urges till they either coalesce into workable dances or pass off.

Taylor seems better able to confide in himself than in his colleagues. In addition to Tacet, he forms attachments to various animals, communes with insects, and lives with a deaf-mute, whose responses to his ideas are childlike and inspired, and never intellectual. Taylor is basically a solitary, but like many people who can't trust their own families, he grows an artificial one around him to fill most human needs. Not only does he work with his dancers every day in the studio, they tour for months every year, sharing countless lumpen meals, feigning nonchalance in flimsy vehicles, warding off injury and illness and crippling fatigue. These, not the delights of tourism, are the bonding experiences of travel for a dancer, and Taylor describes them brilliantly.

His language is as wonderful as his acerbic temperament. "Arriving in Venice, we detrain, unscrunch, and arbitrarily pick a direction that might lead us to a cheap hotel. Along the way we glimpse St. Mark's and other stagy structures through a blurry scrim of sleet. As we've heard, wintertime Venice is a closed-down carnival, laughless and spook-ridden." What they get to see on tour is the inside of theaters, mostly inadequate ones, and by the time they've coped with splintery floors, drafty dressing rooms, and lecherous stagehands, the audience has become a moot point, a virtual abstraction.

Dancers, on the other hand, are distinct and cherished quantities in Taylor's life. His first view of the giants of modern dance, at Connecticut College in 1952, leaves him awestruck but irreverent. In two sentences he captures the elusive Katherine Litz, with whom he danced as a gorilla in a 1963 Central Park duet: "It's composed mainly of masterful oops-and-woops-type catch steps which give the impression of wonderfully vague searchings and daffy aimlessness. Her hands and wrists are adding fili-grees of girlishness, and there is a delicious dose of wanton spinster here and there." Twyla Tharp joins his company and they spar affectionately. He calls her Twerp, and she makes up her own counts to his steps. Other dancers stay longer, but eventually he notices that they are always the same age while he is being stealthily overtaken by "late youth."

Almost imperceptibly, the way it happens in real life, responsibility and physical stress begin to overwhelm Taylor, and the book accelerates toward a disastrous climax—two, actually, several years apart. The first is the 1968 European tour that starts with the company beleaguered by stu-dent strikers in Paris, and ends in a suicidal bender that he describes in gruesome detail. Part two is his collapse onstage at Brooklyn Academy in 1974 after years of booze, pills, and ignoring his body's pleas for attention. Taylor considers this calamity the unofficial end of his dancing career. He quickly winds up the book with a moving and insightful analysis of the transition he had to make, from originating all his dances on his own body first, to "choreographing from a chair." I hope he thinks of this chapter as the prologue to his next book. I do.

Boston Phoenix, 22 May 1998

Every piece on the program of White Oak Dance Project last week-end at the Shubert theater seemed to have at least one other dance behind it. The company itself is a little bit fictitious, provisional. Outside of a few fast-disappearing commissioned works, the dancers and the repertory have all come from somewhere else and are trying to find a way to work for now. You can't help thinking about where they've been and how they happen to be here.

White Oak was started in 1990 to back up the great ballet star Mikhail Baryshnikov, who wanted to ease off the rigors of his native craft but not stop dancing entirely. The eight dancers do small choreographic works interspersed with his showcase solos. The company has been handsomely supported by the late Howard Gilman, and even has a resident string quartet to provide live music. This seems like a fairly standard vanity set-up, along the lines of Nureyev and Friends in the 1970s and several subsequent ballet-company spin-offs. The star draws in the audience and gets to dance some novelties, while giving work to other dancers as well. But White Oak's operating plan contradicts the idea of a star vehicle. There's no artistic director and with an admirable but wholly unrealistic modesty Baryshnikov simply lists himself alphabetically among the dancers.

There's a strange atmosphere of permanent attrition around the company. With Baryshnikov remaining at the center, the dancers seem to change all the time. At first they were all veterans of other companies, and it was a pleasure to see the mature way they interpreted the work. There was a certain amount of turnover built into this, not only because age places a strain on a dancer's ability to withstand and overcome injury. Heavy hitters like David Parsons and Mark Morris would drop in for a season or a few performances, then go on to other commitments. As the White Oak personnel shifted, so did the repertory. The company that came to Boston this time was almost entirely new to me, with Jamie Bishton and Ruthlyn Salomons, I think, the longest-established members. The dancers seemed younger and perhaps hadn't worked together very long, although their biographies in the program didn't always say when the individual came on board.

I felt the lack of ensemble most strongly in Kraig Patterson's *Y*, set to the first three movements of the Debussy String Quartet. Patterson choreographs in the note-for-note manner of Mark Morris, with whom he dances.

Wearing impeccable gray velvet and satin clothes by Santo Loquasto, the five dancers grouped and regrouped, seemingly with no other intention but to fill the stage in varied ways. They gestured severely, kept time with the jittering violins, formed and dissolved partnerships. There seemed to be no center to the dance, except for a tilted, two-foot silver disc that was planted center stage. This was usually ignored by the dancers, but sometimes they would hover over it, as if to warm themselves. Toward the end, they each crossed over it, ritualistically stepping on it as they went. But there was never any real clue as to its meaning.

The shadow dance in *Y* was a version done by Kraig Patterson's own dancers, who apparently created a sense of a family or a community through the way they connected the movements and worked with each other. I only know about this by hearsay, but it would make more sense than the impersonal, almost didactic way White Oak conveyed the piece.

Paul Taylor's *Profiles* is a solid addition to the repertory, bearing the mark of a master who's completely confident of his ability to swim way out beyond the breakwater and take the audience with him. *Profiles* is even more impersonal than *Y*, but its very oddity disarms us; we don't look for family or friendliness, let alone love in the usual expressive sense.

As the string quartet plays Jan Radzynski's minimalist score—a sonorous beehive, with the instruments tacking and buzzing close in around one central tone—two couples shuffle across the space, their feet going one way, their torsos twisted flat. Knees bent, ankles flexed, arms sharply hooked, fingers curled down to the first knuckle, they seem locked into immobility. Yet they're able to yank their limbs different ways to change their shape and direction. They can jump in the air, mount each other's chest or shoulders, carry each other, and even almost embrace. Being so straitjacketed, they seem unusually intense, even touching, in their struggles to connect.

Most people in the audience probably have no idea that *Profiles* is a choreographic sketch for Paul Taylor's pop-art version of *Le Sacre du Printemps*. It had its premiere in 1979, a season before the comic-strip characters, the bizarre, interwoven double plotline, and the Stravinsky two-piano score came together in that amazing work. What predominates in the severely two-dimensional *Profiles* is the ferocious inventiveness that made *Le Sacre* possible.

Opening night at the Shubert, the central attraction was Baryshnikov's solo appearance—there's one on every program. I guess by now the White Oak audience isn't expecting him to do Albrecht from *Giselle*. There's been plenty of hype about his age (fifty), and his search for challenging material to keep him dancing, and the Christopher Janney/Sara Rudner piece *Heart-Beat:mb* that's oh so chic in a nation of avid hypochondriacs.

The idea is that the dancer is hooked up to an electronic monitor that plays his heartbeat through a sound system for all to hear. Janney made the piece for Rudner in 1983, and others have performed it since then. Rather than set choreography, it's a tightly structured improvisation; the dancer really creates the piece each time. According to Rudner, Baryshnikov's is the first "theatrical" version. When it was created, the downtown dancers in New York were beginning to move out of the lofts and were adding smart production elements to their low-budget experiments. Rudner says *Heart-Beat* was one of the most important pieces in her career, and she hopes to perform it again herself in an upcoming season. In the '80s, a thing like a heart monitor would have been part of a serious exploration of movement, not a gimmick.

Well, if anyone can keep the audience's sensationalistic instincts at bay, Baryshnikov can. He was shirtless, so you could see the electrodes taped to his chest, and he looked fit but not hunky the way male dancers do nowadays. He looked like a middle-aged guy going for a checkup. He put himself through the movement equivalent of a doctor's inventory—breathe, now rotate your arms, now start circling the room, now hang over and rest. The monitor thumped reassuringly. When he raised his left arm or tilted so his chest collapsed in a certain way, the monitor rumbled like rocks tumbling into a cave.

As he increased his activity, the heartsound would speed up, then it would slow down again as he gave himself a breather. But it stayed remarkably regular, so regular that he began to use it as a rhythmic accompaniment, dancing little syncopations and ornaments on it as he perambulated. What an idea. Later on, the string quartet played Samuel Barber's familiar Adagio for Strings, and Baryshnikov worked up to some strenuous leaps and jumps that climaxed just as the music did. The monitor was racing but still steady.

Jamie Bishton did a long solo to begin the last piece, Neil Greenberg's *Tchaikovsky Dance*, and it looked lush and romantic after the stringencies of the rest of the program. There was plenty of subtext to this one too. Greenberg danced for years with Merce Cunningham, and has absorbed the Cunningham / John Cage aesthetic. Dancers came and went, did long or short phrases, faced in different directions sometimes and worked in planned ensembles sometimes. At no particular time, the musicians would break into the grandiose finale of some Tchaikovsky quartet.

Then there'd be silence. Once in a while a supertitle would appear on the backdrop, telling us the name of the dancer we were watching, or giving us a bit of personal information. "Jamie was the youngest dancer when he joined the company." "Now he's the oldest (except for Misha)." Halfway through the dance, Baryshnikov and Ruthlyn Salomons entered on opposite sides of the stage. They were out of town until this point in the choreographing, the supertitle told us.

Greenberg's dance reminded me of the playful years of the Cunningham company, when Cage was alive and it was a matter of principle that you let accidents become part of the dance, let the dance take in everybody in their own best ways. And though Baryshnikov has plenty of years to go yet, he provided the kind of sober, attentive presence in the dance that Cunningham projects now—the gentlemanly, paternal desire to blend in with the company, and the knowledge that when he's on stage the audience doesn't see anyone else.

 PLAIN FOLKS' TALES

Boston Phoenix, 5 March 1999

After all this time, Mark Morris still seems to be choreographing anti-ballets. His first adventures in the big time, around 1980, shocked and thrilled people because they had the ambition and theatrical skill of the high-art stage but not the elitist pretensions. Thoroughly musical and meticulously designed, these works nevertheless denied all expectations of approved virtuosity, beauty, and sex. Morris is adored by people who never go to ballet or any other dance performance, and by some of the most discriminating ballet critics. Notwithstanding the success that's allowed him to build a company of eighteen dancers and perform with live music to sellout audiences, Morris subverts the tradition every chance he gets. In his four performances last weekend, his oppositional tactics were on display, and the audience at the Wang Theater hardly noticed them.

Resisting the understandable tendency to harden one's experiments into a style or technique, Morris uses movement from a Fibber McGee closet filled with the world's dance. Instead of an invented vocabulary of steps, what Morris's dancers share is an idea about dancing: a naturalistic way of carrying themselves through whatever steps they're performing. The first thing you might notice is that the legs aren't usually turned out like a ballet dancer's but work in parallel like a skier's or an ordinary person's. Their feet are often flexed, seldom deliberately stretched to a refined point, and they don't try to gain a regal, classical look by elongating and opening their bodies.

With this more or less pedestrian baseline, they can look clunky rather than graceful when they do balletic leaps and turns. We identify with their efforts to overcome inertia, to surpass the limitations of gravity. I don't think they really work any harder than ballet dancers, but they don't have that readiness to start up in their stance. The thing that makes them subversive is that they *mean* to look casual, even indolent. They want us to think this could be just as good a state to dance in as any.

The matter-of-fact approach governs much of Morris's creative decision-making. He picks music for variety and danceability, not for its familiarity to Western ears. He lists dancers alphabetically in the dance credits, even when one of them is the superstar Mikhail Baryshnikov. For the Boston performances, renowned cellist Yo-Yo Ma performed in his 1997 collaboration with Morris, *Falling Down Stairs*, a part of Ma's *Inspired by Bach* film project, but he also played for the other two Morris works on the program. The participants in any Mark Morris enterprise seem to be comrades, like those guys who sit in front of the firehouse and tell stories they all know, trade gossip, help each other solve their problems.

I was thinking about this analogy as a way to explain why, even though each dance is extremely formal and seemingly without expressive coding, somewhere in the middle I often get ideas about narrative. Not a specific story with two or three main characters and their relatives and rejected boyfriends. Nothing about enlisting in the army or getting caught in a storm or celebrating a successful harvest. There aren't even expectant beginnings or neat resolutions. But notions about what these folks are doing together seem to float up in the course of the choreographic conversation and then break off.

In *Falling Down Stairs*, Yo-Yo Ma sits at the side of the stage playing Bach's third suite for unaccompanied cello, and in a flash at the beginning we see a group of dancers on a set of stairs. Almost immediately they cascade down the stairs and fall, all spread out along the floor, except for one person who stays at the top of the stairs. During the rest of the dance the group now and then rushes the stairs and falls back, leaving someone on top. It's like a game of King of the Hill that keeps being interrupted and resumed, with the rules changing slightly each time.

One woman, having almost attained the summit, swan dives off the side into the arms of two waiting rivals. Competition for control of the stairs isn't what the dance is about, it's just an anecdote. They drop this idea and use the stairs as a grandstand; nine people climb up and go through a sequence of rhythmic but cryptic gestures together while the other six people sit on the floor below them. Trading roles, the ones on the stairs sit and the other group plays a game for them. They trade again, only this time the group on the stairs, instead of standing in a diamond shape, make three straight rows. Their gesture pattern is the same but it looks different in this formation.

In *The Argument*, which was having its world premiere in Boston, three couples danced to Robert Schumann's Five Pieces in Folk Style. From Schumann's descriptive subtitles for his not-exactly-authentic folk dances, the composer must have been working in a parodistic mode, or at least a playful one. You could see Morris going for the same thing when Baryshnikov and Marjorie Folkman grabbed and glared at each other, Morris and Tina Fehlandt slowly suppressed the music's sentimentality, and Shawn Gannon and Ruth Davidson mooched up close together but threw slashing punches in opposite directions, all, of course, matched to Schumann's romantic rhythms. But it was in Morris's flamboyant pseudo-mazurka that the joke played best, because it was so fully danced. What's a mazurka, the portly and scraggly Morris seemed to be saying, if you don't throw yourself into it?

Yo-Yo Ma, with Ethan Iverson at the piano, leaned into the dance as if nothing but the cello prevented him from leaping to his feet. Gannon and the women heated up after Morris's outburst of bravura, but Baryshnikov seemed withdrawn and tight, a black-clad apache dancer caught in the wrong century or the wrong nightclub. The whole piece was crammed with detail, and I couldn't see all of it, or hear all the stories, at one view. Perhaps the dancers were testing out the gradations between light comedy, mockery, and burlesque.

The Argument represented the furthest I've seen Morris go in fragmenting his choreographic material. He seemed determined not to let the dance get so deep into any phrase material that it became predictable. Even the costumes—the women's black velvet cocktail dresses, the shirts and pants for Morris and Gannon, and Baryshnikov's turtleneck—clashed stylistically with each other while undercutting the Mittel-Europa rrrrump-pa-pa feeling of the music.

Rhymes with Silver also tumbled together styles and references, but made a more consistent blend of them. This piece, to a long, lush score for piano, percussion, and strings that Morris commissioned from the West Coast master experimentalist Lou Harrison, depends on exotica but plays it down. The sixteen dancers, identically dressed in black silky pants and dark green jerseys, walked sideways on their heels like Cambodian dancers, with bent knees and wide, scooping gestures. They slid back and forth in a grapevine step, in groups of three with pinkies linked. They did a kind of quadrille, where four new people replaced the original group without stopping the dance. To a cakewalk rhythm in two or three different keys, they paired up in a sort of maxixe, one partner behind the other, both of them sliding their legs forward and leaning their torsos back. They line-danced off in a lurching side-step. They pitched themselves into flat, Egyptian zigzag shapes. Guilleromo Resto dithered nonstop around a stationary Kraig Patterson for a long time, but finally sank to his knees and crawled off. At one point, a woman and a man posed like Hindu deities in a cosmic Oriental dance by Ruth St. Denis and Ted Shawn.

The dance seemed as if it would never run out of motifs and new ways to design them, but finally the groups and duets dissipated in a mass crossing of the stage. Instead of linking with any others, the dancers now spun and gestured in their own ecstatic orbits, perhaps fighting off and falling into trancelike states.

The apparent randomness of this, the abandonment of visual coherence, is rare in Mark Morris's work. I can't think of anything that rhymes with silver. Maybe rhyming or dancing with others is unimportant in the momentary attainment of individual bliss.

RECLAIMING THE ORDINARY

Boston Phoenix, 25 May 2001

Mikhail Baryshnikov and White Oak Dance Project deserve accolades for dreaming up PASTForward, an astute and uncondescending look at how the seeds planted in the 1960s continue to forest our dance landscape. Dancers are unaccountably nervous about acknowledging their history, let alone performing it. Basing a whole evening on work that attacked the conventions of dance and dance production is courageous now, maybe even quixotic.

It's as awkward to define the scope of PASTForward as it is to pin down its inspiration, the Judson Dance Theater. Even Judson's chroniclers don't quite agree on who belonged to it or exactly when it functioned. The initial workshops and performances took place in New York at the Merce Cunningham studio and the Judson Memorial Church between 1961 and 1964. But conceptually, "Judson" is a frame of mind that stretches from John Cage, through the first Judson dancers and their subsequent exploits, to attitudes about choreographing and performing right now. Just last Monday, for instance, Boston dancer Marjorie Morgan and three colleagues presented an evening of videos, performance, and discussion based on the structured improvisation work of Deborah Hay, who's still teaching, writing, and choreographing new dance in Austin, Texas.

Hay was one of the original Judson dance makers on the White Oak programs, presented at the Shubert Theater over the weekend by the Celebrity Series. The others were Steve Paxton, Lucinda Childs, Trisha Brown, Simone Forti, Yvonne Rainer, and David Gordon. That's a particular cluster of friends and concerns, not the whole enchilada, but I was happy to have even part of the history so interestingly and persuasively told.

With Baryshnikov as artistic director and David Gordon as writer/director, the show comprised Charles Atlas's documentary film of archival performances and talk, reconstructed early Judson dances and related works made as recently as 2000, and two pieces and two improvisations performed by a large group of local volunteers. What came across most strongly about the Judson aesthetic was the way it focused attention on pedestrian movement. Ordinary bodies, ordinary activity were put on display where they'd never been meant to go, with the intention of opening our eyes to the rich variety and even theatricality all around us.

Steve Paxton's *Satisfyin' Lover* (1967) was the most extreme example of this on the program. Approximately fifty people—men, women, and youngsters including a little girl and a toddler—walk across the space. That's all. Up to forty-two (or eighty-four) performers in six groups work to a score specifying the number of steps each performer takes, when they enter, and the exact timing of pauses and exits. There are a couple of indeterminate instructions, like "falling gradually behind." One or two people are to sit for a certain number of seconds in one of three chairs. The piece lasted six minutes.

You might not think this would be very interesting, but once you see what the pattern is, you realize that the stage is full of differences. Not just of gender, age, and clothing styles, but of body types and the way people hold themselves and focus ahead, and the way they take a step and transfer their weight, and whether their arms swing or their shoulders are stiff, and if they look pleased or worried or eager or calm.

Judson made the acceptable dance vocabulary immensely bigger by reducing the stimulus: with almost nothing to look at, there's suddenly so much more. Anyone could be a performer in this kind of work. Hot disputes raged at the time, of course, whether this was dance or not. Paxton probably didn't care what you called it, but David Gordon got to the crux of the matter in 1979 with *The Matter*. Reducing the choreography even further, to a simple walking lineup. Gordon flagrantly set the whole procession to the music from the opening scene of the Kingdom of the Shades from *La Bayadère*. Ballet is in the eye of the beholder.

In the White Oak performance of *The Matter*, while the volunteers slowly streamed across the front of the stage, you could glimpse Baryshnikov briskly carrying big objects into the space behind them, and Keith Sabado way upstage, frozen in the act of pushing a broom around. By the end, Baryshnikov had built a big sculpture out of boxes and backstage bric-a-brac. Just as the procession and the music ended, the volunteers swarmed back and took all the objects off into the wings with them, leaving the space swept clean.

Sabado's broom dance was one of many pieces where performers interrupted a sequence of movement in freeze-frame, to give the audience time to study what would ordinarily be overlooked in the flow of events. In Paxton's *Flat* (1964), Baryshnikov paced in a circle, sat in a chair, methodically removed his jacket, shirt, pants, shoes, and socks, and put them on again, stopping repeatedly in midmotion without losing his intensity.

Although intensity is just as interesting to concentrate on as anything else a performer does, this was one attribute the Judson dancers stayed away from. They cultivated a kind of indifference—call it objectivity, disengagement, alienation. The kind of attitude that invites the audience's adoration, together with the evidence of skill imprinted on a dancer's body, were to be resisted if dance had any hope of being reformed.

There were plenty of other walking dances and even standing-still or lying-down dances in the '60s and '70s, but the Judson aesthetic often cloaked its didacticism in fun and theatricality. What it rejected for the longest time was dance technique. But there were alternatives. You could borrow movement from sports, movies, fashion shows, animals. You could set up a simple task that would require the performers' own solutions, like Simone Forti's *Scramble* (1970), where several of the volunteers crowded together in the space of an elevator but had to keep moving in what Forti calls "a steady state activity."

Naturally, an improvisational piece like *Scramble*, or Forti's *Huddle* (1961), where one person at a time climbed over the collective shape of eight or ten other people, would be different every time it was performed. In 1966 Yvonne Rainer made up a sequence of nondance but not simple movements that were always performed in the same order. This was *Trio A*, which became almost the trademark dance of the Judson era. *Trio A* was meant to be done by modern dancers, ballet dancers, nondancers, fat dancers, pregnant dancers, people who were learning it, people who had forgotten it, sometimes two or three doing it at the same time.

For White Oak, Rainer set three variations: *Trio A Backwards*, for Rosalynde LeBlanc and Emmanuèle Phuon, who made it a canon because they worked at different speeds; *Trio A Facing*, for Raquel Aedo, with Michael Lomeka running around simply trying to keep the front of his body lined up with hers; and *Trio A Forwards*, for those four plus Emily Coates and Keith Sabado, all together but with small individual interpretations.

Although *Trio A* was not improvised, Rainer worked in both set and indeterminate formats. She liked improbable but suggestive props, like pillows and mattresses, and talking that was unrelated to the moving. In White Oak's version of *Talking Solo* (1963) Lomeka danced while reciting Vladimir Nabokov's description of how butterflies are born. LeBlanc did a variation of his dance and didn't talk.

For others in the Judson group, unexpected juxtapositioning of movement with props, words, music, and media brought forth acres of absurdist and dada entertainment. Emily Coates performed Lucinda Childs's *Carnation* (1964), a deadpan appropriation of mismatched objects that began with putting a lettuce dryer upside down on her head. Live video projected onto the backdrop made her obsessive manipulation of sponges and hair curlers visible to the audience as she sat at a table.

Maybe any group of artists working closely as the Judson dancers did will come up with themes in common, and folding chairs, John Philip Sousa, and the bizarre implications of clothing made frequent appearances on the White Oak program. Trisha Brown's *Homemade* (1965) even converted an eight-millimeter projector into a kind of backpack, which Baryshnikov toted around as he did a duet with himself. Brown made some phenomenal experiments with perception, and in *Homemade*, a film of the same dance becomes a crazily tilting, disappearing partner as Baryshnikov's back-projected image dances off the walls.

PASTForward offered much more to think about, but it still didn't exhaust the provocations and revelations of Judson. What I missed most was a feeling of physicality and risk. White Oak moved with the cool intentionality of cats, like all contemporary dancers, but the Judson ethic fostered a different kind of attentiveness to the body. We might have glimpsed that if they'd shown Trisha Brown's *Leaning Duets* or *Falling Duets* for instance, where people leaned and fell, and looked sensual, beautiful, human.

When Judson reduced performers to working with the uninscribed body, wonderful things could happen. Lucinda Childs's high-energy, post-minimal *Concerto* (1993) closed the White Oak program. At first the dancers looked familiar, leaping, turning, and crisscrossing the space nonstop. But after nine minutes, they tired. Their precision and their invincibility deteriorated. They looked more real. The audience went wild.

POMO RETRO RITE

Hudson Review, Spring 2008

If you were in New York in 2007, you could have seen at least half a dozen different dance versions of *The Rite of Spring* (*Le Sacre du Printemps*). Serge Diaghilev's Ballets Russes premiered the original ballet, with choreography by Vaslav Nijinsky and music by Igor Stravinsky, at the Théâtre des Champs-Elysées in Paris on 29 May 1913, to a volatile audience of aristocrats and aesthetes. After less than ten performances it disappeared, never to be seen again. Stravinsky's score outlived the scandal, consolidating its initial shock into canonical fame, but the ballet itself dissolved into myth. Its loss—and its lurid reputation—have proved an irresistible challenge to choreographers, reconstructors, and historians ever since Léonide Massine remounted the music for Diaghilev in 1920. The composer himself reinforced the myth by issuing contradictory opinions of those first two stagings.

It was the myth, not the ballet, that Yvonne Rainer set out to examine in *RoS Indexical*, commissioned by Performa '07. Rainer's *Rite*, shown twice in November at the Hudson Theater, was a many-layered project that asked the question, what can we know about a legendary dance if it exists only as legend? Rainer's oddly challenging work led me to a universe of *Sacre* far more expansive than the creators could have imagined, but the ballet remained an elusive artifact. Rainer not only destabilized the notion of *The Rite of Spring* as an iconic achievement in dance history; she allowed us to see that a work may live on in greatly altered form, and that its status can actually get validated as it detaches itself from a deceptively permanent identity.

The first thing I thought as *RoS Indexical* began was how really retro it looked. Four women (Emily Coates, Sally Silvers, Patricia Hoffbauer, and Pat Catterson) wandered out, dressed in motley practice clothes, and sat at a small table. Facing each other chattily like lunch companions, they began humming under their breath, as if they were trying to remember a tune, to get it back. On tape, the overture to *Le Sacre du Printemps* was playing. The

RoS Indexical (Rainer). rehearsal. Pat Catterson, Emily Coates, Patricia Hoffbauer, Sally Silvers. Photo © Paula Court, courtesy of Performa.

friends caught bits of its phrases, lost track, agreed on wispy melodic threads, much as Stravinsky's "Introduction" does. They gradually discovered a pulse that cohered into an irregular rhythm, anticipating the barbaric meters of Stravinsky's opening scene, "Auguries of Spring."

But the women seemed oblivious of the urgency and strangeness of the music. Instead, with a fumbly, funny but earnest plainness, a calculated spontaneity, they were reconstituting another lost icon, the signature performing style of the postmodern dance generation. I thought of Yvonne Rainer's low-key but suggestive pedestrian dances of the '60s, and of the improvisational group the Grand Union, which she founded in 1970. By the end of the '70s Rainer had left dance and was making feminist films, fractured, depersonalized narratives of resistance and crisis. Now here was Rainer, choreographing again, retrieving the offhandedness, revisiting the ambivalence about the power games inherent in performing that had propelled a generation of dance revolutionaries. Today's dance avant-garde, if there is one, has gotten over the '60s. New dancers now use the tools of postmodernism—nonlinearity, random mixtures of styles and stimuli, infringement of mainstream values—but they've reclaimed the glamour and physical thrills that were scorned by the postmodernists. Their politics are easier.

Like other choreographic appropriations of the *Rite*, *RoS Indexical* took Stravinsky's music as a text. But rather than adopting a straight-up orchestral accompaniment, Rainer set her dance over the soundtrack of a 2006 BBC feature film, *Riot at the Rite*, directed by Andy Wilson. She eliminated the film's visual image. *Riot at the Rite* was a docudrama about the making of *Le Sacre*, with the last half hour devoted to the ballet's chaotic first performance. As of this writing, *Riot at the Rite* hasn't been released on DVD, but the "Premiere" section could be seen in four parts on YouTube. With the music fading in and out under catcalls, arguments, shrieks of outrage and approval, the film bumps back and forth between a tumultuous audience; an anxious Nijinsky, Diaghilev, and backstage entourage; and dancers of the Finnish National Ballet performing the dance as reconstructed by Millicent Hodson. Well-known English actors are cast as rich patrons, journalists, painters, and ballet notables. Hodson herself can be glimpsed scribbling on a handheld sketchpad as the artist Valentine Gross. Gross's drawings were a major source for Hodson in recovering the *Sacre*'s movement.

Hodson's prodigious research culminated in a full revival, produced in 1987 by the Joffrey Ballet. With backdrops and costumes reproduced by art historian Kenneth Archer from the designs of Nicholas Roerich, the reconstruction was probably the closest thing we'll see to Nijinsky's original. Still controversial, it's been hailed as a miracle by some critics and scholars, dismissed by others as inauthentic. By the time *Riot at the Rite* was filmed, Hodson and Archer had set this version on ten ballet companies in Europe, the United States, and Japan. They were called in to work as consultants on the film from the outset, but the producers' goal of a good story sometimes snagged against Hodson's scrupulous notions of verité. She and Archer published an extended documentation of their involvement with the film in the British publication *Ballet* (February 2006). Tactfully, they didn't say whether they objected to the fact that the ballet surfaced only in brief clips, intercut with the audience's rude response. The complete reconstruction was filmed for Dance in America in 1989, but the very fact that *Riot at the Rite* sacrificed the complete ballet suited the designs of Yvonne Rainer.

RoS Indexical was a palimpsest of absence and recall. Not only did it evoke the innocence and determined iconoclasm of the '60s counterculture, it referred us to the *Rite of Spring* as a potent but forever occluded source of energy. As soon as the music on the TV soundtrack swooped into the eerie cadence that signals curtain-up, Rainer's quartet of women left the table and clustered together facing each other. On the erratic accents of the music they began the stamping, gesturing dance of Nijinsky/Hodson's choreography. Reconstructing the reconstruction, they tapped into the dance that appeared on the invisible film.

I recognized chunks of the choreography in their performance, but as I studied a rehearsal film provided to me by the Performa office, I realized how substantial Rainer's borrowings were, and how they were very deliberately matched to the music and then just as deliberately separated from it. My hunch is that these excerpts were precisely those you could have seen on the film, downsized for four dancers. When the film editors cut away, the *RoS* dancers abruptly left off doing Nijinsky and had to fill in for the missing stage footage. So Rainer's dance is a partial recovery of the BBC's partial portrayal of *Le Sacre*. She filled in the gaps with her own variations on Nijinsky, and with other things. Sometimes the women seemed to ad lib in Grand Union style, using other movement remembered from other movies, or that might have randomly come into their heads. There are other episodes prompted by Stravinsky and Nijinsky/Hodson. During the "Spring Rounds" section, the ritual groups of young men and women throw their upper bodies forward to touch the earth. The Rainer women sit on an overstuffed sofa and double over, as if stretching tense backs or recovering from exertion, on the same music as the originally choreographed foldovers.

There was even an abduction, though nothing like the implied rape scene of Nijinsky's overheated tribal celebrants. It happened during Stravinsky's musical entr'acte. Silvers, Coates, Hoffbauer, and Catterson slumped on the sofa for a minute, then took off their sneakers and encased their feet in Kleenex boxes. They were trying to dance in this extraordinary footwear when a mob of people, including a man and a woman in replicas of Roerich's Russian peasant costumes, rushed up to the stage from the audience, yelling and swarming around them. They picked up Coates and carried her offstage.

One of the things that makes any recovery of *Le Sacre du Printemps* problematic is that it isn't a conventional narrative. Its action is ritualistic, defamiliarized. To observe the return of the sun and ensure its own survival, an ancient tribe enacts certain prescribed dances, games, and commemorations. Finally, it yields up one of its maidens; she dances herself to death, symbolically uniting with the sun in exchange for the renewal of life, the continuation of the tribe. Written notations and descriptions tell us that there were mystic lines, circles, acts of devotion, but nothing spells out exactly how Nijinsky translated these formulas into dancing. For her massive research, Millicent Hodson scoured eyewitness accounts, annotated scores left by Stravinsky and by Nijinsky's assistant Marie Rambert. She looked at drawings and photographs, interviewed survivors, pieced together the enormous canvas that was the original ballet. She also had to exercise a fine judgment, sifting out feverish partisanship, literary license, and imperfect recollections, interpreting poetic images, learning how to move archaic shapes and raucous rhythms, establishing floor patterns for some forty dancers in counterpointed groups. Probably the most reliable and incisive contemporary observer was the critic Jacques Rivière, writing in *La Nouvelle Revue Française*, but even he speaks in aesthetic terms, not graphic ones. The further away from 1913 you get, the less dependable people's memories are, the more the writer is subject to distortion and favoritism. In at least two editions of George Balanchine and Francis Mason's popular *Stories of the Great Ballets*,[7] we get a two-page synopsis of what may be a *Rite of Spring* choreographed in 1962 by Kenneth MacMillan. It differs significantly from the most dependable accounts of Nijinsky's work in the distribution of the personnel, their actions, and the sequence of actions.

The ballet described by Mason and Balanchine interprets the music romantically and adapts the scenario to feature the male-female pairings. In the original, the men's and women's groups were strictly segregated except for brief instances when couples joined in contact during the first act. The later ballet sounds like a modern mating dance instead of a primal invocation of fertility. These notions are similar but not identical. Choreographers ever since have focused on the sexual implications of the *Sacre*. Pina Bausch staged it in 1975 as all-out sex war, with the Chosen One as a battered, martyred victim. Maurice Béjart's 1959 version converted the "Danse Sacrale" into a duet: the men and women of his tribe choose one couple to mate and thus incite a mass orgy. Béjart's 1960 *Bolero* might be seen as an even more suggestive interpretation of Nijinsky's sacrificial dance. A woman undulates on a platform surrounded by lecherous males. This piece was performed in the United States by Béjart's Ballet of the Twentieth Century with a female sex-object, and later with an all-male cast.

These titillating precedents linger on in the 2001 version by Angelin Preljocaj. His "Danse Sacrale" begins as one woman is stripped by the other men and women. Dancing stark naked as they watch, she's brutally groped, lifted, and thrown around, then abandoned. (YouTube X-rated one version of this.) Preljocaj combines Bausch's violent love-pursuit with Béjart's voyeurism, cycling ballet's old equation of sex = death = dancing into the current craze for physically daring duets. In a weird defense of what is on one level an artistic peep show, Preljocaj and dancers in his company have insisted that this *Sacre* is a feminist statement.

Prior to the *Sacre*, Diaghilev's audience had been shocked, then dazzled, by the exotic Fokine/Léon Bakst ballets—*Firebird*, *Schéhérazade*, *Narcisse*—and Nijinsky's sensual *l'Après-midi d'un Faune*. Confronted with the *Sacre*, they were jolted again. It must have been the ballet's refusal of eroticism, as much as Stravinsky's orchestral clangor and broken rhythms, that caused the riot. Far from exploiting sex, *Le Sacre du Printemps* was a venture in dance abstraction. Jacques Rivière begins his famous essay with this remarkable perception: "The great innovation of *Le Sacre du Printemps* is the absence of all 'trimmings.' Here is a work that is absolutely pure. Cold and harsh, if you will, but without any glaze to mar its inherent brilliance, without any artifices to rearrange or distort its contours."[8] Rivière is talking about a theater work that insists on drawing attention to the body but deprives the viewer of anything that sentimentalizes or sexualizes it. Nijinsky's movement was disconnected, asymmetrical, antihistrionic, presenting the viewer with "a thousand complex and mysterious objects that need only to be looked at." Rivière finds himself uneasy, even depressed, despite his appreciation of this achievement. He seems overpowered by the prehuman forces it evokes, the senseless march of evolution, "the terrifying labor of the cells."

Abstraction in dance probably causes the viewer more anxiety than it does in painting. The loss of the figurative is harder to come to terms with when the figure is so palpable before us, insisting on its own effacement or transfiguration. Jacques Rivière speaks of Nijinsky's dancers as severe and centered, containing movement inside the body rather than letting it flow out vaguely, as he thought they did in Fokine's choreography. Any latent eroticism in the *Sacre*'s theme was contradicted by these totemic figures. The dance was impersonal, anti-illusionistic, and in the end pitiless, ageless, and amoral. In its resistance to flattery and romance, its downplaying of individual glamour, and its denial of the audience's expectations of beauty, *Le Sacre* anticipated the postmodern dance of half a century later.

A whole line of dispassionate contemporary renderings of the music have paralleled the flagrant ones, from Molissa Fenley's minimalistic solo marathon (*State of Darkness*, 1988) to *RoS Indexical*. In November Performa 07 produced another *Rite of Spring* inspired by a musical performance of the work, Xavier Le Roy's *Le Sacre du Printemps*. Where Rainer engaged the music and the dance by minimizing them, Le Roy created an additive piece. He learned the movements of Simon Rattle conducting the Berlin Philharmonic Orchestra in a videotaped performance of the *Sacre*, then presented them as a choreographed solo. Dancers learn by imitating their choreographers and teachers. Who was to say Le Roy's performance wasn't a dance? For his accompaniment, he'd placed speakers under the audiences' seats, each playing an electronically separated section of the orchestra. I didn't get to see this piece, but presumably you'd experience being in the orchestra yourself, with Le Roy cuing and prodding you as he simulated the conductor's hyperphysical performance.

One of the postmodern dancers' primary strategies for reform was to declare that anyone could be a dancer. Away with the polish, the star persona, the exclusivity of technique and stage effects. Yvonne Rainer's 1966 *Trio A* is a five-minute paradigm of this democratizing principle. The performer, essentially remaining in place, executes a series of unrelated moves, none of them pantomimic or dancerly, but all of them precisely choreographed and requiring some skill. The performance must be continuous but without emphasis or special accents, without smiles, twinkles, or any other sign that would arouse the spectator's feelings. Rainer filmed the dance in 1978, taking particular care to avoid meeting the eye of the camera that was standing in for an audience. *Trio A* could be done by any type of professional dancer or civilian, and in *RoS Indexical*, it didn't look at all out of place as the four women did a few of its phrases huddled together in a *Sacre*-like grouping. In some bizarre leap of imagination, I can almost see *Trio A* as a Danse Sacrale for our times.

The postmodern agenda dissipated, and dancing returned to its highly specialized, glamorous ways. But the anyone-can-dance idea persists. Besides giving dancers like Xavier Le Roy a set of nontechnical options, it has filtered out into pageantry and community events. In a highly visible form of outreach, *Le Sacre du Printemps* made still another appearance in New York in November, when Simon Rattle, the Berlin Philharmonic Orchestra, and choreographer Royston Maldoom restaged their 2003 Rite of Spring Project for the Berlin in Lights Festival. Since 1980, when he began choreographing for teenagers and laypersons, Royston Maldoom has developed community dance projects in Britain, Europe, and Africa, often working with socially challenged populations like street gangs and prison inmates. More than a hundred New York public school students were enlisted to learn Maldoom's choreography and to make their own musical variations on Stravinsky. In a three-disc documentary of the original project released as "Rhythm Is It!" Maldoom exhorts a studio full of German teenagers. "Don't think we're just doing dancing. You can change your life in a dance class!"

Yvonne Rainer envisions no such transformation. In the second act, the four women dance quite strenuously, recovering parts of the ritual dances that lead up to the accidental selection of the Chosen Maiden. Sally Silvers trips twice as they weave in and out of their pattern. But instead of becoming a sacrificial victim, she rejoins the other women, to perform zany gestural solo turns and more remnants of the *Sacre* group work. The sofa where they've retreated more than once to rest or kill time becomes the site for some feminist parody. During one of the musical buildups, they form a line behind the sofa, then one by one they slither down over its arm into unmistakable Odalisque poses. They return to their gesturing solos, but as the music signals the expiration of the Chosen Maiden and the end of the ballet, Emily Coates does a sudden swan dive onto the sofa. She has literally overturned the posture in which painters like Manet fixed their models as objects of desire.

Coates's action also reminds me that another sofa played a prominent part in Diaghilev's next great transgressive ballet, *Les Biches* (1924) by Bronislava Nijinska. The sister of Nijinsky had returned to Russia after *Le Sacre du Printemps* and worked there for nearly a decade, alongside the constructivists and theater experimenters of the pre-Stalin period. When she returned to the Ballets Russes in 1923 she had become an innovative choreographer, applying modernist ideas to the classical ballet vocabulary. *Les Biches*, set in a sophisticated house party in the south of France, proposes unconventional gender relationships including a lesbian duet. It isn't the only Nijinska ballet that subverts traditional gender designations.

Despite its '70s look of disaffection and randomness, *RoS Indexical* makes me think about how long-term change happens, how the triggers get lost while the remnants get fixed onto film and other substitutes for firsthand experience. Rainer could have chosen any pantomimic movements for her gestural solos; her models were the extremists, Sarah Bernhardt, Groucho Marx, Robin Williams. She could have used anything as a prop—the sofa could have been four motorcycles or a mattress. In identifying with *Les Biches* at the climax, rather than Nijinsky's depersonalized sacrificial victim, Yvonne Rainer denies us the pleasure of a woman dancing herself to death, and rewrites the history of *Le Sacre du Printemps* yet another time.

Notes

CHAPTER 1: LEGENDS

1. Cyril W. Beaumont, *Complete Book of Ballets*. New York: G. P. Putnam & Sons, 1938, 651.
2. Horst Koegler, ed. *Concise Oxford Dictionary of Ballet*. London: Oxford University Press, 1977, 428.
3. See Millicent Hodson, *Nijinsky's Crime against Grace*. Stuyvesant, N.Y.: Pendragon Press, 1996. Hodson and Archer have published and lectured extensively on their Nijinsky research.
4. For the most recent, see Joan Acocella, "The Lost Nijinsky," *New Yorker*, 7 May 2001, 94–97.
5. Their research and an account of this production is the subject of "A Revival of Nijinsky's Original L'après-Midi d'un Faune," ed. Jill Beck. *Choreography and Dance*, Vol. 1, Part 3. London: Harwood Academic Publishers, 1991.
6. Igor Stravinsky, *An Autobiography*. New York: W. W. Norton, 1936, 46–52.
7. "Footnotes in the Sands of Time," *New Yorker*, 23 Nov. 1987, 141–148.
8. "Joffrey's Stupendous 'Sacre,'" *Washington Post*, 2 Oct. 1987.
9. "Joffrey Stages Nijinsky's 'Sacre du Primtemps,'" *Los Angeles Times*, 2 Oct. 1987.
10. "Nijinsky's 'Rite,' 1988: Scholarship and Theater," *International Herald Tribune*, 5–6 March 1988.
11. Reprinted as *Four Centuries of Ballet: Fifty Masterworks*, New York: Dover, 1984.
12. Lincoln Kirstein, *Nijinsky Dancing*. New York: Knopf, 1975, 42.
13. Lynn Garafola, *Diaghilev's Ballets Russes*. New York: Oxford University Press, 1989, 50–51.
14. "Lady Ottoline describes in her journals how she came out one day into Bedford Square with Bertrand Russell, Nijinsky, and Léon Bakst; they saw Duncan Grant and other lithe young men playing tennis in the Square. 'Quel décor!' murmurs Bakst . . . Nijinsky echoes him." Leon Edel, *Bloomsbury—A House of Lions*. New York: Avon Books, 1980, 209.
15. Cyril Beaumont, *Bookseller at the Ballet*. London: C. W. Beaumont, 1975, 131–132.
16. Irina Nijinska and Jean Rawlinson, eds., *Bronislava Nijinska: Early Memoirs*. New York: Holt, Reinhart and Winston, 1981, 442–443.
17. Ibid., 445.
18. Robert Greskovic, *Ballet 101*. New York: Hyperion, 1998, 64.
19. "Flesh as Stone," in *Nijinsky Legend and Modernist—The Dancer Who Changed the World*, ed. Erik Näslund. Stockholm: Dance Museet, 2000, 112.
20. In *Choreography: Principles and Practice*. Report of the Fourth Study of Dance Conference, 4–7 April 1986. Guildford, Surrey: National Resource Centre for Dance, 1987, 80–92.

21. Millicent Hodson, *Nijinsky's Crime against Grace—Reconstruction Score of the Original Choreography for* Le Sacre du Printemps. Dance & Music Series No. 8, General editor, Wendy Hilton. Stuyvesant, NY: Pendragon Press, 1996.

22. Joan Acocella, ed., *The Diary of Vaslav Nijinsky: Unexpurgated Edition.* Translated from the Russian by Kyril Fitzlyon. New York: Farrar, Straus and Giroux, 1999.

23. Transcript, "The Connection." WBUR (National Public Radio, Boston), 1 April 1999.

24. Joan Ross Acocella, "The Reception of Diaghilev's Ballets Russes by Artists and Intellectuals in Paris and London, 1909–1914" (unpublished PhD dissertation, Rutgers University, 1984).

25. *Diary*, 73.

26. Peter Ostwald, *Vaslav Nijinsky: A Leap into Madness.* New York: Lyle Stuart, 1991.

27. *Diary*, 141.

28. Kirstein, *Nijinsky Dancing*, 13.

29. Tamara Karsavina, *Theatre Street.* New York: Dutton, 1961, 237.

30. *Diary*, 39.

31. *Diary*, xxvi.

32. *Diary*, xxi–xxii.

33. *Diary*, xl.

34. *Diary*, xl.

35. *Diary*, xliv.

36. Lincoln Kirstein, *Dance: A Short History of Classic Theatrical Dancing.* New York: G.P. Putnam's Sons, 1935; reprinted 1969, 283.

37. Lincoln Kirstein, *Movement & Metaphor: Four Centuries of Ballet.* New York: Praeger, 1970.

38. *Diary*, xlv.

39. *Choreography and Dance* (see note 5, this chapter) contains several accounts of the research and translation of this score. In the video *Nijinsky's Faune Restored* (Gordon and Breach, 1991), the dance was filmed in performance by dancers at the Juilliard School.

CHAPTER 2: MOVABLE CLASSICS

1. My essay on the first Bournonville Festival, "A Most Unmelancholy Dane," appeared in *Hudson Review*, spring 1980. "Hoping for Eternal Spring," on the second Festival, was published in *Hudson Review*, autumn 1992.

2. Jennifer Fisher, *Nutcracker Nation—How an Old World Ballet Became a Christmas Tradition in the New World.* New Haven: Yale University Press, 2003.

CHAPTER 3: POSTLUDE AND PRELUDE

1. Arlene Croce, *Going to the Dance.* New York: Alfred A. Knopf, 1982.

2. Bernard Taper, *Balanchine: A Biography.* New York: Times Books, 1984.

3. *Portrait of Mr. B: Photographs of George Balanchine*, with an essay by Lincoln Kirstein. New York: Viking Press, 1984.

CHAPTER 4: BALANCHINE DIASPORA

1. Arnold Haskell, *Balletomania Then and Now*. New York: Knopf, 1977, 95–96. The conversation took place in New York, in January 1934, probably just after Balanchine had seen the ballet presented "very badly" by Serge Lifar's touring company. (Richard Buckle and John Taras, *George Balanchine, Ballet Master*. New York: Random House, 1988, 81.)
2. Cyril Beaumont, *Bookseller at the Ballet* (incorporating *The Diaghilev Ballet in London*). London: Beaumont, 1975, 368.
3. *Dance for a City: Fifty Years of the New York City Ballet*, edited by Lynn Garafola with Eric Foner. New York: Columbia University Press, 1999.
4. Nancy Goldner, *Balanchine Variations*. Gainesville: University Press of Florida, 2008.

CHAPTER 5: BALLET IN TRANSIT

1. "Ain't Misbehavin': Two decades of Twyla," Lecture at the Dance Critics Association annual conference, San Francisco, June 10, 1989.
2. Anna Kisselgoff, "Dance View; When a Choreographer Settles Into a Formula," *New York Times*, 3 July 1988, sec. 2, p. 12.
3. Alastair Macaulay, "Dancing: Vivamus Atque Amemus," *New Yorker*, 20 June 1988, 88.

CHAPTER 7: RIFFS AND TRANSLATIONS

1. "Nutcracker and the King of the Mice" in *The Best Tales of Hoffmann*, edited by E. F. Bleiler. New York: Dover, 1967, 182.
2. Edwin Denby's essay on the original production in 1954 remains a classic explication of its appeal. In Denby's *Dance Writings*. New York: Knopf, 1986, 445–450.
3. Two versions of this choreography are available on videotape. One, filmed in 1989 from Spectator's Bolshoi at the Bolshoi series, features Natalya Arkhipova and Irek Mukhamedov. The other, from Kultur, stars Ekaterina Maksimova and Vladimir Vasiliev.
4. Filmed in 1986 for Paramount and available on videotape from Atlantic Releasing Corp. as *Nutcracker—The Motion Picture*.
5. Roland John Wiley, independently of Sendak, has offered the thesis that *The Nutcracker* is autobiographical. Drosselmeyer, Wiley thinks, represents Tchaikovsky, and the whole story is meant to be seen from their viewpoint, not Marie's. See "On Meaning in Nutcracker," *Dance Research*, vol. 3, no. 1 (autumn 1984), 3–28.
6. Paul Taylor, *Private Domain: An Autobiography*. New York: Knopf, 1987.
7. New York: Doubleday, 1975; London: W. H. Allen, 1978.
8. From "Le Sacre du Printemps," by Jacques Rivière, November 1913. Trans. Miriam Lassman. Reprinted in Lincoln Kirstein, *Nijinsky Dancing*. New York: Alfred A. Knopf, 1975, 164–168.

Index

About the Author

Marcia B. Siegel is the author of six books, including *Howling Near Heaven: Twyla Tharp and the Reinvention of Modern Dance*; *Days on Earth: The Dance of Doris Humphrey*; and the classic study *The Shapes of Change: Images of American Dance*. She was the 2004 Senior Critic Honoree of the Dance Critics Association, and in 2005 she received the Congress on Research in Dance (CORD) award for outstanding contribution to dance research. She has been a resident faculty member in the Department of Performance Studies, Tisch School of the Arts, New York University, and is an internationally known lecturer and workshop leader.